D1275687

Advances
in COMPUTERS
VOLUME 11

Contributors to This Volume

ANTHONY DEBONS

DAVID R. HILL

D. M. JACKSON

HARRY H. JOSSELSON

R. B. KIEBURTZ

E. E. NEWHALL

KLAUS W. OTTEN

Advances in
COMPUTERS

EDITED BY
FRANZ L. ALT
American Institute of Physics
New York, New York

AND

MORRIS RUBINOFF
University of Pennsylvania
and
Pennsylvania Research Associates, Inc.
Philadelphia, Pennsylvania

VOLUME 11

GUEST EDITOR
MARSHALL C. YOVITS
Department of Computer and Information Science
The Ohio State University
Columbus, Ohio

ACADEMIC PRESS · New York · London—1971

ACADEMIC PRESS, INC.
111 Fifth Avenue, New York, New York 10003

United Kingdom Edition published by
ACADEMIC PRESS, INC. (LONDON) LTD.
Berkeley Square House, London W1X 6BA

LIBRARY OF CONGRESS CATALOG CARD NUMBER: 59-15761

PRINTED IN THE UNITED STATES OF AMERICA

Contents

Automatic Translation of Languages Since 1960:
A Linguist's View

Harry H. Josselson

Classification, Relevance, and Information Retrieval

D. M. Jackson

Approaches to the Machine Recognition of Conversational Speech

Klaus W. Otten

Man–Machine Interaction Using Speech

David R. Hill

Balanced Magnetic Circuits for Logic and Memory Devices

R. B. Kieburtz and E. E. Newhall

Command and Control: Technology and Social Impact

Anthony Debons

Contributors to Volume 11

Numbers in parentheses indicate the pages on which the authors' contributions begin.

ANTHONY DEBONS, *University of Pittsburgh, Pittsburgh, Pennsylvania* (*319*)

DAVID R. HILL,* *Department of Mathematics, Statistics, and Computing Science, The University of Calgary, Calgary, Alberta, Canada* (*165*)

D. M. JACKSON,† *Department of Computer and Information Science, The Ohio State University, Columbus, Ohio* (*59*)

HARRY H. JOSSELSON, *Wayne State University, Detroit, Michigan* (*1*)

R. B. KIEBURTZ, *Bell Telephone Laboratories, Holmdel, New Jersey* (*231*)

E. E. NEWHALL,‡ *Bell Telephone Laboratories, Holmdel, New Jersey* (*231*)

KLAUS W. OTTEN, *The National Cash Register Company, Dayton, Ohio* (*127*)

* *Present address:* Department of Electrical Engineering Science, University of Essex, Colchester, Essex, England.

† *Present address:* Department of Computer Science, Cornell University, Ithaca, New York.

‡ *Present address:* Department of Electrical Engineering, University of Toronto, Toronto, Canada.

Preface

This volume continues the precedent set with the previous volume for which a guest editor was selected. It was my privilege to be invited to edit Volume 11 of this prestigious series.

Volume 11 examines in detail a number of different areas in computer and information science that are of particular interest and significance today. The topics were chosen particularly to demonstrate how extensive and diverse is the field commonly known as computer and information science. Each of the papers discusses the background and recent activity and research in a particular area.

Included in this volume is a recent survey of the field of automatic translation of languages. Written by Professor Harry Josselson who has done extensive research on the linguistic structure of the Russian language and who has been concerned with the problems of the machine translation of Russian to English, this survey updates the one by Dr. Y. Bar-Hillel published in the first volume of this series.

Another article in this volume considers some aspects of the problems of classification and their relationship to information retrieval. This chapter was contributed by Dr. D. M. Jackson who has done research in the field at Cornell University, at The Ohio State University, and at Cambridge University in England.

Two chapters are included which are concerned with some of the latest approaches to speech recognition and the applications of these approaches to the interaction between people and computers. Contributing these chapters are Dr. Klaus Otten, who has worked for a number of years on various problems involved with speech recognition at the National Cash Register Company, and Professor David Hill, who leads a research program in this area at the University of Calgary.

Some new techniques involving balanced magnetic circuits for both logic and memory devices are discussed by Dr. R. B. Kieburtz and Dr. E. E. Newhall of the Bell Telephone Laboratories. These balanced circuits, developed at Bell Labs, are flexible, efficient, economical, and easy to construct. Because of their simplicity, they appear to have considerable application in the computer field.

Finally, command and control, generally considered to be an important military function, is considered from a broad viewpoint with regard to its previous accomplishments and toward its application to the civilian and scientific sectors of society. In particular, command and control is shown to be a special case and a specific example of information science. The author is Dr. A. E. Debons who has had a distinguished career both as a military officer and as an information scientist. Debons has done research on, and contributed to development of, command and control systems for both the Air Force and the Navy.

I should like to thank the contributors of this volume who have given extensively of their time and effort to make this a timely and vital publication in the field of computer and information science. I should also like to thank Academic Press for giving me the opportunity to serve as a Guest Editor. It has been a most rewarding undertaking.

January 1971   M. C. YOVITS
                                                  Guest Editor

Automatic Translation of Languages Since 1960: A Linguist's View

HARRY H. JOSSELSON

Wayne State University
Detroit, Michigan

1

1. Introductory Remarks

1.1 Some Difficulties of Machine Translation

Many changes have occurred in the field of machine translation since 1960.[1] It has been generally acknowledged, as first pointed out by Bar-Hillel, that fully automatic high-quality translation (FAHQT) is exceedingly difficult, if not impossible, to achieve. The human mind can draw inferences which a machine, even one with an encyclopedic dictionary, cannot do [1]. To restate this in terms of linguistics, the science that deals with that aspect of human behavior which manifests itself through language, the primary reason for the unattainability of FAHQT is the very nature of language itself. This fact escaped many early researchers in machine translation, particularly those who were hardware-oriented and who proceeded from the very naive position that since everybody speaks a language, everybody should, theoretically at least, be able to deal with any processes which involve language.

Language was considered just a "bunch of words" and the primary task for early machine translation (MT) was to build machines large enough to hold all the words necessary in the translation process. The fact that words in one language had no counterparts in another and that in some cases one word in one language had to be expressed by a group of words in another (which as linguists know is due to the fact that speakers of a language view the world that surrounds them in terms of the structure of their language)[2] was completely ignored [2]. Overlooked also was the fact that two given languages may have completely different structures. Thus there sometimes exists between languages a lack of one-to-one correspondence of what is known as "parts of speech." The way sentences are put together in languages also differs greatly, even among such genetically related languages as French and Italian. And last, the MT researchers were confronted, and still are, by what came to be loosely termed as "semantics"—the fact that words have more than one meaning, and that sometimes groups of words or even whole sentences may have more than one

---

[1] The present survey of the state-of-the-art in machine translation is based primarily on the author's work in the field, his contacts with researchers, and on the examination of pertinent literature. His research in MT has been supported by the Information Systems Branch of the Office of Naval Research.

[2] Whorf ([2], p. 93) contrasts Hopi, an Indian language of the American Southwest and what he terms Standard Average European (including English, French, and German). He maintains that there are "... connections between cultural norms and linguistic patterns," and that "... there is a relation between a language and the rest of the culture of the society which uses it."

meaning in a language. Generally speaking, all the translation problems that were not solved by applying rules derived from grammar were lumped together under the heading "semantics," with an indication that since these were difficult theoretical problems they were to be solved later by various devices. These means included the printing out of the several possible solutions of ambiguous text segments to let the reader decide for himself the correct meaning, printing out the ambiguous source language text, and other temporary expedients.

1.2 The Nature of Language and Problems of Language Description

All these difficulties, which of course gave rise to clumsy and what is worse, sometimes outright incorrect translations, were due to the fact that before one can deal successfully with MT, which after all involves language, one must know much more about language. Particularly one must understand the rules under which such a complex system as human language operates and how the mechanism of this operation can be simulated by automatic means, i.e., without any human intervention at all. The first task, linguistic description, is an enormous one that has required and will continue to require a great deal of effort on the part of many serious researchers. Today these efforts are greatly aided by the computer, which assists in formulation of the problem, in testing the proposed solutions, and in proper storage and retrieval of the acquired linguistic information.

The second problem, the simulation of human language behavior by automatic means, is almost impossible to achieve, since language is an open and dynamic system in constant change and because the operation of the system is not yet completely understood. Suppose it were theoretically possible to achieve a complete description of how a given language operates. In the time it would take to compile this description the language would have changed again. It becomes clear, therefore, that the best possible solution for MT, both theoretically and practically, is symbiosis between man and machine.

1.3 MT as Symbiosis between Man and Machine

This man–machine interaction is not to be limited to post-editing of machine-produced texts alone. Rather it is to be viewed broadly as a collaboration between the two in all phases of MT, each partner doing what he can do best most efficiently at a given stage of the translation process, as already suggested by Bar-Hillel (see [1] pp. 95–98). Before my views concerning the details of this partnership are spelled out (see Section 6.2), it might be of interest to discuss briefly some of the ideas concerning man–machine interaction in MT advanced by Bar-Hillel in 1960. He states that as soon as one concedes that any system for production of some sort of qualitative MT output will require a collaboration between man and machine, then the "greatest obstacle to practical MT is overcome" ([*1*], p. 95). The obvious corollary to this is, in his words, that, "As soon as the aim of MT is lowered to that of high quality translation by a machine–post-editor partnership, the decisive problem becomes to determine the region of optimality in the continuum of possible divisions of labor" ([*1*], p. 95).

1.4 Practical MT Problems and Some Tentative Solutions

1.4.1 *Use of Automatic Print Reader*

Bar-Hillel discusses first the necessity for the development of "a reliable and versatile mechanical print reader" ([*1*], p. 96) and speculates about the difference in cost between introducing text into the machine by keypunching and automatic print reading. Although admittedly there is no doubt whatsoever that the latter process will eventually be developed and should turn out to be in the long run cheaper than keypunching, it should be pointed out that any cost estimates of any part of the practical MT process are highly conjectural and should certainly not figure in the determination of the practicality of MT at the present time. Any research and development is a very expensive process and lowering of costs comes only after "the show gets on the road." It is simply premature even today to justify or dismiss MT for financial reasons alone. It will be shown in Section 6.2 that practical, quality MT is realizable even today within certain limits. Next, to Bar-Hillel's prerequisite of an automatic print reader for MT must be added the notion that besides the purely hardware aspect of developing the mechanical reading mechanism there also exists the software aspect—the development of programs necessary for the resolution of some of the text problems for correct input into the computer. For instance, a program must be developed to distinguish between the various uses of the period—end-of-sentence marker, initials indicator, abbreviation, and others. In the case of a print reader for Russian–English MT or the reverse, programs must be written to distinguish for input certain letters common to the Roman and Cyrillic alphabets, like A, B, E, H, O, P, C, X, some of which are identical, like O, and some different, like H, which is N in Russian.

1.4.2 *Problem of Dictionary Storage and Retrieval*

Bar-Hillel also dwells on the need to compile the necessary dictionaries in a form most suitable for computer storage and retrieval. It now seems that the earlier practice of some research groups of completely ignoring existing dictionaries and of compiling dictionaries from scratch, so to speak, has been superseded by efforts to construct computer-stored bilingual glossaries by first reorganizing the published dictionaries in a format specifically designed for the subsequent MT automatic procedures,[3] such as look-up of words, source language sentence analysis, target language sentence synthesis, and all other information incorporated in what is termed the "grammar code" of each lexical entry. Also, during the translation process, in addition to language information normally contained in the grammars and lexicons, the human translator uses other important information not contained in these two traditional sources of compiled linguistic knowledge, information he carries around "in his head" which enables him to solve many complex problems of translation. All this additional information has to be discovered, and stated in rules storable in the computer. Automatic procedures for discovery of this information as well as for augmenting the quantitative content of computer-stored dictionaries from texts also have been proposed [3].

1.4.3 Practical MT: Microgrammars and Microglossaries

It is also now generally recognized that the most efficient way to achieve quality translation and to construct translation rules that will hold true for the overwhelming majority of the material to be translated is to confine oneself to a very narrow segment of technical or scientific literature. The narrower the scope of these materials, the easier it is to construct the microglossaries and grammars for each field and to compile rules for resolution of ambiguities through contextual analysis. In this connection perhaps a comment should be made concerning the form in which source language lexical entries should be stored in the dictionary. Bar-Hillel indicates three possible ways of doing this: (1) the exact letter sequence in which they occur in the text, (2) the so-called canonical form, i.e., infinitive for verbs, nominative singular for nouns, or (3) the canonical stems. In the latter case a portion of the lexical entry is considered as a stem and stored separately from the inflectional endings, necessitating various routines for splitting the text entry into stem and ending and routines for recombining them later during sentence analysis. Bar-Hillel insists that this question must be solved before mass MT production begins

---

[3] For example, by 1960, automatic dictionaries based on Russian text had already been compiled by the following MT research groups: Georgetown, Berkeley, RAND, Harvard, Ramo-Wooldridge *et al.* For a description and list of these computer-stored dictionaries see Josselson [3]. For a detailed account of an experiment in reversing bilingual dictionaries by means of computer processing see Josselson [4].

([1], p. 97) and I am inclined to agree with him. The procedure for storing dictionaries I believe to be most fruitful at the present stage of development of computer technology is given in Sections 3.5.1 and 3.6.1.

2. MT Since 1960: Aims and Growth

2.1 Change in Research Aims and Approaches

Perhaps it would be useful now to restate the aims of machine translation research as it is viewed by those who believe that a reasonable solution to producing a quality machine translation product is possible. Then we will review very briefly the history of MT in the United States, in terms of both the shift of emphasis of the philosophy of approach and the activities of the individual research groups. The primary aim of MT research today is to produce the best possible translation, automated wherever feasible, from one language (the source language) into another (the target language) through the combined efforts of linguists, programmers, and research associates from other related fields. A secondary aim at the present, more an outgrowth of early research than an objective in itself, is to develop as far as possible, a complete description of the way language, and more specifically, individual languages operate. Accumulation of such data is invaluable for subsequent efforts to refine and develop MT output. The acquisition of this linguistic information is of the greatest interest to other fields in the area of information science, such as automatic abstracting, indexing, and content analysis, as well as to linguists and language teachers.

It can be said, therefore, that the mechanical translation process is envisaged as a joint endeavor by linguists, mathematicians, programmers, computer engineers, and systems engineers to develop an over-all program which utilizes high-speed digital computers and other peripheral automatic equipment, such as printers and eventually hopefully also automatic print-readers, to make possible translation from one language into another. The general aim of serious researchers today has shifted, as urged by Bar-Hillel among others, from fully automatic translation to achieving a relatively good quality product. This ideally should be as close to human translation as possible, but as is conceded by many, it will never equal human translation. This translation product will be, as it is to a certain degree even today, useful to those who are interested primarily in acquiring information from the source language, not in a never-to-be-achieved elegance of translation. An exceedingly practical subsidiary aim of machine translation is to produce an output which ideally will not exhibit at least the same degree of errors in interpreting source language as committed by a human translator.[4] Thus, to repeat once more, the machine translation process should be viewed as a process in which automatic equipment plays a major role in the symbiosis between man and machine.

In reviewing the history of machine translation in the United States, one should probably start in 1946, when Warren Weaver and A. D. Booth first discussed the possibility of machine translation. A fuller discussion of the early history of MT appears in Booth and Locke [5]. In the early days machine translation was viewed as another illustration of the "intellectual capability" of computers [6].[5] Computer technology was beginning to develop successfully and there was a desire to prove that the machine was capable of solving all the problems that man can solve. However, the first experiments in machine translation, starting with the trial run in 1953 by Leon Dostert, Director of Georgetown University Institute of Languages and Linguistics, really did not prove anything, particularly as far as the possibility of FAHQT is concerned. This was due to the fact that the first MT experiments were carried out on very limited small texts, with bilingual glossaries and grammars specially tailored for these texts, thus in effect creating an ideal, closed linguistic system in contrast to the openness and dynamics of natural language. The computer programs specifically designed for these small texts, of course, guaranteed the success of these experiments. As a consequence early MT researchers arrived at the conclusion that all that was necessary to achieve practical results in MT was to increase the size of the dictionary and to expand the grammar.

Consequently, the majority of efforts of the MT research groups in the United States and elsewhere were limited to such tasks as construction of schemes for machine-stored bilingual dictionaries; development of grammar codes[6] for dictionary entries, syntactic analysis, including automatic sentence parsing routines; and automatic language

---

[4] As is well known, the three components of human translation are (1) knowledge of the target language, (2) knowledge of the source language, (3) expertise in the subject matter to be translated. These are considered of equal importance in the translation process and a deficiency in any of these can impair the quality of translation.

[5] Similar views were also expressed by Yu. A. Shreider in a report to the meeting entitled "Automatic Translation: Illusions and Reality," cited in [6]. I am greatly indebted to the discussion in [6] in my further discussion of the state of early MT research.

[6] In MT parlance, the term "grammar code" refers to all morphological, syntactic, semantic, and other linguistic information stored in the computer for each dictionary entry which is necessary for further MT processing.

recognition routines in general, routines for contextual resolution of text ambiguities and other information thought necessary for the development of automatic procedures adequate to handle the translation process. By 1962, according to the National Science Foundation, twelve research groups were actively engaged in these tasks in the United States. The same was also true for machine translation groups in Great Britain, France, the Soviet Union, and on a smaller scale in Italy, Germany, Japan, and other countries.[7] The total number of MT groups in the world reached 48 that year [7].

2.2 Federally Supported Cooperation among MT Groups in the United States

Only a few short years after the first organized research efforts in MT were initiated, research personnel and techniques had greatly expanded. Several pioneer researchers, in collaboration with their Federal sponsors (notably, The U.S. Office of Naval Research, The National Science Foundation, and the U.S. Air Force), began to feel the need for cooperative exchange of information among the various research groups to minimize duplication of certain tasks and to attempt to develop MT along more efficient and productive lines. The idea for arranging such an exchange of views about the immediate problems confronting MT researchers took more definite shape in the course of informal discussions among some of the participants at the National Symposium on Machine Translation[8] held at the University of California at Los Angeles in 1960 and led to a series of machine translation conferences organized by Wayne State University [8].

2.1.1 First MT Conference at Princeton

The first conference of federally sponsored machine translation groups was conceived of as a working conference to encourage open discussion and cooperation among participating groups. This spirit of mutual exchange prevailed and established the pattern for what became a series of highly successful "Princeton-type" meetings, as

[7] The activities of all research groups, in the United States as well as abroad, conducting investigations of MT-related problems (encompassing software, hardware, and linguistic theory, description and analysis) were documented in a series published by the National Science Foundation's Office of Science Information Service between 1957 and 1966. This series, entitled *Current Research and Development in Scientific Documentation*, also includes descriptions of research activities in areas of related interest, e.g., language analysis, systems design, pattern recognition, and information storage and retrieval.

[8] Summaries of the proceedings of these meetings were prepared, printed, and distributed to the participants. Copies of these summaries are on file at the Slavic Department of Wayne State University, Detroit, Michigan.

they came to be called. The first meeting was held in Princeton in 1960 and included 26 official participants and several invited visitors, with representatives from MT research groups in the United States, England, and Italy. While the general theme of this conference was dictionary design and the general problem of MT grammar, discussions included such topics as programming strategies, and possibilities for the interconvertibility of the materials, codes, and formats of the various groups. Appraisals were also made of the status of text analysis, dictionary compilation, and grammar coding.

2.2.2 Second MT Conference, Georgetown: Grammar Coding

The second conference was convened at Georgetown University in 1961 and was devoted primarily to problems of grammar coding and the optimal content of the grammar codes of Russian–English automatic dictionary formats. Two representatives from each of the following MT groups came to this meeting: Berkeley, Georgetown, Harvard, M.I.T., National Bureau of Standards, Ramo-Wooldridge, RAND, and Wayne State University. The specific aims of this meeting were (1) to discuss codes, coding procedures, and approaches of Russian–English MT groups in the United States; (2) to consider the prospects for the automatic conversion of coded materials among the various groups; and (3) to decide what material was to be coded and thought to be appropriate for entry into the code. Determination was made of the extant and proposed dictionary coding. Special investigations of Russian grammar by the various groups were noted and listed.

2.2.3 Third MT Conference, Princeton: Syntactic Analysis

The third meeting was held at Princeton in 1962 and concentrated on MT-oriented syntactic analysis. The meeting was held to enable the groups to examine together the main problems that had come to light in syntactic analysis, to compare solutions, and in general to clarify, interpret, and compare the results of various individual endeavors. The discussions included consideration of syntax problems not only in Russian, but in such other languages as Arabic, Chinese, and Japanese. One entire session was devoted to discussion of theoretical models used in syntactic analysis. MT groups, not previously represented, present at this conference were IBM, Ohio State University, and University of Pennsylvania.

2.2.4 Fourth MT Conference, Las Vegas: Semantic Analysis

This meeting held in 1965 dealt exclusively with computer-related semantic analysis. It included a keynote address by the President of the Association for Computational Linguistics, Winfred Lehmann of the University of Texas, and thirteen papers. Besides discussions immediately following the presentation of the above papers, two sessions were scheduled for informal discussion. Six foreign scholars participated: three from the United Kingdom, and one each from Hungary, Israel, and Italy. In addition to observers, eleven federally sponsored groups working in MT and related areas were represented. Also in attendance were representatives of several interested United States Government agencies.

It was generally felt that these meetings benefited all participants in terms of the climate of cooperation created, the informal exchange of views, and the precise definition of problems to be resolved. Various independent scholars and key representatives of research groups were able to examine together the problems of either a linguistic or computational nature that have confronted serious researchers. Also, conference participants were able to compare solutions, question one another on particular points, and in general, pool the results of individual endeavors.

2.3 International Conferences

In addition to the above meetings, two simultaneous developments growing out of the same climate of cooperation should be mentioned. These are (1) the organization of international meetings on automatic language analysis and computational linguistics, and (2) the establishment of a professional society called the Association for Machine Translation and Computational Linguistics (known since 1968 as the Association for Computational Linguistics).

As to the first development, the following international meetings were held and included papers and discussions on machine translation, among other topics.

(1) First International Conference on Machine Translation of Languages and Applied Language Analysis, held in September 1961 at the National Physical Laboratory in Teddington, Middlesex, England. The papers presented at this conference were published in two volumes (*Proc. 1st Intern. Conf. Machine Translation of Languages and Applied Language Analysis*, H.M. Stationery Office, London, 1962).

(2) 1965 International Conference on Computational Linguistics held in New York. The papers presented at this meeting were made available in the form of preprints only.[9]

---

[9] These preprints are available from the Slavic Department at Wayne State University, which functioned as secretariat for this meeting.

(3) Second International Conference on Automatic Language Processing held in August 1967 at Grenoble, France. The papers from this conference were bound in one volume.[10]

(4) The 1969 International Congress on Computational Linguistics held in September 1969, Sanga-Saby, in Sweden.

2.4 Formation of a Learned Society

An ad hoc Committee was set up in 1960 to create a professional society to be called the Association for Machine Translation and Computational Linguistics (AMTCL). The members of this committee were participants in research groups working in MT and related areas. The Committee met at Teddington in 1961 at the First International Conference on Machine Translation and Applied Language Analysis.[11] It was moved and seconded at this meeting that the proposed society be formed and the proposed constitution be adopted. Signing of the constitution as well as the balloting and installation of officers took place at the Third Princeton (Syntax) Conference in 1962. Later the same year, the Executive Committee met at the Massachusetts Institute of Technology and planned the first annual meeting which was held in Denver, Colorado, in 1963. Since that time, annual meetings have been held and membership has grown to approximately 650 at the date of present writing. To reflect the interest of its membership, the location of the annual meetings is alternated between the sites of the meetings of the Linguistic Society of America and the Association of Computing Machinery, being held either immediately preceding or following the sessions of these societies. As already indicated above, the name of the society was changed to Association for Computational Linguistics at the sixth annual meeting held at Urbana, Illinois in July 1968. The Association has two publications MT (*Mechanical Translation*) and tFS (*the Finite String*).[12]

---

[10] The papers presented at this meeting were bound together under the title *2ème conference internationale sur le traitement automatique des langues* and were distributed to conference participants.

[11] The following charter members attended this session: H. Brownson, L. Dostert, H. Edmundson, P. Garvin, D. Hays, K. Harper, H. Josselson, S. Lamb, W. Lehmann, A. Oettinger, E. Reifler, R. See, and V. Yngve.

[12] Information concerning these publications can be obtained from: *Mechanical Translation* (Victor Yngve, Ed.) Graduate Library School, University of Chicago, Chicago, Illinois, 60637; and *the Finite String* (A. Hood Roberts, Ed.) Center for Applied Linguistics, 1717 Massachusetts Ave. N.W., Washington, D.C. 20036.

3. Linguistic Problems in MT Research

3.1 Inadequacy of Early Linguistic Models

It was during early MT investigations that most of the researchers became aware, as was predicted by serious-minded linguists, how little was known about the structure and usage of the language they were working with—even about Western European languages, though there has accumulated over the last two centuries a vast amount of detailed description. All this accumulated linguistic information, it turned out, was incomplete, and it became clear that the theories underlying those machine translation efforts fell far short of both the goal of obtaining satisfactory practical results and the attempt to solve the problem of providing adequate models for the operation of languages. The first MT procedures were obviously of an extrapolation type. They were constructed, as indicated above, on the basis of the examination of a certain number of texts and the resulting rules were then transferred (or extrapolated) to other texts. These were clearly *ad hoc* rules, not based on a thorough investigation of the structure of language (see p. 28 of [6]).

3.1.1 Quest for Operational Linguistic Models

The emphasis of MT research, therefore, shifted in the mid-sixties to the second, far more important aim, namely, finding out more about how language operates and creating language models. For a brief discussion of contemporary linguistic theories see among others [9]; for models see [10]. Just as prior to launching a satellite successfully into outer space a mathematical model of the dynamics of the path of the rocket must be constructed, or before measures for controlling the path of the economy of a nation can be instituted a model of the economic activity of a country must be developed, it is necessary to have an adequate model of language before a quality MT product can be obtained. The fact that language is essentially a biologically based system adds to the difficulty of developing language models, and compounds the complexity of the nature of the translation process. Written texts are an output of the operation of linguistic processes governed by language structures. Therefore, every model of language must reflect the operation of linguistic structure. The fact that the actual processes governing language behavior are not well known explains both the difficulty of constructing adequate language models and the necessity of pursuing serious efforts in this direction (see p. 28 of [6]).

3.2 Some Linguistic Problems Facing MT

Some of the specifics of the linguistic problems which have confronted the MT research groups in the United States will now be discussed along with a general overview of attempts to solve them, touching both on theory as well as on practical solutions. Most of the illustrations will be cited from the area of Russian–English MT, since this is the area in which the author and the majority of MT groups in the United States have been working.[13]

3.2.1 Area and Units of MT Analysis

Most of the machine translation groups in the United States and elsewhere confined themselves to the translation of materials in natural science—physics, chemistry, biology, and mathematics; social science, such as economics; and occasionally newspapers, such as articles in the Russian language newspaper *Pravda*. Generally speaking, the translation unit was the sentence, which in the course of analysis was further subdivided into phrases, words, and morphemes. Automatic analysis of units larger than a sentence were envisaged, e.g., a paragraph, chapter, or book, but up to the present, machine translation research, in the United States at least, has operated within the limits of a sentence. This imposed some limitations upon the resolution of certain morphological ambiguities. For instance, the Russian possessive pronoun его means "his" or "its," depending upon the antecedent. When the latter is not present in the sentence which is being translated, sentences preceding the one containing его have to be scanned for the possible resolution of this ambiguity.

3.2.2 Contrastive Grammatical Analysis

The differences in grammatical structure of the input and output languages also contributed to the difficulties in machine translation. In fact, major efforts of linguists were directed to this problem, both on the analysis and the synthesis levels. Essentially, the linguist in machine translation has had to construct a scheme of contrastive analysis between the source and target languages. It has been pointed out by many linguists that the analysis of a language from the point of view of that language alone will produce one type of scheme. But when one language is analyzed side by side with another, that is, when

---

[13] The ensuing discussion closely parallels the materials contained in my paper "Linguistic basis of mechanical translation: contributions of standard linguistic theory," presented at the Seminar on Mechanical Translation, held under the auspices of the U.S.-Japan Committee on Scientific Cooperation at Tokyo, Japan, April 20–28, 1964.

one language is mapped into another, a different analytical scheme is found to be more useful. In machine translation, contrastive analysis yields the best results. The source language is analyzed not only in terms of itself, but also with a view towards expressing its structure in terms of the target language.

3.2.3 The Lack of One-to-One Correspondence between Languages

As anyone who has engaged in translation from one language to another knows, one of the difficulties in translating, generally speaking, is the frequent absence of one-to-one correspondence between languages on the lexical, morphological, syntactic, and semantic levels. For instance, the Russian adjective used as a noun, зрячий has no exact one-word equivalent in English and has to be translated by a phrase such as "one who sees." Russian lacks the class of article, which English has. Consequently, in translating from Russian into English, one faces the problem of inserting into English, *a, an, the* wherever these are needed in the English text. In Russian, the conjunction пока in the meaning "until" is always followed by the negative не while in English the equivalent construction is affirmative: сиди здесь, пока я не приду—"Sit here until I come." The Russian verb бренчать has the general meaning "to tingle." But the sentence деньги бренчат в кармане, is translated into English as "Money is jingling in the pocket," not "tingling." Coins "tinkle" in Russian just as a piano "tinkles," but in English coins "jingle" and a piano "tinkles." The difficulties that all the above absences of one-to-one correspondence will cause in mechanical translation from Russian into English are quite apparent from the above examples and these problems must be dealt with, if good translation is to be obtained.

Let me cite a few examples indicating how machine translation linguists have attempted to handle the lack of class equivalents between two languages. Frequently the machine is instructed to search the context of a lexical item in the source language in order to render a suitable translation in the target language. Whole classes missing in the source language can also be suppressed, at least partially, in the target language. Lexical items belonging to certain classes can be inserted into the target language as translations for morphemes present in the source language, but missing in the target language. In English, prepositions will sometimes have to be inserted for certain Russian case endings, "of" for the genitive case ending, "to" for the dative, and so on. Words which are followed by negation in Russian, and their equivalents which appear in affirmative English constructions, are appropriately marked in the source language, Russian, accompanied by appropriate instruction to the computer for handling this situation in the target language, English.

Ideally, any translation, human or mechanical, should transfer the content of any utterance, from one language into another. Roman Jakobson expresses this notion succinctly when he says, "Most frequently, translation from one language into another substitutes messages in one language not for separate code units, but for entire messages in some other language" (see [11]). At the present stage of development of machine translation, this ideal state has not quite arrived yet, because of the difficulties of establishing interlingual class equivalents by mechanical means. Yuen Ren Chao, in a paper delivered at the Ninth International Congress of Linguists, pointed out a temporary solution for this problem. ". . . Certain cases of non-correspondence, or at least complicated patterns of correspondence will, at the present state of the science, have to be left to non-machine translation [i.e., human post-editor]. I have in mind such cases where one language has one form of structure, say Subject-Verb-Object, and the other language has a similar structure for certain instances, but a different structure for other instances, conditioned by non-structural, but lexical factors" [12].

3.2.4 Nested Structures

Another problem encountered in machine translation is nesting, a phenomenon which may occur in any language that grammatically allows sentence structures containing discontinuous constituents. Nesting has been defined as the interruption of a main clause by an embedded phrase or clause, followed by the resumption of the main clause. As has been pointed out by Murray Sherry, of the Harvard Machine Translation group, ". . . a *level* of nesting or a *depth* of nesting can be assigned to every phrase and clause in a sentence" [13]. Hence, deeper levels of nesting may be identified when the embedded phrase or clause itself contains an embedded structure. For example, consider Sherry's illustration in English: "The man who came to dinner ate heartily." On the first level one finds—"The man ate heartily," "who came to dinner" is on the second level, and "to dinner" is on the third and deepest level. If one accepts the above definition of nesting, then the nested structure of the following Russian sentence may be identified: Система, параболическая в смысле И. Г. Петровского, удовлетворяет условию.—"The system parabolic in I. G. Petrovsky's sense satisfies the condition." Here, the main clause система удовлетворяет условию —"the system satisfies the condition" has been interrupted by a modifier phrase.[14]

---

[14] The nesting concept, the depth hypothesis, and schemes related to the identification of embedded structures have also been discussed by the following: Alt [14], Yngve [15], and Sager [16].

An interesting discussion of major types of embedding constructions in Japanese is made by Charles J. Fillmore, of the Ohio State group [17]. He points out that one of the main characteristics of Japanese syntax is the embedding transformation analogous to the English relative clause embedding rule, which attaches sentences to nouns. Since in Japanese the relative clause precedes the noun it modifies, and since the transformation may be repeatedly applied in the generation of a single sentence, multilayered Japanese sentences appear to have a constituent structure which is not altogether compatible with the depth hypothesis. To illustrate his argument, Fillmore analyzed a Japanese sentence which appeared to exhibit a considerable amount of left branching, as opposed to English which branches to the right.

It is, therefore, quite clear from the foregoing that a significant share of the effort of the American linguist working on machine translation has been devoted to the analysis of the grammatical structures of the languages involved; I shall now discuss the models underlying the analysis as well as the specific approaches and procedures employed by various MT groups both in the United States and abroad.

3.3 Linguistic Theories Underlying Automatic Syntactic Recognition

Following the compilation of grammar-coded, automatic dictionaries, automatic syntactic recognition and analysis became the primary objective which MT research groups shared in common. Researchers concluded from the beginning, either intuitively or empirically, that the development of syntactic recognition algorithms could only proceed from the establishment of a specific approach to grammar, i.e., within the framework of arriving at a well-defined system of language structure and organization. Moreover, the needs of MT made unprecedented demands for a grammar of precisely formulated specifications.

3.3.1 Theoretical Language Models for Syntactic Analysis

The following approaches to grammar have been adopted by practically all MT research groups since at least 1960. The grammatical models themselves may be distinguished according to traditional linguistic criteria as either formal (theories) or descriptive (approaches) in nature. Garvin [9] prefers to label the former strongly model-oriented grammars, and the latter weakly model-oriented grammars. In essence, the four major theoretical language models are dependency theory (see, e.g. [19]), stratificational theory (see, e.g. [20]), transformational theory (see, e.g. [21, 23]), and formational theory (see, e.g. [22, 23]).

Dependency theory, which has primarily been employed in the MT activities of the RAND Corporation and Georgetown University, was elaborated by David Hays, and is in principle based on the assumption that words in a sentence are mutually dependent in a hierarchical way.

Stratification theory, which was applied to the MT experiment of the Berkeley research group, is predicated on a concept of language, of which the structure may be said to consist of several hierarchical levels or strata, the lowest of which is sound, and the highest is meaning.

Transformational theory, notably articulated by Noam Chomsky among others, is the basic approach of such MT research groups as the Center for the Study of Automatic Translation at Grenoble, France, and the University of Montreal. This theory proceeds from the belief that a language has certain basic types of sentences called kernel sentences from which the remaining, more complex sentences of the language may be derived by application of transformation rules. A language, therefore, consists of kernel sentences and their transforms.

Formational theory, applied in MT experiments at the Linguistic Research Center at the University of Texas, appears to be closely related to transformational theory. It is based on the assumption that it is possible to formulate a mathematical theory of the formation of symbol strings. Also involved is the necessary creation of meta-languages for processing object languages.

3.3.2 Grammatical Approaches to Syntactic Analysis

Some of the better known grammatical approaches to syntactic analysis are predictive analysis,[15] immediate constituent analysis [9], the fulcrum approach,[16] clump theory,[17] and the correlational grammar (see [24]).

Predictive analysis was introduced by Ida Rhodes of the National Bureau of Standards MT group, and further elaborated by the Harvard University group headed by Anthony Oettinger. It is based on the assumption that a Russian sentence can be scanned from left to right, and the syntactic role of a given word in the sentence can be determined on the basis of predictions made during the analysis about the word on its left. The hierarchical function of the word on the right is also predicted based on the word being examined.

---

[15] *Predictive analysis*, various reports of the MT research groups at the National Bureau of Standards and Harvard University's Computation Laboratory.

[16] *Fulcrum*, various reports of the MT group at the Bunker-Ramo Corporation.

[17] *Clump theory*, various reports of the MT group at the Cambridge Language Research Unit in England.

The immediate constituent analysis is based on the view that, taking the sentence as the largest linguistic unit, by a series of consecutive sectionings and subsectionings such an analysis can yield increasingly smaller sentence constituents. This procedure entails multiple, back and forth, scans of the sentence, particularly when automatized.

The fulcrum approach, in opposition to the immediate constituent theory, commences analysis with the smallest constituent of the sentence and proceeds to group constituents into increasingly larger units. This approach, developed by Paul Garvin, has been the basis for syntactic analysis at the Bunker-Ramo Corporation, and a modified version of it has been used in MT research at Wayne State University.

Clump theory was formulated and used at the Cambridge Language Research Unit by A. F. Parker-Rhodes and Roger Needham. This technique for syntactic analysis performs multiple scanning of a sentence and, on the basis of dependency and government relationships, groups related sentence constituents.

Correlational grammar was first developed by Silvio Ceccato in his MT experimentation at Milan in what came to be known as the Italian Operational School. The approach in this system is based on relations created between individual lexical items and their constructed constituents. Basic to this theory is the creation of a table of finite relations that the human mind sets up between the individual items in a train of thought. There is an attempt to correlate human thought with verbal expression.

3.4 Differences between Traditional and MT Grammar

The question that arises quite naturally at this juncture is how machine translation grammar differs from traditional grammar. The differences are conditioned by the fact that the analysis is performed by the computer and not by the human being. The latter has recourse to bilingual dictionaries and written grammars, as well as all the information about language in his head, which he has accumulated during numerous previous translation activities. For machine translation this total information from all possible sources has to be compiled and arranged in a form suitable for processing by the computer. No ambiguities in description will be tolerated by the computer. Every rule must be precisely formulated; all exceptions to rules must be explicitly specified; no "et ceteras" can be allowed, since the computer will not be able to understand them. Linguists traditionally described, but never attempted to test the precision of their grammars. Machine translation has provided the first real challenge to test the power of grammars constructed by the linguists in the course of their research.

3.5 Components of an MT System

The principal steps in the MT process, based primarily on the procedure employed by the Wayne State University group will now be discussed. For the most part, however, these procedures, with a few variations, were in general use by other MT groups as well.

3.5.1 MT Dictionary Compilation

Generally speaking, the first step in machine translation involves the compilation of a bilingual glossary containing all the lexical, morphological, and syntactic information about each entry, and eventually also semantic information necessary in the translation process. To reduce the complexity of some of the problems encountered in the course of this compilation, these dictionaries dealt usually with a specific science subfield—chemistry, physics, mathematics—the so-called microglossaries. Dictionary information was first punched on IBM cards, and then stored on magnetic tape or in core memory, or both, for dictionary look-up by the computer. Words of the incoming language text to be translated were also keypunched, put onto magnetic tape and then by means of appropriate programs looked up. Lexical items found to be missing during the dictionary look-up process were either transliterated, or computer routines were developed to generate, by speculating on their location in the sentence and on their morphemes, the grammatical information of the missing forms. These forms were appropriately coded by human translator and then inserted into the existing dictionary tape. Using all these devices an updated dictionary tape was produced. This text tape with the looked-up information was then processed by syntactic programs especially developed for this purpose.

3.5.2 Syntactic Analysis

These syntactic programs further analyzed the input language sentences by employing various parsing routines, which depend to a large extent on the linguistic theory utilized by the MT groups discussed above. The main purpose of these procedures was, of course, to establish the hierarchical relation between these sentence units, viz., subject, predicate, object, and other components.

3.5.3 Target Language Synthesis

After the components of the source language have been identified and appropriately tagged, the target language equivalents of the source language lexical items are printed out in target language order.

Next, appropriate target language items missing in the source language are inserted; in the case of Russian-to-English translation, these items are articles, prepositions, various forms of the verb "to be," "to do," and other function words. Some source language lexical items have to be deleted in the target language. As an example of deletions in the case of Russian-to-English translation, Russian emphatic particles, же, да, and others can be cited. The lack of structural class equivalents between the two languages has also to be dealt with. Resolution of homography has also to be attempted. And finally, the source language items have to be rearranged in target language order.

3.5.4 Treatment of Idioms and Lexical Units

One way of dealing with the lack of one-to-one correspondence referred to above between languages on the lexical level is to establish a class of lexical units called idioms. Groups of words in the source language have as their lexical equivalent in the target language one or more words. An idiom can also be defined as a group of words the lexical meaning of which is different from the lexical meanings of the words constituting it. Thus, the Russian idiom, несмотря на, the literal translation of which is "not looking at," is best translated into English by "in spite of."

The way idioms were handled by machine translation groups in the United States is related to the dictionary look-up schemes used by them. Some groups, among them Georgetown, RAND Corporation, and Bunker-Ramo, stored idioms in a separate list or table and looked them up prior to the main dictionary look-up operation. The Wayne State University group stored idioms as ordinary dictionary entries, and looked up incoming text in text order. The idioms were identified according to the so-called "longest match scheme," in which a check was first made to determine whether all the constituent parts of an idiom were present. In other schemes, the incoming source language text was first sorted out, either alphabetically or according to some other scheme, e.g., an arrangement of words in an order of descending frequency of use. Idioms were looked up in a special table, as pointed out above, and then the rest of the lexical units of the incoming text were identified.

In glossaries which consisted of full words and stems plus affixes, the full words were looked up first by a matching procedure. For words not found by direct look up, the word was first split into a stem and affixes according to special routines devised for this purpose. An attempt was then made to find a matching stem by checking with a special table of stems. The endings were then also matched against a special table of possible inflectional endings. If a perfect match was obtained in both instances, the full word was again reconstituted and the stored grammatical information attached to it. If a complete match was not obtained, the source language lexical items found were inserted in the eventual printout according to some prearranged scheme, indicated above, i.e., either transliterated, their grammatical information generated, or looked up by a human being.

After the lexical units of the source language, be they full words, stem, affixes or idioms, have been identified, information needed for further translation processing by the computer, which is usually termed "grammar code" by some machine translation groups, has to be attached to them. The way this information was arranged was governed to a major extent by the linguistic theory employed in the grammatical analysis of the sentence (since, as pointed out above, the translation unit of most machine translation groups has been the sentence), as well as by computer considerations. Here one must distinguish carefully between the linguistic theories which are used by the various machine translation groups, either in expressed form or in a form implied in their statements, and the approaches and procedures used by them in the course of analysis and subsequent computer processing.

3.6 Wayne State University MT Procedures

3.6.1 Wayne State University Grammar Code

The lexical units which comprise the Wayne State Machine translation dictionary are coded with respect to their function in the sentence. Although morphological information is used, the basic criteria for the classification employed are syntactic. Nine form classes are established in the Wayne State University grammar code: (1) *nominals*, which comprise all those words that function as nouns (included here are also personal pronouns and the pronouns кто—"who" and что—"what"); (2) *modifiers*, which include all words that can modify a nominal (adjectives, certain pronouns, e.g., possessive and demonstrative), numerals and verbal participles; (3) *predicatives*, which consist of all words that can be used as predicates, including finite verbs, short form adjectives, comparatives of adverbs used predicatively, words denoting the so-called "category of state" in Russian—категория состояния—жаль—"it is a pity," можно—"one can," надо—"it is necessary"—; (4) *gerunds*; (5) *verbal infinitives*;[18] (6) *adverbs* and *particles*, which are grouped together for the sake of convenience

---

[18] Gerunds and infinitives are separated out from the rest of the verb because they differ from the latter in the manner in which they function in the Russian sentence.

since relatively little is done with them in the course of sentence structure determination; (7) *conjunctions*; (8) *prepositions* (these are treated the same as in traditional grammar); and (9) *declined relatives* which consist of relative pronouns like какой, который.—"which," чей—"whose" and which are separated from the other pronouns because of their property of serving as part of an initial clause boundary marker.[19]

The grammatical information thought to be necessary for automatic translation is first entered by coders on appropriate coding sheets and later keypunched onto IBM cards. In the Wayne State University scheme there are two IBM cards for each dictionary entry, one containing the Russian word and the accompanying grammatical information, the other the English equivalent or equivalents of the Russian word. The IBM cards are subsequently stored on magnetic tape, as already indicated.

The first 24 columns of the Russian dictionary card are reserved for the Russian form. Column 25 contains an indication of the form class to which the Russian word belongs. Columns 26 and 27 are used for storing information about homographs.[20] Column 26 indicates the type of the homograph, while column 27 indicates to how many form classes a homograph belongs. Thus the homograph что—"that, what, which"—belongs to four form classes, nominal, adverb, conjunction, and declined relative. Other morphological information contained in the grammar coding sheets pertains to gender, number, case, animation, tense, mood, voice, person, for inflected forms, while the non-inflected forms contain information characteristic of them. Thus, for the adverb гораздо—"considerably"—there is an indication that it must be always followed by a comparative. In case of the prepositions, there is an indication as to whether they can be used postpositionally, like спустя—"later," ради—"for the sake of," вслед—"after." Conjunctions are marked as to whether they are coordinating or subordinating, ambiguous or nonambiguous, paired or not paired.

Syntactic relationships like agreement and government are also coded wherever applicable. The agreement code indicates what the requirements are for the subject of a given predicative, or the possible cases, numbers, and genders which a nominal, a modifier, or a declined relative may have in all possible contexts. The government code is used to indicate which cases are governed by prepositions. There are

[19] This classification scheme was first proposed by Paul L. Garvin, of the Bunker-Ramo group and later adopted, with modification, by the Wayne State group.

[20] A homograph in a given language is a word which, when projected into all possible contexts, may function in more than one part of speech category, e.g., English "hit" which may function as a noun, adjective, and verb.

indications of what specific cases are governed by prepositions, modifiers (аналогичный—"analogous"), and nouns (подарок брату—"a gift for brother"). For predicatives, infinitives, and gerunds, in addition to the indication of cases which they govern, there are also marked cases of what can be labeled complex government, which is said to exist when a predicative governs more than one case, one of which may be a prerequisite for the others: Его выбрали секретарём—. "They elected him as a secretary," the instrumental is required when the accusative is present. Determination of the presence of agreement and government relationship is vitally important in grouping lexical items into sentence units, as will be shown later. Syntactic information about punctuation and formulas occurring in the text is also coded. For example, if formulas serve a predicative function in the sentence, they are appropriately coded in the predicative class.

Target language equivalents of source language dictionary entries are, of course, also entered. In the English IBM card of the Wayne group the first 24 columns contain the Russian form. Column 25 has an indication of the form class of the Russian form, column 26 has the number of translations, column 27 is blank, and columns 28–72 contain the English equivalents. All the above information is then put on magnetic tape and read into the core memory of the computer.

3.6.2 Wayne State University Automatic Syntactic Analysis

After the lexical units of the source language have been looked up in the automatic dictionary, properly identified, and supplied with all the stored grammatical information, syntactic analysis of the source language beings.

The Wayne group employs as the first phase of its syntactic analysis, procedures called blocking, the purpose of which is to identify certain sentence elements that are considered to be important, and to group them with certain adjacent elements that are considered to be linked to these elements in a complementary way. This blocking procedure is useful because it results in the creation of a sentence image, with fewer elements, which simplifies subsequent sentence analysis for the identification of main sentence units, subject, object, predicate.

Essentially, the blocking procedure changes the sequence of lexical units into a sequence of grammatically meaningful blocks (which may consist of just one word). Taken in isolation, without reference to the rest of the sentence, these blocks may still be ambiguous on this level, since the computer does not possess the speaker's intuitive ability to assign them their correct role in the sentence. The present Wayne procedure, called HYPERPARSE, permits the systematic establishment of a sentence profile (by proceeding from the blocking level to the phrase level, and from that to the clause level, each time utilizing the information derived from the previous level). This results in the identification of the kernel of the Russian sentence (subject, verb, object) and the adjunct elements related hierarchically to the kernel. On the phrase level, by means of appropriate routines, the blocks are first divided into four classes. The first class contains predicatives and all potential clause markers, such as conjunctions and punctuation marks. The second class contains potential candidates for subject and object, i.e., possible nominative and accusative constructions. Blocks identifiable as genitives constitute a third class, which serves as a transitional class between the potential kernel elements and adjuncts, while the fourth class contains all prepositional blocks, adverbs, all datives and instrumentals, and all other phrases which are identifiable as potential adjuncts.

After the blocks have been divided into the above four classes, the syntactic analysis on the clause level begins with the systematic investigation of the contents of the first class. This provides information about the structure of the entire sentence, and results in the selection of procedures for analysis of the membership of the other three classes, which are analyzed in turn. Agreement and government checks are used wherever appropriate in the course of analysis, the final result of which is the establishment of the constituents of the sentence in a hierarchical fashion. This analysis is designed specifically for the morphological and syntactic features of Russian, and, furthermore, its results provide an output from which the synthesis proceeds, and which involves, as pointed out above, a contrastive treatment of Russian and English.

3.7 Other MT Syntactic Analysis Techniques

Another type of syntactic analysis called predictive analysis was used by two machine translation groups in the United States: National Bureau of Standards and Harvard University. The notion of predictive analysis was introduced by Ida Rhodes of the National Bureau of Standards [25]. Her empirical system was later adopted, with modifications, by Anthony Oettinger and Murray Sherry at Harvard [26]. In predictive analysis, the syntactic analysis program scans a sentence from left to right, and a storage device called a "pushdown store" is utilized in the "prediction pool," i.e., the list of anticipated structures. The pushdown store is a linear array of storage elements in which information is entered and removed from one end only, so that the last element (prediction) entered is the first one picked up for testing. The technique of predictive analysis subsumes that, in scanning a

Russian sentence from left to right, it is possible both to make predictions about syntactic structures that occur to the right of any word, and to determine the syntactic role of a word itself on the basis of previously made predictions which the word might fulfill.

Mrs. Rhodes has developed a set of predictions describing Russian syntax, some of which are in the glossary and some of which are in the syntactic analysis routine. Each prediction has an urgency number. When a prediction is fulfilled, it is erased. If a prediction is unfulfilled and has a low urgency number, it is also erased. The unfulfilled predictions with high urgency numbers are kept until the end of the analysis, and are used as criteria for evaluating the quality of the analysis. The predictive analysis scheme of Mrs. Rhodes assumes a previous profiling of the sentence to determine clause and phrase boundaries.

Sherry's predictive analysis incorporated provisions for a single path only. His system was found to be inadequate for most sentences, especially for long ones, because of the impossibility of always choosing the correct alternative at each point, particularly in a sentence where syntactic ambiguities exist, and because of the difficulty in tracing back an error known to exist because of inconsistency at some later point in the analysis. In addition, the single path system did not indicate situations where more than one parsing of a sentence was possible. As a result, Warren Plath [27] of Harvard, basing his work on that of Susumo Kuno and Anthony Oettinger of Harvard (in connection with the syntactic analysis of English), developed a multiple-path system of predictive syntactic analysis, which investigates all possible parsings of a sentence, discards the paths which have little likelihood of occurring, and conveniently solves many of the earlier problems involving syntactic ambiguities and error tracing.

Still more research, both on the grammatical analysis of the source language and that of the target language, needs to be done before machine translation output begins to resemble that of a human translator. The contents of language lexicons and what has been referred to above, as contained in the head of the human translator, has to be stated in a form acceptable for computer processing. As an example of this type of endeavor, could be cited the research that the Wayne group is undertaking, for compiling the contents of two Russian lexicons for computer storage and retrieval.[21] To this store

---

[21] Such data were gathered with the support of the National Science Foundation through the activities of two research grants: *Comprehensive Electronic Data Processing of Two Russian Lexicons* and *Computer-Aided Linguistic Analysis of Russian Lexicon: Development of the Grammatical Profile of Lexical Entries.* The two Russian lexicons which served as the corpus for these investigations are: *Tolkovyj slovar' russkogo jazyka* —Lexicon of the Russian Language—(D. N. Ushakov, ed.) Moscow, 1935 and *Slovar' russkogo jazyka*—Dictionary of the Russian Language—Academy of Sciences, USSR,

of information should also be added knowledge about the language which still had not been codified, e.g., which Russian verbs must be always followed by a direct object (obligatory government). Some help for English synthesis is sure to come from attempts to construct generative transformational models of English grammar by disciples of Chomsky and Harris. Contributions in the area of semantics, which has barely begun to be investigated in machine translation, including the Bunker-Ramo [28] and RAND groups [29, 30], and others [31, 32], are sure to come in the future. More investigations of language structure and the development of automatic syntactic recognition and sentence parsing routines are necessary for the implementation of effectively functioning MT systems.

4. Survey of MT Groups Since 1960

When Bar-Hillel's contribution on the status of mechanical language translation was published in volume 1 of *Advances in Computers* in 1960, formally organized MT research activities had been established principally in three countries: the United States, the USSR, and Great Britain. In addition to his discussion of developments by the various MT groups in these countries, Bar-Hillel included some remarks on the status of MT research at Milan, Italy and the Hebrew University at Jerusalem. In the nearly 10 years that have followed Bar-Hillel's survey, reports of official research in MT have emanated from as many as seventy groups in at least fifteen countries: United States, USSR, Great Britain, France, Germany, Japan, Italy, Belgium, Canada, Mexico, Czechoslovakia, Yugoslavia, Rumania, Hungary, and Poland. If efforts of directly related research in computational linguistics or hardware development were included, these figures would be greatly increased.

Moscow, 1957. The main objectives of these investigations were (1) to analyze and process for computer retrieval the pertinent linguistic information contained both explicitly and implicitly in the above lexicons; (2) to compile information contained in each of the dictionaries in the following broad areas: lexical, morphological, and that of function and usage, and then to merge this information; (3) to treat various methodological and theoretical approaches for lexicological research. This information, it is hoped, will provide a useful and rapidly accessible data base for further processing and utilization by grammarians as well as computational linguists. Based on this research, a series of publications was planned, the first of which—*Distribution of Ten Canonical Entry Classes in Two Russian Lexicons*—appeared in January 1967. The second publication in this series by Alexander Viteic, *Russian Substantives: Distribution of Gender*, appeared in the summer of 1969, and deals with the distribution of gender among Russian substantives in the above lexicons.

The present survey will first discuss briefly the status of each of the principal groups covered in Bar-Hillel's survey. Second, several groups which came into being after the publication of Bar-Hillel's article are surveyed. Third, in contradistinction to all the above groups which are essentially research-oriented, the current activities of five production-oriented MT projects are described in some detail.

4.1 MT Groups Covered in Bar-Hillel's Survey of 1960

4.1.1 University of Washington

The Seattle group investigated problems of MT from 1949–1962. Primary emphasis was placed originally on German–English MT, and subsequently on Russian–English MT, but a separate program was also undertaken for Chinese–English MT. At the time of termination, advances in MT research at Seattle included considerable development of dictionary procedures as well as morphological and syntactic analysis routines. A particular effort was made in investigating the problem of automatic resolution of grammatical ambiguity. At the conclusion of this research, machine translation was being simulated as a means for pinpointing system procedures which required improvement, e.g., codification of lexicographical or dictionary data.

In addition to the development of an MT system, the Seattle group conducted collateral research in translation evaluation in investigations of (1) the statistical aspects in translation of scientific language, and (2) machine translation quality and its evaluation.

The principal goals of the Seattle group according to its view of the translation process were (1) selection of the correct target equivalent of the source word, and (2) organization and coordination of these words into a grammatical and semantic form which would be meaningful to the reader in the target language.

To implement the group's evaluation program, three general approaches were investigated:

(1) A study and evaluation of occurrence probability between certain Russian kernel structures and their English equivalents

(2) A study of methods evaluating continuity of meaning among equivalents selected by the translation process

(3) The development and evaluation of a "test" of translation reality.

The Seattle approach of kernel analysis entailed the mechanical location of basic elements in each sentence of a Russian text. These elements are classified according to types based on their grammatical features and word order. English kernels, composed of words in the English translation of the text corresponding to the words of the

Russian kernel, are also mechanically located and classified according to type [*33–35*].

4.1.2 Massachusetts Institute of Technology

The M.I.T. group was engaged in formal MT research for 12 years, 1953–1965. Research efforts were primarily devoted to German– and Russian–English MT; other languages, such as Arabic and French, were also investigated. Since it was felt that for its objectives both source and target languages required complete analysis, the M.I.T. group performed extensive analysis of English as well.

The basic approach to grammatical analysis of this group was based on the phrase structure model. To meet programming needs a new program language was developed by the principal investigator, Victor Yngve. This language, known as COMIT, gained wide acceptance and usage by many MT workers. Various investigations ranged from programming techniques to theoretical linguistics, from morphology and syntax to semantics. An over-all aim of fully automatic quality translation led the group throughout its research period to investigate many problems irrespective of degrees of complexity. A very impressive list of publications issuing from its research appears in the *Final Report* [*36*].

4.1.3 Georgetown University

In his 1960 survey, Bar-Hillel said of Georgetown that no other MT group has been working on such a broad front. In the report on Georgetown's activities from 1952–1963 prepared by R. Ross Macdonald, the full scope of MT research, together with a complete list of publications for that period, is presented in detail.

The Georgetown group committed itself to result-oriented experimental research in primarily Russian–English MT of scientific and technological literature. Since the basic problem of MT was considered to be linguistic in nature, the Georgetown researchers were mainly guided by current linguistic orientation.

The group's main objectives, as stated in the above report, were the following:

(1) The progressive improvement of experimental runs by means of a feedback procedure on the basis of the discernment of lacunae and inadequacies

(2) The processing of scientific and technological language first of all, since it presents fewer problems than general language for automatic translation

(3) Transfer from Russian to English.

Following the publication of the above report, individual papers by various group members have appeared under the series ttile *Occasional Papers on Machine Translation,* see [37]. These papers are numbered consecutively and are available at Georgetown University. They cover a wide range of topics on materials which were generally developed around the Georgetown technique of structural transfer.

Since 1965 MT research has been continued at Georgetown under the direction of R. Ross Macdonald. The objective of this research has been to achieve an operational MT system which will transfer Russian to English without editing, and which will be usable in connection with any effective general purpose computer.

4.1.4 RAND Corporation

The RAND group began its studies in machine translation around 1958 with primary emphasis being placed on Russian–English MT until approximately 1963, when the scope of research was broadened to include problems in theoretical and structural linguistics. The approach to MT taken by this group was based on dependency theory as elaborated by David G. Hays. This method, which Hays called "sentence structure determination," sought to establish dependency relationships among text occurrences in the sentence. Dependency theory, according to Hays, is actually a characterization theory not necessarily associable with any empirical method or principle. It is a theory of grammars with abstract mechanisms for characterizing sets of utterances, and for assigning to them certain structural descriptions called D-trees.

The activities of the RAND group have centered generally around computational linguistic research. The group has produced a great quantity of documentation which has been released periodically over the past 10 years in the form of monographs. Its contribution to machine translation research was indeed of considerable scope and influence [38–41].

Two additional efforts reported in 1966 were studies on predication in contemporary standard Russian, and elaboration of the RAND glossary of Russian physics.

4.1.5 Bunker-Ramo Corporation

This is fundamentally the same group as comprised the Ramo-Wooldridge group (as reported in Bar-Hillel's survey) and the Thompson-Ramo-Wooldridge group. To clear up any confusion, the successive changes in the name of the corporation did not involve either geographic displacement of the group or significant alteration of its research objectives and personnel. The large number of progress reports and other publications since at least 1958 have of course appeared under each of the above names. MT research has centered chiefly around Russian–English MT, but there has been extensive work with other languages as well.

The basic approach of this group centers around the fulcrum theory as enunciated and elaborated by Paul Garvin. Most recent fulcrum techniques have been concentrated significantly on the resolution of semantic problems.

The major research effort at Bunker-Ramo led to the production of an experimental but operational machine translation program which included input, dictionary look-up, syntactic analysis, and printouts of translation of scientific documents as well as selected text from the Soviet newspaper *Pravda*.

Like other MT groups, such as Wayne State University, Texas, and RAND, the Bunker-Ramo group, through its experience, reached the conclusion that high quality machine translation is still not feasible, such output being impeded by many unsolved problems. These problems are linguistic as well as computational. The hope was that the quality of MT output will increase proportionally as these problems are articulated and resolved.

MT research at Bunker-Ramo has involved four major areas:

(1) Linguistic analysis leading to more effective syntactic analysis of Russian

(2) Linguistic analysis directed at improving the quality of the English output

(3) Incorporation of the results of the linguistic research

(4) A continuing programming effort directed at improving the simplicity, dependability, and the speed of the computational aspects of the system.

Although, as mentioned above, the Bunker-Ramo group has been involved recently in deep semantic studies and related problems of multiple meaning, considerable emphasis was also placed on syntactic analysis, specifically Paul Garvin's principle of a heuristic approach to syntax. In this approach, decisions are based on immediate context as tentative, subject to revision on the basis of information from a larger context. In addition to various progress reports, see [42–46].

4.1.6 Harvard University

As pointed out in Bar-Hillel's survey, the Harvard group's primary MT research effort in the late fifties was devoted to the development and implementation of an automatic dictionary, an MT problem to which Harvard, perhaps more than any other research group, devoted considerable experimentation. During that time, the source language was Russian.

By 1960, this group shifted its emphasis from word-by-word translation to sentence analysis. Concomitantly, grammatical analysis of Russian structure was implemented on a broad plane, and an approach to the automatic syntactic analysis of the sentence was formulated. This approach was the predictive method originally formulated by Ida Rhodes, and modified and adapted by the Harvard group. It was tested on English sentences during initial stages, and gradually was extended to Russian as well. The general strategy employed in syntactic analysis came to be known as multiple-path syntactic analysis.

Since 1964, the Harvard group has expanded its investigations to include mathematical models of language in addition to research on automatic syntactic analysis of Russian and English [47–51].

4.1.7 University of Michigan

Research in machine translation by this group was discontinued in 1962. The primary research objective at that time was the development of a theory of translation to form the basis for constructing a "learning" or "self-modifying" program to translate natural languages. See Koutsoudus [52] and Smoke and Dubinsky [53].

4.1.8 University of Pennsylvania

MT *per se* was not the objective of this research group, whose principal investigator, Zelig Harris, was the prime author of the transformation model of language analysis.

The principal aim of this group was automatic syntactic analysis. In the course of its development, the group contemplated computerized syntactic recognition. In this connection, there was some tangential bearing on MT, insofar as this group, as well as various MT researchers, concerned itself with the automatic generation of English output.[22]

4.1.9 National Bureau of Standards

Bar-Hillel briefly described a method of syntactic analysis of Russian devised by Ida Rhodes and applied by the NBS group in their MT experimentation. This method later became known as predictive

---

[22] See various papers printed under series heading University of Pennsylvania. Transformations and Discourse Analysis Projects, particularly Sager, Naomi, " Procedures for left-to-right recognition of sentence structure," No. 27, 1960; Harris, Zelig, "Immediate constituent formulation of English syntax," No. 45, April 1963; Holt, Anatol W., "A mathematical and applied investigation of tree structures of computer syntactic analysis," No. 49, June 1963.

analysis, which, as mentioned in the discussion of the Harvard Group, was later adapted and modified by Harvard.

MT research by this group continued until 1964. At that time, work was proceeding on the last of three sections in the long-range program for practical Russian–English MT. The first two sections dealt essentially with (1) the mechanical retrieval of source word grammatical characteristics, and (2) the parsing of Russian sentences using the predictive method. The last section involved a special process of encoding of words called "profiling" [54, 55].

4.1.10 Wayne State University

Research in computer-aided Russian–English machine translation at Wayne State University has led to the development of an experimental system which presently comprises three basic operations—dictionary look-up, syntactic blocking, and HYPERPARSE. At the current stage of development, these three operations are coordinated through the interaction of both human and machine procedures. (See Fig. 1.)

Input to the system generally consists of a technical Russian language text which has been keypunched and read onto magnetic tape. One sentence at a time is analyzed. Each sentence item is looked up in a computer-stored dictionary (a compilation of words as they occur in a text comparable to the input text) and its encoded grammatical characteristics and English equivalent(s) are retrieved. The resultant output tape of looked-up text is used as input to the next operational phase—syntactic blocking or analysis. This procedure endeavors to recognize and to record the functional (grammatical) role played by each sentence constituent.

In syntactic analysis, sentence items (sometimes only one word) which serve the same function in the sentence, e.g., subject, predicate, object, are put into blocks or groups. Each block has a kernel word (noun, verb, preposition) on which other sentence items may be said to depend. For example, blocks would be formed by a noun and its modifiers, a verb and an adverb, a preposition and its object noun, etc. An output tape of blocked sentence is then created and serves as input to the third operational stage, i.e., where the blocked sentence is automatically parsed. This procedure entails determining the functional role (e.g., subject, predicate, object) played by each of the blocks.

To resolve the problem of grammatically ambiguous sentences, the computer program HYPERPARSE (see Section 3.6.2) reduces grammatically ambiguous sentences to the fewest possible interpretations. This is done by means of a mechanically generated matrix which seeks to discover distinctions among the apparently ambiguous blocks. Those noun blocks which do not qualify as either subject or object candidates are grouped as so-called "adjuncts."

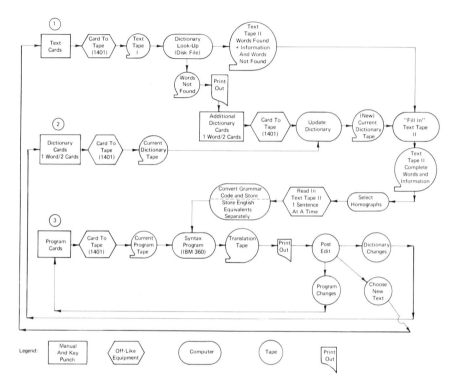

FIG. 1

Experimentation in machine translation at Wayne State University[23] is continuing with two primary objectives: first, to automate additional analytic procedures; and second, to refine previous routines according to insights gathered from each successive experiment. At the same time, translation rules are being formulated which, when written into the system, will improve the quality of the output. For a complete list of all MT publications produced between 1958 and 1968, see [58].

For one year's research, Shogo Ushiyama, from Japan has joined the WSU group. The objective of his research is the design of a system for automatic translation of Japanese–English telegrams.

---

[23] For dictionary problems and grammar coding, see [56]; for a discussion of problems in automatic syntactic recognition, see Steiger [57].

4.1.11 University of California at Berkeley

The particular language emphasis in MT research by this group has been on Russian– and Chinese–English. Extensive research in theoretical studies of linguistic structure has been conducted. It has been the belief of this group that these studies would yield formalisms which might serve as a basis for writing MT algorithms.

The grammatical approach taken by this group was significantly influenced by the stratificational model developed by Sydney Lamb while he was at Berkeley. In his syntactic research, he was primarily interested in developing a system for tactic analysis which presupposes a segmentation of text units in terms of his concept of language as a hierarchy of strata.

A wide range of linguistic problem solving by computer has characterized research during and following the period of primary concentration on the problem of MT. Developments growing out of this research included such studies as production of concordances by computer. For a discussion of Lamb's approach to automatic syntactic analysis, and linguistic models see [59–61]. Efforts to develop a Chinese–English MT system have been continuing under the direction of Ching-Yi Dougherty.

4.1.12 University of Texas

This group documented its activities from 1959–1961 in a series of quarterly progress reports entitled "Machine Language Translation. Study." Since 1962 its activities have been incorporated into the Linguistic Research Center at the University of Texas, under which title group publications have appeared up to the present time.

This research group has always had a slightly different orientation than most other MT research groups in the United States owing to the fact that attention has been focused not only on problems of machine translation, but simultaneously on the general area of linguistic analysis. Efforts have centered around three interrelated tasks directed at refinement of the group's model and approach. These three tasks are (1) descriptive linguistics, (2) programming, and (3) mathematical research.

As reported recently in a pamphlet from the Linguistic Research Center, the approach is concentrated on four points:

(1) The translation process is viewed as independent of specific source and target languages.

(2) The structures of source and target languages are supplied to the computer in the form of grammar codes.

(3) Linguistic analysis produces phrase structure grammars arranged

in a hierarchy (i.e., independent but related grammars are produced for each type of description, e.g., for syntactic and semantic).

(4) Linguistic analysis of source and target languages are independent of each other.

The Linguistic Research Center approach, although geared at the outset to German–English translation, has aimed at developing a translation technique that could be readily adapted to other languages. The group has, in fact, been developing syntactic descriptions of English, Russian, and German, and limited efforts have been made for similar descriptions of Japanese and Chinese. Pilot descriptions of other languages have been made as well to test the generality of the algorithms developed for machine translation.

The group has sought to accumulate comprehensive data including lexical, syntactic, and semantic descriptions of many languages. These data are then retrieved in compact formats required for automatic analysis and synthesis. Around 1965 the Russian Master Dictionary, developed through Air Force support, was incorporated into the research program. The dictionary has permitted the testing and expansion of a Russian–English translation system based on a syntactic translation model that has been developed [62–64].

4.1.13 Birkbeck College, London

As was clearly pointed out in Bar-Hillel's survey, Andrew Booth, the director of this group, was one of the outstanding MT pioneers. It was also indicated that this group placed great hope for successful MT on the development of an interlingua, i.e., an artificial intermediate language; moreover, the group was guided in its experimentation by methods based on mathematical and logical considerations.

Research into MT techniques continued into the mid-sixties. However, there was more progress made in a related area of investigation, viz., the mechanization of certain aspects of literary studies, such as the preparation of word-indexes and concordances. For a sample of this group's work see [65].

4.1.14 Cambridge Language Research Unit, England

It was shortly after the publication of Bar-Hillel's survey, in which he briefly described the newly conceived CLRU approach to grammatical analysis, that there was a final formulation of its lattice theory on which the CLRU syntactic analysis was subsequently based. In addition to syntactic analysis, the CLRU also focused attention on development of its thesaurus approach as well as on an investigation of semantics in general.

Its research progress was reported regularly until approximately 1965. Specifically, during the time between the appearance of Bar-Hillel's survey and 1965, its work in syntactic analysis entailed the development of an automatic parsing program based on the afore-mentioned Parker-Rhodes lattice model of language. A formal bracket-ing (i.e., syntactic blocking) algorithm was developed. For a formal presentation of the lattice theory approach see [66].

In the area of semantics, CLRU research activities included the development of a general interlingual machine translation procedure, and an investigation of the semantics of language based on the "semantic square" model of human communication. A detailed view of the CLRU semantic approach and related discussions may be found in [67]. Margaret Masterman of this research group has served as a consultant to the National Research Council of Canada on problems relating to development of MT in that country. Most recently reported research was focused on English to French machine-aided translation. The group is attempting to develop a system for producing low-level but message-preserving output, based on segmentation of text into natural phrasings (i.e., units of text containing two stress points, or a stress point and a pause), by computer program.

4.1.15 MT in the USSR

In his survey, Bar-Hillel included a discussion of the MT research activities of approximately ten groups which were conducting research at that time in the USSR. He indicated that whereas some groups were theoretically oriented, others were more empirically minded; some advocated FAHQT, while others operated with more modest aims. Not unlike MT in the United States, serious research in the USSR shifted its emphasis and came gradually to recognize the more realistic aim of machine-aided translation. With a clearer understanding of the problems of MT, serious researchers were able to emphasize the need for descriptive studies of languages "from a structuralist point of view" as Bar-Hillel pointed out, and "the only one which makes sense for MT."

Rather than undertake a similar survey here, since the pertinent literature is not so readily available, a comprehensive summary of the state of the art in the USSR, is recommended for the interested reader. It has been translated from the Russian and contains a bibliography of 165 significant references [68].

A portion of the closing statement perhaps best sums up the current view of MT in the USSR, and it bears quoting:

The first results of work on machine translation created an illusion in the scientific community that the solution to the problem was near at hand. This illusion was due not only to the seemingly convincing demonstrations of machine translation capabilities. . . . Nor did these demonstrations have any significant impact in the scientific community. Much more serious is another illusion which was supported by many investigators. This is the illusion that the problem at hand was of an "engineering" nature, that machine translation had already been resolved in principle, and that to be implemented in practice, only considerable organizational efforts were required ([68], p. 43).

The authors went on to add:

An opinion was maintained that large-scale machine experiments with translation using known principles would be capable of making the available theoretical algorithms operational. It turned out, however, that the problem was in fact of a different class, for it concerned the investigation of operating principles of a biological system and the elucidation of how such a complex system as human language is capable of functioning at all. This is a serious problem indeed. Unless it is settled, no successful development of information systems needed for human society seems possible ([68] p. 44.)

4.1.16 University of Milan, Italy

Although the Milan approach of correlational grammar mentioned above was considered unpromising by Bar-Hillel, it endured at least until 1966 at Milan, and has provided a basis for further research at the University of Georgia on the same theoretical model.

Although basically a theoretical approach to MT was favored by the Milan group, many practical activities were undertaken. The group worked primarily on Russian–English translation, but German and Italian output were added to the procedure. An experiment of English–Latin translation of random sentences made with a limited vocabulary was also perfected. Further efforts included the development of a general grammar suitable for the mechanization of every kind of linguistic activity: translation, summarization, and description. For a general view of the Milan effort see Ceccato and Zonta [69] and Ceccato [70]; see also Ceccato [71].

4.2 MT Groups Established After Bar-Hillel's Survey of 1960

These groups, for the most part, are located in countries other than the United States, the USSR, Great Britain, and Italy.

Inasmuch as there was relatively little literature on the activities of these groups available at the time of preparation of this survey, the following discussions are quite brief. The omission of some existing groups from this survey is in no way intended to give the impression that the activities of these groups do not merit mention. It simply means that no pertinent material relating to their work was accessible.

4.2.1 Centre d'Études pour la Traduction Automatique, University of Grenoble, France

This research group has been conducting experimentation in Russian–French machine translation for the past few years. Having first compiled a machine dictionary, the group then proceeded to write a formal recognition grammar for Russian syntactic structures. The transformation model of grammar has been adopted in attempt to develop a metalanguage common to the two main procedural problems: (1) semantic evaluation of syntactic structure in the source language, and (2) generation of French syntactic structures. The group has recently been testing transformation rules written in conjunction with the above grammar for analysis of tree structure.[24]

The group has also been experimenting with German–French and Japanese–French machine translation. Further information is available [72–75].

4.2.2 University of Montreal, Canada

The Department of Applied Linguistics of the University of Montreal has conducted a mechanical translation research project since 1966, sponsored by the Canadian National Research Council. Research efforts have been focused on English–French machine translation. In organizing its program this group maintained close contacts with automatic translation groups at Harvard University and the University of Grenoble, France.

The primary aim, following the compilation of a dictionary in which morphological information is stored, has been to compose a grammar of English in order to be able to perform automatic recognition of syntactic structures. Existing algorithms have been tested to study the comparative efficiency of the respective syntactic analysis systems. The group appears to have expressed a preference for tree structure analysis and is continuing to experiment with grammatical models (e.g., finite state grammar). In addition to the quarterly progress reports of this group, see the following [76–77].

---

[24] A recent report indicates that a stratificational approach has also been incorporated into this group's effort to design an MT system.

4.2.3 Groupe de Linguistique Automatique, Université Libre de Bruxelles, Belgium

This group, headed by Lydia Hirschberg, has worked in cooperation with EURATOM. The analytic procedure has many points of similarity with Zelig Harris' string analysis. The group has also patterned its analytic procedures to some extent on Hays' dependency grammar and its related tree structure. Having developed a morphologically coded dictionary and syntactic analysis procedures, the group, according to its most recent publications, has been investigating semantic problems, e.g., the use of semantic information in the selection of lexical units in microglossaries.

Since at least 1964, this group has also been developing automatic dictionaries for human translators. The group has been working in cooperation with its primary user, the European Coal and Steel Authority. Dictionaries of technical terms and idiomatic structures have been compiled with a view to translation among the four languages of the European Community: French, German, Dutch, and Italian. Dictionary look-up programs accept input sentences, and produce a listing of the vocabulary requested by a translator. There are also programmed provisions for morphological analysis of the source language. Among the various publications of this group, see in particular [78].

4.2.4 Karlova University, Prague, Czechoslovakia

The objective of this group has been the investigation of the Czech and English languages for machine translation. The group's analysis of English has been largely based on a modified version of the predictive method of analysis. In a related project, this group has been developing algorithms for Czech in connection with the generative description of the language. Work has also been done on the synthesis of the Czech language, grammar coding programs have been designed, and an intermediate language, recently developed, is being improved [79].

4.2.5 Computing Centre of the Hungarian Academy of Sciences

The research objective of this group is automatic syntactic recognition of Russian sentences. A procedure called pseudomorphemic syntactic analysis has been developed which is designed to control and minimize the number of grammatical rules to be written. This scheme includes morphological analysis that provides input for syntactic analysis in the form of initial sequences of categories. The number of rules required for these analyses is reduced since separate categories are set up not only for word forms, but for their grammatical properties as well [*80*].

4.2.6 Deutsche Acadamie der Wissenschaften zu West Berlin, Germany

This group has been working on English–German and German–English MT. Its objectives include research on mathematical foundations, development of methodology, and establishment of algorithms as scientific preparation for practically applicable English and Russian machine translation of natural science and technical texts by means of computer techniques. In addition to other group reports, see [*81*].

4.2.7 Japan

Research in machine translation has also been based at several projects in Japan, including the following four groups: (1) Electro-technical Laboratory, Tokyo, Japan; (2) First Research Center, Defense Agency of Japan, Tokyo, Japan; (3) Kyoto University, Kyoto, Japan; (4) Kyushu University, Fukuoka, Japan.

Group 1 has concerned itself with English–Japanese and Japanese–English translation of scientific papers. A generalized and syntax-oriented translation system is its objective. Research has included programming considerations as well as formal descriptive linguistics. For additional information see [*82*].

Group 2 has also concentrated on problems of syntax. Its approach seeks to help linguists construct a less redundant set of rules, and also to give comprehensive account of the algorithms for syntactic analysis, transfer, and synthesis. See [*83*].

Group 3 has a translation procedure from English to Japanese, the principal feature of which is the use of four grammar tables. Analysis is done from the end of a sentence to the beginning, applying these four tables recursively. See [*84*].

Group 4 has been placing current emphasis on the development of a practical procedure for reciprocal English–Japanese translation. Work falls into three areas: (a) the accumulation, analysis, and organization of linguistic information for constructing dictionaries and formalizing Japanese grammar; (b) computer programming; and (c) the introduction of a learning process to the computer program of translation for the automatic analysis of syntax. See [*85*].

4.2.8 Other MT Groups

Research in MT has been conducted at the following centers in some cases since the early sixties. The lack of up-to-date information on the activities of these groups has made it difficult to summarize the results of their research. The names of some of these groups are being listed here so that the reader may at least be cognizant of their existence.

Universidad Nacional Autónoma de México, Mexico

Université de Nancy, France

University of Debrecen, Hungary

University of Saskatchewan, Canada

Research Institute for Mathematical Machines, Prague, Czecho-slovakia

University of Warsaw, Poland

Institut Za Eksperimentalnu Fonetiku, Yugoslavia

Académie de la République Populaire Roumaine, Rumania

4.3 Production-Oriented MT Groups

In contrast to the foregoing discussions of the activities of research-oriented MT research groups, this part of the survey will describe the activities of organizations that have committed themselves to the development and operation of production-oriented machine translation systems.

4.3.1 European Atomic Energy Community (EURATOM)

This organization is located in Ispra (Varese) Italy. The principal director of the Russian–English machine translation program is S. Perschke. This center, which has adopted the machine translation system developed at Georgetown University, has sought primarily to carry out practical machine translation of Russian scientific litera-ture.

The translation system is reported to be operative and to be produc-ing quite acceptable scientific translations. Whenever errors are dis-covered in the output, the dictionary and linguistic operations are updated.

Improvements in the system were contemplated within the past two years, including new procedures for syntactic and semantic analysis[86].

4.3.2 Oak Ridge National Laboratory, Oak Ridge, Tennessee

The machine translation system at Oak Ridge has been essentially adapted from the system developed through experimentation by the Georgetown University machine translation project. The Oak Ridge program pursues two objectives: (1) to provide rapid translation service to scientists and engineers; and (2) to continue MT research in order to improve the existing system. The chief advantage of the system is the ability to produce translations rapidly. Conventional translation by an outside agency requires 4 to 6 weeks, whereas the MT output is obtainable in 1 week, and, if there is urgent need, even overnight service is possible. The cost of translation has turned out to be competitive with human translation.

The group has not yet conducted a rigorous evaluation of the comparative quality of MT output as opposed to human output. However, expressions of opinion have been solicited from many users, and with little exception opinions have been favorable.

In connection with the group's second objective, there has been a concentration of effort on introducing new words into the machine dictionary on the basis of actual texts. Refinement of translation equivalents is also planned, and it is hoped that microthesauri in specialized fields will be developed.[25]

4.3.3 Foreign Technology Division, U.S. Air Force, Dayton, Ohio

This MT system has been operational for several years, and is based primarily on a dictionary developed by IBM and on a grammar worked out by a research group at the University of Texas, Austin. Science text is processed from Russian to English. The output is examined by human post-editors before it is transmitted to user agencies.

An evaluation of machine-aided translation activities at the Foreign Technology Division was made in 1965 in terms of quality, cost, and timeliness [87]. The quality of the output of the machine-aided translation system, for the group's purposes, was considered comparable to standard human translations. The main cost components in the process, i.e., post-editing and recomposition, accounts for 70% of the cost, but over-all comparative costs between human and machine-aided translation were competitive. In terms of time spent, it was found that machine output often required less than half the amount of time for human translation.

It was concluded that the "MT system in both is technically and economically feasible," and that it should be continued and operated as a production facility devoted to providing high-quality service to users of translations.

4.3.4 National Physical Laboratory, Teddington, England

Research in MT which has been in progress for several years at this facility was recently concluded (see McDaniel et al. [88]). The primary aim of this group had been to demonstrate the practicability of translation

---

[25] Information about activities at Oak Ridge was obtained through personal correspondence between the author and Francois Kertesz of the Oak Ridge group.

by computer of Russian scientific and technical texts in the fields of electrical engineering, mathematics and physics into English. Experimentation and goals have been directed toward the simulation of a translation service, and in this respect the most recent efforts may be construed as operational machine translation techniques. The ultimate experiment involved a procedure for evaluation of the usefulness of machine output which was not subjected to human post-editorial treatment. This evaluation experiment, in which 34 evaluators commented on 19 distinct papers, has a range scale from 8 down to 0, viz. from "fully adequate" to "mostly very good" to "fair" to "poor" to "useless." A majority verdict which was produced may be paraphrased as "mostly good enough, with a few obscurities."

A broader evaluation exercise has been contemplated which would be conducted over a wider range of potential readers, and which, it is hoped, might lead to a strenghtening of the above verdict, thus making it possible to decide on the viability of a production machine translation service based on the NPL system.

It is felt that many components of the NPL system have been developed so that each may be of considerable independent importance. For example, the automatic Russian–English dictionary, covering all forms of around 17,000 Russian words, and available on punched cards, is perhaps capable of wider application. Included among other components of similar value are the scheme of comprehensive morphological representation, methods of Russian syntactic analysis, and a computer model of linguistic structure.

4.3.5 Central Research Institute for Patent Information, Moscow, USSR

Since 1964 this agency has been involved in developing and operating a system of "automatic translation" of patent literature from English into Russian. All programming has been done on the Soviet URAL-4 computer; source text has been taken from the *Official Gazette*, the weekly publication of the United States Patent Bureau.

This system is quite sophisticated and therefore it may be profitable to examine it to see how at least one operational MT system is conceptualized and structured.

An algorithm based on segment analysis provides for the delineation of operational units of text (syntagmas) such as noun groups and verbal combinations. The translation is carried out with the aid of a compiled dictionary of specified patterns of syntactic constructions. In contrast to patent formulas, trade marks are not compiled in the text, but are examined separately.

The program for this system is comprised of approximately 20,000 instructions and consists of sixteen subroutines, enumerated below:

I. Text preparation
   1. program to arrange words
   2. program to search for words in the dictionary
   3. program to analyze unknown words (i.e., not found in the dictionary)
   4. program to process idioms
   5. program for homograph selection
   6. program to segment text
   7. program to segment text into phrases
II. Syntactic analysis of segments
   1. program for locating pronominal antecedents
   2. program for working out case information (morphological)
   3. program for analysis of predicative units of text
   4. program for analysis of noun word combinations
III. Synthesis of Russian text
   1. program for synthesis of Russian text and alphabetic printout of translation
IV. Auxiliary programs
   1. master program
   2. program for writing information on magnetic tape
   3. program to transfer information from tape to drum storage
   4. program for printout of intermediate program results

For details see Kravec *et al.* [*89*].

5. ALPAC Report

5.1 Industry's Exaggerated Claims for MT Success

As evidenced from the above discussion, by the mid-sixties most MT researchers were beginning to move along the path of learning how language operates and of attempting to incorporate the results of their research into the design of automatic procedures for the translating processes. There were in the United States, however, a few groups (notably Bunker-Ramo, Georgetown University, and IBM) whose primary aim in addition to the above objectives, was the development of a functioning MT system. Industry also jumped on the bandwagon, aiming primarily at developing a marketable MT system which would serve clients in need of translation. Its exaggerated claims for success raised hopes, later proved to be premature, and presented a false picture both to the general public and to government agencies, which by 1965 had given support to what was presented as MT to an amount close to $20,000,000 [*90*]. James P. Titus [*91*] gives the following very graphic description of industry's deep, but, as it turned out, rather misdirected interest in MT:

In industry an entirely different picture presents itself. In the early days—ten years ago—optimism for machine translation ran at a high pitch. Advertising, which eventually damaged the cause, glowed with promises of quick, clean translations. Marketing plans were laid for such adventures as automatic translating service centers, and one was opened by Itek Corporation in New York City. But it closed in a few months. Gradually, industry's enthusiasm for machine translation dwindled until it was either abandoned or submerged in other linguistic research.

IBM was one of the most enthusiastic supporters of machine translation ten years ago, and it had a considerable effort under way. With funds of its own and funds of the government, it built four translation machines based on photo-storage and special-purpose, lexical processors: the Mark I, Mark II, the Research Language Processors—which was used at the 1964–65 World's Fair, and Alps, the Automatic Language Processing System. Two of these machines, Alps and Mark II, are still operating in the government.

5.2 Establishment of ALPAC

These exaggerated advertising claims, as well as the previously unheard of large expenditures of government funds in such a comparatively esoteric area as language, led in October, 1963 to the request by Leland Haworth, Director of the National Science Foundation to Frederick Seitz, President of the National Academy of Sciences:

> ... to advise the Department of Defense, the Central Intelligence Agency and the National Science Foundation on research and development in the general field of mechanical translation of foreign languages [90].

Replying to this request, Seitz in April, 1964 appointed the Automatic Language Processing Committee (ALPAC).[26] The committee carried out its investigation by examining the following three areas: (1) the need for translation in government agencies and the scientific community; (2) the satisfying of these needs by the then existing human translation facilities, government and private; and (3) the advantages, shortcomings, and perspectives for machine translation, including comparison between human translation product, and MT output—in terms of both quality and cost. In the course of its investigation the committee conducted a number of studies trying to evaluate the quality of translations, cost estimates, types of errors discovered in translation output, and other aspects of translation in general. It also interviewed seventeen witnesses, including translators, linguists, industry representatives, translation output users, and other invited people.[27]

---

[26] For the membership of the committee consult the appropriate page of the ALPAC report.

[27] For a list of persons who appeared before the committee see the ALPAC report, p. 24.

5.3 ALPAC's Recommendations

The ALPAC report, entitled *Language and Machines* [*90*] was released to the public in November, 1966 and recommended expenditures in two distinct areas: (1) computational linguistics, and (2) improvement of translation. It also suggested by inference that pursuit of FAHQT is not a realistic goal in the immediate future, as reported in *the Finite String*:

The committee sees, however, little justification at present for massive support of machine translation *per se*, finding it—overall—slower, less accurate and more costly than that provided by the human translator [92].

The committee also finds that

. . . without recourse to human translation or editing. . . . there has been no machine translation of general scientific text, and none is in immediate prospect ([90], p. 19).

5.4 Reactions to ALPAC Report

5.4.1 German Reaction to ALPAC Report

Probably one of the most incisive points of the comments directed at the ALPAC report is, in the view of its critics, the contention that the committee's findings are based on a comparison of outdated machine translation output of 1964 vintage, ignoring more recent, improved MT output, which was then generally available, with products of human translators, some of whom were highly skilled professionals. Also ignored was the fact, in view of some, that if it is assumed that MT and human translation serve two different objectives—the former of transmitting essential information, the latter of providing a full translation of a given text—then a completely different picture emerges [*93*]. The same critic, Friedrich Krollman, Director of the Translation Service of the Federal Armed Forces of West Germany at Mannheim, calls attention to the fact that the overwhelming part of the ALPAC report deals with the general problems of translation, such as quality, cost, service; the number, background, and availability of human translators; the rise of English as a language of science; the prospects of American scientists learning Russian—factors which relate, at best, only peripherally to MT. He finds it most astonishing that of the total 124 pages of the ALPAC report only six deal with the state of MT at that time. Of these six, only two-and-a-half pages discuss MT *per se*, with the remainder devoted to the reproduction of samples of MT output. Krollman thinks that more space in the report should have been devoted to the discussion of MT, its scope, objectives, and problems [*94*].

5.4.2 Soviet Reaction to ALPAC Report

Krollman [95] also questions whether ". . . the sometimes rather categorical conclusions of the ALPAC committee are valid for all future times and for all kinds of translation."[28] A similar view is also echoed in a review of the ALPAC report which appeared in the authorative Soviet journal dealing with information processing generally, *Nauchno–Tekhnicheskaja Informatsija* (Scientific–Technical Information) which declares that while the findings of the committee may be applicable to the conditions in the United States, they certainly are not relevant to the Soviet Union and, at any rate, the state of the MT art in the USSR should also be investigated by an appropriate authorative committee. The Soviet journal also finds that the ALPAC group has underestimated the progress of MT research and makes the following observation [96]:

> It just seems to us that in the evaluation of the importance of this [MT] research the Committee displayed—perhaps in a most vexatious manner—a certain narrowness and pragmatic single mindedness, which is characteristic of the report. Those ideas which have originated and are originating in connection with MT are a contribution not only to the development of a MT system (a problem which is probably not acute in the United States) but also advance the resolution of one of the most important problems of the 20th century—the problem of symbiosis of man and machines.[29]

5.4.3 Reactions to ALPAC Report in the United States

Probably the most thoroughgoing commentary of the ALPAC report in the United States is contained in a memorandum, the draft manuscript of which was made available to me by Zbigniew L. Pankowicz, of the Griffiss Air Force Base, Rome, New York. In it he challenges the committee's report on the following grounds:

> . . . (1) inferior analytical work resulting in factual inaccuracies; (2) hostile and vindictive attitude toward machine translation; (3) use of obsolete and invalid facts and figures as a basis for condemnation of machine translation; (4) distortion of quality, speed and cost estimates in favor of human translation; (5) concealment of data reflecting credit on machine translation (*suppressio veri suggestio falsi*), and (6) wilful omission of dissenting statements on machine translation, presented to the Committee by some experts in this field ([97], p. I).

Pankowicz states very carefully that the views expressed in this memorandum are his own and do not represent the opinion of the Rome Air Development Center, at which he is employed. He marshalls

---

[28] Translation from German is by the author.
[29] Translation from Russian is by the author.

an array of documented evidence which controverts the accuracy of
some of the data of the committee, points out some contradictions and
omission of some of the evidence gathered by the committee and
finds that, "It is obvious that machine translation has been con-
demned by the committee prior to a sufficient and full examination
of the case" ([*97*], p. II) thus echoing in general the feelings of other
critics cited above.

I should like to mention just one more commentary[30] on the ALPAC
report in the United States by someone not in any way connected with
MT. James P. Titus reports arguments against two conclusions of the
committee by a group of government research administrators who met
in Washington 2 months after the ALPAC report was released. They
asserted that there was no surplus of translators, as claimed by the
ALPAC report, and that, contrary to other findings of the committee,
MT was produced at five facilities around the world. He then asks:

> Why should two intelligent groups of men, all seated in chairs of responsibility,
> come to such divergent views on the same subject? The main reason seems to
> be that they are examining different information to form their conclusions. The
> government research administrators are looking at their projects as they exist
> today. The ALPAC group looked at data that was probably 2 years old. And that
> is the basic weakness of the ALPAC report ([91], p. 189).

But perhaps the best critique of the ALPAC report is to be found
in the observation that the committee not only deprecated the importance of the achievements of MT, but also ignored its future poten-
tialities by implying that MT has no future. Titus ([*91*], p. 191)
concludes that

> . . . it seems premature to abandon support of machine translation after only 12
> brief years, especially if the abandonment is based only on the findings of the
> ALPAC committee. Even the critics of machine translation admit its contribution
> to the knowledge of linguists. Who can say what contributions lie ahead?

He then cites the following comment by a distinguished linguist and
serious MT researcher:

> As W. P. Lehmann, Director of the Linguistic Research Center at the University
> of Texas, put it: "If Dr. Michael E. DeBakey devises a heart pump and it is not
> immediately successful in its application, the biological community does not raise
> a great hue-and-cry and returns to theoretical research, shelving the heart
> pump. It continues experimentation" ([91], p. 191).

---

[30] For another commentary on the ALPAC report, see Garvin [*98*] in which he advo-
cates a "reasonable middle ground" for MT.

6. Conclusion

6.1 Justification for Continuing MT

It now becomes clear from the foregoing that even if one admits that FAHQT is not realizable, there is still abundant justification for continuing both MT research and efforts to advance the development of functioning MT systems along the lines carried out by the five groups mentioned in Sections 4.3.1–5 of this survey. The primary objective of the latter would be to transmit information, particularly in the area of natural sciences, from one language to another without regard to established rules of grammar in the target language. In Russian, for example, adverbs of quantity which in English would require the plural can be used with a singular verb, so that one can very easily obtain in English a translation of the type "many industrial zones is situated . . . ." It goes without saying that one of the major aims of developing a functioning MT system should be to avoid mistranslations, but one should not expect that practical MT should be more rigorous in this respect than human translation. It is obvious, too, that MT research should also be continued since it contributes to the expansion of our knowledge of how language operates, as already pointed out numerous times in preceding discussions. For instance, research in development of automatic recognition procedures on the syntactic and semantic levels is of help not only in sentence analysis but also in constructing rules for generation of sentences. The implication of the latter for practical MT, information storage and retrieval, and language teaching are quite obvious. Last, MT, generally speaking, is the most important area where symbiosis between computer and man can be most successfully advanced.

6.2 Practical MT as an Application of Symbiosis between Man and Machine

This interaction between man and machine can and should also be applied in the development of a practical MT system. This co-operation should not be limited to the areas of post-editorship of machine produced texts alone. Even after automatic print readers have been developed, certain areas of the input process, like resolving of textural ambiguities will be best left to man, who can handle them more efficiently than the machine can. In the area of dictionary look-up, words of incoming text not found in the glossary stored in the computer, should be translated and grammar coded by man, who again can do it more efficiently than the computer by using his own built-in enormous storage and retrieval system. After the machine stored dictionary has been thus updated, the chances of fouling up the developed syntactic routines are considerably reduced, since even one missing lexical item in the sentence can render the parsing routines inoperative. It is also quite obvious that in the case of failure of resolution of contextural ambiguities by the computer, when two or more target language equivalents for source language lexical items are printed out the man can easily cross out those translations which do not apply. The computer has failed here, but in some cases the resolution of this difficulty by man can be incorporated into the MT system.

6.3 Development of a Guide to Read "MTese"

Since it is quite obvious that the product of any functioning MT system will never look the same as human translation man will also have to expend some effort in reading the output. This process will, however, require less effort than the acquisition of reading skill of another language, which is generally recognized as the easiest to achieve of the three areas of learning a second language, reading, writing, and speaking. Consequently, MT output will have to be accompanied by a brief guide how to read the translation. In essence, these instructions will be statements detailing those structural differences between the source and target languages, obviously from the point of view of mapping the source language into the target language, which have defied automatic analysis at the time of the MT run. These directions will, of course, change as the MT system advances. The compilation of these reading instructions again will be performed by man with the help of the computer, which will indicate to him where these statements are needed.

6.4 MT Most Effective in Small Subarea of Language

One more element in the implementation of functioning MT systems must be mentioned, the carrying out of the translation activities in a small subarea of language, usually a subfield in the natural sciences, e.g., solid-state physics, marine biology, partial differential equations in mathematics, and others. The smaller the area of language, the greater will be the success in practical MT. One has only to cite the eminently solid results achieved in the Soviet Union in automatically translating American patent literature into English mentioned in Section 4. For this purpose microgrammars and microglossaries have already been and will be created. Appropriately tagged, these computer-stored microgrammars and microglossaries can be modified, expanded, and merged whenever necessary, so that they can be available to all needing them. The computer is, of course, eminently suited to aid substantially in this activity.

To sum up, concentration on small subfields of language expression, creation of guides for reading "MTese" and appropriate division of labor between man and machine are all necessary ingredients for the successful operation of a functioning MT system. Since computers will not go away and are, quite obviously, here to stay, it makes no sense to renounce their application in such an important area of human behavior as language output. You don't throw away an important tool: you use it.

SELECTED BIBLIOGRAPHY[31]

There has been no attempt here to compile an exhaustive bibliography of documents related to the field of automatic language processing. The references contained herein were selected primarily for the purpose of providing a source of general information on, and broad coverage of, research in mechanical translation. Readers who are interested in the particular work and publications of individual MT research groups described in this survey should address their inquities directly to the pertinent groups.

PROCEEDINGS AND CONFERENCES

Abstracts of papers presented at the Second (1964), Fourth (1966), Fifth (1967), Sixth (1968) Annual Meetings of the Association for Computational Linguistics (formerly the Association for Machine Translation and Computational Linguistics) available at the Slavic Department, Wayne State University, Detroit, Michigan 48202.

Edmundson, H. P., ed., *Proc. Nat. Symp. Machine Translation, Los Angeles, 1960.* Prentice-Hall, Englewood Cliffs, New Jersey 1961.

1965 International Conference on Computational Linguistics, New York, 1965. Reprints available at the Slavic Department, Wayne State University, Detroit, Michigan 48202.

Proceedings of the 1961 International Conference on Machine Translation of Languages and Applied Language Analysis, National Physical Laboratory, Teddington, England 1961, Vol. I-II. London, H.M. Stationary Office 1962.

Proceedings of the Conference on Computer-Related Semantic Analysis. Machine Translation Research Group, Wayne State University, Detroit, Michigan, December 1965.

Second International Conference on Computational Linguistics (2ème Conference Internationale sur le Traitement Automatique des Langues), Grenoble, France, August 23–25, 1967.

Summary of the Proceedings of the Wayne State University Conference of Federally Sponsored Machine Translation Workers. Machine Translation Research Group, Wayne State University, Detroit, Michigan, July 1960.

[31] See also references contained therein.

Summary of the Proceedings of the Russian-to-English Grammar Coding Conference. Machine Translation Research Group, Wayne State University, Detroit, Michigan, April 1961.

Summary of the Proceedings of the Conference of Federally Sponsored Machine Translation Groups on MT-Oriented Syntactic Analysis. Machine Translation Group, Wayne State University, Detroit, Michigan, June 1962.

PERIODICALS

Computational Linguistics. Computing Centre of the Hungarian Academy of Sciences, Budapest, Hungary.

The Finite String. Newsletter of the Association for Computational Linguistics (formerly the Association for Machine Translation and Computational Linguistics). A. Hood Roberts, ed., Associate Director, Center for Applied Linguistics, 1717 Massachusetts Ave. N.W., Washington, D.C. 20036. (Each issue includes a list of recent publications in computational linguistics and machine translation.)

Foreign developments in machine translation and information processing. U.S. Department of Commerce, Office of Technical Services, Joint Publications Research Service (JPRS), Washington, D.C. 20025.

KVAL. Research Group for Quantitative Linguistics. Fack, Stockholm 40, Sweden.

Mechanical Translation. Published at the University of Chicago Press for the Association for Computational Linguistics. Victor Yngve, ed., Graduate Library School, University of Chicago, Chicago, Illinois 60637.

The Prague Bulletin of Mathematical Linguistics. Karlová Universita, Prague, Czechoslovakia.

Prague Studies in Mathematical Linguistics. Academia, Czechoslovak Academy of Sciences, Prague, Czechoslovakia.

Revue Roumaine de Linguistique. L'Académie de la République Socialiste de Roumanie, Bucharest, Rumania.

Statistical Methods in Linguistics (SMIL). Skriptor, Fack, Stockholm, 40, Sweden.

La Traduction Automatique, Bulletin trimestriel de l'Association pour l'étude et le Développment de la Traduction automatique et de la Linguistic appliquée (ATALA), 20, rue de la Baume, Paris 8e, France.

Two leading Soviet references *Научно-техническая Информация* (Scientific-Technical Information), Academy of Sciences, USSR, Moscow. Issues starting with 1968 include tables of contents and summaries of each article in English translation.) *Реферативный Журнал* (Abstract Journal), Academy of Sciences, USSR, Moscow. This journal also appears completely in English translation.) See especially the section headed Автоматический перевод текстов (Automatic Text Translation]

GENERAL REFERENCES

Akhmanova, O. S., Mel'chuk, I. A., Frumkina, R. M., and Paducheva, E. V. *Exact Methods in Linguistic Research.* Hays, D. G., and Mohr, D. V., The RAND Corporation, Transl. Santa Monica, California, September 1963.

Booth, A. D., Brandwood, L., and Cleave, S. C. *Mechanical Resolution of Linguistic Problems.* Academic Press, New York, and Butterworths, London 1958.

Delavenay, E., *An Introduction to Machine Translation.* Thames and Hudson, London, 1960.

Garvin, P. L. and Spolsky, B., eds. *Computation in Linguistics, A Case Book.* Indiana Univ. Press, Bloomington, Indiana, 1966.

Hays, D. G., Research Procedures in Machine Translation. RAND Research Memo. RM-2916-PR, December 1961.

Hays, D. G., ed., *Readings in Automatic Language Processing.* American Elsevier, New York, 1966.

Hays, D. G., *Introduction to Computational Linguistics.* American Elsevier, New York, 1967.

Language and Machines (The ALPAC Report). Computers in Translation and Linguistics. Automatic Language Processing Advisory Committee Report, Publication 1416. Behavioral Sciences, Nat. Acad. Sci.–Nat. Res. Council, Washington, D.C., 1966.

Lehmann, W. P., *Machine Translation Research During the Past Two Years*, p. 10. Eric Document 020503, 1968. Information concerning ERIC publications is available from ERIC Document Reproduction Service, 4936 Fairmont Ave., Bethesda, Maryland.

Locke, W. N., and Booth, A. D., eds., *Machine Translation of Languages.* M.I.T. Press, Cambridge, Massachusetts, 3rd printing, 1965.

Машинный перевод. Труды Института точной механики и вычислительной техники АН СССР, Москва, вып. 1, 1958 г.; вып. 2, 1961 г. [*Machine Translation.* Institute for Precision Mechanics and Computational Technology of the Academy of Sciences of the U.S.S.R., Moscow, Issue 1, 1958; Issue 2, 1961.]

Машинный перевод и прикладная лингвистика. Труды Московского государственного педагогического института иностранных языков, Москва, вып. 8, 1964. [*Machine Translation and Applied Linguistics.* Moscow State Foreign Language Pedagogical Institute, Moscow, Issue 8, 1964.]

Мельчук, И. А., *Автоматический синтаксический анализ.* Редакционно-издательский отдел сибирского отделения АН СССР, Новосибирск, 1964. [Mel'chuk, I. A., *Automatic Syntactic Analysis.* Department of the Siberian Branch of the Academy of Sciences of the U.S.S.R., Novosibirsk, 1964.]

Мельчук, И. А. и Равич, Р. Д., *Автоматический перевод*, 1949—1963. Винити, Институт языкознания, Москва, 1967. [Mel'chuk, I. A. and Ravich, R. D., *Automatic Translation*, 1949–1963. All Union Institute for Scientific and Technical Information, Linguistics Institute, Moscow, 1967.]

Nida, E. A., *Toward a Science of Translating.* E. J. Brill, Leiden 1964, see, especially, the chapter entitled Machine translation.

Oettinger, A. G., *Automatic Language Translation.* Harvard University Press, Cambridge, Massachusetts, 1960.

Papp, F., *Mathematical Linguistics and Mechanical Translation in the Soviet Union.* Mouton, The Hague, The Netherlands, November 1965.

Ревзин, И. И. и Розенцвейг, В. Ю., *Основы общего и машинного перевода*, изд-во «Высшая школа», Москва, 1964. [Revzin, I. I. and Rozentsveyg, V. Yu., *Principles of General and Machine Translation.* Higher Education Publishing House, Moscow, 1964.]

Vauquois, B. A survey of formal grammars and algorithms for recognition and transformation in mechanical translation. IFIP Congress, 1968 Preprints, North-Holland Publ., Amsterdam, 1968.

Yngve, V. Implications of mechanical translation research. *Proc. Am. Phil. Soc.* **108**, No. 4, 275 (1964).

REFERENCES

1. Bar-Hillel, Y., The present status in automatic translation of languages. *Advan. Computers* **1**, 160–161 (1960).
2. Whorf, B. L., The relation of habitual thought to language in *Language, Culture and Personality* (L. Spier, ed.), pp. 75–93. Sapir Memorial Publ. Fund, Menasha, Wisconsin, 1941.
3. Josselson, H. H., Automatization of lexicography. *Cah. Lexicol.* **9**, 73–87 (1966).
4. Josselson, H. H., Lexicography and the computer, in *To Honor Roman Jacobson*, pp. 1046–1059. Mouton, 's-Gravenhage, The Netherlands, 1967.
5. Booth, A. D., and Locke, W. N., Historical introduction, in *Machine Translation of Languages*, pp. 1–14. M.I.T. Press, Cambridge, Massachusetts, 3rd Printing, 1965.
6. Kuznetsov, V. I., Preamble *Proc. Symp. Machine Translation Budapest, October 1967*, see *Nauch. Tekh. Inform.* (Scientific-Technical Information) **2**, No. 6, 28–30 (1968).
7. *Current Research and Development in Scientific Documentation* **11**. Nat. Sci. Found. Washington, D.C. 1962.
8. Edmundson, H. P., ed., *Proc. Nat. Symp. Machine Translation, Los Angeles, 1960*. Prentice-Hall, Englewood Cliffs, New Jersey, 1961.
9. Garvin, P. L., An informal survey of modern linguistics. *Amer. Doc.* **16**, 291–298 (1965).
10. Models and Theories Session, *Proc. Conf. Federally Sponsored Machine Translation Groups MT-Oriented Syntactic Analysis, Princeton, 1962*, pp. 83–92. MT Research Dept., Wayne State University, Detroit, Michigan, 1962.
11. Brower, R. A., ed., *On Translation*. Harvard Univ. Press, Cambridge, Massachusetts, 1959.
12. Chao, Y. R., Translation without machine, pre-publication copy of paper delivered at the IX International Congress of Linguists, August 27–31, Cambridge, Massachusetts, p. 6.
13. Sherry, M., The identification of nested structures in predictive syntactic analysis. *Proc. 1st Intern. Conf. Machine Transl. Lang. Appl. Lang. Anal., Teddington, England, 1961*, pp. 143–155. H.M. Stationery Office, London 1962.
14. Alt, F., Recognition of clauses and phrases in machine translation of languages. Nat. Bur. Stds. Rept. 6895, Washington, D.C. 1960.
15. Yngve, V., A model and an hypothesis for language. *Proc. Amer. Phil. Soc.*, **104**, 444–446 (1960).
16. Sager, N., Procedure for left-to-right recognition of sentence structure. Transformations and Discourse Analysis Proj. Rept 27. University of Pensylvania, Philadelphia, Pennsylvania, 1960.
17. *Proc. Conf. Federally Sponsored Machine Translation Groups MT-Oriented Syntactic Analysis, Princeton, 1962*, pp. 79–82. Wayne State University, Detroit, Michigan, 1962.
18. Hays, D. G., Dependency theory: A formalism and some observations. RAND Memo RM 4087-PR, July 1964; for an earlier discussion of a related topic, see Tesnière, L., *Esquisse d'une Syntaxe Structurale*. Klincksieck, Paris, 1953.
19. Lamb, S. M., *Outline of Stratificational Grammar*. Georgetown University Press, Washington, D.C., 1966.

20. Bach, E., *An Introduction to Transformational Grammars*. Holt, New York, 1964.

21. Senechalle, D., Introduction to formation structures, Rept. LRC63 WTM-2. University of Texas, Austin, Linguistics Research Center, April 1963.

22. Estes, W. B., Holley, W. H., and Pendergraft, E. D., Formation and transformation structures, Rept. LRC63 WTM-3. University of Texas, Austin, Linguistics Research Center, May 1963.

23. Ceccato, S., ed., *Linguistic Analysis and Programming for Mechanical Translation*. Gordon and Breach, New York, 1961.

24. Dutton, B., An introduction to the theory and practice of correlational grammar. Georgia Institute for Research, Athens, Georgia, October 1968.

25. Rhodes, I., A new approach to the mechanical translation of Russian, Nat. Bur. Stds. Rept. 6295. Washington, D.C., February 1959.

26. Sherry, M., Mathematical linguistics and automatic translation, Nat. Sci. Found. Rept. 5. Harvard University, Cambridge, Massachusetts, August 1960.

27. Plath, W., Mathematical linguistics and automatic translation, Nat. Sci. Found. Rept. 12. Harvard University, Cambridge, Massachusetts, June 1963.

28. Machine translation studies of semantic techniques, RADC-TR 61–72. Ramo-Wooldridge, Canoga Park, California, February 1961.

29. Studies in distributional semantics, in Six tasks in computational linguistics, Chapter 2, RM-2803-AFOSR. RAND Corporation, Santa Monica, California, October 1961.

30. Hays, D. G., Research procedures in machine translation, pp. 18–25, 33–36, 40–48. RM-2916-PR. RAND Corporation, Santa Monica, California, December 1961.

31. Householder, F. W., Jr., and Lyons, J., *Fourth Quart. Rept. Automation Gen. Semantics*, pp. 8–9. Indiana University, Bloomington, Indiana, February 1961.

32. *Proc. Conf. Computer-Related Semantic Analysis, Las Vegas, Nevada, 1965*, held under the auspices of Wayne State University.

33. Linguistic and engineering studies in automatic language translation of scientific Russian into English, Tech. Rept, RADC-TN-58-321, ASTIA Doc. AD-148992. Dept. Far Eastern and Slavic Languages, and Dept. Electrical Engineering, Univ. of Washington, Seattle, Washington, June 1958.

34. Translation study, Final Rept., AF30(602)–2131, RADC-TR-61-235. Dept. Electrical Engineering, Univ. of Washington, Seattle, Washington, August 28, 1961.

35. The Chinese-English machine translation project, Vols. I and II. Final Rept. Dept. Far Eastern and Slavic Languages and Literatures, Univ. of Washington, Seattle, Washington, September 1962.

36. Yngve, V., *MT at M.I.T., 1965*. Research Laboratory of Electronics, Mass. Inst. Technol., Cambridge, Massachusetts, June, 15, 1965.

37. Macdonald, R. R., General report 1952–1963, Occasional papers on machine translation, No. 30, Georgetown Univ. Machine Translation Res. Proj. Georgetown University, Washington, D.C., June 1963.

38. Hays, D. G., Research procedures in machine translation, Memo. RM-2916-PR. The RAND Corporation, Santa Monica, California, December 1961.

39. Harper, K. E., Hays, D. G., and Scott, B. J., Studies in machine translation bibliography of Russian scientific articles, Memo. RM-3610-PR. The RAND Corporation, Santa Monica, California, June 1963. (This publication includes a list of RAND studies in machine translation on page 97.)

40. Hays, D. G., Annotated bibliography of RAND publications in computational linguistics, Memo. RM-3894-PR. The RAND Corporation, Santa Monica, California, March 1964; see also Computational Linguistics Bibliography, 1967, Memo. RM-5733-PR, June 1968.

41. Hays, D. G., Dependency theory: A formalism and some observations, Memo. RM-4087-PR. The RAND Corporation, Santa Monica, California, July 1964.

42. Machine translation studies of semantic techniques, Final Rept. AF30(602)–2036. Ramo-Wooldridge Div., Thompson-Ramo-Wooldridge, Canoga Park, California, February 22, 1961.

43. Fulcrum techniques to semantic analysis, Final Rept. AF30(602)–2643. TRW Computer Div., Thompson-Ramo-Wooldridge, Canoga Park, California, March 5, 1963.

44. A syntactic analyzer study, Final Rept AF30(602)–3506. Bunker-Ramo Corp., Canoga Park, California, July 31, 1965.

45. Adaptation of advance fulcrum techniques to MT production system (Russian-English), AF30(602)–3770. Bunker-Ramo Corp., Canoga Park, California, November 1, 1966.

46. Computer-aided research in machine translation, Final Rept. NSF-C372. Bunker-Ramo Corp., Canoga Park, California, March 31, 1967.

47. Oettinger, A. G., *Automatic Language Translation*, Harvard Monographs Appl. Sci., No. 9, Harvard Univ. Press, Cambridge, Massachusetts, 1960.

48. Sherry, M., Comprehensive report on predictive syntactic analysis, in Mathematical Linguistics and Automatic Translation, Rept. No. NSF-7, Section I. Harvard Computation Laboratory, Cambridge, Massachusetts, 1961.

49. Oettinger, A. G., Automatic syntactic analysis and the pushdown store. *Proc. Symp. Appl. Math.* **12**. Am. Math. Soc., Providence, Rhode Island, 1961.

50. Mathematical linguistics and automatic translation, Rept. No. NSF-13. Harvard Computation Laboratory, Cambridge, Massachusetts, March 1964.

51. Mathematical linguistics and automatic translation, Rept. No. NSF-21. The Harvard Russian Syntactic Analyzer Manual, Harvard Computation Laboratory, Cambridge, Massachusetts, May 1968.

52. Koutsoudas, A., Machine translation at the University of Michigan, in *Information Retrieval and Machine Translation*, Part II (Allen Kent, ed.), pp. 765–770. Interscience, New York, 1961.

53. Smoke, W., and Dubinsky, E., A program for the machine translation of natural languages. *Mech. Transl.* **6**, 2–10 (1961).

54. Rhodes, I., A new approach to the mechanical translation of Russian, NBS Rept. 6295. U.S. Department of Commerce, Nat. Bur. Stds., Washington, D.C., February 6, 1959; see also, A new approach to the mechanical syntactic analysis of Russian, NBS Rept. 6595, November 10, 1959.

55. Alt, F., Recognition of clauses and phrases in machine translation of languages, NBS Rept. 6895. U.S. Department of Commerce, Nat. Bur. Stds., Washington, D.C., July 11, 1960.

56. Research in machine translation, Ann. Repts. 3, 4, and 5. Wayne State University, Detroit, Michigan, 1961, 1962, and 1963.

57. Steiger, A. J., Parsing by matrix. MT Research Dept., Wayne State University, Detroit, Michigan, 1965.

58. Ten year summary report, MT Research Dept., Wayne State University, Detroit, Michigan, May 1968.

59. Lamb, S. M., and Jacobsen, Jr. W. H., A high-speed large-capacity dictionary system. *Mech. Transl.* **6**, 76–107 (1961).
60. Lamb, S. M., On the mechanization of syntactic analysis. *Proc. 1st Intern. Conf. Machine Transl. Lang. Appl. Lang. Anal.*, *Teddington, England, 1961*, paper 21. H.M. Stationery Office, London, 1962.
61. Lamb, S. M., Outline of stratificational grammar. University of California, Berkeley, California, 1962.
62. Final report on machine translation study, Rept. No. 16. Linguistics Research Center, University of Texas, Austin, Texas, June 1963.
63. Tosh, W., *Syntactic Translation.* Mouton, 's-Gravenhage, The Netherlands, 1965.
64. Research on syntactic and semantic analysis for mechanical translation, Final Rept., Linguistics Research Center, University of Texas, Austin, Texas, April 1967.
65. Levison, M., The Mechanical analysis of language. *Proc. 1st Intern. Conf. Machine Translation Lang. Appl. Lang. Anal.*, *Teddington, England, 1961*, paper 29. H.M. Stationery Office, London, 1962.
66. Parker-Rhodes, A. F., A new model of syntactic description. *Proc. 1st Intern. Conf. Machine Translation Lang. Appl. Lang. Analysis*, *Teddington, England, 1961*, paper 34. H.M. Stationery Office, London, 1962.
67. Masterman, Margaret, Semantic algorithms. *Proc. Conf. Computer-Related Semantic Analysis*, Machine Translation Res. Proj., Wayne State University, Detroit, Michigan, 1965. See also Karen Spark Jones, Semantic classes and semantic message forms, same conference.
68. Linguistic problems of scientific information, ICSU-UNESCO, Joint Project on the Communication of Scientific Information, Moscow, November 19, 1968.
69. Ceccato, S., and Zonta, B., Human translation and translation by machine. *Proc. 1st Intern. Conf. Machine Machine Translation Lang. Appl. Lang. Anal.*, *Teddington, England, 1961*, paper 30. H.M. Stationery Office, London 1962.
70. Ceccato, S., Automatic translation of languages. *Inform. Stor. Retrieval* **2**, 105–158 (1965).
71. Ceccato, S., Correlational analysis and MT, in *Progress in Mechanical Translation*. North-Holland Publ., Amsterdam, The Netherlands, 1966.
72. Nedobejkine-Maksimenko, N., and Torre, L., Modèle de la Syntaxe Russe, Centre d'Etudes pour la Traduction Automatique, Grenoble, France, December 1964.
73. Rapport d'Activité pour l'Année 1966, Centre d'Etudes pour la Traduction Automatique, Grenoble, France, 1966.
74. Baille, A., and Rouault, J., Un Essai de Formalisation de la Semantique des Langues Naturelles, Centre l'Etudes pour la Traduction Automatique, Grenoble, France, December 1966.
75. Veillon, G., Veyrunes, J., and Vauquois, B., Un Métalangage de Grammaires Transformationelles, Centre d'Etudes pour la Traduction Automatique, Grenoble, France, 1967.
76. Querido, A., Deux Modèles de Description Syntaxique, Centre d'études pour le traitement automatique des données linguistique, University of Montreal, July 1966.
77. Friant, J., Grammaires Ordonées—Grammaires Matricielles, Centre d'études pour le traitement automatique des donneés linguistiques, University of Montreal, October 1968; Langages Ultralinéaires et Superlinéaires Nouvelles Caracterisations, Centre d'études pour traitement automatique des donneés linguistiques, University of Montreal, November 1968.

78. Hirschberg, L. Dictionnaires Automatiques pour Traducteurs Humains. *J. Traducteurs*, Brussels, 1966.

79. Konečná, D., Novák, P., and Sgall, P., Machine translation in Prague. *Prague Studies in Mathematical Linguistics*, No. 1. Czechoslovak Academy of Sciences, Prague, Czechoslovakia, 1966.

80. Varga, D., Towards a new system of automatic analysis. *Computat. Linguistics* **6**, 123–136 (1967).

81. Kunze, J., Theoretical problems of automatic translation. *Z. Mat. Logik Grundlagen der Matematik*, **12**, 85–130 (1966).

82. Nishimura, H., The YAMATO and the experimental translation, 46 pp. Electrotechnical Laboratory, Tokyo, Japan, May 1964.

83. Sakai, I., Some mathematical aspects of syntactic description, paper presented at the International Conference of Computational Linguistics, New York, May 1965.

84. Sakai, T., Models and strategies for MT, presented at the U.S.–Japan Seminar on MT, Tokyo, Japan, May 1964.

85. Tamati, T., Syntactic description of Japanese grammar, presented at the U.S.–Japan Seminar on Mathematical Translation, New York, 1965.

86. Brown, A., *The "SLC" Programming Language and System for Machine Translation*, Vol. 1: *Programming Manual* (rev. ed.); Vol. 2: *Utility Programs*, Rept. No. EUR2418, Euratom, Brussels, Belgium, 1964.

87. *An Evaluation of Machine-Aided Translation Activities at FTD*, Arthur D. Little, May 1, 1965.

88. McDaniel, J., *et al.*, Translation of Russian Scientific Texts into English by Computer. Final Rept., Autonomics Div., National Physical Laboratory, Teddington, England, July 1967.

89. Kravec, L. G., Vasilevskij, A. L., and Dubickaja, A. M., Eksperimental'naja sistema automaticheskogo perevoda publickacij iz Amerikanskogo patentnogo ezhenedel'nika "Official Gazette." *Nauch.-Tekh. Inform.* **Ser. 2**, No. 1, 35–40 (1967).

90. Language and machines, computers in translation and linguistics, Publication 1416, pp. 107–112. Automatic Language Processing Advisory Committee Report, (ALPAC Report), Nat. Acad. Sci. Nat. Res. Council, Washington, D.C.

91. Titus, J. P., The nebulous future of machine translation. *Commun. Assoc. Comput. Machinery* **10**, No. 3, 190 (1967).

92. *The Finite String*, **3**, October/November 1966.

93. Krollman, F., *Der Sprachmittler*, No. 3, 85 (1968).

94. Krollman, F., *Der Sprachmittler*, No. 4, 121 (1967).

95. Krollman, F., *Der Sprachmittler*, No. 2, 43 (1968).

96. Nauchno-Tekhnicheskaja Informatsija. Scientific Technical Information, Ser. 2, No. 8, 24 (1968).

97. Pankowicz, Z. L., Draft of a Commentary on ALPAC Report, Part I. Rome Air Development Center, Griffiss Air Force Base, Rome, New York, March 1967.

98. Garvin, P. L., Machine translation—fact or fancy? *Datamation* pp. 29–31, 1967.

Classification, Relevance, and Information Retrieval

D. M. JACKSON[1]

Department of Computer and Information Science
The Ohio State University
Columbus, Ohio

---

[1] Now at: Department of Computer Science, Cornell University, Ithaca, New York.

1. Introduction

To treat the relationship between classification, relevance, and information retrieval, it is first desirable to consider briefly some of the more important events that have taken place in the field of information retrieval. A brief account of the field follows.

One of the earliest references to the problem, which has since become central to information retrieval, was made by Bush [8] in 1945. Commenting on the inadequacies of contemporary library classifications and of the resulting tendency to neglect existing information on research work, he remarked: "Even the modern great library is not generally consulted: it is nibbled away at by a few ... our ineptitude at getting at the record is largely caused by the artificiality of systems of indexing." Since that time, work has progressed in a number of different directions and has achieved a number of goals, all falling within the general area of information retrieval. All have the common problem of extracting or retrieving information, although for different purposes, from a corpus of natural language text or from a prepared set of data. Darlington [13], for example, shows how certain English problems can be translated into logical terms and treated subsequently by formal methods. Bobrow [5] deals with the linguistic problems that arise while analyzing those English statements which describe mathematical relationships. The "word problems" are translated directly into algebraic expressions. Simmons [60] finds answers in an indexed natural language text by means of grammatical dependencies. Raphael's [51] SIR (Semantic Information Retrieval) demonstrates how conversational and deductive abilities may be obtained by using a model which represents semantic content from a variety of subject areas. Green's [22] BASEBALL answers questions posed in ordinary English about the data in store and determines what information is given about the data being requested. An important distinction must be made here between these systems and those in which the computer acts primarily as a repository for records of information (medical or insurance records, for example) and delivers the correct record once a suitable tag (the patient's or customer's name) has been provided. In the systems under consideration, the linguistic relationships between the request and the set of data being interrogated are examined to establish a response. In the others, no such relationships are determined—the tag addresses directly the information to be retrieved. Throughout this chapter, the term "information retrieval" will be taken as synonymous with "document retrieval" (*sensu* Cooper [11])—that is, a system which refers the user to documents which may be of interest to him, by examining a request which indicates his area of interest. This is, therefore, contrasted with retrieval systems that deliver specific items of interest in the subject area of interest in response to a user's request. This usage agrees with that of Salton [57] and Cleverdon [10] and many others.

Since the importance of the problem was recognized, mainly in the United States, a number of retrieval systems have been designed, suggested, and even used. The use of high speed digital computers profoundly affected the field and permitted the mechanization of certain stages of the retrieval process. Computers were most effective in the stages which were purely routine in character and which could be performed equally well without the participation of the "intelligent" mind. The recording of the removal or return of books, the issuing of "overdue" notices, the calculation of fines and the verification of the identity of a library user and his status to access restricted regions of the library are examples of such stages. The University of Pittsburgh, for example, has mechanized some of these stages and the system is now in constant use.

The development of large capacity storage media accessible to computers has also resulted in innovations in the area of information retrieval and this has had its attendant problems. The difficulties of scanning large interdependent files of information at a cost comparable with the present manual systems, the updating and verification of the integrity of the information, and the preserving of the complete system for recovery after a computer breakdown are all problems to which people have addressed themselves.

Attention has not, however, been confined to these areas alone. The systems referred to earlier aim at identifying information contained within written text in order to perform some appropriate action. Few systems deal with English text of unrestricted structure. The counterpart in information retrieval is the isolation of information contained within documents[2] written in natural language to specify what the text is "about," and the subsequent use of this information to assist in the retrieval of only relevant[3] documents in response to the user's request. In doing so, the computer has been used to perform a task which has been the subject of long investigation by librarians. Maron [37] speculates on the direction in which this type of work may progress:

> To correctly classify an object or event is a mark of intelligence; a mark of even greater intelligence is to be able to modify and create new and more fruitful categories, i.e., to form new concepts. (Perhaps one of the really dominant characteristics of the intelligent machine will be that of creating new categories into which to sort its "experiences".)

---

[2] *Document* here is used in the generic sense, namely, a piece of natural language text.

[3] *Relevant* is used, for the moment, informally. The dictionary definition "bearing on, pertinent to, the matter in hand" will suffice in the present context.

The information retrieval systems that have been suggested and used involve the following stages, some of which may be wholly or partially mechanized:

(a) The documents added to the system are examined to determine information about them which will facilitate their retrieval.

(b) The requests are examined to determine the information essential for the retrieval of documents relevant to them.

(c) The information provided by (a) and (b) is then compared or matched in such a way that the document collection may be partitioned into two sets, namely, the set of documents relevant to the request and the set of documents not relevant to the request. Alternatively, the documents are ordered according to their relevance to the request, according to some scale of relevance.

(d) Access to the relevant documents is provided by divulging their reference numbers.

In connection with these, two principal subjects of research arise, both of which have been studied extensively in the last two decades. These are

(1) What information should be extracted from documents and requests so that algorithms may be designed to achieve (c) above?

(2) Which stages may be mechanized, and how?

More recently, a third area of research has arisen. That is the following.

(3) In what ways may retrieval systems be evaluated in terms of their ability to retrieve relevant documents in response to users' requests?

There have been two main approaches to the first stage of information retrieval, namely the processing of documents to be added to the system. These approaches are described in the following two sections. Question (3) is discussed in Section 1.4.

1.1 The Classification Approach

Documents are classified or grouped into a particular order, according to a predetermined classification scheme. The documents may be grouped physically on shelves. This is the principle upon which most conventional library classifications are based [e.g., Dewey, Universal Decimal Classification (UDC)]. This principle of classification makes a number of presuppositions. The following are taken from Shera [59] and adapted for discussion of the classification of knowledge in general.

(a) *Linearity* of subject arrangement. This is necessary in order physically to arrange books on shelves.

(b) Complete *covering* of all knowledge.

(c) *Meaningfulness* of terms and meaningful *differences* between terms.

(d) Provision for a *specific place* for every topic or field.

Such classifications encounter difficulties which do not seem to be soluble, even by revision of the classification which is used. Thus, when it is unclear into which of several categories a document should be placed, rules have to be devised to permit the selection of one class in favor of another. These are essentially arbitrary for they are exterior to the general principle of the classification scheme. Without duplicate copies of documents or an adequate set of cross-references, documents which relate to the subject area of a particular class may, nevertheless, not appear in that class and therefore may be missed in retrieval. Thus the limitations of the traditional classifications are that they are inconsistent in their organization and therefore excessively complex in structure, and are unable to adapt to the advance of knowledge.

The way in which such a classification is established owes a great deal to the Aristotelean method. Such an approach is *a priori* in character. A method is given for the analysis of classes by enumerating their contents and distinguishing each from the others. Thus, starting with the *genus*, a series of *differences* is stated. The *species* are then listed according to their different characteristics or *properties*. A close parallel may be drawn between the classifications used in libraries and the development of botanical classifications. In botanical classification, the major subdivisions were determined by considerations which, on an *a priori* basis, seemed to be of paramount importance in contemporary science. There was no attempt at experiment, and as a result, there was considerable diversity of opinion about the criteria which were important in making the major divisions. A number of different classification schemes arose. Caesalpino (1519–1603) paid chief attention to the fruits of the plant. Tournefort (1656–1708), however, based his classifications on the character of the corolla. Linnaeus (1707–1778), on the other hand, regarded the variations of the sexual organs of plants as the main consideration in making the divisions. The systems grew in complexity, as have the library classifications of the present day, as exceptions to them were found and recorded in the classification. As Adanson (1727–1806) observed, there appeared to be little consistency between the classifications.

The difficulty of fulfilling requirements (a)–(d) of this section is plain. Even in the case of (c), the problem is not straightforward, for it is not always clear what constitutes a meaningful difference. The following, taken from Diogenes Laertius [15], is sufficient to illustrate the point briefly:

Plato had defined Man as an animal, biped and featherless, and was applauded. Diogenes plucked a fowl and brought it to the lecture-room with the words "Here is Plato's man." In consequence of which there was added to the definition, "Having broad nails."

A more serious criticism of the *a priori* method of library classification arises in connection with requirements (b) and (d), namely complete *covering* of all knowledge, and the provision for a *specific place* for every topic of field. It is as if all the objects of the universe had been distributed into lists or parcels, and a common name given to the objects of each list until all the general names in language had been invented, thereby covering all knowledge. To decide whether a certain general name may be truly predicated of a particular object, it is necessary, as it were, only to read the role of objects which have the name to see whether the object appears among them. Mill [40] remarks: "So absurd a doctrine will be owned by nobody when thus nakedly stated; ..." He adds: "General names are not marks put upon definite objects; classes are not made by drawing a line round a number of given assignable individuals. The objects which compose any given class are perpetually fluctuating." Thus if the meaning of a general name is the set of things which have the name, no general name has a fixed meaning. In discussing the meaning of general names he asserts:

The only mode in which any general name has a definite meaning, is by being the name of an indefinite variety of things; namely, of all things, known and unknown, past, present, or future, which possess certain definite attributes. When, by studying not the meaning of words, but the phenomena of nature, we discover that these attributes are possessed by some objects not previously known to possess them (as when chemists found that the diamond was combustible) we include this new object in the class. We place the individual in the class because the proposition is true; the proposition is not true because the object is placed in the class.

In information retrieval one is confronted with the problem of assigning documents to a set of categories which are not necessarily exclusive or independent. Maron [37] clearly points out the difficulty:

The problem arises because the categories are not defined extensionally. That is, a category is not defined by enumerating its members (documents), but, rather, the situation is reversed. Based on some more or less clear notion of a category, we must decide whether or not to assign a document to it.

Needham [42] remarks in this connection:

If we are to assign a document to a class automatically, we must have (a) a list of facts about the classes which will make ascription possible; (b) an algorithm, usually some sort of matching algorithm, to tell us which class best suits a document. Given a classification like the UDC, it is not at all obvious that (a) and (b) exist, or even, if they can be found. (a) and (b) imply a degree of uniformity about the classification which may just not be there.

1.2 The Indexing Approach

The purpose of indexing is to describe or characterize the content of a document to ensure its retrieval by the appropriate request. Consideration is confined exclusively to indexing methods in which relational operators between terms are not used. A detailed comparison of the other class of methods is given by Soergel [62]. One of the most commonly used methods was "multiple aspect" indexing. Here a document was described by a list of terms. The terms were regarded as unordered and unrelated. A request, processed in much the same way, was compared with a document to determine whether it should be retrieved or not in response to the request. A decision to retrieve or not was taken, possibly after a number of further operations, by determining whether the term list of the document contained the terms of the request. As such, the systems were realizable on punched cards and, in principle, terms common to the request and the document were detected by sensing holes in identical positions on two cards by superimposing the cards. There were two main approaches. The "Uniterm" endeavored to restrict the thought required of the indexer to a minimum. The indexer recorded the terms which he considered were characteristic of the document, and in doing so a term vocabulary was gradually accumulated *a posteriori* from his lists. Originally, no effort was made to record synonyms or near-synonyms. The vocabulary grew in size without any firm internal structure. The virtue of such a system was in its simplicity, and its merit lay in its attempt to reduce work on the part of the indexer to a minimum. For general use, however, the system proved to be ineffectual.

The "thesaurus" approach attempted to remedy the ills of the Uniterm system by controlling the internal structure of the vocabulary. The method is generally associated in its original form with Luhn [35]. A term vocabulary was determined in advance, and terms were included in it for their effectiveness in describing the subject matter of the document collection as a whole. The indexer was instructed to select terms from this vocabulary that were appropriate to the documents he examined. This approach proved to be considerably more successful than the Uniterm system. Its disadvantages, however, lay in the difficulty of extending the system to deal with the accumulation of documents which were gradually added to the collection, thereby altering its original character. Thus new terms needed to be added to the term vocabulary. Some of the old terms needed to be more specific in their meaning to distinguish between the new concepts introduced by the new documents. To achieve this it was necessary to replace the offending terms by a number of new terms. To include these changes, the complete document collection had to be re-examined to reassign to them the terms of the new vocabulary. The resemblance between a structured vocabulary of this type and the present day technical thesaurus is strong. At the time, however, no such thesaurus existed. Roget's *Thesaurus*, with its complete lack of technical terminology, was inappropriate for document collections concerned with specific research topics in technical fields.

A similar attempt to exercise some control over the term vocabulary was provided by the *association map* or *library lattice* of Doyle [*16*]. It was successful in dealing with synonyms and provided a means of replacing an arbitrary term by a more specific term or a more general term. Giuliano [*20*] remarked about their use:

> Automatic index term techniques are needed to improve the recall of relevant information, to enable indexers and requestors to use language in a more natural manner, and to enable retrieval of relevant messages which are described by different index terms than those used in the inquiry.

The lattice is a partially ordered set and the ordering relation was that of the generic to the specific. Thus synonyms were identified in the lattice with the same nodes. Near-synonyms were represented by nodes that were close together in the sense that their least upper bound was a few arcs above them. The replacement of a term or a set of terms by a more general term related to it in the lattice had the anticipated effect of increasing the number of documents retrieved but ran the risk of retrieving documents which were not relevant. The general term comprised the word senses which were isolated and distinguished in the dependant nodes lower in the lattice. The replacing of a term by a more specific term had the reverse effect. Fewer documents tended to be retrieved, but the relevance of these was hopefully enhanced. The price of this was that a number of documents relevant to the request were lost. This inverse relationship characterizes all attempts at automatic retrieval.

Needham [*43*] has proposed and experimented with an ordering relation which differs from the "generic-specific" relationship mentioned above. Needham's relationship was expressed informally by the slogan: "If, when you ask for a document about A you cannot reasonably complain if you get a document about B, then A should be above B in the ordering." The ordering relation was therefore more clearly related to the retrieval process in that the relation itself involved a rudimentary assessment of the relevance of documents to subject categories. The ordering relation, nevertheless, still depended strongly upon subjective decisions. What, for example, constitutes a "reasonable complaint"? In the use of this ordering relation may be seen the beginning of a "mechanistic" approach to the construction of term classifications for information retrieval. In such an approach, attention is focused primarily on reproducing the expected responses by the system as requests are presented to it, without the anterior assumptions of the utility, in retrieval, of particular linguistic relationships between terms. The determination of the linguistic character of the classes of a classification, developed as the result of a purely mechanistic approach, would, therefore, be posterior to the construction of the classification.

A number of methods have been proposed to generate automatically the lattice dependencies between the items of the term vocabulary. Some of the techniques have involved a syntactic analysis of the text with a subsequent manual screening to select the unique correct analysis for each sentence. The relationships between nouns located in this analysis were then computed with reference to the co-occurrence of terms within sentences and within syntactic structures. Such a method is only partially automatic since it involves the manual stage of selecting the correct syntactic structure. In addition, the syntactic analysis of large quantities of text with which methods must be capable of dealing in the future, may scarcely be contemplated unless the methods are greatly refined.

The measurement of the co-occurrence of pairs of terms within documents has been used by Stiles [67], and by Borko and Bernick [7] in factor analytic methods. These methods have aimed either at the assignment of documents to subject categories, in the case of Borko and Bernick, or at the reformulation of users' search requests by Stiles. The reformulation of the request expanded it by the addition of statistically associated terms to refine the original request. Factor analytic methods have proved effective in many of the reported experiments. Their principal drawback is that they are not amenable to the examination of large document collections. Their computational requirements as determined by the existing eigenvector methods make such procedures impracticable for such a purpose.

The statistical methods that have been outlined briefly above represent a significant departure from the indexing methods of the 1950's. The earlier methods were concerned more closely with the behavior and meaning of words within a more extensive area than that covered by the particular document collection being used in retrieval. They were concerned with the meaning and use of words in natural language as a whole. The whole experience of the indexer, as a person well versed in the language in which the document was written, was brought to bear when he indexed the collection. The statistical techniques, at least those concerned with term association, deal only with the vocabulary of the document collection and the ways in which the words relate within the document collection.

Again, a parallel may be drawn between the developments of the last two decades in library classification and the gradual recognition, in post-Linnaean botanical classification, of the importance of observation. The dictatorship of the Aristotelean method, with its notion of arriving at the truth by reason unaccompanied by experiment, was on the decline during Bacon's lifetime. In its stead followed the extensive and detailed examination of plants and the painstaking recording of botanical observations. Classification was to be achieved by the comparison of as many features of the plants as possible. Adanson [1] wrote of this method:

> La vrai fisique des Plantes est donc celle qui considère les raports de toutes leurs parties & qualités, sans excepter une seule; elle réunit toutes les Plantes en Familles naturels & invariables, . . .

Sneath [61] has discussed Adanson's contribution to the development of modern taxonomy in detail.

The use of word frequency statistics for the analysis of the content of documents is ascribed to Luhn [35]. His work, begun in 1957, was concerned with the analysis of single documents, and it was not until 2 years later that the statistical approach was extended beyond the single document stage. The use of computers and the popularity of coordinate indexing, in which terms were assigned to documents without differentiating between the relative importance of the terms in describing the content of the documents, led to "associative indexing." Maron and Kuhns [38] recognized the inherent unsoundness of undifferentiated terms in coordinate indexing and explained:

> The correspondence between the information content of a document and the set of tags is not exact as it is difficult to express precisely the subject content of a document by means of one or more index terms. There is no strict one-to-one correspondence between the set of index terms on the one hand and the class of subjects they denote on the other hand. We say that there is semantic noise in the index terms.

The semantic noise occurs, they claim, because the meaning of the terms is dependent upon their context and function within the documents. "The grammatical type, position and frequency of other words help to clarify and specify the meanings of a given term." The use of Boolean combinations of the index terms of requests has been suggested for reducing semantic noise. If, for example, two terms are connected conjunctively, the subject area is narrowed and more closely specified. The disjunction of terms, on the other hand, broadens the scope of the request. Thus, by the appropriate use of logical combinations, the retrieval of irrelevant documents or the missing of relevant documents would, hopefully, be avoided. The conjunction of terms in the request, although it decreases the chance of obtaining irrelevant documents.

has the effect of increasing the chance of missing relevant documents The converse holds for the disjunction of terms in the request. Verhoeff [75] has demonstrated this behavior, and the resulting inapplicability of Boolean functions in general to information retrieval systems.

The associative methods rest on the assumption that sufficient information may be obtained from the documents by counting word and word-pair frequencies to represent adequately the information content of the documents. The assumption, if it is appropriate, relieves us of the detailed and costly work of examining the context and function of terms within documents in order to resolve the " semantic noise " referred to by Maron and Kuhns. Maron *et al.* [39] defend the principle as follows:

> Whereas the semantical relationships are based solely on the meaning of terms and hence are independent of the " facts " described by these words, the statistical relationships between terms are based solely on the relative frequency with which they appear and hence *are* based on the nature of the facts described by the documents. Thus, although there is nothing about the meaning of the term " logic " which implies "switching theory," the nature of the facts (viz. that truth functional logic is widely used for the analysis and synthesis of switching circuits) " causes " a statistical relationship. Another example might be the terms "information theory " and " Shannon " . . .

Doyle [18] remarks in the same connection: " When pairs of words co-occur strongly in text it should not be surprising to find the members of the pairs associated in the minds of the authors of books in which they occur." Thus, in short, the basis for associative indexing is the assumption that strongly co-occurring terms are likely to be conceptually related.

The associative methods led to " probabilistic indexing ", in which a weight is given to each term assigned to a document giving the probable relevance of the index terms to the document. Dissimilarity measures between documents, significance measures for index terms, and closeness measures between the terms were required, together with the *a priori* probability distribution data. Classes of documents were retrieved and ranked according to their " computed relevance numbers ". Thus, in addition to avoiding the disadvantages of coordinate indexing with its use of undifferentiated terms, Maron tried to make the retrieval process a natural extension of his statistical approach. However, there appears to be no clear distinction between indexing and classification. Thus Maron [37] states: " This enquiry examines a technique for automatically classifying (indexing) documents according to their subject content." Later he states: " This approach to the problem of automatic indexing is a statistical one. It is based on the rather straightforward notion that individual words in a document function as clues, on the basis of which a prediction can be made about the subject category to which the document most probably belongs." The method relies on the existence of established subject categories to which the documents are to be assigned. The categories are not generated automatically. This subject classification is an *a priori* one, with the result that the method is limited by the refinement and sophistication of the classification.

1.3 The Evaluation of Retrieval Systems

Although the work done during the last two decades on automatic subject classification and automatic indexing has been considerable,[4] little progress has been made in the evaluation of retrieval systems until recently. The problems associated with evaluation, however, have been recognized for some time. The earliest comparative experiment, using a coordinated uniterm index, was reported by Gull [23] in 1956. The need for more adequate evaluative procedures has been made apparent by the progress in automatic clssification and indexing tech- niques. Research in information retrieval will soon reach the point where, hopefully, sufficient experimental evidence will have been col- lected about existing classification and indexing methods to provide the basis for the establishing of a formal theory. Indeed, a theoretical approach may be regarded as a natural stage in the evolution of re- trieval systems, starting from the early days of Bush's MEMEX and the mechanical approach, and progressing through the experimental stage of the late fifties and early sixties. The aim of such a theory would be to distinguish between "good" and "bad" retrieval practice in the design of retrieval systems, and to allow some sort of estimate to be made of the operating characteristics of a, retrieval system once its design had been specified. Such a theory is not yet available, although the research associated with the SMART system and with the Cran- field Project is progressing in this direction. Evaluation serves two important purposes. First, it provides a means of choosing between a number of possible systems on the basis of the excellence of their per- formance as retrieval systems. Second, it provides a means of judging the effect on performance of variations in the techniques used in retrieval or the variations in experimental design. This is essential if research in information retrieval is to progress.

Cleverdon [10] has suggested a number of criteria of importance in the evaluation of retrieval systems.

(a) The ability of the system to present all relevant documents (i.e., recall):

(b) The ability of the system to withhold all nonrelevant documents (i.e., precision):

---

[4] See, for example, the state-of-the-art report by Stevens [66].

(c) The interval between the demand being made and the answer being given (i.e., time):

(d) The physical form of the output (i.e., presentation):

(e) The effort, intellectual or physical, demanded of the user (i.e., effort).

Cleverdon has further argued that of these (c) and (d) offer the least problem since both may be improved by more sophisticated or more appropriate hardware. The evaluation of (e) may be achieved by the straightforward observation of a number of users of the system. The main intellectual difficulties of evaluation reside in providing suitable methods of estimating (a) and (b), namely, recall and precision.

In a retrieval system which is to be operable on an industrial scale, an evaluation measure would supposedly strike an economic balance between the quality of the performance, judged in terms of recall and precision, and the cost of achieving this. Supposedly, some reduction in quality might be tolerable provided that the cost of maintaining the system decreased appreciably. Such considerations, however, may be deferred until the task of designing a system that exhibits good performance in terms of recall and precision has been accomplished. Accordingly, throughout this chapter, the performance of a retrieval system is discussed solely in terms of recall and precision. Their appropriateness for evaluating retrieval performance is strongly defended by Cleverdon: "The unarguable fact, however, is that they [i.e., recall and precision] are fundamental requirements of the users, and it is quite unrealistic to try to measure how effectively a system or subsystem is operating without bringing in recall and precision."

An evaluation measure gives an estimate of the system's ability to retrieve all documents relevant to the users' requests. Ideally, for effective comparisons to be made between systems, this estimate must be characteristic of the system itself, and therefore independent of the characteristics of the user population the system serves. There are a number of difficulties associated with this. The evaluation of a retrieval system requires that a set of requests be available, together with a set of decisions giving the relevance of each document in the collection to each request. The response of the system to the set of requests is compared with the expected response, and the agreement or disagreement between these is used to evaluate the performance of the system. Provided that the comparison is made over enough requests, it may be supposed that evaluation is independent of the particular choice of test requests. Performance of a given system may change with the subject area covered by the document collection, as the SMART system has shown. The evaluation also depends on the individual decisions concerning the relevance of each document of the collection to each request, and these decisions are essentially subjective. Mooers [41] is emphatic on this point: "There is no absolute 'relevance' of a document. It depends upon the person and his background, the work and the date. What is not relevant today may be relevant tomorrow." In the last analysis, relevance may only be defined in terms of what the user considers appropriate as responses to his request. Relevance, nevertheless, for all its disagreeable and apparently arbitrary properties remains central to any discussion of evaluation. As Doyle [19] aptly and succinctly remarked: "Relevance is a thought crutch; with it we may think inaccurately about the retrieval problem, but without it (or something better) we couldn't think at all."

A number of attempts has been made to examine the question of relevance and its applicability and suitability as a basis for the determination of retrieval system performance. Cuadra and Katter [12] remark: "Relevance judgments have been used as a basis for measures designed to evaluate the effectiveness of information retrieval systems.... There is reason to believe, however, that as ordinarily obtained, they [i.e., the relevance judgments] may be unreliable and sensitive to a number of conditions of measurement that have not been carefully controlled in previous evaluation studies." In their study, a number of criteria or "implicit use orientations" are defined, on the basis of which subjects (judges) are invited to assess the relevance of documents to requests. Not surprisingly they report: "It was found that the particular use orientations assumed by the judge has a marked effect on relevance judgments." The use orientations enabled the judges to adopt a particular "assigned point of view" about relevance. If a judge is instructed, for example, to determine relevance according to the "stimulative value"[5] of documents then his judgments would, in all likelihood, differ from those where he judges according to the "hard-factual"[6] nature of documents retrieved. A request offered to a retrieval system seldom specifies in sufficient detail the actual intention or motivation of the user in submitting the request. However, the difficulties raised by Cuadra and Katter might be lessened, although not eliminated, if the "use orientation" were incorporated explicitly into the request. To assess relevance of documents to request according to first one "user orientation" and then according to a second, for example, is to submit two, possibly substantially different, requests. Cuadra and Katter conclude:

These findings support the belief that relevance scores are very likely to be artifacts of particular experimental instructions and conditions and should not

---

[5] Stimulative value, i.e., wants articles that will have "idea-stimulative" value for himself.

[6] Hard-factual, i.e., fact-oriented and very chary of "theory and speculation;" is interested in "hard results."

be offered or viewed as absolute numbers. This conclusion does not invalidate experiments in which a given group of judges makes relevance appraisals for a specific system. However, it does call in question any comparative evaluations (between systems or subsystems) in which the attitude of the judges about the intended use of the materials was not considered and *controlled*, either experimentally, or statistically.

Resnick and Savage [52], as do Cuadra and Katter, support the use of relevance as the basis of evaluation for a given system. In one of their experiments they have set out "... to compare the relative inter- and intrasubject consistency of humans when judging the relevance of documents to their general interests on the basis of (a) citations, (b) abstracts, (c) index terms and (d) total texts." Briefly, a number of randomly chosen subjects, informed in the topic areas, were directed to choose from a number of documents, randomly selected from a set of internal publications, those documents which were relevant to their interests. Their decisions were based on the complete document, citations, abstracts, or index terms. The experiment was repeated with the same judges and materials after the lapse of a month. The results of the two experiments were compared to determine

(1) The ability of humans to judge consistently the relevance of items to their general interests.

(2) The effect on these judgments of different kinds of lexical material (documents, citations, abstracts, and index terms).

(3) The ability of humans to recall previous judgments of relevance. The results showed that "... under the conditions of this experiment, humans are consistent in their judgment of relevance and that this consistency is independent of the kind of material on which this judgment is based, except in the case of abstracts. This anomaly associated with abstract judgment appears to have no simple explanation." They conclude, "The high consistency of the human judgments observed in this study may put to rest those criticisms of the reliability of evaluations of text processing systems based on such judgments." They also agree with Cuadra and Katter about the artificiality of relevance numbers giving the degree of relevance of a document to a request, and observe: "What does remain as a problem is a procedure for the quantification of the results of human judgments. . . . The scores [i.e., relevance scores], however, still cannot be shown to lie on a metric scale, and we are not yet justified in assuming that a score of 50 is twice as high as a score of 25. The problem awaits further analysis."

Taube [72] also agreed that, although judges may be selfconsistent in their judgments of relevance, it is not clear that they are consistent among themselves. He remarks:

When relevance is used to characterize a document or characterize the relationship between a document and the subjective requirements of a searcher, its meaning is as clear as any other psychological predicate; that is, we may accept the supposition that the searcher uses the term relevance with fair consistency in referring to his own responses. When it comes to assessing the consistency of usage for all searchers, we are on much shakier ground.

Taube, like Cuadra, Katter, Resnick, Savage and others has warned against current practices in the measurement of relevance. He has objected that, while relevance is widely agreed to be a subjective notion, reasonably consistently assessed by a single judge but admitting considerable variation between judges, it has nevertheless been calculated in many experiments to a degree of arithmetic precision which is unreasonable and inappropriate. In addition, since relevance assessments may not be consistent between users, relevance-recall values may not be taken as characteristic of the retrieval system itself. In this connection, Taube asserts,

> When . . . discussion shifts to the *relevance-recall* ratio, relevance is assumed to characterize or describe, not psychological states, or the relation of a particular document to a particular question, but the system as a whole. It is supposedly an indexing or IR system as a total complex which is characterized or ranked according to its relevance and recall performance. It may be said that the system's performance is measured by subjective responses, . . .

Thus, if the evaluation of performance is sensitive to changes in the assessment of relevance of the type which may occur between competent and informed judges, then certainly the evaluation is not characteristic of the system. Taube has also questioned the use of recall and precision on procedural grounds. "A subjective response may be trusted to determine that a certain percentage of items retrieved are not *relevant*, but such a response cannot establish a percentage of recall because the subject does not know what other documents there are in the collection which might be relevant to his question." This criticism cannot be made if sufficient care has been taken before evaluation to ensure that the relevance of each document to each request has been examined.

Recent studies by Salton [57] have clarified some of Taube's criticisms. The purpose of the study was to determine the effect of variations in relevance assessments on the average recall and precision values used in measuring retrieval performance. Briefly, four sets of decisions were obtained from a number of judges giving the relevance of each document to each of the requests. Two of the sets were the set of relevance decisions obtained by the originators of the requests, and the set of relevance decisions obtained by a person other than the originator of the requests. The decisions were dichotomous, and indicated only the relevance or nonrelevance of a document to a request. In addition, the criterion on which the judges were instructed to assess relevance was strict. A document was to be judged relevant to a request only: "if it is directly stated in the abstract as printed, or can be directly deduced from the printed abstracts that the document contains information on the topic asked for in the query." Three different retrieval procedures were used and these were ranked according to their retrieval effectiveness computed for each of the sets of relevance judgments in turn. Salton asserts, "... it appears reasonable to conclude not only that the performance methods are ranked in the same order, no matter which of the four sets of relevance judgments is used, but also that the actual performance differences resulting from differences between author and nonauthor judgments are negligible." The relative insensitivity of the evaluation of the retrieval methods to relatively large differences in the relevance judgments is ascribed to the calculation of recall and precision averages over the set of requests. Salton concludes:

> ... it can be stated that, if the relevance assessments obtained from the query authors used in the present study are typical of what can be expected from general user populations of retrieval systems, then the resulting average recall-precision figures appear to be stable indicators of system performance which do in fact reflect actual retrieval effectivenesss.

Similar conclusions have been reached by Cleverdon [9] in connection with the ranking of a number of indexing languages according to their retrieval effectiveness. Cleverdon concludes, "Insufficient analysis has been done to make any detailed comments, but it is clear that the relevance decisions did not significantly effect the comparative results of Cranfield II."

2. Term Classification in Information Retrieval

2.1 Intersubstitutability, Co-occurrence, and Stability

The merits of indexing by "uniterms" has already been discussed in Section 1.2. Both the simplicity with which uniterms may be used and the lack of sophistication required of the indexer in assigning them to documents lessen the cost of the initial stage of document processing. Of the methods reviewed in Section 1 for representing the information content of the document collection, the use of uniterms is at least economically the most practicable on a large scale. The complete absence of any structure between them, however, makes them on their own entirely unsuitable for information retrieval. The "thesaurus" approach discussed in Section 1.2, however, provides a structure between terms which may profitably be used in retrieval. The difficulty of extending the thesaurus or lattice as the document collection increases in size and the necessity of reindexing the complete collection if terms are added to the vocabulary, are the principal obstacles to the thesaurus in information retrieval. Provided that these disadvantages may be overcome, it is appropriate to examine a retrieval system which combines the simplicity of the uniterm approach with the organized structure of the thesaurus. Accordingly the function of the library lattice will be examined in greater detail to determine how the difficulties may be resolved.

Suppose that for a particular document collection a lattice has been constructed. The system may be realized on punched cards, a card being set aside for each term in the vocabulary. Each card also contains an indication of the terms above and the terms below the term represented by the card. The system is operated in the following manner. For each term in a request presented to the system the appropriate cards are selected and superimposed. The documents which are to be retrieved are indicated by the presence of a hole in each card in the same position. This may be sensed by optical or mechanical means. The output of such a system may be increased by replacing some or all of the cards representing request terms by the cards which correspond to those terms immediately above the request terms in the lattice. These terms are available on the cards corresponding to the request terms. "Above" and "below" are interpreted in terms of the ordering relation which induced the lattice. In a lattice in which the ordering relation is from the "specific" to the "generic", the replacement of a term by a term above it in the lattice corresponds to a broadening of the request. The replacement of a term by a term below it in the lattice corresponds, on the other hand, to a narrowing of the request. All documents indexed under a particular term will also be indexed under the less specific term above it in the lattice.

Suppose for example that Fig. 1 is a fragment of a lattice giving the relationship between the terms t_1, t_2, t_3, and t_4 and t_5. A request which contains the term t_1 may be broadened by replacing it by t_4. Not only

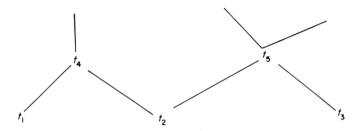

Fig. 1. Fragment of a lattice.

are the documents containing t_1 retrieved, but also those documents containing the term t_2, which is also directly below t_4 in the lattice. Thus, considering the replacement by t_4, t_1, and t_2 may be regarded as *intersubstitutable* since the output of the system will be unchanged by replacing t_1 by t_2 in the request.

The retrieving of a document is unaltered if one of its terms t_1 is replaced by another of its terms t_2. Thus, considering the retrieval of a specific document, the terms which occur together in the document are intersubstitutable. A specific pair of terms are intersubstitutable over the whole document collection provided only that the terms occur together in documents of the collection. This is unlikely to occur in practice and this requirement of intersubstitutability must therefore be relaxed. Instead, complete intersubstitutability over the whole document collection may be approximated by those terms which occur together in a significant number of documents of the collection. More generally, groups, rather than pairs, of terms are required which comprise terms showing a marked tendency to occur together in documents. Pairs of terms taken from the same group will be assumed to be intersubstitutable, although this assumption may only be supported in practice if the tendency to co-occur is sufficiently strong for each pair of the group. The construction of the lattice has therefore been reduced to a classification problem which, hopefully, is more tractable.

The groups of terms whose members show a marked tendency to co-occur resemble, in usage, the groups of terms that are closely related in the lattice, although there may be little resemblance between the constitutions of the groups. The groups of terms may be regarded as descriptors and the complete set of descriptors as a classification of the term vocabulary. The descriptors are, as it were, one level removed from the document text itself. Words extracted from the document text itself are more closely related to the text than a descriptor, for a descriptor may never appear in the text. The similarity in function between groups of terms sharing the same upper bound in the lattice and groups of terms whose members show a strong tendency to co-occur may be seen from Fig. 1. Just as a document or a request containing t_1 may be expanded to increase recall by substituting for t_1 the nearest term above it given by the partial ordering relation, so t_1 may be replaced by the descriptor corresponding to the class containing t_1. In addition, the other terms in the same class as t_1 are involved in the substitution in the same way that t_2 was involved by replacing t_1 by t_4. The document and request are, in effect, expanded by the addition of all terms which occur in the same class as terms in the document or terms in the request. Thus the descriptors, defined by the classification of the term vocabulary, are used for coordinate indexing, although the search techniques which will be used in retrieving documents will be different from those used, for example, with the UDC.

From the original term descriptions of the documents the relative frequency of co-occurrence of terms within documents may be derived. On the basis of this information about the interrelation of terms it is proposed to construct a classification. A document may not, however, have a unique index description in that the decision to assign a term or keyword to a document, particularly with the uniterm system, rests with the discretion of the indexer. Although two indexers, indexing the same documents, may produce descriptions which agree with each other substantially, it is nevertheless likely that there will be points of disagreement. Accordingly, it is necessary that two term classifications derived from the same document collection, indexed separately by two different indexers, should not differ substantially. That is, the classification technique must be stable with regard to small changes in the document descriptions. Thus, for example, it would be unreasonable to suppose that the addition of a single document to the collection would result in a serious reorganization of the classification. Borko [6] makes a covert reference to the stability requirements of term classifications when he remarks:

> One of the claims for mathematically derived classification systems is that the categories so derived are descriptions of the documents used in the analysis. However, if the categories prove to be so unique that they describe only the one document set and no other, they would be of little value.

Needham and Sparck Jones [45] make a similar observation: "We want to be able to update our classification: we should be able to add new terms without radically altering the system if there are only a few of them." This requirement is a constraint on the classification technique and providing the technique is stable with respect to small changes in the term descriptions, significant differences in term classifications, should they occur, are attributable only to the inadequacy of the indexing. Assuming, however, that the documents have been indexed adequately, the use of term classifications in retrieval has the important property of reducing the effects of bad or faulty indexing decisions.

Classification is a process in which the individual differences between the objects to be classified are suppressed in order to derive more general properties which are characteristic of groups of objects. Two questions therefore arise in the present context:

(1) Has too little information been lost, in that the classification permits distinctions to be made between terms which uselessly distinguish between certain documents?

(2) Has too much information been lost, in that the classification

does not enable appropriate distinctions to be made between certain documents?

If too much information has been lost then the performance of the retrieval system will doubtless suffer, and this will be shown in the evaluation of the system. If, on the other hand, too little information has been lost, then effort has been wasted in making distinctions which are redundant for the purposes of retrieval. It is important that this waste of effort should be avoided in a system that is intended to be viable on a large scale. Questions (1) and (2) may be summarized by adapting the terminology of the requirements of Section 1.1; that is, are the classes obtained *meaningful* and are there *meaningful differences* between classes which enable the appropriate, and only the appropriate, distinctions to be made between terms?

These questions may be answered in full only after the classification has been set up and documents have been retrieved from the collection in response to requests submitted to the system. Evaluation of the response of the system based on the ideas of Section 1.3 may be used to determine the adequacy of the classification. A partial answer may be given to the first question, however, on the basis of the type of information that will be used in the construction of the term classification. A classification constructed from the co-occurrence of terms in documents is less likely to make redundant distinctions between terms than a human classifier since there would be no information on the basis of which these could be made. The human classifier, on the other hand, has available additional sources of information about the terms and, on the basis of this, he is able to make distinctions between terms which in fact serve no useful function in indexing the collection.

2.2 Retrieval Characteristics of Term Classifications

The use of the relative frequency of occurrence of terms within documents has been arrived at by considering only the intersubstitutability of terms in the library lattice. Maron *et al.* [*39*] and Doyle [*18*], among others, have supported the use of relative frequency of co-occurrence for determining groups of semantically associated words. Terms that occur together in the same document may not have any obvious semantic relationship, and, accordingly, the linguistic character of the classes derived from term co-occurrence will not be obvious. The terms within a class will not be more strongly related than "topically" related, in that they may meaningfully be used in connection with the same topic area within the subject area of the collection. Accordingly, it is reasonable to suppose that groups of intersubstitutable terms will consist of those terms that relate to topic areas within the field covered by the document collection. The classification of the term vocabulary into groups of terms whose members show a strong tendency to occur together in documents enables document and request descriptions to be expanded to include terms related to the topic areas of the request. For each document or request there are, therefore, two specifications: the first using manually assigned terms from the term vocabulary, and the second using automatically assigned descriptors defined by the constructed term classification. The extent to which a document relates to a request is determined by the degree to which the document and request specifications conform with each other. Provided that the assignment of terms to documents of the collection is adequate for characterizing their content, the greater the conformity between document and request specifications then the greater the relevance of the document to the request. The degree to which a document and request conform may be determined by a function called the *match function*. A number of different match functions may be defined, each of which represents a different way of uniting term and descriptor specifications to improve the performance of the retrieval system. The match functions must all exhibit, however, the same general behavior with respect to the term and descriptor specifications of documents and requests as was described above, namely, the greater the agreement between term specifications and between descriptor specifications then the greater the value of the match function. Given a particular document and a particular request, there are four specifications—two term specifications and two descriptor specifications—that may be used by the system to determine whether or not the document should be retrieved in response to the request. The probability that a descriptor will be shared both by the request and the document is higher than the probability that there will be a shared term, since a descriptor is shared provided at least one term from the request belongs to the same class as at least one term from the document. Accordingly, as has been asserted above, descriptors have the effect of increasing the recall of the system. The same assertion may be made on intuitive grounds, for the expansion of the term descriptions by using descriptors enables the system to retrieve those documents which relate to the same topic area as the request. Thus the use of a term classification in information retrieval may be regarded as a recall device, to compensate for the failure in term matching between document and request.

A term classification may also serve as a device for improving the precision of the retrieval system. Suppose that the classification is such that classes are permitted to overlap freely. A term may, therefore, belong to more than one class. The different senses of a term or the different contextual uses of a term may therefore be identified by determining the term's different class affiliations. The class membership of a term specifies the term's affiliations to the topic areas of the document collection. The senses are indistinguishable if simple term descriptions of documents are used. The same conclusion has been reached by Vaswani [73] who states: "For the purposes of document indexing a word might usefully occur in more than one cluster to allow it to be clustered with sets of words with which it may associate in different meanings. . . . The optimum degree of overlap may have to be found by experiment."

Both recall and precision are affected by the sizes of the classes of the classification. If the classes are large, then the probability of a descriptor occurring both in the document specification and in the request specification is high, since a descriptor will be shared if there is at least one term in the request which belongs to the same class as at least one term in the document. Precision is low for large classes since the document and request have, in effect, been augmented by a large number of terms. For smaller classes, the probability of a shared descriptor decreases so that the recall decreases accordingly. Precision, on the other hand, may be higher since the document and request specifications have not been augmented by terms which may result in the retrieving of nonrelevant documents. As has been seen above, a term classification may be used both as a recall and as a precision device. The problem of constructing classifications for information retrieval is to ensure that they are increased simultaneously.

2.3 Limit on Attainable Retrieval Performance

The approach to information retrieval discussed above enables improvement to be made in the performance of a retrieval system by utilizing a classification of the term vocabulary. The classification is constructed automatically from information which is assumed to be adequate in representing enough of the content of the documents for the purposes of information retrieval. The retrieval performance is to be assessed on the basis of the evaluation methods outlined in Section 1.3 in which the responses of the system to a set of requests are compared with the expected responses of the system.

The retrieval system, however, may be such that, given the general specification of permissible term classifications and document-request match functions, the required response of the system to the base set of requests may never be realized. That is, no choice of classification and no formulation of the document-request match function, within the general design of the retrieval system, may achieve perfect performance. The highest performance attainable by the system lies somewhere below this ideal. Part of the difficulty lies in designing a system with sufficient flexibility to accommodate all the vagaries in relevance judgments made by users of the system. Salton [57] has made the observation that "The gap between the complete human search and a perfect search ... appears to be due to ambiguities in query formulations and to the difficulties of reconciling the user's view of a subject area with the subject classification provided in a given document collection. This latter gap may never be bridged by any search and retrieval system likely to come into existence in the foreseeable future." This is not, however, the only difficulty. There may be a limit on the attainable performance imposed by the design of the retrieval system irrespective of the set of relevance judgments, and this may be a significant contribution to the observed gap between actual performance and perfect performance. There has been little reference in the literature to the existence of a limiting value of achievable performance for a retrieval system, and, certainly, no methods have been proposed for determining it. It is important, at least in information retrieval research, to know the limits imposed on performance by the actual design of the system. Detailed discussion of this and associated problems is deferred to Section 4.

The properties of term classifications required in information retrieval may now be summarized.

(1) The classification is to be based on information relating to the relative frequency of co-occurrence of terms within documents.

(2) The classes comprise those terms which show a marked tendency to occur together in the same documents.

(3) The classes may overlap freely and are arranged nonhierarchically.

(4) The membership of terms to classes is not quantified by probabilistic weights. A term either belongs to a class or does not belong to a class.

(5) The classification must be stable with respect to small changes in the term descriptions.

Methods for generating classifications conforming to these requirements are now considered.

3. The Construction of Term Classifications

3.1 General Requirements

The type of classifications discussed are unusual in that classes are intentionally allowed to overlap. The role of overlap between classes of terms as a possible precision device in information retrieval was referred to in Section 2. In many applications, however, it is a requirement that the objects to be classified should be assigned to disjoint classes, and the clustering and hierarchical methods for achieving this comprise the main bulk of classification techniques. In plant taxonomy, for example, where the objectives are somewhat different since categorical differences between the objects to be classified are of primary importance, Williams and Dale [76] are skeptical about the use of overlapping classifications. Techniques appropriate to these applications are given by Sokal and Sneath [63]. Nevertheless, the techniques to be described below for constructing overlapping classifications have been applied, with some success, by Parker-Rhodes [46] and Parker-Rhodes and Jackson [47] to mycological data containing ecological and meteorological descriptors.

In information retrieval, classes of terms must be formed in such a way that they may be used to achieve an increase in retrieval performance. There is, however, no *a priori* reason for claiming that a particular classification, in which the members of the classes are related in some specific way, is better than any other classification of the terms. The value of a classification is determined empirically by evaluating the effect on retrieval performance when the classification is incorporated into the system. Thus, in constructing classifications for information retrieval, the Platonic concept of error in the assignment of terms to classes is entirely absent. That is, there is no prior classification which automatic techniques are intended to reconstruct in detail; and there is, therefore, no basis for the probabilistic assignment of terms to classes to give the extent that properties of particular terms in the vocabulary are inferable from a knowledge of the classes to which each belongs. Sutcliffe [68, 69] has attempted to replace the Platonic concept of error by comparing, statistically, a large number of classifications of the same population to determine the typical and atypical allocation of objects to classes. The stringent conditions under which observations on the objects must be made so that atypical class allocation may be adopted as an indication of error, make this approach inapplicable here.

Certain classifications suggest themselves as devices for improving retrieval performance, and it is quite consistent to assert that these improve retrieval performance provided that such an assertion is phrased in terms of a hypothesis that is susceptible to testing. It may be supposed, for example, that a classification of the term vocabulary into groups of synonyms can be used to improve the performance of a retrieval system beyond that obtained with other classifications. Gotlieb and Kumar [21] propose another classification based on the *a priori* (pre-assigned) semantic relationships between terms rather than on the co-occurrence of terms within documents. In their scheme, the " closeness " of two terms is determined from the sets of all immediate semantic relatives of each term (i.e., all terms in the vocabulary which reference each term and which are referenced by each term). Their method requires a cross-reference mapping giving the "see also" references, as is provided, for example, in the Library of Congress' *Subject Headings* [*34*].

The assertion that a particular classification improves performance for a particular collection may be tested directly by evaluating the effect of the classification on retrieval performance, and the validity of the assertion for document collections in general may be determined provided sufficiently many document collections are examined. However, the success with which terms have been arranged into groups of synonyms must be determined by inspection of the classes and an intuitive assessment of the constitution of each class. As a relation between terms, synonymy is quite strong and, indeed, methods have been proposed for isolating groups of synonyms automatically by Sparck Jones [*64*] and by Lewis *et al.* [*33*]. Topical relatedness, suggested by the arguments of Section 2, is however less definite. The answer to the question whether two terms are topically related—that is, the two terms may relate to the same topic area—as opposed to synonymously related, is less obvious. In probabilistic classification, the probability of the assignment of terms to a class gives the reliability of the information conveyed by asserting that the term belongs to the class. Topical relatedness is not sufficiently definite a relationship in the first place to permit the calculation of probabilities with any degree of accuracy. Accordingly, a classification in which the assignment of terms to classes is nonprobabilistic is more appropriate for dealing with topical relatedness.

The classifications which we consider consist of classes of terms that show a marked tendency to occur together in the documents of the collection. The classes formed by this criterion will, hopefully, specify topic areas within the field covered by the collection, and accordingly, terms that appear together in the same class will be said to be topically related. The criterion on which classes are formed is a weak one in that classes are to be composed of terms that *tend* to co-occur; co-occurrence between every pair of terms in a class is not demanded. The criterion is therefore less restrictive than for cliques in which the classificatory criterion must be exhibited between every pair of objects belonging to a clique. A clique is a maximal complete subgraph of a graph in which the presence of an arc between a pair of nodes indicates that the nodes are related. The degree of relatedness may be specified by the strength of the arc. A further requirement of the classification is that the classes be self-generated in the following sense. Classes are defined as sets of terms which satisfy the classificatory criterion, and the complete vocabulary must be explored to find such classes. It is inadmissible to specify a set of possible topic classes initially and subsequently to distribute the terms to the most appropriate of these since, first, these classes must be treated as unknown, second, significant yet intuitively obscure classes would not be located, and third, the number of classes required is unknown. Such procedures, for example, Sebestyen's [58], might, however, be adopted as an economical means of updating an existing classification to avoid complete reclassification of the term vocabulary as the document collection expands. In terms of the general statement of the "classification problem," we want to construct classes of objects such that objects more strongly resemble objects of the same class than they do objects not in the same class. The objects are terms and the degree of similarity is determined by the relative frequency of co-occurrence of terms within documents. Accordingly, a matrix giving the similarity between pairs of terms of the vocabulary is required. This commits the order of the classification procedure to be at least n^2 in the number of objects to be classified. Methods exist which avoid the use of such a matrix. Doyle's [17] algorithm, for example, which locates clusters of documents, does so by comparing each document with a profile of the class to determine whether or not to assign the document to it. It is, however, necessary to specify in advance the number of clusters required in the final classification. Doyle's algorithm has been shown not to converge in certain cases. Dattola [14] has improved Doyle's algorithm and has obtained convergence. The convergence of a general class of classification procedures, akin to Dattola's has been demonstrated by Needham [44]. Dattola's algorithm is of order $n \log n$ in the number of objects to be classified. The conditions imposed on the determination of similarity between terms will now be given.

The objects to be classified are described or defined in terms of measurements or observations made upon them and the information is characteristically conveyed by specifying the qualitative[7] or quantitative[8] attributes which the objects possess. A great deal of discussion in taxonomic literature has been devoted to the problems arising from the interdependence of attributes. Suppose, for example, that the binary attributes "black" and "white" were used in describing the objects of a population. Then, provided that these attributes were relevant to the population, the value of one of the attributes would determine the value of the other. A less obvious example is given by the use of

---

[7] These are sometimes called "qualities." The attributes may be two-state, indicating the presence or absence of the quality; or may be multistate. The attribute "leaf-shape," for example, in which linear, obovoid, and pandurate must be distinguished, is three-state. Note the independence of the states.

[8] For example, "leaf-length," possibly averaged over a suitable sample.

"carnivorous" and "ungual." Here the dependence is not a logical one. Sokal and Sneath [63] are of the opinion that dependencies between attributes which are known without recourse to analysis must be eliminated before the objects are classified. Williams and Dale [76], while admitting that such dependencies may dominate the analysis, consider that their use in classification is a matter of taste—the sole criterion is the interest or otherwise of the user. Thus, since the dependence between "carnivorous" and "ungual" has been established, subsequent users can afford to be more sophisticated in their choice of initial attributes. The problem corresponds in information retrieval to the presence of terms which co-occur frequently compared with the frequency of occurrence of either term. The acceptability of the dependencies must be determined by their effect on retrieval performance. There is evidence that they have a deleterious effect. The dependence, however, is not a logical one.

3.2 Constraints on Classification Procedure

Suppose that x and y are two objects of a population U and suppose that $d(x, y)$ is the similarity between x and y. Then the following conditions are imposed:

$$d(x, y) = d(y, x) \qquad \text{for all } x, y \text{ in } U \tag{1}$$

(symmetry)

$$d(x, y) \geqslant 0 \qquad \text{for all } x, y \text{ in } U \tag{2}$$

$$d(x, y) = 0 \qquad \text{if } x = y \text{ for } x, y \text{ in } U \tag{3}$$

(indistinguishability of identical objects)

$$d(x, y) = 0 \qquad \text{only if } x = y \text{ for } x, y \text{ in } U \tag{4}$$

(distinguishability of nonidentical objects)

$$d(x, z) \leqslant d(x, y) + d(y, z) \qquad \text{for all } x, y, z \text{ in } U \tag{5}$$

(triangle inequality).

A system which satisfies (1)–(5) is called Euclidean. A system in which (5) is not everywhere true is called a quasimetric. A system in which (4) is not everywhere true is called a pseudometric (or a semimetric). Systems have been examined in which (5) is replaced by the more restrictive condition:

$$d(x, z) \leqslant \max\,(d(x, y), d(y, z)) \qquad \text{for all } x, y, z \text{ in } U. \tag{5'}$$

Systems in which (5′) is imposed are called ultrametric. Taxonomic hierarchies using ultrametrics have been discussed by Johnson [29], and by Jardine et al. [28]. A number of functions satisfying some or all of (1)–(5) have been proposed for information retrieval, for example, by Kuhns [30], and for wider applications, for example, by Ball [2].

A number of "distance coefficients" which satisfy some or all of (1)–(5) have been extensively applied in ecology and anthropology. Typical among these coefficients are those of Pearson [49], Mahalanobis [36], and Rao [50]. These coefficients are intended for use when the descriptions of the objects to be classified themselves result from the statistical determination of the mean and variance of a character or attribute over a sample of all instances of the object in the population. The counterpart in information retrieval is the determination of the "distance" or similarity between index terms, taking account of the variability in the assignment of terms to documents by a sufficiently large number of indexers independently indexing the collection. The uniterm indexing scheme was considered because of its simplicity and cheapness to apply in practice. The possibility of repeated indexing of the same collection would add grossly to the cost of obtaining the initial index descriptions, and accordingly cannot be considered.

Observations on the terms of the vocabulary consist of the names (call numbers) of those documents to which the terms have been assigned. Since the documents of the collection are indexed using uniterms, each document may be characterized by a vector whose components, one or zero, indicate whether or not a particular term has been used in indexing the document. The complete collection may therefore be represented by a rectangular array D, the ith row of which gives the index description of the ith document. $D_{ij} = 0$ indicates that document i has not been indexed by term j, while $D_{ij} = 1$ indicates that it has. Since it is the terms that are to be classified by their co-occurrence in documents, the terms are the objects of the universe (the document collection) while the documents are two-state or binary attributes. D is called the document array or the document matrix. Co-occurrence of terms within documents may be determined from the matrix D quite simply. Consider two terms t_j and t_k. Then the frequency of co-occurrence of the terms is given by

$$|D_{.j} \wedge D_{.k}|$$

where $D_{.j}$ is the jth column of the document array D. This will be called the *mutual association* of t_j with t_k. The *self-association* of t_j is defined as the number of documents in which it occurs and is given by

$$|D_{.j}|.$$

These quantities arise naturally in discussions of computational methods for generating similarity matrices. The relative frequency of co-occurrence of terms within documents may now be defined as

$$s_1(t_j, t_k) = |D_{.j} \wedge D_{.k}| / |D_{.j} \vee D_{.k}|. \qquad (6)$$

This is a quasimetric and varies between 0, when t_j and t_k never co-occur, and 1, when t_j and t_k always co-occur. The function, which arises naturally in information retrieval, is ascribed to Tanimoto [71]. It is biassed in favor of positive occurrence of terms in documents. The common nonoccurrence of terms in a document does not contribute toward the similarity of the two terms. As has been already seen in Section 2, intersubstitutability of terms is based on actual occurrence of terms in documents. A symmetrical form of the function may, however, be defined. A function with similar properties is the correlation coefficient, defined by:

$$s_2(t_j, t_k) = \left[\frac{|D_{.j} \wedge D_{.k}|^2}{|D_{.j}| \cdot |D_{.k}|} \right]^{1/2}. \qquad (7)$$

It is clear that other functions may be defined for calculating the similarity between pairs of terms based on their frequency of co-occurrence within documents. Account may be taken, for example, of the variation in the numbers of terms assigned to documents. The functions defined above, however, have the substantial practical advantage of making the manual inspection of classes, member by member, a relatively straightforward matter. As an example of these functions, suppose that in a collection of 5 documents, t_1 appears in documents 1, 2, and 4 while t_2 appears in documents 1, 2, 3, and 5. Then t_1 and t_2 are given vectorially by

$$t_1 = (1,1,0,1,0)$$

and

$$t_2 = (1,1,1,0,1).$$

Therefore $s_1(t_1, t_2) = 0.4$ and $s_2(t_1, t_2) = 1/\sqrt{3}$.

The classification procedure which is needed must construct classes of intersubstitutable pairs of terms. Intersubstitutability has already been expressed in terms of the co-occurrence of terms within documents, from which a value of the similarity between the two terms may be computed. These values, for all pairs of terms in the vocabulary, form a matrix which provides the information about the terms from which classes are to be constructed. The following are constraints generally placed on classification procedures:

(a) The classification must be *well defined*. That is, application of the algorithm must supply a single result.

(b) The classification must be *stable*. That is, the classification must not be grossly affected by small changes in the data.

(c) The procedure must be unaffected by a permutation of the names of the terms. That is, the procedure must be independent of the *labeling* of the terms.

(d) The procedure must be independent of *scale*. That is, the procedure must be unaffected by multiplication of the similarity matrix by a positive constant.

The need for stability has been remarked already, for it enables the classification to be reasonably insensitive to faulty indexing of the document collection. Independence of scale is an obvious requirement since the scale of the similarity function is essentially arbitrary. The stronger condition of invariance under a monotonic transformation of the similarity function has also been suggested.

For example, a number of methods have been proposed in which distances or similarities between objects are largely irrelevant. The methods rely on the inequalities between pairs of objects. Similarity functions induce a partial ordering on the set of objects to be classified. A classification is constructed such that a partial ordering derived from it agrees as closely as possible with the partial ordering induced on the data. The measurement of agreement is given by Benzécri [3]. The methods are accordingly insensitive to monotonic transformations of the similarity functions with the result that, according to Benzécri [4], " ... the host of indexes enumerated by S. and S.[9] is essentially reduced to two, which differ mainly (and do definitely differ) according to the part played by NN matches ... " An NN match is a match in which a given attribute is recorded as absent in both objects compared. Such a match may or may not be allowed to contribute toward the total similarity between the two objects. Benzécri distinguishes the two cases. An overview of these methods is given by de la Véga [74].

Independence of labeling requires that a classification should not be dependent on the order in which the terms are treated, and is demonstrable only in a classification in which all classes which satisfy the criterion are enumerated. For the algorithm to be proposed, it cannot be shown that all of the classes are found. A permutation of the names of the terms would result in a classification which, although sharing a substantial number of classes, would differ in a number of classes. The failure of (a) and (c) are related. Relabeling enables more classes to be found, and examination of all permutations corresponds

[9] Sokal and Sneath.

to inspecting all subsets of the terms to determine which satisfy the classificatory criterion. It is clearly impracticable to examine all subsets since there are too many of them. Provided a large enough number of classes is found the failure of (a) and (c) is unimportant.

It is not easy to give a precise meaning to "large enough." Certainly, the least number of classes required to distinguish all of the terms is the binary logarithm of the number of terms in the vocabulary. A rough guide is provided by requiring that the classes, used as descriptors, should provide a more economical description of the objects than the original attributes.

3.3 The Classificatory Criterion

It is now possible to give a more detailed specification of the classification criterion; that the classification should consist of classes such that each term resembles terms of the same class more than it does terms not in the same class. Two things are needed. First, a means of measuring the overall similarity of a term to a class; second, a means of deciding to which, among a number of classes, a given term has the greatest similarity. Care must be taken in specifying how this decision is made to avoid presupposing the existence of a fixed number of classes among which the term is to be distributed. This presupposition violates the requirement that classes be self-generating. The difficulty may be resolved quite simply as follows. Suppose that A is a set of terms and that B is the complement of A with respect to U, the term vocabulary. Suppose further that A is a putative class of the classification. The construction of A progresses by deciding, for each term, whether to admit a term into the putative class or to reject it; that is, by deciding whether to assign the term to A or to B. Thus, membership to B is by default and corresponds to rejection from A. In general, B will not be a class of the classification.

Suppose that A is a set of terms. Suppose also that x is a term and that $s(x, A)$ is the similarity between x and the class A. It is not clear that any strict rules may be laid down for the design of $s(x, A)$. Lance and Williams [32], in their treatment of hierarchical systems, have examined the effect of object–set and set–set similarity functions on local geometry. They argue that the spaces defined by such functions do not necessarily have the same properties as the space defined by the interobject distances. Certain classification strategies will behave as though the space in the immediate vicinity of a group has been distorted (that is, contracted or dilated). *Space contraction* corresponds to an apparent movement of a group on formation toward some or all of the remaining objects. *Space dilation* corresponds to a movement away from other objects. Lance and Williams warn against the use of space-contracting systems. These concepts also apply to clustering systems which optimize intragroup homogeneity given by Lance and Williams [*31*].

However, a number of points are clear. The similarity between x and A is the same as the similarity between A and x. The similarity between a term and a set must reduce, in the case where the set consists of one term, to the similarity between the two terms. This is equivalent to the definition of *compatible* by Lance and Williams [*32*] in their work on hierarchical systems. A compatible strategy is one in which the similarity between two sets reduces, in the case where the sets are single membered, to the similarity between the two members. Also, the similarity between x and A must increase when another term with non-zero similarity to x is added to A. Finally, the similarity between x and A must depend only on the individual similarities between the terms of A and x. This requirement arises naturally in Section 2. Lance and Williams [*31, 32*] refer to strategies with this constraint as *combinatorial*. A non-combinatorial strategy, on the other hand, is one in which the attributes of the objects must be reconsulted in determining similarity. The distinction is primarily concerned with the computational aspects of classification and is of little theoretical interest except where, for example, the comparison of certain attributes requires human judgment.

An appropriate function which fulfills these requirements is

$$s(x, A) = \sum_{y \in A} s(x, y).$$

Analogous requirements may be placed on the similarity between two sets A' and A, and an appropriate definition is:

$$s(A', A) = \sum_{x \in A'} s(x, A),$$

where A' and A are disjoint and

$$s(A, A) = \tfrac{1}{2} \sum_{x \in A} s(x, A) \qquad \text{[each } s(x, y) \text{ counted only once].}$$

Suppose that A and B are sets of terms defined as above. Suppose also that q is the scale of the term–term similarity function so that $0 \leqslant s(x, y) \leqslant q$. The scale of similarity will be normalized by choosing $q = 1$. The following relationships hold for any such A, B:

$$s(A, A) + s(A, B) + s(B, B) = \text{const.} \tag{8}$$

for the term vocabulary and the document collection. This may be shown as follows:

$$s(A, A) + s(A, B) + s(B, B) = \tfrac{1}{2} \sum_{x \in A} \sum_{y \in A} s(x, y) + \sum_{x \in A} \sum_{y \in B} s(x, y)$$
$$+ \tfrac{1}{2} \sum_{x \in B} \sum_{y \in B} s(x, y)$$
$$= \tfrac{1}{2} \sum_{x \in A} \left(\sum_{y \in A} + \sum_{y \in B} \right) s(x, y)$$
$$+ \tfrac{1}{2} \sum_{y \in B} \left(\sum_{x \in A} + \sum_{x \in B} \right) s(x, y)$$

by symmetry for term–set similarity.

$$= \tfrac{1}{2} \sum_{x \in A} s(x, U) + \tfrac{1}{2} \sum_{y \in B} s(U, y)$$

$= s(U, U)$ by symmetry for set–set similarity
$= $ constant for the term vocabulary and the document collection
$= S$, say.

Let $s^*(A, A)$ be the value of $s(A, A)$ when all terms in A are maximally similar to each other. Then

$$s^*(A, A) = \tfrac{1}{2} N_A (N_A - 1) \tag{9}$$

where $N_A = |A|$ since

$$s^*(A, A) = \tfrac{1}{2} \sum_{x \in A} \sum_{\substack{y \in A \\ y \neq x}} s^*(x, y)$$
$$= \tfrac{1}{2} \sum_{x \in A} \sum_{\substack{y \in A \\ y \neq x}} 1 \qquad \text{for maximum similarity}$$
$$= \tfrac{1}{2} N_A (N_A - 1).$$

Similarly

$$s^*(B, B) = \tfrac{1}{2} N_B (N_B - 1) \tag{10}$$

where $N_B = |B|$. Also

$$s^*(U, U) = \tfrac{1}{2} N(N - 1) \tag{11}$$

where $N = |U|$.

Let $s^*(A, B)$ be the value of $s(A, B)$ when all terms in A are maximally similar to all terms in B. Then:

$$s^*(A, B) = N_A \cdot N_B \tag{12}$$

since

$$s^*(A, B) = \sum_{x \in A} \sum_{y \in B} s^*(x, y)$$
$$= \sum_{x \in A} \sum_{y \in B} 1 \qquad \text{for maximum similarity}$$
$$= N_A \cdot N_B.$$

It follows trivially that

$$s^*(A, A) + s^*(A, B) + s^*(B, B) = s^*(U, U). \tag{13}$$

For completeness:

$$N_A + N_B = N. \tag{14}$$

The tendency of terms of A to be strongly similar to each other is indicated by

$$I_A = s^*(A, A)/s(A, A). \tag{15}$$

I_A decreases to one as the number and magnitude of the similarities between terms in A increases. The tendency for terms of A to be more similar to the terms in B than to other terms in A is indicated by

$$E_A = s(A, B)/s(A, A). \tag{16}$$

E_A decreases to zero as the number and magnitude of the similarities of terms in A to terms in B decreases. I_B and E_B are defined analogously. The strength of the similarity between A and B compared with the maximum is given by

$$E_{AB} = s(A, B)/s^*(A, B). \tag{17}$$

E_{AB} decreases as the number and magnitude of the similarities between A and B decrease.

The quantities I_A, I_B, E_A, E_B, and E_{AB} are independent of the scale of similarity, q, since all numerators and denominators are homogeneous and of the same degree in the term–term similarities $s(x, y)$. Minimizing I_A corresponds, therefore, to maximizing the number and magnitude of the similarities between the terms of A. Minimizing E_A corresponds to minimizing the number and magnitude of the similarities between terms in A and terms discarded from A, namely those in B. Thus minimizing I_A and E_A jointly corresponds to constructing classes of terms which have the general character that terms belonging to a class are more strongly related to the other terms in the class than they are to terms not in the class. The universe of terms is therefore partitioned into two disjoint sets A and B by minimizing jointly I_A and E_A. The function of I_A and E_A which expresses the relationship between them as they are jointly minimized is not yet specified, but may be stated in the following general form:

$$c_A = f[s(A, A), s(A, B), s(B, B), N_A, N_B].$$

This function is called the *cohesion function*. c_A is the value of the cohesion across the boundary between the sets A and B. A set of terms which minimizes the cohesion is called a clump as defined by Parker-Rhodes and Needham [48].

Accordingly, the classification of the term vocabulary U into groups of similar terms will be defined in terms of minimum cohesion as follows. A class A is a clump provided that the cohesion for A is *locally minimum*. The cohesion for a class A of terms is locally minimum if the cohesion of each set in the k *locality* of A is not greater than the cohesion for A. A set P_i of terms is in the k locality of A provided that P and A differ in at most k terms, where k is a positive integer constant which may be chosen arbitrarily. Thus A is a clump if

$$c_A < c_{P_i} \qquad \text{for all } P_i \text{ such that } |P_i \wedge \overline{A}| + |\overline{P}_i \wedge A| < k.$$

The classification consists of the set of classes which satisfy this criterion. The membership of a term to a particular clump does not affect its membership to other clumps. Clumps may therefore overlap. However, the extent to which pairs of clumps may overlap, and the number of clumps in the classification is affected by the value of k. The number of local minima of the cohesion function, and therefore the number of clumps, cannot be determined since it depends upon the values of the individual similarities between pairs of terms. However, the following remarks may be made:

(1) Clumps may not differ in k terms or less. (For, if two sets differ in k terms, then each is in the k locality of the other. The set which has the smaller cohesion is a clump.)

(1′) As a corollary: if there is a clump with k' terms, where $k' < k$, then there cannot be another clump with $k - k'$ terms or less, since if there were they would differ in k terms or less.

(2) The number of sets of terms in U which differ in more than k terms decreases with k. The number of clumps in U, therefore, decreases with k.

(3) The number of sets in the k locality of an arbitrary set increases with k.

For each putative clump A, all the sets in the k locality of A must be examined to establish that the cohesion for A is a local minimum. It follows from (3) that the amount of computation required to test that A is a clump, is least for classifications based on $k = 1$. It follows from (1) that, for classifications based on $k = 1$, clumps must differ by at least two terms. The choice $k = 1$ therefore imposes least restriction on the structure of the classification, both in terms of the number of clumps which may be constructed, from (2), and in terms of the differences in composition of the clumps. For these reasons, the classifications are based on $k = 1$.

In the design of suitable cohesion functions, care must be exercised in selecting appropriate combinations of $s(A, A)$ $s(A, B), s(B, B), N_A, N_B$ to minimize. The following rules[10] determine the general behavior which must be exhibited by cohesion functions. The quantities $I_A, I_B, E_A, E_B, E_{AB}$ and their interpretation in terms of interset similarities have already been defined.

(4) If the value of E_A for a putative clump A is increased by the removal of terms from A or by the addition of terms to A, then the cohesion must increase.

(5) If the value of I_A for a putative clump A is increased by the removal of terms from A or by the addition of terms to A, then the cohesion must increase.

(6) The cohesion must be independent of a change in scale of term–term similarities.

(7) A set, none of whose terms are similar to terms outside the set, must be a clump. In graph theoretic terms, the components of the undirected graph representing the term–term similarities must satisfy the criterion. Note that the components need not be maximally connected. This is achieved provided that

(7′) The cohesion is always positive.

(7″) If $s(A, B) = 0$ then $c_A = 0$.

(8) The cohesion function must have the property that

$$f[s(A, A), s(A, B), s(B, B), N_A, N_B]$$

is either always greater than or always less than

$$f[s(A, A), s(A, B), s(B, B) + K_1, N_A, N_B + K_2]$$

for each partition A, B of the term vocabulary, where K_1 and K_2 are positive or negative constants.

Requirement (8) is necessary as a consequence of the requirement that the addition of a set of documents, indexed only by a set of terms which do not belong to the vocabulary, should not disturb the classification of the vocabulary. Suppose that the term vocabulary U of a document collection D is classified. A number of documents D' are

---

[10] The definition of clumps in terms of local minima of cohesion has certain computational advantages. Rubin [54] constructs a set of rules for the design of "splitting functions" (analogous to cohesion functions) whose purpose is to define the "best" partition of a population into a number of disjoint sets. The search for the best partition progresses by maximizing the value of the partition function for each level of similarity. Rubin considers the danger in his algorithm of encountering local maxima which hinder the detection of the global maximum, and lists a number of heuristic techniques which help in this situation. The comparable difficulty with minima is not encountered in the construction of clumps, since clumps are defined in terms of local minima within a well-defined k locality.

appended to D to form a collection D''. The set of documents D' is indexed by a set of terms U' which includes none of U. The enlarged term vocabulary is denoted by U''. We require that a classification of U'' should include all the clumps of a classification of U together with a classification of U'. None of the terms of U' may occur in the clumps of U since, on the basis of co-occurrence of terms in documents, no term in U is similar to any term in U'. Suppose that A is a clump belonging to a classification of U. The effect of adding the terms U' to U is to increase N_B by K_2, where $K_2 = |U'|$ and to increase $s(B, B)$ by K_1, where $K_1 = s(U', U')$. $s(A, A)$ and $s(A, B)$ remain unchanged in value. Provided that requirement (8) holds, minimization will be unaffected so that A will be a clump in U''. Similarly, the removal (corresponding to K_1, $K_2 < 0$) of the set of terms U' from U'' does not disturb the classification of the remaining terms of U''. Condition (8) is important computationally, for it implies that a set whose terms are similar to no terms outside the set may be excised from the term vocabulary and classified separately. The number of sets in the k locality of a putative clump in the excised set is smaller than the number of sets in the k locality of the putative clump considered as a clump of the complete term vocabulary. The amount of computation needed to establish that the class is indeed a clump is therefore reduced.

A number of cohesion functions have been designed which satisfy conditions (4)–(8). These are

$$g_1(A) = s(A, B)/[s(A, A) + s(B, B)]. \tag{18}$$

Its intended action is to locate sets of terms A which are well separated from their complements. However, it has certain disagreeable properties. From Eq. (8), $g_1(A)$ may be reduced to

$$g_1(A) = s(A, B)/[S - s(A, B)]$$
$$= 1/([S/s(A, B)] - 1).$$

Minimizing $g_1(A)$ therefore corresponds to minimizing $s(A, B)$. There is a strong tendency for classification methods based on this function to obtain the null set as a clump, since there is nothing to prevent $s(A, B)$ from decreasing progressively, as terms are removed from A, except fortuitous similarities. A more workable function which has the same intended action is

$$g_1'(A) = s(A, B)/N_A \cdot N_B$$

that is,

$$g_1'(A) = E_{AB}.$$

The tendency of $g_1'(A)$ to decrease as terms are removed from A is now counterbalanced by the factor $1/N_A$ which increases $g_1'(A)$. Both $g_1(A)$ and $g_1'(A)$ are symmetrical in A and B, so that if A is a clump then so is B.

$$g_2(A) = s^2(A, B)/s(A, A) \cdot s(B, B) \qquad (19)$$

Its intended action is to separate the class A from its complement and to increase, at the same time, the number and magnitude of the similarities between terms in A. It may be expressed in the form:

$$g_2(A) = E_A \cdot E_B.$$

The function is symmetrical in A and B. If A is a clump then the complement B of A is also a clump. The universe is therefore partitioned into two sets, both of which satisfy the criterion. The cohesion function has, in addition, the following property. Classifications are unchanged by a transformation of the term–set similarities of the form:

$$s'(x, A) = h(N_A)s(x, A)$$

where $h(N_A)$ is a function of N_A which is never zero, since:

$$\begin{aligned} g_2'(A) &= s'^2(A, B)/s'(A, A) \cdot s'(B, B) \\ &= [h^2(N_A)h^2(N_B)/h^2(N_A)h^2(N_B)] \cdot [s^2(A, B)/s(A, A)s(B, B)] \\ &= g_2(A). \end{aligned}$$

Classifications based on this cohesion function therefore seem to be singularly unaffected by space distortion.

$$g_3(A) = N_A(N_A - 1)[s(A, B)/s^2(A, A)]. \qquad (20)$$

This may be reduced to the form:

$$g_3(A) = E_A \cdot I_A.$$

This function is not symmetrical in A and B. It may be argued that it is overrestrictive to require that a necessary condition for a class to be a clump is that the complement should also be a clump. The action of $g_3(A)$ is similar to that of $g_2(A)$ apart from the symmetry requirement. A is constructed to be well-separated from its complement (measured by E_A) and to have a large number of strong similarities between its terms in proportion to its size (measured by I_A). However, classifications based on this function have tended to consist of large, heavily overlapping classes of loosely related terms. It appears therefore that the factor I_A has not been given sufficient emphasis during minimization.

$$g_4(A) = \frac{s(A, B)}{s(A, A)} \left[\frac{N_A(N_A - 1)}{2s(A, A)} - \frac{2ps(A, A)}{N_A(N_A - 1)} \right]. \qquad (21)$$

This may be expressed in the following form:

$$g_4(A) = E_A[(I_A - p/I_A)]$$

where $0 \leqslant p \leqslant 1$.

Its action is to achieve a more flexible balance between the well separatedness of A from its complement B and the number and strength of the similarities between terms in A in proportion to its size. For small sets, the factor E_A dominates in value. As terms are added to A, the factor $(I_A - p/I_A)$ dominates in value. The minimum value of I_A is 1, and corresponds to complete and maximal similarity between all terms of A. As classes become more amorphous (i.e., fewer terms are similar and the similarities between the terms of A and itself become smaller) with the addition of terms from B, $(I_A - p/I_A)$ increases by an amount which is smaller the larger p is. In minimizing $g_4(A)$, terms in A are reallocated to reduce the magnitude of this factor and therefore to increase the strength and number of similarities between A and itself. The contributions of the two effects may be balanced by adjusting the value of p at the start of classification. Classifications are found to differ for $p = 0$, $\frac{1}{2}$, and 1 in a way predicted by the above analysis. Clumps for $p = 1$ tend, on the whole, to be better separated from their complements and to have stronger similarities between their members than for clumps based on $p = 0$. The effects of the values of p smaller than $\frac{1}{2}$ are negligible, and in the limit as p tends to zero, classifications are identified with those constructed with $g_3(A)$.

3.4 The Classification Algorithm

The strategy for detecting clumps of terms for an arbitrary cohesion function satisfying conditions (4)–(8) in Section 3.3 consists of three separate procedures, each of which will now be considered. The procedures are the *starting procedure*, dealing with the initiation of the search for a clump; the *assignment procedure*, dealing with the allocation and reallocation of terms to a putative clump; and the *stopping procedure*, dealing with the conditions under which the search for a clump may be terminated.

A clump has been defined as a set of terms for which the cohesion is locally minimum in the sense that, for all sets in the k locality of the clump, the clump has the least cohesion. For reasons given earlier, the clump finding strategy will deal only with the case $k = 1$. To find all of the clumps in a given population it is necessary to examine all the binary partitions (into sets A and B such that $A \cup B = U$ and $A \cap B = \emptyset$) of the population. A theoretically possible starting procedure, therefore, consists of enumerating all of these partitions. The clumps are a selection of those which satisfy the criterion of locally minimum cohesion. For a large population, however, complete examination of all binary partitions cannot be contemplated since the amount of computation required to do this is prohibitively large even if it is assumed that the components of the graph representing the term–pair similarities have been found.

One possible starting procedure consists of examining a subset of the total number of binary partitions of U into the sets A and B. Instead of testing whether A is a clump and discarding it if it is not, the composition of A is altered by the addition or removal of terms to improve the suitability of A as a clump. The terms which are added or removed are determined by the assignment procedure. Thus the testing of each partition for minimum local cohesion is replaced by the enumeration of a subset of the partitions of U into A and B and by the adjustment of A to conform with the criterion of minimum local cohesion. Since there is no *a priori* way of deciding whether a given partition eventually may be transformed into a clump by a series of adjustments, the choice of initial partition is arbitrary. Accordingly, the simplest initial partitions are examined, namely those for which $|A| = 1$. The single term which belongs to A is called the *starting element*. Thus clumps are constructed by accretion to a single term. The total number of initial partitions with $|A| = 1$ is $|U|$, the number of terms in the vocabulary. With such a starting procedure, it cannot be guaranteed that the total number of clumps present in the universe has been found. However, provided sufficient information about the relative similarities between terms may be recovered from the classification, we may assert that a sufficient number of clumps have been located. From a practical point of view, one is interested in constructing classes of terms for a specific application, and it is immaterial whether or not all of the classes have been discovered providing that the set actually found is adequate for the application.

Suppose that A is a putative clump and that t_i is a term. t_i belongs either to A or to B, the complement of A. For definiteness, suppose that t_i belongs to A. Suppose also that the cohesion for A is c_A. Consider then a new partition of U into the disjoint sets A', B' (i.e., $A' \cup B' = U$, $A' \cap B' = \emptyset$) formed by removing the term t_i from A and placing it in B. Thus $A' \wedge t_i = A$ and $B \wedge t_i = B'$. Suppose that $c_{A'}$ is the cohesion for A'. If $c_{A'} < c_A$ then the cohesion is reduced by the removal of t_i from A. Accordingly, A' is a more suitable candidate as a clump than A. Suppose, on the other hand, that $c_{A'} \geqslant c_A$, then the cohesion is increased by the removal of t_i from A'. A is therefore a more suitable candidate as a clump than A'. A comparable argument holds for the case where t_i belongs to B and is moved into A to form a new partition of U. The operation is repeated for the next term and one of A and A', whichever has the lower cohesion. The calculation of $c_{A'}$ necessitates the calculation of $s(A', A')$, $s(A', B')$, $s(B', B')$, $N_{A'}$, $N_{B'}$. It is unnecessary to reconsult the whole similarity matrix to do this, since the transition from the partition A, B to the partition A', B' involves the addition or removal of a single term t_i. Instead $s(A', A')$, $s(A', B')$, $s(B', B')$, $N_{A'}$, $N_{B'}$ may be calculated quite straightforwardly from $s(A, A)$, $s(A, B)$, $s(B, B)$, N_A, N_B as follows. There are two cases.

(a) Suppose that t_i belongs to A. Then:

$$s(A', A') = s(A, A) - s(t_i, A)$$
$$s(A', B') = s(A, B) + s(t_i, A) - s(t_i, B)$$
$$s(B', B') = s(B, B) + s(t_i, B)$$
$$N_{A'} = N_A - 1 \qquad\qquad (22)$$
$$N_{B'} = N_B + 1.$$

(b) Similarly, suppose that t_i does not belong to A. Then:

$$s(A', A') = s(A, A) + s(t_i, A)$$
$$s(A', B') = s(A, B) - s(t_i, A) + s(t_i, B)$$
$$s(B', B') = s(B, B) - s(t_i, B) \qquad\qquad (23)$$
$$N_{A'} = N_A + 1$$
$$N_{B'} = N_B - 1.$$

The values of $s(t_i, A)$ and $s(t_i, B)$ may be determined simultaneously by a single scan of the ith row of the similarity matrix. This technique may also be applied to the calculation of $s(A, A)$, $s(A, B)$, $s(B, B)$ for the starting partition A, B where $|A| = 1$. Suppose that t is a starting element. Then:

$$s(A, A) = 0$$
$$s(A, B) = s(t, B) \qquad\qquad (24)$$
$$s(B, B) = S - s(t, B)$$

where $S = s(U, U)$. The calculation of S involves a scan of the complete matrix. By using the above relations, a scan of the complete matrix once for each starting partition is avoided. During the course of classification, the matrix need be completely scanned only once.

Suppose that the term vocabulary U consists of the terms $t_1, t_2, \ldots, t_n$. Suppose also that A_0 is the putative clump. The assignment procedure constructs the sets $A_1, A_2, \ldots, A_{n+1}$ such that:

$$A_i \wedge t_{i+1} = A_{i+1} \qquad \text{(i.e., addition of } t_{i+1} \text{ to } A_i \text{ reduces cohesion)}$$

or

$$A_{i+1} \wedge t_{i+1} = A_i \qquad \text{(i.e., removal of } t_{i+1} \text{ from } A_i \text{ reduces cohesion).}$$
$$(25)$$

or

$A_{i+1} = A_i$ (i.e., neither addition nor removal of t_{i+1} reduces cohesion).

Suppose that m is the number of pairs of sets (A_i, A_{i+1}) such that $A_i \neq A_{i+1}$, that is, m is the number of terms which have been added to A_0 or removed from A_0 during a complete examination of U. As i goes from 1 to n, $A_{i+1} \wedge t_{i+1} = A_i$ and $A_i \wedge t_{i+1} = A_{i+1}$ generate all the sets A_{i+1} in the k locality of A_0, where $k = 1$. Thus A_0, by definition, is a clump provided $m = 0$, since no set in the k locality ($k = 1$) of A_0 has smaller cohesion. If $m = 0$ the construction of A_0 is terminated, while if $m \neq 0$, A_{n+1} is offered as a more suitable candidate as a clump than A, and the procedure is repeated.

4. Pseudo-classification and Information Retrieval[11]

4.1 The Use of Relevance in an Evaluative Retrieval System

It seems evident from the work of Salton [56], and of Sparck Jones and Jackson [65] that a certain measure of improvement in performance[12] over simple term retrieval may be obtained by using classifications generated automatically. It has been established, independently, that small tightly structured classes of terms constitute a classification favorable to retrieval applications, but it is as yet unknown whether the improvement gained by using such classifications may be increased still further. The classes used in these experiments have in the main been generated automatically by making use of the co-occurrence of terms in documents.

In the preceding sections, attention has been focused specifically on the effect of automatically generated classes on retrieval performance. Consideration has been given to both classification and information retrieval, and has been directed toward finding classification and retrieval algorithms which yield improvements in performance beyond

---

[11] This material originally appeared in [25]. Permission to make use of it here has been granted by the American Society for Information Science.

[12] Performance here relates only to the retrieval or nonretrieval of relevant or nonrelevant documents. No account is taken of "hardware factors." Thus, for example, the amount of effort expended in extracting relevant documents is not taken into consideration.

that obtained by simple key-word coordination. An assessment of the effect of two different classifications of the same document collection and the same set of requests on retrieval performance involves a comparison between the two recall-precision curves. This may be achieved by direct comparison of the recall-precision curves since the principal interest was in an overall improvement for all coordination levels. When the curves for two experiments crossed, improvement was regarded as uncertain. Salton and Lesk [55] have used statistical methods to establish whether a limited number of classifications and thesauri display consistent improvement over a number of different document collections. Other evaluative measures have been developed by Swets [70], who uses a decision theoretic approach, and by Romerio and Cavara [53].

The experimental studies outlined above are similar in a number of respects. First, they use the term descriptions of the documents in the collection to produce term co-occurrences, and then a classification of terms. Second, they attempt to evaluate the performance of the retrieval procedure by using the base set of requests and a table of documents relevant to each request. Third, there is no attempt to adjust a classification on the basis of information gathered during evaluation. This is not intended as a criticism of these approaches, for they set out to establish whether classifications derived solely from co-occurrences of terms within documents can improve performance. A subsequent adjustment to the classification is, therefore, outside the terms of reference of these investigations. Finally, none gives a clear indication of the best performance that theoretically may be obtained from the retrieval systems, given the document collection, the base set of requests, and the table of documents relevant to the base set of requests. Some work in this general direction, however, has been done by Cleverdon and Keen [10], who have examined the exhaustivity and specificity of several index languages.

There are four sources of information for an evaluative retrieval system, namely, the document collection, the term classification, the base set of requests, and the table of documents relevant to the base set of requests. The latter, together with a performance measure, enables an evaluation of the system to be made by comparing lists of documents actually retrieved with lists of documents which should be retrieved. Not all of the four sources of information are independent of each other. Under the hypothesis that:

(a) *Co-occurrence of terms within documents is a suitable measure of the similarity between terms,*
a classification may be generated automatically. This hypothesis will be referred to as the *Association Hypothesis*. Alternatively, the classi-

fication may be produced manually. The dependence between the document collection, the base set of requests, the term classification, and the table of relevant documents is, however, less tractable. Suppose, for example, that a match function, which measures the coefficient of matching between a document and a request, is designed, and that this coefficient varies with the coordination level of a match both on terms and on classes. Then with the hypothesis, which will be called the *Relevance Hypothesis*, that:

(b) *Coordination is positively correlated with external relevance (i.e., that relevance may be defined algorithmically),*

a classification and a match function could be imagined which retrieved all and only relevant documents, namely those with high match coefficients. In practice, however, this position is seldom attained; partly because the match function is an imperfect approximation to that function which actually corresponds to external relevance, if such exists; partly because the classification is defective; partly because there may, in fact, not be sufficient information provided to the system to achieve the best[13] performance; and partly because the notion of relevance may not be well formed and may result in inconsistencies of some sort. The difficulty is that the external judging of relevance is simulated by using an assortment of classification algorithms based on the association hypothesis and an assortment of match functions based on the relevance hypothesis. Moreover, the simulation is undirected since there is no guide as to how a better simulation may be achieved. Information has been injected into the system by introducing hypotheses, rather than by utilizing the information available in a more economical fashion. It is the utilization of the available information more economically and the ideas to which this leads which will now be examined.

4.2 The Use of Relevance in Pseudo-classifications

The relationships which hold between the categories of information used in an evaluative retrieval system have been described briefly. To make descriptions of this type more precise it is convenient to introduce the notion of a *model*. Suppose that a set of experiments is designed to examine a particular aspect of information retrieval. Functions and processes are designed according to a set of rules and these, when taken together, form the retrieval system. The set of rules which govern the construction of each part of the system represent a description of a particular approach to the solution of information retrieval. These

---

[13] Best performance is used here in the sense of complete agreement with the document-request relevance table.

rules themselves are hypotheses within the field of information retrieval and an evaluative retrieval system allows these hypotheses to be tested. A complete knowledge of the set of rules gives, ideally, complete knowledge of a particular approach to information retrieval. The set of rules is called a model and may be such that a number of quite different systems can be constructed to conform to them; each such system is called a *representation* of the model. Within a model of information retrieval there will be models, or *submodels*, for each of the logically distinct processes which together comprise the system. Thus, for example, there will be a *classification model* if classification is required as an adjunct of the retrieval system. There will be an *information model* describing the categories of information required by the system, together with statements of the assumptions made about these categories; a *relevance model*, containing statements about the way in which external relevance is simulated by the system; and finally, an *evaluation model*, containing statements of the assumptions made about the evaluation of the output of the retrieval system. Once the model has been defined, it may be found that experiments can be designed to test the validity of the complete model, that is, all representations within the model, rather than the validity of a single representation.

Section 4.1 contained an informal specification of part of a particular model of information retrieval in its reference to the association and relevance hypotheses [Section 4.1(a) and (b)] and the interrelation of the four categories of information listed in that section. In this model, the classification and match function are used together with the document descriptions to simulate the external judgments of relevance for the base set of requests. The information contained in the relevance table is disregarded in the construction of the system and is used *post facto*, evaluatively, to corroborate or contradict the result of the classification algorithm or the match function. Instead, suppose that each request is taken in turn and a classification of the terms is gradually constructed which confers a high match coefficient on those documents judged relevant and a low match coefficient on documents judged irrelevant. This presupposes that the requests are well-formed, and that the table of relevance appropriate to those requests is incontrovertible. The match function may be defective but it is assumed to be an approximation to an intuitive notion of relevance. Each constructive step consists of an operation altering the membership of selected terms to selected classes of the classification. Furthermore, a subsequent alteration of the classification to accommodate the relevance judgments of another request is prevented from affecting the classification in a way detrimental to the requests already examined. The grouping so constructed is a classification of the terms only since it consists, *de facto*, of classes of terms. There is little reason to assume that such a classification will consist of classes of terms which represent generic concepts associated with the document collection. Subsequent analysis, for example, by comparison with a classification generated from term co-occurrences, might demonstrate that this is so. In the absence of this, however, a distinction is drawn between these two classifications by referring to the former as a *pseudo-classification*, and it is to be regarded as a purely formal construction. Performance for the base set of requests will be, by construction, the best attainable for all representations of the classification model, given the particular model of retrieval.

5. The Use of Pseudo-classifications in Retrieval

5.1 The Predictive Use of Pseudo-classifications

The procedure outlined here constructs limiting pseudo-classifications, which produce the best performance when used in conjunction with the apparatus of information retrieval. A distinction has been drawn between a pseudo-classification and a classification, for the former is a pure construction, while the latter is, as far as classification technique permits, a more fundamental grouping based on the resemblances between terms. The problem arises of predicting the effect of a pseudo-classification on retrieval performance when a new set of requests, distinct from the set used in constructing the pseudo-classification, is offered to the system. There is no guarantee that the system will respond in anything but a perverse way, since the pseudo-classification is derived from a particular set of requests and a particular set of relevance judgments over the whole document collection. It is hoped that the procedure has generalized the notion of relevance from a number of specific instances of relevance of documents to requests and has stored it in the pseudo-classification in such a way that the system may predict which documents bear the same relationship to subsequently presented requests as certain prescribed documents bear to the base set of requests; that is, by repeated analogical statements such as "the relationship between D_1 and R_1 is the same as the relationship between D_2 and R_2," where it is known that document D_1 is relevant to request R_1 and document D_2 is relevant to request R_2. Although generalization may take place, this cannot be assumed as the following hypothetical set of requests and relevance judgments demonstrates.

Suppose that each request is disjoint from all other requests, each request has one document relevant to it and no document is relevant to more than one request of the base set of requests. A possible pseudo-classification for this configuration is the assignment of each term to a class by itself and such a configuration does not extend to an arbitrary request. There are a number of reasons that indicate that this is unlikely, although experimental demonstration is required to show it in practice. The first point is that the match function is designed to reflect an intuitive notion of relevance formulated in the relevance hypothesis (b) in Section 4.1. The classification is constructed by operations involving the assignment of terms to existing classes and the creation of new classes by the assignment of terms not yet gathered together into a class. Pairs of terms within a class are used in retrieval as if they are *intersubstitutable* as defined in Section 2.1, and it is the intersubstitutable pairs, which yield good retrieval performance, that are to be located.

Although there may be some choice available in the selection of terms and classes to operate upon, and although these terms may be brought together into such classes randomly, in the event of no other basis for decision, it is reasonable to suppose that, as the classification develops it will become more determinate in that the opportunity for random assignments will diminish, since the number of assignments to be made is finite. Also, it is reasonable to suppose that the later assignments of terms to classes may have the effect of diminishing the deleterious effect of the random assignments made during the early stages of the construction of the classification provided that terms may be removed from classes. The problem of extending the system to deal with new requests will be referred to as the *problem of generalizing*.

The only satisfactory solution is to choose a base set of requests in such a way that the set is *representative* of all future requests to be submitted to the system. There are a number of ways of doing this. Suppose, for example, that a statement may be made about the distribution of terms in the requests that may be submitted to the system. Probabilities are assigned to the ouput of the system to indicate that, although a document may be deduced relevant to a request, it is only guaranteed relevant by the system with the specified probability. This is not the same as *degree of relevance* since the document may be entirely irrelevant to the request, and is unsatisfactory compared with the system's good response to requests of the base set.

Another possibility is that each request must satisfy prescribed conditions. The pseudo-classification is constructed only with requests satisfying these, and the system, in turn, is required to respond only to requests that are of this type. Such conditions may contain a statement about a classification of terms with reference to their co-occurrence within requests. Thus, while attempting to base a retrieval system on considerations that do not involve classification techniques *per se*, a classification is required in order to ensure that the procedure will generalize to subsequent requests.

Finally, there may be available a large collection of requests and the associated relevance judgments, and although it cannot be demonstrated categorically, they are highly likely to represent a typical and representative sample of all the requests that may be put to the system in future, in that all the different kinds of requests are adequately represented. Although this remark is pragmatic, this state of affairs nevertheless may happen in a practical application.

5.2 The Evaluative Use of Pseudo-classifications

The use to which pseudo-classifications may be put in evaluating retrieval performance will now be considered by means of the following experiment. An information retrieval system is designed to conform to some model, and a match function is specified that measures the relevance of a document to a request. The design of this function is based on intuitive ideas about relevance and is an internal analog of relevance as judged by the users of the system. The function may be good or bad, according to its ability to retrieve relevant and only relevant documents, and may be subject to change and modification as ideas about the internal representation of relevance change. There are also a number of algorithms for producing term classifications conforming to a model of classification. It is necessary to isolate the classification, which, when used in conjunction with the match function, results in highest retrieval performance. There remains, however, the problem of evaluation. Although the use of precision-recall curves for this purpose seems to be well established, there is still criticism of them and there is no one method which is generally accepted. For example, Cleverdon and Keen [10] compute recall and precision without regard to the order in which documents are retrieved. Salton [56], on the other hand, is interested in determining whether the relevant documents are retrieved first. Suppose that a certain match function is decided upon for the experiment. Classifications are produced by a number of algorithms and among these the algorithm is to be found which yields the best retrieval performance, for a particular way of measuring performance. Accordingly, each of these classifications, in turn, is used in the retrieval system, and the resulting performances are compared to determine the best. These results may suggest a variation in classification technique and by experimentation of this kind it is hoped eventually to arrive at a classification algorithm that will give the best performance.

There is a serious difficulty with this approach. For a given document collection, base set of requests, and table of relevance there is a best possible level of performance, according to some measure of performance, the given match function, and the classification model. The measures of performance customarily used do not relate the performance of a retrieval system to the best theoretical performance for the retrieval model, with the result that there is no indication of the extent to which the system may be improved, or the direction in which such improvements may occur. Suppose, however, that it were possible to examine all the pseudo-classifications, in turn, which satisfied the classification model. The maximum theoretical performance for the model is then given by the classification which resulted in performance better than any of the other classifications, since all possible representations in the model would have been examined to make this assertion. Such a classification is the limiting pseudo-classification since it is the one that agrees most closely in retrieval with the relevance table for the base set of requests. Moreover, the pseudo-classification does not depend upon the measure of retrieval performance but more directly on the extent to which the relevance judgments set out in the relevance table have been reproduced by the system. The effect of the pseudo-classification may be assessed subsequently by choosing a particular measure of retrieval performance which uses this information, and the numerical values which result will represent the best possible performance obtainable with the given models.

The problem, however, cannot be approached in this way for, although the number of partitions, and, therefore, the number of classifications, of a finite number of terms is itself finite, the amount of computer time needed for evaluating them all is prohibitively large. Instead of enumerating them all, a method is needed for isolating those that are the best for the particular retrieval experiment. The extraction of classifications in the sense of linguistically coherent groups of terms is no longer of primary interest. Only formal groups of terms that result in good retrieval performance are of interest, because it is the hypothesis that a particular classification technique is the best for a specific retrieval experiment which is to be tested. These partitions are the pseudo-classifications, an algorithm for the construction of which has been alluded to earlier in Section 4.2.

The following way of measuring retrieval performance is suggested by the foregoing remarks. A particular match function and performance measure are chosen. A pseudo-classification is constructed (by algorithm rather than by selection from a complete enumeration of the representations of the classification model) which, when used in retrieval, gives rise to a particular level of performance. This is the theoretical best for the data, for the classification and retrieval models, and for the match function. The proposed measure of performance measures the departure of the performance in a particular case from this theoretical best. If this departure is small, little improvement may be gained by changing the classification technique, indicating that further experimenting in this direction is unprofitable. The introduction of another match function, however, results in a different pseudo-classification and a different estimate of the theoretically best performance. If this is better than the optimum for the previous match function, then the choice of match function may be regarded as more useful in retrieval than the previous one in that it permits the system, at least theoretically, to achieve an improvement in performance. If the measure of retrieval performance is changed, it is not necessary to regenerate the pseudo-classification, since this does not depend on the formulation of the measure. The following definition is, therefore, made.

The difference in performance in retrieval of the pseudo-classification and the automatically generated classification (according to some measure of performance) gives an estimate of the *improvability* in performance of the retrieval model for the match function and classification algorithm which have been applied.

Although the use of this performance measure may indicate whether it is more profitable to improve performance by changing either the classification algorithm or the match function, no indication is given of how this is to be done. In spite of the fact that the classification of the model that gives the best performance is known, there is no means supplied for deriving it without recourse to the relevance judgments of the base set of requests. In spite of this, its usefulness as an evaluative device for experimental models is not impaired.

5.3 The Isolation of Inconsistencies in Relevance Judgments

The practicability of constructing a pseudo-classification must now be raised. It may happen that, after the classification has been constructed to give the correct response to a number of requests of the base set, a request is encountered whose processing conflicts diametrically with some of the conditions set up to prevent deterioration of the classification with respect to previously processed requests. It is possible that this results from an inconsistency in the judgment of relevance of documents to requests as supplied by experts in the field covered by the document collection. However, it is expected that the assessment of external relevance by an individual does not lead to serious inconsistency and that the same is true for the determination of relevance by consensus of opinion. Detailed work by Resnick and Savage [52] on the consistency of human judgments of relevance support this view. It may transpire that the number of conditions that have to be constructed to prevent deterioration, or the number of decisions that have to be taken and which are represented by the assignments of terms to classes, increases at such a rate with the number of requests processed that the classification becomes overdetermined at an early stage of construction. The best that can be done with a request that leads to an inconsistency is to reject it and tolerate a small decrease in performance over the base set of requests. The origins of the inconsistencies may be difficult to locate, but at least it will be known that a particular document-request pair cannot be manipulated in the pseudo-classification to satisfy the conditions set up for earlier pairs without impairing retrieval performance. This itself serves as a guide to subsequent work on the construction of classification and match algorithms within the retrieval model.

On a purely practical level, there is little defense against inconsistent judgments of external relevance. If relevance judgments were to be completely idiosyncratic, a retrieval system would have to be constructed for each user, and the only way forward would be by interactive techniques. If relevance judgments were to be arbitrary, no system could function at a predictable level of performance. A fixed, that is, noninteractive system relies on a consensus of opinion of users as to the relevance of documents to requests.

6. A Retrieval Model

6.1 The Information Model

An information model is a statement of the categories of information used to describe the system followed by a statement of the assumptions made about these categories. Within this model, algorithms may be designed to perform specified operations, and they must not refer directly or indirectly to information which is outside the model.

Section 4.1 referred to the four sources of information required by an evaluative retrieval system. These are

(1) $\underline{D}$, the set of documents defined extensionally by terms. This is the document collection.

(2) $\underline{R}$, the set of requests defined extensionally by terms. This is the base set of all requests.

(3) $\underline{Z}$, the set of requests defined extensionally by the documents relevant to them. This is the set of relevance judgments.

(4) $\underline{C}$, the set of classes defined extensionally by terms. This is the term classification.

These are similar in that each defines one set of elements extensionally in terms of another set of elements. Each, therefore, may be regarded as a rectangular incidence array giving the occurrence of an element of one type with an element of another type. The underlining indicates that we are considering the set of elements defined in terms of another set (i.e., an array) rather than a single element defined in terms of a set of elements. Attention is confined to documents indexed using simple term coordination, and document collections indexed probabilistically, for example, by the methods of Maron and Kuhns [38], are not considered. The reasons for this are threefold. First, the document collection used is not indexed probabilistically, although some attempt might be made to rectify this. Second, it is felt that tests with undifferentiated terms, logically, should precede any experimenting with term weighting in order first to establish a basis for comparison. Third, the construction of pseudo-classifications is simpler in this case since a single operation on the classification involves the dichotomous choice between the removal or insertion of a term. The probabilistic case is more complex since the choice of a value to be assigned to the weight is no longer dichotomous.

The terms which specify the requests also appear unweighted as do, for quite different reasons, the documents relevant to the base set of requests. It may be possible to construct a scale of relevance and assign degrees of relevance according to this scale. Instead, those documents have been selected that have been judged of highest relevance. Therefore, in this study, the scale of relevance as applied externally has two values, namely, "relevant" and "not relevant". It is realized that the external judgment of relevance is more complex than this and that there is no simple division of documents into those relevant to a request and those not relevant. The insertion of a third category would be more realistic, and such a category, namely "of unspecified relevance," would serve to separate the polarities of relevance more clearly. The quantification of the degree of relevance of documents to requests has further difficulties of quite a different nature. Suppose, for example, that it were possible to place in order of increasing relevance to a particular request all the documents of the collection. As soon as numerical values are assigned to each document to quantify its degree of relevance, metric properties are assumed about the scale of relevance. During the course of retrieval, arithmetic operations on degrees of relevance are performed which tacitly assume the truth of statements like, for example: "document D_1, whose degree of relevance to a request R is i, is i/j times as relevant to R as document D_2, whose degree of relevance to R is j." Until a metric has been established for degrees of relevance such statements remain indefensible. Resnick and Savage [52] have proposed to make a study of this question. For these reasons it is decided to work with categories of relevance rather than degrees of relevance; that is, with a qualitative scale rather than a quantitative scale. The two-valued scale has been adopted since the main body of data for testing purposes is reducible to this form.

6.2 The Classification Model

The model by which classifications to be constructed are constrained is as follows. Membership of terms to classes is a binary property; the object either belongs or does not belong to a class. The probabilistic assignment of terms to classes is excluded. All assignments of objects to classes are *a priori* independent, and overlapping classes are allowed. Finally, the classification is nonhierarchical. It should be noted that the classes of the classification are defined extensionally. Terms are not assigned to classes according to their satisfying a known condition on the class. It may, nevertheless, transpire that classes have useful properties in terms of the character of the vocabulary.

The model of retrieval, therefore, is such that all sets encountered are defined extensionally and nonprobabilistically. For explanatory purposes we shall refer to Section 6.1 Statements (1)–(4) as the *retrieval environment* [see (26)].

6.3 The Relevance Model

The match functions applied only make use of the information contained in or derivable from the environment. Thus:

$$l = M[D, R, f(D, \underline{C}), f(R, \underline{C})] \tag{26}$$

where l is the match coefficient corresponding to the match function M applied to an arbitrary document D in $\underline{D}$ and an arbitrary request R in $\underline{R}$ using the classification $\underline{C}$. f is a function which produces from a description of a set, specified using terms, a description using classes. The purpose of f is to provide a means of recovering in class matches the term matches that were missed on simple matching of the term descriptions for R and D because a term was used in one of these and a variant of this term in the other. The relationship between these terms may or may not be one of actual synonymy in natural language. The intention is that the classification should contain classes of terms mutually intersubstitutable and which result in good retrieval performance.

In accordance with the relevance hypothesis (Section 4.1), M is required to be a monotonically increasing function of the number of terms or classes in common between R and D. Its behavior with respect to the terms belonging to one of them, but not to the other, is not specified. This is a subject for precise formulation in a specific realization of M which satisfies the conditions mentioned. The modifications to the pseudo-classification as it is being constructed will be seen, from

Section 7.3, to involve the addition of terms to classes already defined or the grouping of terms to form new classes. The size of the classes and their number will, therefore, vary during construction and no particularly relevant interpretation may be put on these quantities. In addition, if the match function is allowed to depend on them explicitly, the classification will be unalterable or will certainly deteriorate with respect to already processed requests, as new requests are examined. The dependence of the match function on these two quantities is, therefore, explicitly proscribed.

The values resulting from application of the match function to a document that is absolutely relevant to a request, and to a document that is absolutely irrelevant to a request, may be specified at will. Although absolute irrelevance is not as precise an intuitive concept as absolute relevance (for a reason can always be found for saying that a document is slightly relevant to a request in a collection of restricted subject matter), it will suffice simply to regard it as being that relationship which exists between document and request at the lowest value of the match coefficient. A corollary of the relevance hypothesis is that this coefficient must increase monotonically to its maximum value which represents absolute relevance. It is, therefore, required that the bounds of the match function be finite and that these bounds are attained, at least in theory, by the function. The additional conditions on the match function are, therefore:

(a) M is a monotonically increasing function of the number of terms or classes in common between R and D.

(b) M is independent of the size of any class in $\underline{C}$ and of the number of classes in $\underline{C}$.

(c) l is bounded above and below, and attains its bounds.

Once the classification has been constructed using the base set of requests, it may still be underdetermined, but additional requests and their appropriate relevance judgments could be used to complete the classification only if the match function does not depend on the number of requests in the base set. Similarly, additional documents could only be added to the collection provided the match function does not depend on the size of the collection. Since both of these are valuable properties of a retrieval system, the following conditions on M are imposed:

(d) M does not depend on the size of $\underline{R}$.

(e) M does not depend on the size of $\underline{D}$, or on the size of the term vocabulary.

So far, there is no criterion of relevance in the model. Any criterion is bound to be arbitrary to a certain extent, for it is never possible to have complete knowledge, either of the document collection, or of the mind of the user of the system. To use the complete document unprocessed is as far from the solution as hoping to provide a complete analysis of the document, revealing in detail the complexity of the structural and semantic relationships between all the linguistic elements in the document. It is necessary to use approximations which hopefully will reveal the salient features of the collection for the purposes of automatic retrieval. In the model, the upper and lower bounds of the match coefficients that represent the polarities of relevance are known. By (26), a scale of relevance between these poles has been established and somewhere along this scale a value is defined, above which documents are retrieved and below which they are suppressed. This value is called the *critical value* of the match coefficient. Categories rather than degrees of relevance are assigned, therefore, to retrieved documents. In the absence of any evidence to the contrary, it will be assumed that the values of the match coefficient are distributed over the document collection in such a way that the critical value is the value midway between the extrema of the match coefficient. Subsequent experiment may require a revision of this assumption. Thus, for deciding on a suitable value for the critical point in the scale of relevance, the following hypothesis is made:

(f) The critical value is the arithmetic average of the upper and lower extrema of the match coefficient.

This will be referred to as the *critical value hypothesis*.

The following notation is introduced in connection with the above assumptions. Suppose that l^+ and l^- are the upper and lower bounds of the match coefficient l, respectively, and suppose that l_0 is the critical value of l. In accordance with the above hypothesis, l_0 is defined as:

$$l_0 = \tfrac{1}{2}(l^+ + l^-). \tag{27}$$

The binary asymmetrical relations $@$ and $\cancel{@}$ are used to denote "relevant to" and "not relevant to," respectively. Thus:

$$\begin{aligned} l \geq l_0 &\Leftrightarrow D \ @ \ R \\ l < l_0 &\Leftrightarrow D \ \cancel{@} \ R. \end{aligned} \tag{28}$$

For completeness, the binary asymmetrical relations $@^*$ and $\cancel{@}^*$ are introduced to denote "absolutely relevant to" and "absolutely irrelevant to", respectively. Thus:

$$\begin{aligned} l = l^+ &\Leftrightarrow D \ @^* R \\ l = l^- &\Leftrightarrow D \ \cancel{@}^* R. \end{aligned} \tag{29}$$

7. Methods for Constructing Pseudo-classifications

7.1 Two Approaches

Within the model of retrieval set out in Section 6, two approaches in the construction of pseudo-classifications may be distinguished. The first approach may be regarded as an attempt at an *analytic solution* by determining the "inverse" of the match function. This is seen more clearly from (26) which, in the context of Section 6.3, defines the match coefficient in terms of other elements of the model. This relationship is open to a more general interpretation in which it is regarded as an equation connecting l, D, R, and $\underline{C}$ by the functions f and M, which are given. Providing only requests of the base set are considered, the values of l, or at least their magnitudes with respect to the critical value of the match coefficient, are known. In the construction of pseudo-classifications, $\underline{C}$ is unknown so that (26) may now be interpreted as an implicit definition of $\underline{C}$. Such a solution, however, depends on whether M possesses the requisite algebraic properties which enable the inversion to be performed. Even if these properties were known, the method involves an amount of matrix manipulation—for $\underline{D}$, $\underline{R}$ may be regarded as rectangular binary matrices—which makes such a solution uneconomic for the scale of document collection eventually to be processed.

An alternative solution is by the method of *perturbations*, which has the advantage that less analysis of the match function is required. The classification is subjected to a number of alterations involving the insertion and deletion of terms from classes until the appropriate response to the base set of requests is elicited from the system. The alterations are carried out by *perturbation functions*.

7.2 General Outline of a Method

Suppose that it is possible, by a suitable perturbation, to cause the system to give the correct response, "relevant" or "not relevant", to a specific document-request pair. With a suitable convergence theorem, it would be possible to treat each document-request pair independently of the others. The response for one document-request pair might be destroyed or impaired by later adjustments to accommodate other pairs but at worst it would be necessary to examine each pair a number of times. The convergence theorem would ensure that although a number of responses may be impaired, gradual convergence would nevertheless set in. Without such a theorem, it is necessary to use a method in which each document-request pair is examined once only and in which conditions are set up to prevent a response from being obliterated by the processing of subsequent pairs. The degrading of responses by adjustment of the classification to accommodate subsequent document-request pairs is called *deterioration*. The conditions necessary to prevent the destruction of a response are referred to as *deterioration conditions*.

An outline of a method for constructing pseudo-classifications may now be given as follows:

(a) Let $\underline{C}'$ be the state of the pseudo-classification.

(b) Perturbations are applied to $\underline{C}'$ until the correct response is given by the system to a particular (D, R). The state of the pseudo-classification is then $\underline{C}''$.

(c) Deterioration conditions are set up for (D, R) with respect to $\underline{C}''$.

(d) The process is repeated for the next (D, R).

7.3 Design of Perturbation Functions

Deterioration conditions for the method described in Section 7.2 are effective only if all the perturbations which might lead to deterioration have been examined. It is, therefore, necessary that the perturbations which affect the match function are exhaustively enumerated and that there are few enough of them to make the method practicable. For each document-request pair, all perturbations which might lead to deterioration must be examined. It is required, as a practical constraint on the method, that the number of deteriorating perturbations be less than the number of document-request pairs to be considered. The algorithm for constructing pseudo-classifications is, therefore, of order two in the number of document-request pairs.

The operations which are appropriate to altering the classification are

Assignment of terms to classes:

$$a(\{x_i\}^p \to \{y_i\}^p); \qquad \langle \text{condition on } \{x\}^p, \{y\}^p \rangle \qquad \text{for all } i \leq p. \qquad (30)$$

Removal of terms from classes and their assignment to other classes:

$$r(\{x_i\}^p: \{y_i\}^p \to \{z_i\}^p); \qquad \langle \text{condition on } \{x\}^p, \{y\}^p, \{z\}^p \rangle \qquad \text{for all } i \leq p \qquad (31)$$

where $\{x\}^p$ is an ordered set of p terms and $\{y\}^p$, $\{z\}^p$ are ordered sets of p classes, and where the conditions limit the choice of operands for a and r. x_i, y_i, z_i are the ith members of the sets $\{x\}^p$, $\{y\}^p$, $\{z\}^p$, respectively. p is called the *step length* of perturbation. A complete enumeration of the perturbations with *step length* P which affect the classification involves the enumeration of all perturbations of smaller step lengths (i.e., $P-1$, $P-2$, ..., 2, 1).

Another possible perturbation is the simple removal of p terms from p classes. This, however, might result in the complete evacuation of terms from the classification. The removal of terms from classes is provided for in (31) and since, in this case, terms are reassigned to classes, there is no possibility of complete evacuation of the classification. For these reasons the simple removal of terms from classes without reassignment is not considered.

The effect of (30) on the classification is to *classify* terms (i.e., to insert terms into classes of the pseudo-classification) while the effect of (31) is to *reclassify* terms (i.e., to redistribute terms among the classes of the pseudo-classification). A further distinction is drawn. The classes mentioned in (30) and (31) are of two kinds. A class may already exist in the classification so that the effect of (30) and (31) is to add or remove terms. The effect, therefore, is to alter the constitution of a class. The number of classes in the classification remains unchanged or decreases. The classes may, however, be new in the sense that it is only when the functions have been applied that the classes enter the classification. They are not modifications of already existing classes since the number of classes in the classification increases. The effect of (30) and (31) when applied to such classes is to *create* new classes within the pseudo-classification. These distinctions are made use of in Section 7.5, where a method is proposed for selecting the appropriate perturbation to apply to a given document-request pair.

The choice of perturbation is further determined by the response which must be simulated for a given document-request pair. Suppose that the response of the retrieval system to the pair (D, R) is "not relevant" and that "relevant" is the correct response. A perturbation is applied to the classification which has the effect of increasing the value of the match coefficient for (D, R) to a level greater than the critical value. To facilitate this selection, the perturbations are grouped into those which increase the match coefficient, those which leave the match coefficient unchanged and those which decrease the match coefficient. The following terms are therefore used:

(a) *Increasing* perturbations have the effect of increasing the match coefficient for a given document-request pair.

(b) *Level* perturbations have the effect of leaving unchanged the match coefficient for a given document-request pair.

(c) *Decreasing* perturbations have the effect of decreasing the match coefficient for a given document-request pair.

Once perturbation functions have been grouped according to their effects on the match function, it is clear how the deterioration conditions should be determined. If it is necessary to apply an increasing perturbation to accommodate a particular document-request pair, then conditions are set up to inhibit the application of the decreasing perturbations which may lower the match coefficient below the critical value. Similarly, if a decreasing perturbation is applied then conditions must be set up to inhibit the action of increasing perturbation functions.

The number of perturbations of the form (30) and (31) increases with the step length p. In order to satisfy the practical constraints on the model only single-step ($p = 1$) perturbations will be examined in detail.

7.4 Deterioration Conditions

Suppose that t_i is a term and that C_j is a class in the classification. It follows from the model of classification defined in Section 6.2 that either $t_i \in C_j$ or $t_i \notin C_j$ and that membership is nonprobabilistic. The classification $\underline{C}$ may, therefore, be represented by a binary array indicating the incidence of terms in classes. Thus,

$$C_{ij} = 1 \Leftrightarrow t_i \in C_j$$
$$C_{ij} = -1 \Leftrightarrow t_i \notin C_j \tag{32}$$

where C is used to denote both the classification and the array. During the construction of the classification, however, another possibility of membership of terms to classes is used. The value $C_{ij} = 0$ is to imply that, on the basis of the information used so far, no decision may be taken about the membership of t_i to C_j although, at a later stage of construction, a definite choice may be made. During the construction of the classification the array is tri-valued. The values $1, 0, -1$ are referred to as *status values*.

During the construction of the pseudo-classification, perturbations are applied which affect the membership of terms to classes and accordingly change the corresponding status values. A change in the status value is called a *transition* and is defined as:

$e_i \to e_j$ status value e_i is changed to status value e_j in the
                  pseudo-classification.   (33)

The *transition table* T_{ij} gives the set of permitted transitions and is defined by:

$$T_{ij} = 0 \Leftrightarrow e_i \to e_j \qquad \text{not allowed}$$
$$T_{ij} = 1 \Leftrightarrow e_i \to e_j \qquad \text{allowed} \tag{34}$$

where $e_i, e_j \in (-1, 0, 1)$. From (30) and (31) the single-step perturbations are of the form:

$$a(x \to y); \qquad \langle \text{conditions on } (x, y) \rangle \tag{35}$$

$$r(x: y \to z); \qquad \langle \text{condition on } (x, y, z) \rangle. \tag{36}$$

The deterioration condition associated with (35) is "x must never be assigned to y." This is achieved by forbidding the membership of term x to class y and by forbidding any transition from the status value -1. The effect on the pseudo-classification is, therefore:

$$C_{ij} = -1 \qquad \text{where } x = t_i \text{ and } y = C_j$$

and the required values in the transition table to ensure that this is never revoked are

$$T_{-1,1} = 0 \quad \text{and} \quad T_{-1,0} = 0.$$

The change to the classification is effected if

$$T_{0,-1} = 1.$$

The deterioration condition associated with (36) is "if x is in y then x may not be assigned to z." This condition is recorded in the *condition table* $Q(k: i, j)$ defined by:

$$Q(k: i, j) = 0 \Leftrightarrow r(t_k: C_i \to C_j) \qquad \text{allowed}$$
$$Q(k: i, j) = 1 \Leftrightarrow r(t_k: C_i \to C_j) \qquad \text{not allowed.} \qquad (37)$$

These conditions may not be revoked in a later stage of the construction of the pseudo-classification. That is, within the condition table, the change from 1 to 0 is not allowed.

The effect of (35) on the pseudo-classification is

$$C_{ij} = 1 \qquad \text{where } x = t_i \text{ and } y = C_j$$

and for this to be possible the transition $0 \to 1$ must be allowed:

$$T_{0,1} = 1.$$

The effect of (36) on the pseudo-classification is

$$C_{ki} = 0, C_{kj} = 1 \qquad \text{where } x = t_k, y = C_i, z = C_j$$

and for this to be possible the transition $1 \to 0$ must be allowed:

$$T_{1,0} = 1.$$

The remaining transitions $e_i \to e_i$ for $e_i \in (-1, 0, 1)$ and $1 \to -1$ are allowed since they are not explicitly excluded by the above analysis. These results are collated below. The transition table, therefore, may be indicated as

	j		
	-1	0	1
-1	1	1	1
i $\quad$ 0	0	1	1
1	0	1	1

$$(38)$$

The effect of (35) on the classification array is

$$C_{ij} = 1. \tag{39}$$

The effect of (36) on the classification array is

$$C_{ki} = 0, \qquad C_{kj} = 1. \tag{40}$$

The deterioration condition for (35) is

$$C_{ij} = -1. \tag{41}$$

The deterioration condition for (36) is

$$Q(k: i, j) = 1. \tag{42}$$

Two functions a' and r' are now introduced, which have the effect of setting up the deterioration conditions (41) and (42) associated with the functions a and r, respectively. The functions are called *conditional perturbations* and are defined as:

$$a'(x \to y); \qquad \langle \text{condition on } (x, y) \rangle \tag{43}$$

whose effect is $C_{ij} = -1$ where $x = t_i$ and $y = C_j$ [see (41)]

$$r'(x: y \to z); \qquad \langle \text{condition on } (x, y, z) \rangle \tag{44}$$

whose effect is $Q(k: i, j) = 1$ where $x = t_k$, $y = C_i$, $z = C_j$ [see (42)].

7.5 Precedence of Perturbations

It has been seen in Section 7.3 that perturbations may be grouped in two different ways: according to their effect on the match coefficient and according to their general effect on the classification. The selection of an appropriate perturbation to apply for a given document-request pair is determined, to a certain extent, by the system's response and the response specified in the relevance table. If, for example, the match coefficient for a document-request pair is lower than the critical value and it is known that the document is relevant to the request, then an increasing perturbation function is required. The choice of perturbation function is further determined by establishing a *precedence* between perturbations according to their effect on the pseudo-classification, namely *classifying*, *reclassifying*, or *creating* [see Section 7.3]. These three groups of perturbations will be denoted by c, r, and n, respectively. This is not, however, an exclusive grouping since a particular perturbation may be, for example, both r type and n type, that is, its effect is both to reclassify and to introduce a new class. A complete exclusive grouping consists of the group c (classify), r (reclassify), cn (classify and create new class), and *rn* (reclassify and create new class). The *type* of a perturbation is, therefore, defined as:

$$type = c \text{ or } r \text{ or } cn \text{ or } rn. \tag{45}$$

The first precedence to consider is that between *r* and *c*. During the construction of the pseudo-classification, it is advantageous first to attempt to reclassify the terms already classified until no further reclassification is possible. At this point more terms are admitted to the classification and are subsequently reclassified as appropriate. The precedence rule which achieves this effect is:

$$r > c.$$

The same argument holds for *rn* and *cn*, to obtain the rule:

$$rn > cn.$$

A final requirement is that the classification be constructed with as few classes as possible to achieve the required distinctions among the terms. This position is approached, at least in principle, if the perturbations involving the creation of new classes have the lowest precedence. Accordingly, the precedence of the types of perturbation is given by:

$$precedence = r > c > rn > cn. \tag{46}$$

The selection of perturbations according to precedence and according to their effects on the match function does not lead to a unique function. There may be a number of perturbations which fulfill the conditions and for each of these there may be a number of possible choices of operands satisfying $\langle$condition on $(x, y)\rangle$ or $\langle$condition on $(x, y, z)\rangle$ [see (30) and (31)]. It will be seen that the perturbations change the match coefficient by an amount that is independent of the choice of arguments from among those which satisfy the appropriate conditions. Therefore:

(1) The arguments for the perturbation are chosen at random from the class of suitable operands.

To prevent the classification from becoming overdetermined at an early stage of construction (in the sense described in Section 5.3):

(2) The smallest number of perturbations are selected which together produce the required change in the match coefficient.

8. Concluding Remarks

The analysis given provides the basis of a method for constructing the classification, that is the limiting classification, which enables the best retrieval performance to be achieved for a given set of relevance judgments and for a particular set of requests. Naturally, it is unrealistic to rely on the availability of relevance judgments, and the problem arises of constructing the limiting classification from the document collection alone. This problem remains unanswered at present. The most logical way in which to proceed is to examine the classes of the limiting classification to determine whether or not the members of each class are more strongly related to themselves than they are to terms outside the class. This question may be resolvable by comparing the limiting classification with classifications constructed on the basis of the association hypothesis by techniques discussed in Section 3. Methods for comparing classifications are already available [24, 27]. Once the limiting classification is known, it is hoped that the methods outlined in this chapter will lead to the formulation of classification techniques which will be more applicable to the specific classification problems presented by information retrieval, than are those available at present.

ACKNOWLEDGMENTS

The author is indebted to Dr. R. M. Needham (University Mathematical Laboratory, Cambridge University, England) and Dr. K. Sparck Jones for their encouragement and advice throughout the course of the work presented here. He also wishes to thank Mr. D. S. Linney for his helpful criticisms.

This work is the result of research conducted on classification techniques for Information Retrieval supported in part by Grant Number GN-534.1 from the Office of Scientific Information Service of the National Science Foundation to the Computer and Information Science Research Center, The Ohio State University, and in part by a grant from the Office of Scientific and Technical Information of the United Kingdom.

REFERENCES

1. Adanson, M., *Famille des Plantes*, 2 vols., Preface, III Partie, 1ᵉʳ Article, p. *clv.* Vincent, Paris, 1763.
2. Ball, G. N., Data analysis in the Social Sciences: What about the details. *Proc. AFIPS Fall Joint Computer Conf., Las Vegas, 1965.*
3. Benzécri, J. P., *Sur les algorithmes de classification.* Texte multigraphié, 1965.
4. Benzécri, J. P., Statistical analysis as a tool to make patterns emerge from data in *Methodologies Pattern Recognition* (S. Watanabe, ed.), pp. 35–74. Academic Press, New York, 1969.
5. Bobrow, D. G., Natural language input for a computer problem solving system. Ph.D. Thesis, Mathematics Dept., M.I.T., Cambridge, Massachusetts, 1964.
6. Borko, H., Studies on the reliability and validity of factor analytically derived classification categories. *Proc. Symp. Statistical Methods Mechanized Documentation, Washington, 1964.* Nat. Bur. Stds. Misc. Pubs., No. 269, pp. 245–251.
7. Borko, H., and Bernick, M., Automatic Document Classification. *J. Ass. Comput. Mach.* **10**, 151–162. (1963).
8. Bush, V., As we may think. *Atlantic Monthly*, **176** (1), 101–108, July 1945; The Growth of Knowledge, in *Readings on Organization and Retrieval of Information* (M. Kochen, ed.), pp.23–35. Wiley, New York, 1967.

9. Cleverdon, C. W., Report on effect of relevance decisions on comparative performance of index languages. College of Aeronautics, Cranfield, England, 1970.

10. Cleverdon, C. W., Keen M., Mills, J., Factors determining the performance of indexing systems. Aslib Cranfield Research Project, 1966, Vol. 1 (Parts 1 and 2) and Vol. 2, Cranfield, England.

11. Cooper, W. S., Fact retrieval and deductive question-answering information retrieval systems. *J. Ass. Comput. Mach.* **11**, 117–137 (1964).

12. Cuadra, C. A. and Katter, R. V., Opening the black box of "relevance." *J. Doc.* **23**, 291–303 (1967).

13. Darlington, J., Translating ordinary language into symbolic logic. Memo MAC-M-149, Project MAC, M.I.T., Cambridge, Massachusetts, 1964.

14. Dattola, R. L., A fast algorithm for automatic classification. *J. Libr. Automat.* **2**, 31–48 (1969).

15. Diogenes Laertius, *Lives of Eminent Philosophers* (R. D. Hicks, Transl.), Loeb Classical Library, 2 vols. W. Heinemann, London, 1925.

16. Doyle, L. B., Semantic road maps for literature searchers. *J. Ass. Comput. Mach.* **8**, 553–578 (1961).

17. Doyle, L. B., Breaking the cost-barrier in automatic classification. Systems Development Corporation paper SP-2516, 1966.

18. Doyle, L. B., Indexing and abstracting by association. *Amer. Doc.* **13**, 378–390 (1962).

19. Doyle, L. B., Is relevance an adequate criterion in retrieval system evaluation? *American Documentation Institute: Automation and Scientific Communication. Ann. Meeting Amer. Doc. Inst., Chicago, 1963*, Part 2, p. 200. Amer. Doc. Inst., Washington, D.C., 1963.

20. Giuliano, V. E., Automatic message retrieval by associativ etechniques, in *Joint Man-Computer Languages*, p. 10. Mitre SS-10, Mitre Corporation, Bedford, Massachusettes. 1962.

21. Gotlieb, C. C., and Kumar, S., Semantic clustering of index terms. *J. Ass. Comput. Mach.* **15** 493–513 (1968).

22. Green, B. F., Wolf, A. K., Chomsky, C., and Laughery, K., BASEBALL: an automatic question answerer, in *Computers and Thought* (E. A. Feigenbaum, and J. Feldman, eds.), pp. 207–216. McGraw-Hill, New York, 1963.

23. Gull, C. D., Seven years of work on the organization of materials in the Special Library. *Amer. Doc.* **7**, 320–329 (1956).

24. Jackson, D. M., Comparison of classifications. in *Numerical Taxonomy* (A. J. Cole, ed.), pp. 91–111. Academic Press, New York, 1969.

25. Jackson, D. M., Basis for an improvability measure for information retrieval. *Proc. 32nd Anner. Conv. Amer. Soc. Information Science, San Francisco, 1969*, pp. 487–495.

26. Jackson, D. M., A note on a set of functions for information retrieval. *Inform. Stor. Retrieval* **5**, 27–41 (1969).

27. Jackson, D. M., Automatic classification and information retrieval. Ph.D. Thesis, Faculty of Mathematics, Cambridge University, England, 1969.

28. Jardine, C. J., Jardine, N., and Sibson, R., The structure and construction of taxonomic hierarchies. *Math. Biosci.* **1**, 173–179 (1967).

29. Johnson, S. C., Hierarchical clustering schemes. *Psychometrika* **12**, 241–254 (1967).

30. Kuhns, J. L., The continuum of coefficients of association. *Proc. Symp. Statistical Methods Mechanized Documentation, Washington, 1964*. Nat. Bur. Stds. Misc. Publs., No. 269, pp. 33–39.

31. Lance, G. N., and Williams, W. T., A general theory of classificatory sorting strategies. II. Clustering Systems. *Computer J.* **10**, 271–277 (1967).

32. Lance, G. N., and Williams, W. T., A general theory of classificatory sorting strategies. I. Hierarchical systems. *Computer J.* **9**, 373–382 (1967).

33. Lewis, P. A. W., Baxendale, P. B., and Bennett, J. L., Statistical discrimination of the synonym/antonymy relationship between words. *J. Ass. Comput. Mach.* **14**, 20–44 (1967).

34. Library of Congress. Subject Headings, 6th Ed. Washington, D.C., 1957.

35. Luhn, H. P., A statistical approach to mechanised encoding and searching of literary information. *IBM J. Res. Devel.* **1**, 309–317 (1957).

36. Mahalanobis, P. C., On the generalised distance in statistics. *Proc. Nat. Inst. Science India*, **2**, 49–55 (1936).

37. Maron, M. E., Automatic indexing: an experimental enquiry. *J. Ass. Comput. Mach.* **8**, 404–417 (1961).

38. Maron, M. E., and Kuhns, J. L., On relevance, probabilistic indexing and information retrieval. *J. Ass. Comput. Mach.* **1**, 216–244 (1960).

39. Maron, M. E., Kuhns, J. L. and Ray, L. C., *Probabilistic Indexing.* Data Systems Project Office, Ramo-Wooldridge, Los Angeles, California. Tech. Memo. No. 3, 1959.

40. Mill, J. S., *System of Logic*, Vol. 1. J. W. Parker and Son, London, 1851.

41. Mooers, C. N., Summary of Lectures No. 1 and No. 2. Presented at the *NATO Advan. Study Inst. Automat. Doc. Analysis, Venice, July 1963.*

42. Needham, R. M., The place of automatic classification in information retrieval. Rept No. ML 166, Cambridge Language Research Unit, Cambridge, England, 1963.

43. Needham, R. M., Classification and grouping. Ph.D.Thesis. University of Cambridge, England, 1961.

44. Needham, R. M., The termination of certain iterative processes. Memo. No. RM-5188-PR. Rand Corporation, Santa Monica, California, 1966.

45. Needham, R. M., and Sparck Jones, K., Keywords and Clumps. *J. Doc.* **20**, 5–15 (1964).

46. Parker-Rhodes, A. F., Statistical aspects of fungus forays. *Trans. Brit. Mycol. Soc.* **38**, 283–290 (1955).

47. Parker-Rhodes, A. F., and Jackson, D. M., Automatic classification in the ecology of the high fungi, in *Numerical Taxonomy* (A. J. Cole, ed.), pp. 181–215. Academic Press, New York, 1969.

48. Parker-Rhodes, A. F., and Needham, R. M., The theory of clumps. Rept. ML 126, Cambridge Language Research Unit, Cambridge, England, 1960.

49. Pearson, K., On coefficients of racial likeness. *Biometrika* **18**, 105–117 (1926).

50. Rao, C. R., *Advanced Statistical Methods in Biometric Research.* Wiley, New York, 1952.

51. Raphael, B., SIR—A computer program for semantic information retrieval. *Proc. AFIPS Fall Joint Computer Conf., San Francisco, 1964*, pp. 577–589.

52 Resnick, A. and Savage, T. E., The consistency of human judgements of relevance. *Amer. Doc.* **15**, 93–95 (1964).

53. Romerio, G. F., and Cavara, L., Assessment studies of documentation systems. *Inform. Stor. Retrieval* **4**, 309–325 (1969).

54. Rubin, J., Optimum classification into groups: an approach for solving the taxonomy problem. Rept No. 39.014. IBM, New York Scientific Center, 1966.

55. Salton, G., and Lesk, M. E., The SMART automatic document retrieval system—an illustration. *Commun. Ass. Comput. Mach.* **8** (6), 391–398 (1965).

56. Salton, G., Computer evaluation of indexing and text processing. *J. Ass. Comput. Mach.* **15** (1), 3–36 (1968).
57. Salton, G., and Lesk, M. E., Relevance assessments and retrieval system evaluation. *Inform. Stor. Retrieval* **4**, 343–359 (1969).
58. Sebestyen, G. S., Recognition of membership in classes. *IRE Trans. Information Theory*, **IT-7** 44–50 (1961).
59. Shera, J. H., Libraries and the organization of knowledge. 1965 (D. J. Foskett, ed.). Archon Books, Hamden, Connecticut, 1965.
60. Simmons, R. F., Klein, S., and McConlogue, K., Towards the synthesis of human language behavior. *Behavioral Sci.* **7**, 402–407 (1962).
61. Sneath, P. H. A., Mathematics and classification from Adanson to the present, in *The Bicentennial of Michel Adanson's "Famille des Plantes."* The Hunt Botanical Library, Carnegie Institute of Technology, Pittsburgh, Pennsylvania, 1964.
62. Soergel, D., Some remarks on information languages, their analysis and comparison. *Inform. Stor. Retrieval* **3**, 219–291 (1967).
63. Sokal, R. R., and Sneath, P. H. A., *Principles of Numerical Taxonomy.* Freeman, San Fransisco, 1963.
64. Sparck Jones, K., Synonymy and semantic classification. Ph.D. Thesis, University of Cambridge, 1964.
65. Sparck Jones, K., and Jackson, D. M., Current approaches to classification and clump-finding at the CLRU. *Computer J.* **10**, 29–37 (1967).
66. Stevens, M. E., Automatic indexing: A state-of-the-art report. NBS Monograph No. 91, Natl. Bur. Stds., *U.S. Dept. Commerce*, U.S. Gov. Printing Office, Washington, D.C., 1965.
67. Stiles, H. E., The association factor in information retrieval. *J. Ass. Comput. Mach.* **8**, 271–279 (1961).
68. Sutcliffe, J. P., A probability model for errors of classification. I. General considerations. *Psychometrika* **30**, 73–96 (1965).
69. Sutcliffe, J. P., A probability model for errors of classification. II. Particular cases. *Psychometrika* **30**, 129–155 (1965).
70. Swets, J. A., *Effectiveness of Information Retrieval Methods*, Rept. 1499. Bolt Beranek and Newman, Cambridge, Massachusetts, April, 1967.
71. Tanimoto, T. T., An elementary theory of classification and prediction. *IBM Report*, Yorktown Heights, New York, 1958.
72. Taube, M. A., Note on the pseudo-mathematics of relevance. *Amer. Doc.* **16**, 69–72 (1965).
73. Vaswani, P. K. T. A technique for cluster emphasis and its application to automatic indexing, Booklet G, pp. 1–4. *IFIP Conf., Edinburgh, Scotland* North-Holland Publ., Amsterdam, 1968.
74. de la Véga, W. F. Techniques de classification automatique utilisant un indice de ressemblance. *Rev. Fr. Sociol.* **8**, 506–520 (1967).
75. Verhoeff, J., Goffman, W. and Belzer, J. Inefficiency of the use of Boolean functions for information retrieval systems. *Commun. Ass. Comput. Mach* **4**, 557–558, 594 (1961).
76. Williams, W. T., and Dale, M. B. Fundamental problems in numerical taxonomy. *Advan. Botan. Res.* **2**, 35–68 (1965).

Approaches to the Machine Recognition of Conversational Speech

KLAUS W. OTTEN

The National Cash Register Company
Dayton, Ohio

1. Introduction

During the past years, several papers have described automatic speech recognition and the role it might play in various man–machine communication situations, (for example, [1, 2]). Great hopes have been expressed that one might soon converse with computers by speech, and that the traditional keyboard might be replaced as an input by a microphone with an automatic speech recognition device.

127

Some successful demonstrations of automatic word recognition devices of a limited nature (for example, [3–8]) have nourished the belief that the recognition of strings of spoken words, and ultimately that of conversational speech, is mainly a matter of additional engineering efforts or of proper programming for large computers. Unfortunately, this is not the case. The recognition of a limited knowledge of isolated spoken words is a pattern recognition problem in the conventional sense. The recognition of conversational speech, in contrast, is a much more complex problem. The complexity of the problem has its origin in the need for pattern formation, an operation which has to be successfully performed before the actual pattern recognition operation can be undertaken.

This chapter is concerned with the analysis of those problems that have to be solved to achieve machine recognition of conversational speech. The analysis of the problems is followed by a discussion of possible avenues along which the design of conversational speech recognition systems are likely to proceed.

2. Reasons for Interest in Machine Recognition of Conversational Speech

2.1 Definition of "Machine Recognition of Conversational Speech"

Machine recognition of speech is the translation of the continuously varying acoustical speech signal into a sequence of discrete symbols representing linguistically defined units. These units have to be capable of conveying the full meaning of the spoken utterance. Examples of these units are characters, phonemes, morphemes, syllables, words (see Fig. 1).

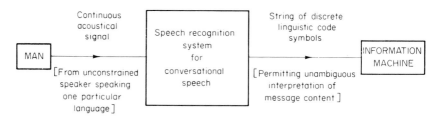

Fig. 1. Input–output characteristics of speech recognition system for conversational speech.

Machine recognition of conversational speech implies that the translation process can be performed with conversational speech. Conversational speech is usually poorly articulated speech and differs, often significantly, from the accepted standard speech expressed by a sequence of phonetic events (for example, the phonetic transcription found in a pronunciation dictionary). The redundancy of the language permits the speaker to be imprecise with his articulations: The listener can "get the message" because he can reconstruct a meaningful correct message from correctly recognized fragments of the speech. He can do this solely because of his understanding of the rules of the language and the semantic context of the verbal communication.

Hence, procedures for the machine recognition of conversational speech must account for man's speaking habits and must provide capabilities similar to those of the listener who is familiar with the language spoken. The magnitude of the problems implicit in these requirements will be outlined in the following sections.

2.2 Reasons for the Interest in Speech Recognition

There are three primary reasons for the strong interest in machine recognition of conversational speech.

(1) Interest in an understanding of the mechanics of the human speech production and speech perception process.

(2) Interest in an understanding of natural languages as communication codes.

(3) Ability to translate human speech into a machine code as basis for man–machine communication via speech.

The first two reasons satisfy our academic curiosity, the third practical needs. Our understanding of the mechanics of the speech production and speech perception process is still rather meager. One can argue that to succeed in the design of a speech recognizer, one must have this presently lacking understanding of the human neural encoding and decoding process. Should, on the other hand, engineers succeed in modeling a working speech recognizer, the functioning of the machine may suggest explanations for the functioning of the human speech communication process. Hence, the attempts to devise speech recognition machines stimulate basic research on speech production, speech perception, and natural languages.

The third reason for the interest in speech recognition is the most direct one: Man wants to communicate with his information machines (computers) as he communicates with his human fellows; that is, by speech, the fundamental expression form of human languages. A speech recognizer for conversational speech forms the basis for both verbal man–machine communication and for instantaneous automatic language translation of speech and can, therefore, become of great practical importance as part of the computer utility concept.

In the following, we will analyze the speech recognition problem from the standpoint of the designer of man–machine communication systems in support of future computer and information utilities.

2.3 Speech Recognition in Man–Machine Communication

The communication problems in man–machine communication situations stem from the differences between man (with his natural language) and an information machine or computer (with its algorithmically organized machine language). The semantics of the computer are a (small) specialized subset of the semantics of man. Depending on the type and size of the subset, man will use only a certain part of his natural language as far as semantics and specialized words and concepts are concerned. However, as far as linguistic structures (grammar) and phonological coding (inaccuracy of articulation) are concerned, there is little difference between a narrow highly specialized or a wide general subject field of man–machine communication.

Recognition of conversational speech in man–machine communication, therefore, must provide means for accepting all normally expected ranges of speech variations independent of application. Differences in the vocabulary size and the semantic decoding ability which are associated with different man–machine communication tasks, do affect the information processing capability of the machine, but not the capability of the speech recognition system.

The speech recognition system must be capable of translating any speech signal into appropriate discrete linguistic units, units which permit the machine to decipher the meaning of the utterances. This deciphering has to be unambiguous, but only with respect to the content (meaning of the message), not with respect to its form.

3. Fundamentals of Speech Recognition

3.1 Speech Recognition as a Mapping Operation

Speech recognition can be viewed as a mapping operation. Conversational speech is represented as a continuous acoustical signal. The result of the speech recognition process is a discrete description in the form of a linguistic code which conveys the semantic content of the message. Hence, speech recognition requires the mapping of the physical continuous speech signal from the acoustical domain into discrete linguistic descriptors of a linguistic code domain. This discrete description is only the transcription of the utterance, not its semantic decoding. However, this transcription is sufficient to decode the semantic content of the information by mapping it into the semantic domain in a second mapping operation. We can think of speech recognition (as we will be concerned with it) as the first part of a two-step mapping process (Fig. 2a). In the first step—the speech recognition process—the acoustical speech signal is mapped into a linguistic code. The continuous signal is translated into a sequence of linguistic code symbols. In the second step—the semantic interpretation process—this linguistic transcription of the speech is interpreted within the framework of the semantics of the communication situation. It is important to realize that the speech recognition according to our definition (i.e., the first of the two mapping operations required for semantic message decoding) is successful only if the resulting linguistic transcription permits the unambiguous semantic decoding. It is for this reason that the first mapping operation has to be analyzed always in the context of the two consecutive and interdependent mapping operations. Speech recognition, in our sense, is only complete if the recognition results allow the information machine (computer) to derive the semantic information content consistently with a small number of errors.

3.2 Requirement for Recognition: Code Knowledge

Speech recognition is a decoding process. Correct decoding requires complete knowledge of the code. Speech is the physical (acoustical) form of linguistically encoded information. Two basic types of encoding processes are involved in speech production—the semantic encoding of information into a linguistic code (message encoded as strings of words, phonemes, or characters), and the acoustical encoding (strings of words or phonemes encoded as a continuous acoustical signal).

Speech recognition is only one part of the speech decoding process in man–machine communication by speech. If we refer to our definition, speech recognition is not equivalent to the entire speech decoding process, it is only the first part of a two-step mapping operation (Fig. 2a and b). The first mapping operation, and hence, speech recognition, can be viewed as an acoustical decoding process, a process complementary to the acoustical encoding process. The code, according to which the decoding process has to function, has to be known to the speech recognizer. However, this code is at least partly determined by the second step.

The extent and performance of the second mapping by the information machine, which we may accordingly name semantic decoding, determines the requirements for the acoustical decoding that is performed in the speech recognition process. Specifically, the choice of the linguistic units from which the semantic interpretation can be made

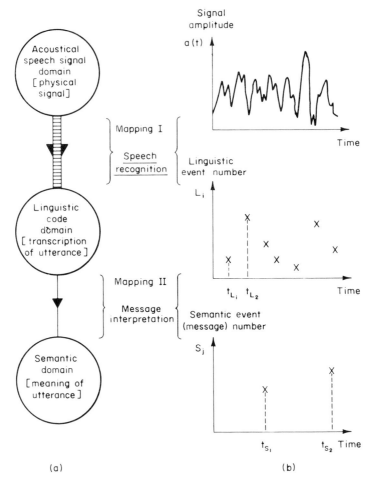

Fig. 2. (a) Speech recognition as a mapping operation: the mapping operations. (b) Speech recognition as a mapping operation: results of mapping operation.

unambiguously, determines the complexity of the speech recognition process: Phonemes as units, require different recognition complexity than do syllables as linguistic units.

What are the codes that have to be known by the information machine and by the speech recognizer? The code, which has to be known to the semantic classifier (information machine), is the code that translates semantic units into strings of linguistic units. This code is the abstract description of the language at the semantic and linguistic levels: It is a set of lexical and grammatical rules and a list of correspondences. This language knowledge must be available to the information machine with which man wants to communicate by means of the speech recognizer.

The code knowledge needed by the speech recognizer is different from the language knowledge required by the information machine. To perform the acoustical decoding, the receiver must know the rules for interpretation of the acoustical signals as strings of linguistic symbols: The rules for mapping of the acoustical signals into the chosen units of the lingustic domain implies a code which must be derived from the knowledge of the human speech production process, and, to a limited degree, of the language structure. Note that this code is determined, in part, by the choice of the linguistic units used to describe the message content.

3.3 Speech Recognition as the Complement to Speech Production

Human speech production as an encoding process can be viewed as a mapping operation. Like the speech decoding operation, this mapping is a two-step mapping as illustrated in the upper part of Fig. 3. In the first step the speech is formulated by mapping from the semantic domain into the linguistic domain. In the second step the acoustical speech signal is produced by mapping from the linguistic domain into

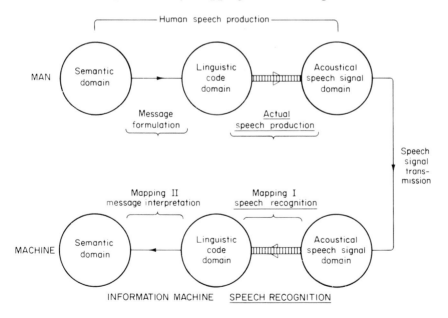

Fig. 3. Speech recognition process as complement to speech production process.

the acoustical domain. If we compare this model presentation of the total speech production process with the mapping model of the speech decoding process (lower part of Fig. 3) the complementary nature of the (acoustic) speech production process and of the speech recognition process becomes evident.

The hypothesis that speech recognition is the complement to speech production deserves further discussion. In Fig. 4, refined models of

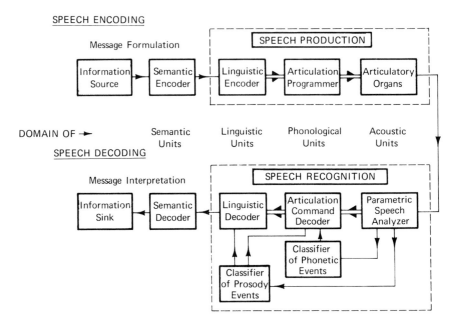

FIG. 4. Model of speech production and speech recognition process.

human speech production and of speech recognition, are confronted. We recognize corresponding functional blocks of the models in four domains: The semantic, linguistic, phonological, and acoustical domains. The two models illustrate the (one-way) man–machine communication process employing human speech and automatic speech recognition.

In the human mind, the information is selected (semantic units, e.g., concepts, numbers, as output of information source). As part of the speech formulation process, these units are linguistically encoded (linguistic units, e.g., morphemes, as output of semantic encoder.) These units are further encoded in terms of structural linguistic units (e.g., syllables or phonemes as output of the linguistic encoder).

At this level, further encoding becomes part of the actual speech production process. The articulation programmer translates linguistic symbol sequences into phonological production programs (time table of commands for the excitation of muscles of the articulatory apparatus). In response to these commands, and smoothed by the inertia of the articulatory organs (transfer function of the mechanoacoustical articulatory system) the continuous acoustical signal is produced. Notice that the translation from the discrete into a continuous description takes place in the last encoding process because of the inertia inherent in the speech production mechanism.

In the speech recognizer steps of decoding corresponding to those of the actual speech production take place. In a parametric speech analyzer, the speech signal is interpreted in terms of parameters which describe the speech production characteristics, such as pitch frequency, resonant frequencies (formant frequencies) of the vocal tract, etc., as continuous functions of time. Based on the analysis of these descriptors, phonetic and suprasegmental events are classified and an attempt is made to reconstruct the articulation program used by the speaker. This hypothesized articulation program and the tentative classification results are used by the linguistic decoder. It formulates a description of the recognized speech in terms of linguistic units. These can then be interpreted by the semantic decoder, the information machine connected to the recognition system.

4. Problems in the Recognition of Conversational Speech

4.1 Four Major Problem Areas

The preceding discussion of the fundamentals of speech recognition will allow us to recognize the existence of four major problem areas:

(1) Selection of suitable linguistic units for the description of the semantic message content (problem of selecting and defining recognition units)

(2) Consistent translation from the continuous signal domain into the discrete symbol domain (problems of segmentation)

(3) Consideration of the variability of the acoustical characteristics of speech (problems of detecting and utilizing invariants in speech)

(4) Means and methods of utilizing language redundancy in the decoding process (problems of recognition error detection and correction)

Each of these problem areas is further analyzed in the following sections.

4.2 Selection and Definition of Recognition Units

In the man–machine communication process employing speech (and hence speech recognition) there appear to be five types of classification (or recognition) units involved. The relations between these units of speech are shown in Fig. 5.

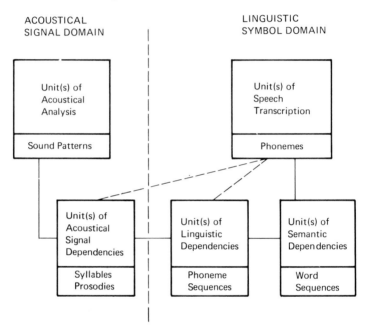

FIG. 5. Units of speech in speech recognition.

Only two sets of units can be defined in the acoustical signal domain —unit(s) of acoustical analysis (sound patterns) and unit(s) of acoustical signal dependencies (syllables, prosodies).[1] Acoustical correlates to the units permit, at least in principle, the segmentation of the acoustical signal into units of these two types solely by an analysis of the acoustical signal without reference to linguistic information.

The goal of the speech recognition process is, however, the translation of the acoustical signal into linguistic code symbols that permit the interpretation of the meaning of the utterance. This implies that

---

[1] Sound patterns are units which are distinguishable by differences in the acoustical signal properties without reference to phonological meaning. Units of acoustical dependencies are characterized by acoustically defined boundaries and dependencies for the sequences of sound patterns representing these units, either because of articulatory constraints or because of phonological rules.

the speech recognition system must describe speech in terms of units of the linguistic symbol domain. All three types of units of the linguistic domain [unit(s) of speech transcription, of linguistic dependencies and of semantic dependencies] do not have acoustical correlates and hence cannot be identified directly by an analysis of the speech signal.

The desired unit of the speech recognizer output is the unit of speech transcription, the phoneme. It is attractive as a recognition unit because phonemes are the smallest linguistic units permitting the almost unambiguous transcription of speech of a particular language and because (what follows logically) of its small alphabet size as compared to the "alphabet sizes" of other linguistic units, such as morphemes or words.

The identification of units of speech transcription in the speech signal is indirect. It has to be based on the direct identification of acoustical signal domain units and the interpretation of these units in terms of linguistic information (rules of the language) as units of the linguistic symbol domain. The desired units of speech transcription (phonemes) hence emerge as the result of a sequence of interdependent operations at both lower levels (sound patterns, syllables, prosodies) and higher levels (phoneme sequences, word sequences) within the hierarchy of speech units. It should be noted that this identification of phonemes is only possible if the recognizer is "knowledgeable" of the rules of the language in terms of the units introduced: The recognition systems must store in memory the complete set of language production rules and the strategies for resynthesizing legitimate linguistic symbols from identified acoustical signal domain units.

In summary, speech recognition of conversational speech is not a pattern recognition process by which the speech signal is segmented into one single class of segments which are thereafter classified. In contrast, it involves the sequential classification of interdependent units within a hierarchy of units.

The need for interdependent units of speech may become more evident in considering the complex of segmentation problems.

4.3 Segmentation: Direct and Indirect Segmentation Approaches

4.3.1 Concept of Direct and Indirect Segmentation

The translation of the continuous speech signal into a discrete linguistic symbol sequence involves, directly or indirectly, segmentation —a discrete symbol sequence represents (possibly overlapping) segment sequences.

The translation process can take two extreme forms. In the first form segments are first formed by direct segmentation and then classified. In the second form the signal is continuously matched with a set of reference patterns. Whenever a match is achieved, the presence of a classification unit is indirectly detected, and by the knowledge of the matching pattern, this unit is automatically classified.

The first process involves direct segmentation, the second indirect segmentation; the associated recognition methods can be named segment classification methods and continuous pattern match methods.

4.3.2 Differences between Direct and Indirect Segmentation

The two extreme classification methods differ significantly as do the associated segmentation performances.

In its extreme forms segment classification methods provide segmentations whenever segmentation criteria are detected in the continuous signal. As a result, segments (which may overlap) are formed. Thereafter, each segment is classified as a member of the alphabet chosen for the particular set of segments. Note that a classification has to be made for each segment, hence, the segmentation process determines the number of classifications.

In the continuous pattern match methods the unknown signal (or its description in terms of a continuous signal analysis such as a continuous spectrum description) is compared with corresponding reference patterns. These patterns describe properties of the speech units in terms of continuous parameters. For each unit of the recognition alphabet, a reference pattern is stored. All reference patterns are compared with the unknown signal and measures of the individual pattern matches are computed. Whenever this match measure exceeds a threshold, the existence of an acceptable pattern is signaled and the pattern is classified as belonging to the class of the best matching reference pattern. Note that the match measures are derived continuously for all reference patterns. It is, therefore, possible that at any time more than one measure may exceed the threshold. Ambiguous multiple classifications can result.

Figure 6 may help in demonstrating the differences between the segment classification method and the continuous pattern match method. The same acoustical signal $a(t)$ leads to different numbers of speech unit classifications: 5 units (C_1 through C_5) are identified by the segment classification methods, 6 units (M_1 through M_6) are recognized by the pattern match method. Note that there is not only a difference in the number of recognized units, but also in the timing of the recognitions.

In the segment classification approach, segment boundaries (B_0

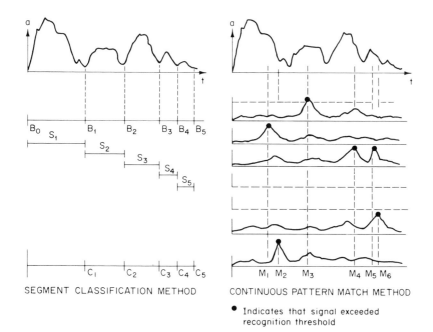

SEGMENT CLASSIFICATION METHOD   CONTINUOUS PATTERN MATCH METHOD

● Indicates that signal exceeded
recognition threshold

Fig. 6. Segment classification method and continuous pattern match method.

through B_5) are detected by analysis of the speech signal. They lead to the formation of acoustical signal segments (S_1 through S_5). The characteristics of the signal of each segment then lead to the (forced) classification of the segments (C_1 through C_5).

In the continuous pattern match approach, the signal is continuously matched with reference patterns. For each matching operation, a continuous match measure is derived. Five of these match measure signals are shown. Each of those shown exceeds at least once the critical threshold value and, hence, indicates a speech unit recognition (M_1 through M_6). Note that for one recognition, two measures exceed the threshold simultaneously: The result is two different classifications (or an ambiguous recognition).

It might be interesting to note that the detection of the boundaries in the segment classification method involves a process that is equivalent to the continuous pattern match process—segmentation criteria are continuously matched with reference criteria. One might ask, therefore, is there a significant difference between the two approaches?

The answer is affirmative. Direct segmentation methods are based on the existence of reliable and consistently occurring segmentation criteria with the criteria for segment classification being less consistent. On the other hand, in the continuous pattern match approaches, no reliably derivable segmentation exists. Hence, one has to rely on the indirect detection of the units by recognizing the existence of the characteristic properties.

4.3.3 The Segmentation Processes in Conversational Speech Recognition

Direct segmentation requires the existence of consistently observable boundary criteria in the acoustical signal. These seem to exist at three levels: Boundaries between sound elements, boundaries between syllables, and boundaries between phrases.

Units of speech which are directly segmentable are represented by segments of signals for which certain properties remain relatively unchanged or change slowly. These segments are separated by boundaries that are identified by rapid changes in one or several properties of the signal. For example, boundaries between sound elements are indicated by changes in the spectral composition of the signal, those between syllables by changes in the signal intensity and certain spectral changes and, finally, those between phrases by short cessations in the signal.

Direct segmentation and the associated classifications of segments may be used to assist in the derivation of the classification at those levels for which only indirect segmentation is possible. Figure 7 shows how indirect phoneme segmentations and classifications are obtained

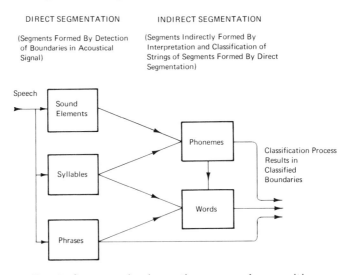

FIG. 7. Segmentation in continuous speech recognition.

by reference to the results of direct segmentations and classifications. Phonemes can be classified by interpretation of sound element sequences within the frames of recognized syllable boundaries. Phonemes are indirectly recognized as sound element sequences and as building blocks of syllables. Similarly, recognition is possible if those laws are known that describe the composition of syllables in terms of defined sound elements, even though not necessarily as part of the speech recognition process. In turn, words can be interpreted as sequences of phonemes within the framework of recognized syllable and phrase boundaries.

4.4 Variability of Acoustical Characteristics of Speech

4.4.1 Causes for Variation of Characteristics

We can make the idealized assumption that speech can be consistently segmented into some kind of speech units. For this assumption, recognition can only be successfully achieved if the characteristics of the speech signal segments contain invariants that permit positive differentiations. Unfortunately, there appears to be no set of invariants for a particular level of speech units. Instead, our ability to recognize speech seems to be based on the interpretation of sequences of variables that are only constrained in the range of variability (rather than invariant for a particular event). The acoustical characteristics of speech, the basis for the recognition, can, for the same speech event, vary over wide ranges. Fortunately, most of these variations are, in some form or other, explainable and nonrandom, and hence can be considered systematically.

The causes for the variation in the speech characteristics can be realized if one considers the speech production process. The mapping of the message content from the semantic domain into the acoustical signal varies: The speaker has freedom in the choice of his message formulation and phonological expression.

Figure 8a shows an oversimplified model of the speech generation process. The information source represents the message content selection in our mind. The content is then linguistically encoded according to the rules of the particular language spoken. This is a two-phase encoding operation that provides information to the articulatory control system. In the supralinguistic encoding phase momentary articulation speed, loudness, and other prosodic features are selected as needed for the expression of the message. In the linguistic encoding phase the message is structured in terms of abstract linguistic code symbols—it involves the formulation of the message in terms of phonemes or morphemes or other suitable linguistic units.

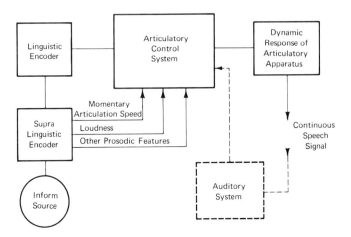

FIG. 8(a). Model of speech signal generation.

In the supralinguistic, as well as in the linguistic encoding phase, the speaker has considerable freedom of choice. The supralinguistic coding allows great variation in timing and intensity without affecting the semantics conveyed by a particular linguistic code (a particular sentence structure). In the articulatory control system (a part of the brain) the articulatory program is composed. It is the translation of the linguistic code and the supralinguistic command information into a specific schedule of commands to the particular muscles involved in the speech production process. Because of the inertia of the articulatory organs, the response is not instantaneous. The initially (at one early level) discrete commands result in the production of a continuous acoustical signal which is determined jointly by the articulatory program and the dynamic response (transfer function) of the physical articulatory system. It should be noted that the signal production involves a feedback loop—the produced signal is fed back to the articulatory control system via the auditory system. As the result of detecting deviations between program instructions and their execution, minor changes in the timing can be initiated.

4.4.2 Manifestations of Variations in Characteristics

Figure 8b may help in an understanding of the causes and resulting forms of variations of the acoustical speech signal characteristics. With reference to the model of the speech signal generation, the effect of the speaker's physical constitution on the speech characteristics is apparent. The anatomy of the individual speaker is reflected in the spectral composition of the produced signal. The dimensions of the

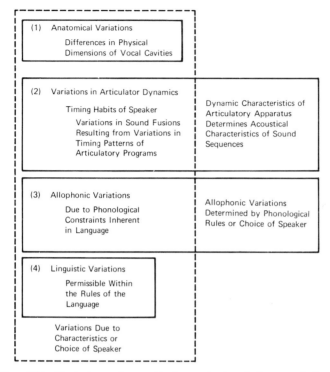

Fig. 8(b). Variations of acoustical speech signal characteristics.

vocal cavity determine the range of variations of spectral energy distributions and of formant frequencies.

The dynamic characteristics of the articulation apparatus (inertia of articulatory motions) introduces time-dependent variations of the characteristics. The time constants associated with the various articulatory organs, or members thereof, determine the speed by which one can transit from one articulatory position to the other. If the available time for the motions is less than the natural transit times, incomplete articulations result. The time allotted for each sound production is determined by the articulation programmer in response to supra-linguistic encoding of the overall speech timing (average articulation speed). Hence, various forms of sound fusions, of incomplete articulations (vowel reduction), and of co-articulation are exhibited as functions of the articulation speed, with the speaker's dynamics of the articulatory apparatus as parameters.

Phonological constraints inherent in the particular language are another source of quasi-systematic variations of the speech characteristics. Allophonic variations of phonemes are context dependent—the same phoneme has phonetically different forms dependent on specific preceding or following sounds.

Another cause for variations of the characteristics are linguistic constraints. The preceding causes of variations are, at least partially, predictable, given the physical characteristics of the speaker, timing information, and empirically determined allophonic laws. Changes of characteristics due to linguistic constraints, that is, due to the set of rules specifying the constructions of syllables, words, and sentences, provide a language with a great amount of coding redundancy. As a result a listener, provided he knows the rules of the language in the same form as the speaker, can decode the message even if many message elements are missing or mutilated. We can easily read a poor copy (that is, decode the message) of a document even if many characters are badly mutilated and unrecognizable. Language redundancy permits us to write in longhand and assume that an unknown reader will get the message even though he may not be able to identify all of the individual characters and words. This same redundancy of the language permits a speaker to be imprecise in his articulations and even to omit speech elements without endangering the human speech communication process. These improper articulations and omissions are largely unpredictable. While they are easily detected, compensated for, and corrected in the speech decoding process of a human listener, these latter speech variations cannot be handled by a machine interpreter unless the machine is equipped with a listener-like language knowledge and has the capability to apply this knowledge for the detection and correction of recognition errors.

4.4.3 Considerations of Variations in the Recognition Process

Each of the four major causes of speech variations requires a special form of consideration in the man–machine communication process. The anatomy of the speaker and the dynamics of the articulatory apparatus are unique features of each speaker. (These features, together with the not-so-unique timing patterns of speech productions, have been used to identify persons by "voice prints." Voice prints are speaker-unique spectrographic patterns of specific utterances—like fingerprints.) Because of these speaker-dependent features, the same message spoken by different people is acoustically different. But, there exists a deterministic relationship between anatomy, dynamic transfer function of the articulation apparatus, and the actual produced speech signal itself. Therefore, it is, at least in principle, possible to normalize the speech signal. We can think of a "standard" speaker with "average" anatomy and dynamic characteristics. Assume that the recognition characteristics are optimized for this hypothetical "standard" speaker. Any real speaker whose speech is to be recognized has to be analyzed first with respect to the deviations of his anatomy and dynamic characteristics from that of the hypothetical "standard" speaker. This can be done indirectly by the analysis of specific sound sequences. Because of the deterministic relationships between speech characteristics and anatomy and speech dynamics, the recognition characteristics originally derived for the "standard" speaker can then be modified and "adapted" to be optimal for the real speaker. For example, the recognition characteristics for sustained vowels in terms of formant frequencies may have to be changed to reflect the different anatomy of the speaker relative to that of the standard speaker.

The second major cause of speech variation manifested by vowel reduction, co-articulation, and other forms of sound fusions can be considered in a similar form. Adaptation, however, is not to the characteristics of the speaker, but rather to the timing pattern of the speech surrounding the particular event. This implies that timing information is continuously derived from speech. An example may illustrate the required consideration. Vowel reduction is the result of shortening the time available for the production of a vowel. Vowel reduction is a systematic shift of formant frequencies as a function of available time and of (consonantal) environment. The same formant frequencies may represent different vowels depending on the consonantal environment and the time available for the production. Consequently, vowel reduction can be considered only in the form of an adaptation of the formant frequency interpretations. These interpretations become functions of consonantal environment and measured time, as determined for the particular speech sample. This indicates the need for a bootstrap operation—a hierarchal processing involving decision feedback. It implies that the consonantal environment has to be classified before the interleaved and possibly reduced vowels can be identified.

The third cause of speech variations indicates a need for a sequential decoding of tentatively classified sound sequences. By applying known allophonic rules, the classifications can, within limits, be modified to satisfy the rules.

The fourth cause of speech variations, linguistic constraints, has to be considered primarily outside of what constitutes, according to our definition, the speech recognition concept. Omission of speech elements or improper articulations will often result in incorrect or incomplete phonemic recognition in speech recognition systems, even if the first three causes of speech variations are being considered as suggested. However, errors in the incorrect phonemic transcription of speech can be detected and corrected by the information machine engaged in speech interpretation. This is possible because of two factors: the high redundancy of the languages as codes and because of the systematically introduced omissions and distortions. Improper articulations may occur at random, but whenever they occur they are related to the "standard" correct articulations. For example, if the "standard" articulation calls for an $|s|$ the actual articulation is unlikely to be that of a vowel or a stop consonant, it is most likely another speech element similar to $|s|$ with fricative properties, perhaps resembling the phonemes $|z, f, \phi|$, etc. Hence, when the phoneme sequences are examined in view of linguistic and semantic language rules, these phonemic classification errors can be, and usually are, indirectly detected and corrected—by achieving the only correct interpretation of phoneme strings as words and sentences.

4.5 Means and Methods of Utilizing Language Redundancy

In the message interpretation process, which is performed by the machine connected to the speech recognizer, the language redundancy is utilized. As such, the utilization of language redundancy is only of indirect concern in the discussion of speech recognition problems. It is of importance to know what factors control this indirect error detection and correction process in the message interpretation. These factors permit us to determine the trade off between perfecting the speech recognition system (for example, to approach an error-free phonemic transcription) and transferring part of the recognition problem to the error detecting and correcting message-interpreting machine.

In the one extreme, the close-to-perfect speech recognizer provides an essentially correct phonemic transcription of speech which is interpreted by the connected machine in a relatively straightforward process. Phoneme sequences are interpreted as words, word sequences as sentences, and these are translated into meaning. The techniques involved are related to those developed for computer answering of questions in which the questions are provided in an essentially error-free computer language statement.

In the other extreme, the speech recognition system can be less complex and is permitted to provide speech transcriptions which are only coarse approximations to a standard (e.g., phonemic) transcription. The message interpretation by the connected machine is now a considerably more complex process. In addition to the operations already indicated, each speech recognizer output must (directly or indirectly) be checked for agreement with the rules of the language.

Speech element sequences which do not agree with the rules of the language (for example, those which do not represent actual words) indicate recognition errors and have to be corrected. An error, for example, at the level of phonemes, can be detected only by analyzing higher order units of the language, e.g., syllables or words. If a particular phoneme sequence does not make sense in view of the known complete set of occurring syllables or words, the existence of one or more errors is assured. The next step, in which it is determined which phoneme of the sequence is in error, is considerably more complex. First, one has to recognize that the error can be the result of a wrong classification, an omission (no recognition of an actually existing phoneme), or an addition (recognition of one single actual phoneme as a sequence of two). Error identification is closely related to the error correction: Knowing the rules of the redundant language, hypothetically related phoneme sequences have to be formed. Considering the likelihood of making certain recognition errors (this likelihood is a function of the recognition method and of the properties of the language) one can determine probabilities for having made various mistakes. These probabilities state how likely it is that the available incorrect phoneme sequence is the result of erroneous recognition of a variety of similar, but linguistically acceptable, and therefore potentially correct phoneme sequences. The particular phoneme sequence (which must be a legitimate unit of the language) for which the likelihood of recognition as the available phoneme sequence is highest, is then chosen as the most likely correct phoneme sequence. Potential correction of the error(s) is achieved by replacing the incorrect sequence by the supposedly correct sequence.

Let us assume that the unit of correction was a syllable. The sequence of corrected syllables may still not agree with the word formation and sentence formation rules. The process explained for the correction of incorrectly recognized phonemes is now repeated for the next higher level of linguistic units, that is, for wrongly corrected phoneme sequences (syllables): The basis for error detection and correction becomes now the set of word and sentence generation rules.

The example points out the problems of utilizing language redundancy:

(1) It requires a message interpretation machine which knows the rules for generating legitimate units of the language at various levels (e.g., syllables, words, sentences)—consider the memory problem!

(2) Means for checking the validity of unit sequences in terms of more complex unit structures must be available.

(3) Strategies for replacing an incorrect sequence by the most likely legitimate higher order structural element must be available. This

implies probabilistic processing and knowledge of the performance of the speech recognizer (conditional error distribution matrix) and of the speaker (conditional articulation error distribution matrix).

Language redundancy permits, in principle, the correct message decoding from an imperfect speech recognition output. It may be utilized by the message interpreter in the future if certain conditions are met:

(a) Compact algorithmic descriptions of the language rules are available.

(b) Methods for hierarchical linguistic and semantic decoding have been perfected.

(c) Probabilistic error correction strategies for hierarchical processes have been developed.

(d) Computer processing and storage capabilities to perform the comparison and correction operations in real time are available.

In short, efficient error-correcting message interpreters may permit the use of realistic, that is, nonperfect and technically feasible, speech recognition systems in man–machine communication. The postulated interpreters will exist once we have "computerized" our human ability to get correct messages from mutilated transcription.

5. Operational Requirements for Speech Recognition Systems

5.1 Identification of Recognition Operations

Based on the preceding explanation of the problem areas in speech recognition, we can identify the operations required in the recognition process performed in man–machine communication.

We must first assume that the recognition criteria have been determined for the particular speaker who provides the input. The actual recognition process involves three major interdependent operations:

(1) Pattern formation

(2) Tentative adaptive pattern classification

(3) Correction of tentative and potentially incorrect classification results

The first operation, the pattern formation operation, has to achieve two objectives: (a) Extraction of acoustical correlates of segmental and of suprasegmental speech elements; (b) Formation of speech units at various levels.

The extraction of acoustical correlates can be interpreted as the partial removal of the acoustical signal redundancy. (Acoustical signal redundancy is the direct result of the carrier nature of the speech signal.)

The pattern formation operation is based on the analysis of the acoustical signal with little or no reference to linguistic (structural) information unique to the language spoken.

In the second operation, the speech units at the lower levels (patterns of acoustical correlates) are tentatively classified in an adaptive process. In this process, knowledge of the speech production process is used extensively, e.g., in the consideration of vowel reduction and co-articulation. Phonological as well as some linguistic rules (statistics of sound sequences) may be utilized depending on the type of classification units chosen (sound element or phone, phoneme, etc.). For most practical cases, these first two operations describe the functioning of speech recognition systems according to our definition.

The last operation, the correction of classification results, is the indirect error-detecting and -correcting process involved in the message interpretation of the "human-like" machine with which we want to communicate ultimately by speech. This last operation, however, may also take place in the tentative adaptive pattern classification process, in particular if the classification process is hierarchal and involves two or more levels of recognition units (such as sound patterns and phoneme-like units expressed in terms of sound pattern sequences).

5.2 Sequence of Operations

The interdependence of operations implies that certain operations are dependent on the results of other operations. Therefore, the recognition operations have to be performed in proper sequence.

In Fig. 9 the sequence of recognition operations is shown schematically. As is to be expected, the pattern formation process has to precede any classification attempt. Classification of patterns at the lowest level in the hierarchy of recognition units are made first and are tentative in nature. These tentative classifications permit the adaptation of recognition criteria for the classification of patterns at the next higher level. For example, the adaptation of the recognition criteria at the phoneme-like levels to compensate for vowel reduction and co-articulation can be attempted only after more elementary speech elements (sound patterns) have been classified. However, this adaptation and the next higher level classification can take place only if the next higher classifications units have been formed as patterns to be recognized. This required pattern formation may be influenced by the tentative classification results at the level of the lower recognition units. Note that pattern formations, tentative classifications I and II, and the intermediate operation of recognition criteria adaptation are

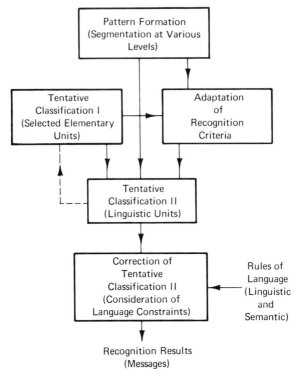

FIG. 9. Sequence of recognition operations.

based on information derived from the acoustical signal, on descriptions of the speech production processes, and on selected phonological rules of the particular language.

Speech recognition as defined in our discussion ends with the classification of units at a linguistic level, for example, at the phoneme-like level. In man–machine communication, the recognized string of linguistic units has to be interpreted as semantic units. This is done by the interpreting machine by applying linguistic and semantic rules. In this semantic decoding operation the language constraints permit the detection of some classification errors. These are corrected in one of two forms. If the decoded linguistic symbol string is in disagreement with the rules of the language, then minor phonological corrections (a replacement of one phoneme by a phonologically similar phoneme) may lead to a meaningful decoding. In this case the language redundancy permitted the correct semantic decoding without direct reinterpretation of the acoustical signal. The correction is inherent in the semantic decoding process.

On the other hand, if minor phonological corrections do not lead to meaningful semantic interpretations, the tentative classifications I and II have to be re-evaluated. This can be achieved by making major hypothetical phonological corrections which would lead to meaningful interpretations. These corrections, before being accepted as corrections, have to be tested as hypotheses: Changes of classifications II have to be justified in terms of different adaptations of recognition criteria; these different adaptations have, in turn, to be justified in terms of different classifications I, and these changes may require a different original pattern formation. Several of these hypothetical corrections may have to be tested until one is found that makes sense in view of permissible interpretations of the acoustical signals.

To simplify the explanation only two levels of tentative classification prior to the linguistic–semantic decoding were assumed. In practice, the process described may take place between any two or more of the hierarchical levels which may be involved in the complete machine interpretation of speech.

5.3 Information Manipulated

The speech recognition process requires the manipulation of large quantities of information (data). The recognition process implies, in some form or other, the comparison of the information describing the unknown acoustical signal with the complete set of information describing how the particular speaker could have produced not only the message to be decoded but any message in the language of concern. The latter set of information is (if "complete") of tremendous magnitude. If we are concerned with speech recognition in the narrow sense, it represents, in abstract form, our knowledge of the speech production process. On the other hand, if we are viewing the entire semantic decoding process of the speech interpreting machine, it includes our knowledge of the language. This monumental set of information is often referred to as the "recognition criteria" without recognizing the magnitude of what is involved.

The information derived from speech is obtained continuously and is the result of redundancy-reduction signal processing. This information is represented by sets of continuously varying parameters—acoustical correlates of segmental and suprasegmental speech elements.

The set of parameters describing the unknown speech signal is continuously "compared" to the set of reference information. The reference information is stored in the recognition system. This storage can be in direct form (e.g., in a memory unit) or in indirect form (e.g., as the specific processing properties of filters, comparators, logic).

In addition to the reference information, process control information has to be stored. This information specifies the methods and alternate avenues by which the unknown signal can be compared with selected sets of the reference material to decode the spoken message. Basically the process control information consists of process strategies. The most important strategies are those applied for adaptation of recognition criteria and for the detection and correction of errors.

In Fig. 10, the forms of information manipulated and used in the speech recognition process are summarized.

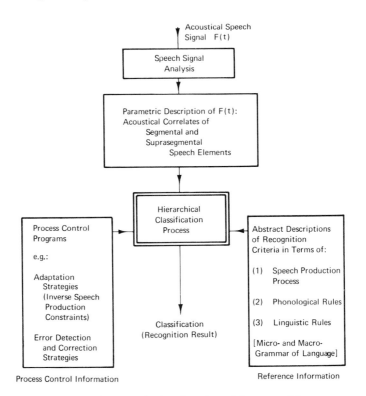

FIG. 10. Information manipulated and used in recognition process.

6. Approaches toward the Recognition of Conversational Speech

6.1 Recognition Concepts Instead of Recognition Systems

In the preceding sections, we attempted to introduce the reader to the magnitude of the problems associated with the recognition of conversational speech. It was suggested that the speech recognition process must be, at least in part, complementary to the speech production process. Furthermore, it can be argued that the recognition performance of an automatic recognizer, if operating together with a message interpreting computer, must be comparable to the speech perception performance of the human listener.

Since our knowledge of the mechanics of speech production, and even more, that of the speech perception mechanics is very incomplete, it is not surprising that we have not succeeded in engineering any acceptable machine capable of recognizing conversational speech. Instead of recognition systems, we have recognition concepts and a few attempts of implementing simplified versions of these concepts.

The variety of recognition concepts is great. The concepts are conditioned, in part, by the knowledge of speech characteristics, speech production, and speech perception, and, in part, by state of the art of the technologies available at the time of the concept formulation. In analyzing the various concepts, a few philosophies for approaching the continuous speech recognition problem can be identified. Rather than describing the various recognition concepts, only three major approach philosophies will be analyzed. These approach philosophies are indicative of possible directions for future, more comprehensive, developments.

6.2 Approach Philosophies

The approaches to the recognition of conversational speech show wide ranges in three major areas:
  (a) Segmentation and classification
  (b) Consideration of speaker variations
  (c) Information processing
A few comments will show that often significantly different approaches may have valid reasons for serious consideration.

As explained before, speech segmentation can be direct or indirect. In the direct segmentation approach, criteria derived from the acoustical signal are used to form defined segments of the speech signal. Each segment is then classified according to classification rules. These rules have been established for the particular type of segments which result from the chosen segmentation process. In the indirect segmentation approach, segmentation is only the indirect result of the classification process. This classification process is a property filtering action: a classification is achieved whenever certain combinations of classification criteria are detected. In this approach, no segments, per se, are formed—the continuous speech is directly translated into a sequence of detected speech elements.

Early attempts at speech recognition applied direct speech segmentation. Examples are the experimental speech recognition devices by Dreyfuss-Graf [9] and by Olsen and Belar [10]. A later attempt at continuous speech recognition by Martin *et al.* [*11, 12*] was based solely on indirect segmentation. Direct segmentation approaches adapt readily to digital processing techniques favoring quantized information. Indirect segmentation approaches, in contrast, are particularly suitable for predominantly analog processing techniques. Martin's recognition approach is based on an analog model of a neuron (analog threshold detector) as the elementary unit in the information processing recognition network which, combined with some logic, became a special purpose hybrid computer.

The second area in which approach philosophies differ is in how the variations of speech characteristics of individual speakers are considered. The two extreme approaches are (1) recognition concepts assuming the "adaptation" to the individual speaker and (2) recognition concepts designed to accept the speech from any speaker without special preparation or "self-adaptation."

Recognition concepts which can be adapted to (that is, be programmed for) any one individual speaker, require that the characteristics of the particular speaker are known. However, this speaker characterization has to be very specific; it has to be in terms of those parameters for which the recognition system has adaptation capabilities. Therefore, speech recognition approaches with adaptation to the speaker imply that the recognition operation cannot begin unless speech samples of the particular speaker have been analyzed and the analysis results have been translated into the reprogramming of the actual recognition machine. In other words, the recognition system has to be supplemented by a "speaker analyzer" and a "programming controller or recognition adapter" whenever the recognition device has to operate with more than one speaker. If the speaker analysis and adaptation are implemented as an integral part of a "learning" or "self-adaptive" recognition system, then this approach to conversational speech recognition appears to be related to human speech perception. When we listen to a person with a strong accent, we analyze and learn his particular deviations from normal speech and gradually "adapt" our perception function.

The other extreme in approaches to cope with the variety of speakers are attempts of basing speech recognition on only those very broad and general criteria that are not speaker-dependent. If those speaker-invariant criteria (inherent in the acoustical speech signal) could be found, and if different criteria combinations exist for all speech elements chosen as recognition language (for example, for all phonemes), one set of recognition criteria would allow the recognition of speech from any speaker. This is unlikely to be the case for elementary speech elements. However, for speech segments corresponding to complex units such as syllables or words, this might be possible. If it were possible, the number of criteria combinations would be extremely large, as would the memory problem. The recognition success would depend on how well linguistic context can be considered. This approach could be pursued with chances of success if the speech recognition system would be merged with the message interpretation system. This would mean that the emphasis would shift from a detailed acoustical signal analysis to a speech pattern interpretation with the interpretation relying on linguistically conditioned general constraints.

The third area of major differences in approach philosophies concerns the form chosen for information processing. The convenience of digital processing techniques as a factor in considering direct segmentation over indirect segmentation methods (favoring analog processing) has been mentioned. The readily available large processing power of general purpose computers has a strong influence on the choice of recognition approaches. Approaches which can be readily translated into simulation programs for general purpose computers seem to be preferred over approaches involving complex analog parallel information processing.

Another aspect of information processing can lead to different approaches—the choice between serial or parallel processing. The large volume of information to be compared and processed for each recognition decision can be achieved by either real-time parallel processing (e.g., as described in [11]) or in a high-speed serial operation as required when a general purpose computer is used. Closely related to the choice between parallel and serial operation is the approach to storage of the reference information needed for recognition. In a parallel processing implementation, the information may be stored indirectly in the form of the particular processing structure. In a serial processing approach, information storage in an addressable memory appears more appropriate.

This short review of the variety of approach possibilities in only three major areas indicates that, at this time, no statement can be made on the definite emergence of one particular approach philosophy to be more promising than any other.

Three approaches which appear to have chances for successful implementations and which have the potential of conversational speech recognition (when operated in connection with a powerful message interpretation system) are described in Sections 6.3, 6.4, and 6.5. The "continuous dynamic pattern match" has been implemented in one form [11, 12]. The second approach (phonological parametric decoding) is an extension of the first approach. It is more complex in the method by which it takes the speech production constraints into account. This approach has not been implemented. The third approach (phonological digital decoding) uses direct segmentation and sequential decoding methods and can be implemented by digital techniques. In some aspects it represents further improvements over the second approach. Variations of the phonological digital decoding approach may be investigated in the near future since the concept can be investigated readily with a general purpose computer.

6.3 Continuous Dynamic Pattern Match

In this approach, the unknown signal is continuously analyzed to determine its resemblance to specific dynamic patterns characteristic for speech events (or elements), hence the name continuous dynamic pattern match. The presence of a pattern is detected by property filters, i.e., nonlinear filters which determine the resemblance between the properties of the transformed unknown signal and the properties of the various patterns representing speech events. There are as many property filters as there are distinguishable speech events. The outputs of the property filters are signals which are nonlinearly proportional to the degree of resemblance between unknown signal and reference pattern. Whenever the filter output signal exceeds an empirically determined threshold, the particular speech event is classified accordingly. Classifications can be based on logic or analog connections (or combinations) of various filter outputs where some represent basic properties common to various speech elements and others are specific for a particular speech element.

In one form this approach was implemented and described in detail by Martin et al. [11, 12]. These descriptions refer to early phases of the development when the approach was used successfully for the recognition of nonconnected speech.

Figure 11 shows schematically the principle of the continuous dynamic pattern match approach. The speech signal is analyzed and translated into a set of parametric descriptors. These can be the outputs of filters from a filter bank, parameters describing speech characteristics such as formant frequencies, or indirect descriptors of spectrum shape properties such as the slope of the spectrum between filter center frequencies [11]. These descriptors (continuous functions of time) are then interpreted by an interpretation processor. This processor consists of networks of interdependent measuring circuits and adaptive filters. Functionally, the processor can be represented as a battery of interconnected property filters. Note that these property filters are more than what one usually refers to as a filter; they produce an output whenever the signal has particular properties which may be

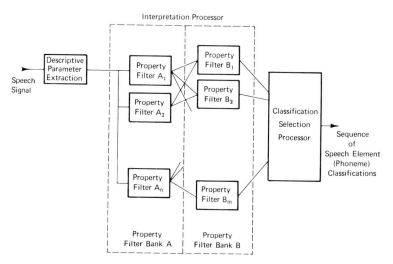

FIG. 11. Functional block diagram of continuous dynamic pattern match operation.

defined in the frequency domain, in the time domain, or in both. In Fig. 11, two layers of such property filters are shown in cascade. The first set of n property filters, for example, can be designed to detect properties common to several speech elements, the second set of m property filters to detect those specific to individual speech elements. The outputs of the property filters are fed into the classification selection processor. If more than one property filter connected to the classification selection processor responds at any one time or within a time interval shorter than that considered the minimum between two successive detectable speech elements, this processor selects the most likely correct classification. Figure 11 is intended to show only the principle of operation. In an actual implementation, there is likely to be no clear separation between various layers of property filters, nor is there a fixed number of property filters for the classification of any specific speech elements. Some elements may be detected by only one filter, others may require the interactive operation of several filters.

6.4 Phonological Parametric Decoding

As the name implies, recognition is achieved in this approach by a decoding process which is parametric and which is based on phonological criteria. The approach is an extension of the continuous dynamic pattern match approach. It differs from the dynamic pattern match approach in that it uses decision feedback to achieve adaptation to phonological conditions which determine the variations of acoustical correlates to phonological events.

The continuous dynamic pattern match recognizer, as described, achieves recognition by forward processing without feedback. It is relatively inflexible, it will recognize properly as long as the acoustical correlates of speech events can be translated into property filters and are relatively invariant. In connected speech, however, the acoustical correlates of phonological events do vary somehow systematically as a function of context and articulation speed, among others. If the controlling variables—such as context and instanteous articulation speed—are known, one can compensate for the variation of the acoustical correlates in the recognition process. This compensation can be referred to as an adaptation to the phonological conditions.

Adaptation to phonological condition is attempted in the phonological parametric decoding process. In contrast to the continuous dynamic pattern match approach which has forward processing without feedback, this approach makes use of decision feedback: final classification decisions are made only after the classification rules have been adapted for the particular phonological condition. The phonological condition indirectly described by context and articulation speed can be determined from an interpretation of those varying parameters which allow the analysis of co-articulation, vowel reduction, and articulation speed variations. The phonological parametric decoding approach, therefore, implies a three-step processing: first, the phonological conditions have to be determined, then the recognition parameters have to be adjusted, and finally the particular acoustical signal segment can be recognized as what it represents in the particular phonological condition.

Figure 12 is a functional block diagram of a phonological parametric decoder. Continuous descriptive parameters are extracted from the speech signals in the same form as for the dynamic pattern match approach.

These parameters are then simultaneously fed into a transit storage device and an interpretation processor. The transit storage device is a memory of the delay line-shift register type: at any time it stores the parameters describing the speech of the past several hundred milliseconds, the exact time determined by the "width" of the acoustical context to be considered in the adaptation process. The interpretation processor is a network of interconnected property filters as described for the dynamic pattern match recognizer. But instead of having property filters for speech elements, it has property filters for more general, and hence less variant, characteristics of speech elements.

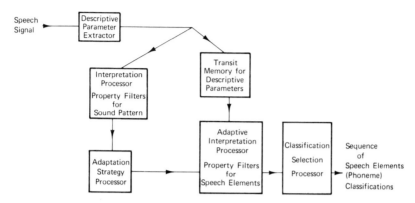

Fɪɢ. 12. Functional block diagram of phonological parametric decoder.

These filters respond to signal properties such as "voiced, spectral type X, rapidly increasing intensity, etc." Sequences of these generalized acoustical or phonetic classifications then become the basis for the determination of the phonological condition—classification sequences are analyzed as sound patterns which characterize the acoustical environment and the timing pattern.

In the adaptation strategy processor the recognized phonological condition is translated into weight adjustments of the property filters which are similar to those of the dynamic pattern match recognizer as far as filtering properties is concerned, however, with one significant difference—the filtering characteristics can be changed by the adaptation strategy processor to reflect the phonological condition.

As an example, assume that the general classifications made by the interpretation processor yield a sequence of segments with the following characterizations: frication period, stressed vowel, silence, plosive segment, in that order. The timing of events in this sequence permits the development of a strategy for the proper interpretation of the stored (delayed) descriptive parameter values. Those values representing the center section of the sequence (the vowel) can now be interpreted as those of a vowel in a particular consonantal environment and with a certain amount of vowel reduction (as determined by the measured duration of the segments). The measured values, e.g., the formant frequencies and their variations, can now be mapped into vowel classifications. These classifications consider, to a certain degree, the acoustical signal variation due to the constraints of the speech production process for connected speech. This design feedback process compensates, in part, the effects of articulatory dynamics on the characteristics of connected sounds. It can work only if the characteristics of connected speech are known to be systematically related to the phonological conditions. Such relationships have been postulated and experimentally demonstrated for vowel reduction [13] and for certain forms of co-articulation [14].

6.5 Phonological Digital Decoding

This digital decoding approach differs from the two preceding approaches in the speech element formation process and in the predominantly digital, rather than analog, processing. In the two preceding approaches, segments were formed indirectly by the property filtering process. Processing was performed parametrically, classification decisions were made only after considering all available information. In the phonological digital decoding approach, in contrast, decisions are made early in the processing. Final classifications are based on the interpretation of preceding classifications. Furthermore, the original speech signal is sampled and the samples quantized thus permitting a digital signal analysis (e.g., by Fast Fourier Analysis) and the convenient storage of the continuous analysis results in a digital transitory memory (shift register). The processing following the initial classifications, that is, the majority of all processing, is performed digitally. Since the decoding is based on phonological criteria, and since the processing is predominantly digital, the approach is named phonological digital decoding.

A functional block diagram of a phonological digital decoder is shown in Fig. 13. The analog speech signal is first sampled and the sample quantized by the analog-to-digital converter. The digitized signal is then analyzed to determine descriptive parameters. These parameters are fed into a shift register-type temporary storage and are further analyzed to determine significant events. Significant events are

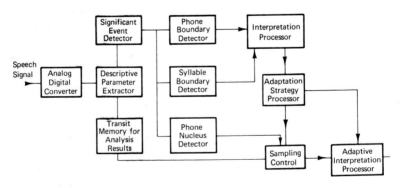

Fig. 13. Functional block diagram of phonological digital decoder.

sensed whenever one or several parameters change significantly or assume extreme values (relative maxima or minima).

The classification of these (acoustical) significant events (according to their physical nature) is the first decision-making operation. All consequent decision-making processes leading to more and more linguistically-oriented decisions are dependent in part on these elementary decisions.

In the next decision-making process the classified significant events are interpreted as specific phonological events: Each significant event is potentially a boundary between phones or syllables or the nucleus of a phone. The analysis of the significant event in the context of its neighbor events and the timing between events permits the classification of some of the events as specific boundaries or as nuclei of phones. These decision-making operations are performed by the phone boundary detector, the syllable boundary detector, and the phone nucleus detector. Each of these detectors is a digital processor which matches significant event classification and timing patterns against patterns known to be associated with specific boundaries or nuclei. The two boundary detectors determine the timing of boundaries. Like the significant event detector, these detectors perform a direct speech segmentation. The significant event detector segments speech into acoustically defined segments, the phone and syllable boundary detectors group these segments together to form phonologically defined segments. The phone nucleus detector identifies the timing of that interval of a phone during which the characteristic values (e.g., specific formant frequencies) are most likely to occur. It performs, therefore, not a segmentation but rather a timing function in support of the segment classification.

The classification of the now defined smallest phonological segment, the phone, is the next step. It results from the interpretation of the two phone boundary classifications. In the boundary pair classification only general classifications are made, such as "frication period of spectral type X, vowel segment type Y," where type X or Y characterize such features as relative duration, spectral composition, and relative intensity.

In the following step the sequence of classified boundary pairs (phones) that fall between two syllable boundaries is analyzed. These syllables form, singly or as pairs, units of phonological context, that is, units within which the acoustical properties of individual phones can only be interpreted in view of the properties of neighbor phones. In a decision feedback process similar to that described for the phonological parametric decoder the tentative classification of phones is replaced by the desired classification of linguistic units such as phonemes.

This final decision process deserves some explanations and comments. The initial tentative classifications are only approximate descriptions of the signal properties of segments. The segments are not necessarily the desired recognition units (e.g., phonemes) but rather building blocks of those. Consequently, the first task is to interpret phone sequences as potential phonemes. This is partially achieved by the interpretation processor which groups the phones within syllable boundaries into phonemes. With the knowledge of phonological context units (syllables) and phone groups which potentially represent phonemes, the adaptation strategy processor can determine how descriptive parameters have to be interpreted in view of the context. This adaptive interpretation information is supplied to the adaptive interpretation processor which makes the final classification. This classification is based on the matching of specific samples of the original analysis results (which have been stored in the transit memory) with the recognition criteria corrected to reflect the context constraints. The samples are taken for those times for which the phone nucleus detector or the adaptation strategy processor determined that characteristic parameter values might have occurred. Note that the interpretation processor forms the recognition units (segment) and that the sampling control provides accordingly for each recognition unit a set of samples for the adaptive interpretation processor. This processor then will make one classification. A classification selection processor, as needed for the previously discussed decoders, is consequently not required.

7. Concluding Comments

The description of the three approaches to conversational speech illustrates the complexity of any implementation attempt as well as the variety of avenues along which one can proceed. The preceding discussion of the problems of automatic recognition of conversational speech gave reasons why we have not proceeded further. We still do not know a great deal about information encoding and decoding in speech communication.

We conclude this survey of approaches to conversational speech recognition by asking: What has been achieved and where will we go? The investigations and experiments of scientists and engineers have given us insight in the problems of speech recognition without finding more than directions toward solutions. The optimism expressed in the mid and late fifties that speech recognition is primarily a matter of developing faster and more powerful computers has been replaced by the realization that we know too little about speech even to specify the computer one would like to have, much less to speak of programming it.

Speech recognition efforts in the near future, therefore, will play probably more the role of providing instrumentation for research in phonetics, phonology, and linguistics rather than that of developing man–machine interfaces. The development of an operational automatic recognition systems for truly conversational speech appears to be a project for the far future.

REFERENCES

1. David, E. E., Jr., Eyes and ears for computers. *Proc. IRE* **50**, 1093–1101. (1962).
2. Lea, W. A., Establishing the value of voice communication with computers. *IEEE Trans. Audio Electroacoustics* **AU-16**,184–197 (1968).
3. Wiren, J., and Stubbs, H. L., Electronic binary selection system for phoneme classification. *J. Acoust. Soc. Amer.* **28**, 1082–1091 (1956).
4. Denes, P., and Mathews, M. V., Spoken digit recognition using time–frequency pattern matching. *J. Acoust. Soc. Amer.* **32**, 1450–1455 (1960).
5. Fatehchand, R., Machine recognition of spoken words. *Advan. Computers* **1**, 193–230 (1960).
6. Kusch, H., Automatische Erkennung gesprochener Zahlen. *Nachrichtentech. Z.* **18**, 57–62 (1965).
7. Musman, H.-G., and Steiner, K. H., Phonetische Addiermaschine, *Arch. Elektrisch. Uebertr.* **19**, 502–510 (1965).
8. King, J. H., and Tunis, C. J., Some experiments in spoken word recognition. *IBM J. Res. Develop.* **10**, 65–79 (1966).
9. Dreyfuss-Graf, J., Phonetograph und Schallwellen-Quantelung, *Proc. Stockholm Speech Communication Seminar, September 1962.* Royal Institute of Technology Stockholm, Sweden, 1962.
10. Olson, H. F., and Belar, H., Phonetic typewriter. *J. Acoust. Soc. Amer.* **28**, 1072–1081 (1956).
11. Martin, T. B., Nelson, A. L., and Zadell, H. J., Speech recognition by analog feature-abstraction techniques. USAF Avionics Lab, Tech. Doc. Rept No. AL-TDR-64-176, August, 1964, (AD 604 526).
12. Nelson, A. L., Herscher, M. B., Martin, T. B., Zadell, H. J., and Falter, J. W., Acoustic recognition by analog feature-abstraction techniques, in *Models for the Perception of Speech and Visual Form* (W. Wathen-Dunn, ed.). M.I.T. Press, Cambridge, Massachusetts, 1967.
13. Lindblom, B., Spectrographic study of vowel reduction. *J. Acoust. Soc. Amer.* **35**, 1773–1781 (1963).
14. Ohman, S. E. G., Co-articulation of VCV utterances: Spectrographic measurements. *J. Acoust. Soc. Amer.* **39**, 151–168 (1966).

Man–Machine Interaction Using Speech

DAVID R. HILL[1]

Department of Mathematics, Statistics, and Computing Science
The University of Calgary, Calgary, Alberta, Canada

[1] Present address: Department of Electrical Engineering Science, University of Essex, Colchester, Essex, England.

165

1. Introduction

1.1 Nature of a Man–Machine Interface Using Speech

What is meant by "man–machine interface using speech"? One could talk instead of a "system–system interface using speech," and thereby avoid the slightly irrelevant question as to which is the man. An interface is a communication boundary between two systems. The essentially *human* character of a speech interface lies in the *nature of speech*, which is also where most of the problems arise. For communication, there must first be transmission of information. Information is characterized in terms of selective power among a set of messages, so the communicants must have message sets in common (which explains why the communication of "new ideas" is so difficult). There must also be some means of ensuring that the information received corresponds to that which was transmitted. *Effective* communication is achieved when the receiver's state following the message transmission is that desired by the sender. The receiver's state (of understanding) may have to be determined indirectly by observing the receiver's *behavior*. The sender, therefore, requires (in the absence of guarantees) feedback concerning the pertinent aspects of the receiver's behavior, to allow modification of what is transmitted until the information received achieves the effect required by the sender. Some basic steps involved in man–man speech communication are indicated in Fig. 1.

It is clear, therefore, that a "system–system interface using speech" implies that *both* systems:

(1) are able to recognize and understand intelligible speech;
(2) are able to generate intelligible speech;
(3) have a common corpus of experience—a common language.

One important aspect of speech is that the sole arbiter of what *is* intelligible speech is the human—preferably, for obvious reasons, in the form of a representative panel of his species. Machine recognition is "successful" if it makes a judgment agreeable to such a panel. Speech units have no absolute existence even within the same language. Speech units are functionally defined entities—two speech phenomena, even though physically (acoustically) dissimilar, are the "same" if they never distinguish two words in the language. A similar philosophy applies at higher levels of language.

1.2 Recognition and Synthesis

Just as the communication situation is symmetric, so there is symmetry in the processes of speech recognition and speech synthesis.

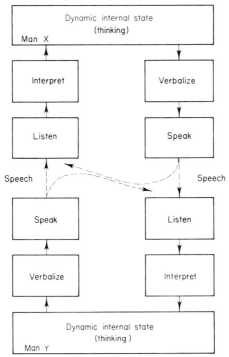

FIG. 1. Steps for man–man speech communication.

Figure 2 illustrates the parallel levels in both. In either case, it is necessary to *describe* speech adequately. This problem corresponds to the "problem of representation" noted by Feigenbaum [36]. He makes it clear that he considers "representation of data and data structures" to be a different problem to the "problem of representation *for problem solving systems*," though he indicates a belief that they have much of importance in common. For those working on speech recognition and synthesis by machine, the "representation of the problem to be solved" and the "data representation" are inextricably interwoven. Much essential research in speech has been concerned with exploration of suitable structures in which to frame worthwhile questions about speech. The problem of representation is the central problem in both speech recognition and speech synthesis in any sense. There are two further problem areas in both recognition and synthesis —implementation and application. These are, perhaps, problems of technology and awareness.

Synthesis is a valuable aid to improving our representation of speech, since we can observe the inadequacy of the synthesized speech, and infer the inadequacy of our representation (see also Section 4.2).

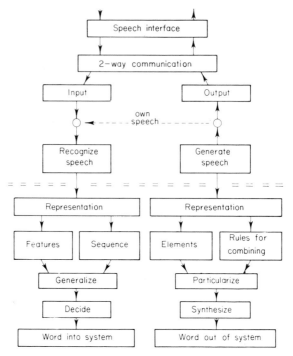

Fig. 2. Symmetry of the speech interface.

In this way synthesis is closely related to recognition, though caution is necessary, for synthesis is *particular*, whereas an adequate representation of speech must be *general*. This is one reason for the advanced state of speech synthesis compared to the rudimentary state of speech recognition; a second reason lies in the efficiency of the human recognition process, which is able to compensate for some inadequacy in the machine generator. A good example of the "particular" nature of synthesis is the "identifiability" of both human and mechanical talkers. Iles at Edinburgh University [71] has adapted Holmes' [64] rules to suit PAT, the synthesizer invented by Lawrence [2]. The resulting synthesis is identifiable with Holmes' rules, and characteristics of PAT are clearly noticeable. Recognition of individual *machine* generated speech would seem to offer little more than a technological problem, but an individual speaker varies more than an individual machine. The principle factor that has underlain continued failure to "solve" the recognition problem has been an inability to give a generalized representation of speech, and the recognition process, which embraces such variation. The representation adopted even restricts what questions may be asked concerning speech.

2. Reasons for Requiring a Man–Machine Interface Using Speech

2.1 Introduction

The reader is entitled to ask why a man–machine interface using speech is so attractive. It cannot be denied that *some* interface is essential, so it is permissible to concentrate on the notion of using speech.

At the 1967 IEEE International Convention, during a panel discussion, J. C. R. Licklider is quoted by Lindgren [90] as saying:

> I am concerned that the assumption is made that people are going to continue to talk mainly with people. Whereas it seems to me, we will have in due course a dynamic, organized body of knowledge, not in anyone's brain, but in some vast machine or chemical thing and, for scientific and technical and intellectual purposes, we'll want to talk mainly with it. Talking among people might be mainly for positive reinforcement of one another, although I suspect that even that could be handled better through some organized reinforcement arrangement.

Licklider speaks with authority, and is among those concerned with making the facts of the future. Even his last remark is fair as may be judged by the fact that some intelligent people could not be convinced that Weizenbaum's [146] primitive automatic psychiatrist—ELIZA— was only a suitably programmed computer. Thus ELIZA passes Turing's test [152] in this restricted context.

Thus the first reason for requiring a *speech* interface, as opposed to any other, is based in the psychology of the human. It is natural, convenient, and indeed, almost expected of any system worth communicating with.

2.2 Advantages

There are, however, a number of very practical advantages. Speaking for the nontechnical man John Lotz (quoted by Lindgren from the same discussion) notes the following advantages of speech communication:

(1) No tool is required;
(2) It can be used in the dark as well as it can in the light;
(3) It does not require a free line of sight;
(4) It can be varied from a (confidential) whisper to a loud (long distance) shout;
(5) It requires very little energy;
(6) It is omnidirectional;
(7) It leaves the body free for other activities.

The last two are, perhaps, the most important advantages from the purely practical point of view. Lea [82] working for NASA translates

these advantages into concrete terms for us. After noting, with Licklider, that the use of speech is rooted deep in man's psychological
makeup, he notes some general advantages of speech communication
and also some advantages of special significance to astronauts. A
speech interface (where numbers following cross-reference prior advantages):

(8) Offers more natural communication;
(9) Allows physical mobility during operation (6, 7);
(10) Increases the communication capacity, by exploiting multi-modal communication [he notes that speaking is, in any case, much faster than
typing];
(11) Gives additional reliability—since channel failure is less a problem when
there are many channels;
(12) Is very suitable for "alert" or "break-in" messages (6);
(13) Allows communication without specialized training (1, 8);
(14) Is essential, when hands and eyes are both occupied, as they often are in
busy space missions (7);
(15) May allow physiological/psychological monitoring of the state of the
operator, at least as a back up to electrical sensing;
(16) May be less affected by acceleration than other channels [there have been
no reports of hearing loss during acceleration].

He notes further considerations of special relevance to astronauts:

(17) In space, the environmental noise is under perfect control [though he
admits it may still be noisy] because no noise can come in from "outside."
(18) In a spacecraft, the speaker population is very restricted.
(19) Voice control allows machinery inside the spacecraft to be operated from
outside without the need to carry around complex communicators.

We may add to these as follows. A speech interface is extremely
compact, the speech interface need take up little or no panel space.
Shortage of panel space has been a problem in some situations, and
especially so in small space capsules, with so many demands for what
little space is available. With voice control of machine functions it
would be easy to monitor *control sequences*. Only a radio transmitter
and receiver would be required. When speech is a normal means of
communication (as in Air Traffic Control) the communication load on
the operator can be reduced if the machine is able to accept input in the
form in which it is normally generated. In currently planned ATC
schemes the controllers must talk to the aircraft and store the same
information in a local computer. Even when ATC is largely computer
controlled, this will remain true in a significant sense. Speech also
offers special advantages for disabled persons (other than those with
speech or hearing difficulties), especially for the blind. The transmission of information by speech is compatible with the cheap and

widely available telephone system. The possibility of "voice dialing" is an additional attraction. Finally, using voice-printing, or similar techniques, identity checks may be performed on the speaker—a potentially valuable security measure. These advantages may be summarized. A speech interface:

(20) Takes up little or no panel space;
(21) Allows simple monitoring of command sequences by remote personnel;
(22) Can allow a single channel to serve more than one purpose (e.g., communication with aircraft at the same time as data entry to a computer);
(23) Allows blind or disabled persons to operate machines easily;
(24) Is compatible with the widely available and inexpensive telephone system;
(25) Allows security checking.

To realize *all* these advantages fully requires better performance than is offered by any equipment now in sight.

2.3 Disadvantages

Lea notes two disadvantages. First, a message from the computer leaves no permanent trace in voice form—but (with a proper interface) presumably the astronaut could ask for a repeat of the message if necessary: from point of view of "the record" all conversation is recorded anyway. Second, if machines are used which are excessively limited (e.g., in terms of vocabulary, or acceptable "accent"), they may be so aggravating to converse with that they will be unusable.

We may add to these as follows. A speech input may be subject to competing inputs—a special case of the noise problem. The recipient of spoken machine output is compelled to progress at the rate dictated by the machine; he may not scan a page, taking note only of the odd sentence, nor reread parts easily. Special care must be taken to verify key messages; a mechanical device, unless it fails, will produce a definite signal; a spoken word, even for the most perfect machine and under completely "noise-free" conditions, may be ambiguous. The problem of ambiguity can be alleviated by careful choice of message structure and vocabulary, and such precautions are normally taken, by the military, even for man–man communication using speech. Thus we may summarize the *disadvantages* of a speech interface:

(1) It is rather susceptible to various sorts of environmental noise;
(2) It could prove aggravating, and therefore unusable, if too far short of perfection;
(3) It is transitory, and requires additional complexity of equipment to allow recording or repetition;
(4) Verification of some messages, prior to execution, might be essential;
(5) A speech output may not be scanned easily.

3. An Outline of Speech Production, Perception, and
Some Related Topics

3.1 Introduction

Speech forms the visible tip of the vastly complex iceberg that is language. Although speech is physically an acoustic phenomenon, it is a gross simplification to consider speech production and perception solely in terms of the speech (acoustic) waveform. Both speech production and speech perception depend heavily on all manner of constraints that form part of the total language process. It would be quite outside the scope of this article, however, to do more than outline the bare essentials of speech production and perception, as far as possible at the acoustic level. It is true that it is not possible to avoid, entirely, some of the higher level processes. We may restrict discussion of production to purely physical terms; perception, on the other hand, is essentially subjective and depends on too many nonphysical circumstances. It is generally accepted that the acoustic waveform does not always contain enough information to be unambiguously identifiable on acoustic criteria alone. A good illustration of the kind of difficulty is the fact that a person listening to a language he or she does not understand is appalled, not because the words cannot be understood, but because very little word structure is even apparent. Though the process of perception depends at least in part on the acoustic waveform, either "now" or as experienced in the past, it depends on other factors within the province of the psycholinguist, the neurophysiologist, the physiologist, the anatomist, and the psychologist. We know less about such factors than we should like to. Even the manner in which we use our past experience of the acoustic waveform is subject to uncertainty of a similar kind, and there is but a tenuous link between the physical properties of the acoustic waveform, and the perception of a sound.

The problems of syntax and semantics, and the problem of how these mediate the production and perception of speech involve formidable new kinds of problems, for which it would seem we require a new insight before we even start to tackle them. Sager [126] has briefly reviewed some approaches to the analysis of syntactic structure, and has presented details of one particular approach. Further significant progress in the way of a practical procedure for syntactic analysis has been made by Thorne and his colleagues [148]. Chomsky and Halle have recently published an "interim" report [17] on their work, aimed at the unification of grammar and phonology, on the basis of a transformational model (originated by Chomsky [16]).

Automatic translation has proceeded, not too successfully, at the syntactic level, because our ability to handle the problems at the semantic level is so restricted. Work at the semantic level has tended to be restricted to word association networks ([*44, 75, 76*], for example), and information retrieval—especially question-answering programs [*46, 170*] and "Advice Taker" type programs ([*91*], for example). Borko [*9*] and also Salton [*129, 130*] provide more recent relevant material. Miller [*103*], Cherry [*14*], and Broadbent [*10*] have provided valuable overviews of the communication process. Meetham and Hudson's Encyclopaedia [*102*] provides useful snapshot information on topics in speech and linguistics. The MITRE syntax analyzer [*163, 164*] is important and there is a forthcoming book by Foster [*41*] on automatic syntactic analysis. Simmons *et al.* [*138*] have considered the problems of modeling human understanding and provide further references. Finally references [*4, 38, 55, 98*] cover aspects of language analysis and semantics. All of this must be declared to be beyond the scope of this article.

Even while confining our attention, in this section, to the acoustic level, much that could be said must be left unsaid. Flanagan's book [*37*] provides excellent, detailed coverage of the hard-core of acoustically oriented speech research in the three areas of analysis, synthesis, and perception. Fant [*33*] is concerned with the acoustics of the vocal tract, and his book is a classic, though unfortunately (at time of writing) out of print. Both these books provide excellent bibliographies. The literature relevant to speech research is widely scattered among electrical engineering, psychology, linguistics, speech and hearing research, physiology, neurophysiology, physics, acoustics, audio-engineering, and a variety of specialist books and journals. Good bibliographies are difficult to compile, and rarely complete. A broad spectrum of papers numbering around 500, and covering up to 1965/ 1966, appear in abstracted form [*57*] but the selection is somewhat inconsistent, and is heavily biased towards automatic speech recognition. Stevens' *Handbook of Experimental Psychology* [*142*] is a valuable reference for many of those areas which are of indirect but vital concern to speech research and, in particular, includes papers on "Speech and Language" by Miller, "Basic Correlates of the Auditory Stimulus" by Licklider, "The Perception of Speech" by Licklider and Miller, "The Mechanical Properties of the Ear" by Bekesy and Rosenblith, and the "Psycho-Physiology of Hearing and Deafness" by Hallowell Davis. A large body of spectrographic data on speech sounds appears in Potter *et al.* [*118*], recently reprinted from a 1948 edition.

Speech communication is surely one of the most interdisciplinary subjects imaginable. This fact creates one of the more formidable problems for those wishing to work in this area, for progress in understanding the process of speech communication will depend on the combined use of skills from many disciplines.

3.2 Speech Production

The human vocal apparatus is depicted, diagrammatically, in Fig. 3. The main constituents are the larynx—in which are the vocal folds (also, mistakenly, called "cords"); the tube connecting the larynx to the mouth—comprising the pharynx and the oral cavity; the nasal

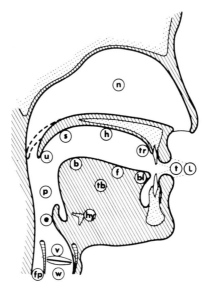

Fig 3. Schematic diagram of the human vocal apparatus: b, back of tongue; bl, blade of tongue; e, epiglottis; f, front of tongue; fp, food passage; h, hard palate; hy, hyoid bone; l, lips; n, nasal cavity; p, pharynx; s, soft palate or velum; t, teeth; tb, tongue body; tr, teeth ridge or alveolar ridge; u, uvula; v, vocal folds (and glottis); w, windpipe.

cavity; the velum—a valve which may open to connect the nasal cavity in parallel with the oral cavity; the teeth; the tongue; and the lips. In the most relaxed articulatory state, and with the velum closed, the larynx, together with the tube to the mouth orifice, may act somewhat like an organ pipe. Forcing air through the glottis (the elongated "slit" between the two vocal folds within the larynx) causes forced vibration of the vocal folds, and provides a harmonic-rich, quasi-periodic source of excitation which sets up standing waves within the vocal tract, as illustrated in Fig. 4. The frequency of these standing waves, or resonances, under these circumstances, depends principally on the length of the tube from the larynx to the lips. This length is about 17 cm for the adult male, and leads to resonances of about 500 Hz, 1500 Hz, 2500 Hz, etc. The energy supplied by the *source* (carried as a modulation of the airflow through the glottal orifice) is concentrated into particular frequency regions by the *filter effect* of the vocal tract, and it is worth considering speech production in terms of the so-called *source-filter* model [*33*]. The Fourier spectrum of a typical glottal volume–velocity waveform (which is, roughly, a train of triangular pulses) falls off with increasing frequency at about 12 dB/octave [*37*]. The behavior of the vocal tract may be regarded as analogous to the behavior of an electrical network in which current represents volume flow, and voltage represents pressure. There is, in fact, a quantitative correspondence: the resonant behavior of the

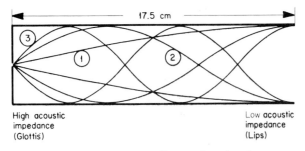

FIG. 4. Standing waves in a uniform tube, closed at one end.

appropriate electrical network, which is based on the assumption that the irregularly shaped vocal tract may be approximated by the electrical equivalent of many short cylindrical sections of varying diameters, parallels that of the vocal tract. To the extent that the model is valid (and there is considerable agreement between model and reality [*33*]) one can investigate the transmission properties of the tract analytically. It is possible to treat the source and filter in terms of network theory to derive expressions representing the output from the vocal tract in terms of the excitation function and the transfer function of the tract [*33, 37*].

The spectral peaks (in a frequency analysis) of the sound radiated from the vocal system are termed *formants*. For most practical purposes formant frequencies may be considered the same as the resonant frequencies of the vocal tract [*33*]. Schroeder [*134*] expresses the distinction between the representation of speech in terms of vocal tract transfer function and excitation function on the one hand, and the representation in terms of spectral envelope and spectral fine structure (of a frequency analysis of the radiated sound) on the other, very clearly.

In the neutral articulation considered above, therefore, the lowest formant, called F1, had a frequency of 500 Hz. The *frequency* of the nth formant is conventionally represented as F_n, thus, for the neutral unstressed vowel under consideration, $F_2 = 1500$ Hz and $F_3 = 2500$ Hz. Such a neutral unstressed vowel occurs in English as the first vowel in "above." The formants higher than F3 are less important for intelligibility of speech, though they affect speech quality, and give clues as to speaker identity. Even F3 is important for only a few sounds, such as the "r" in "three" in general American.

If the vocal tract is constricted at some point, then the resonant properties are modified, and the formant frequencies change, leading to perception, by a listener, of vowels other than the neutral vowel. A very simple view, considering a given formant, is that a constriction at a velocity maximum for that formant, within the tract, decreases the formant frequency, while a constriction at a pressure maximum increases the formant frequency [33]. The constriction may be produced by a tongue "hump" raised at some point anywhere from the front to the back of the oral cavity, the height of rise being anywhere from high (maximum constriction consistent with production of a vowel sound) to low. Vowels are frequently classified in terms of height and place of tongue hump constriction. Figure 5 shows four relatively extreme vowel articulations.

Besides the vowels, produced as a continuous sound with a quasi-periodic source (voicing or phonation) and a relatively unobstructed vocal tract, other sounds may be produced. Some depend on excitation by incoherent noise, produced at a severe constriction in the tract with or without accompanying voicing. These are termed *voiced or unvoiced fricatives* and, for English, include, for example, /v,z,f,s/. Such sounds are characterized by the random source, and the amplitude and frequency of the main spectral peak(s). Strevens [144] has published some data on English fricatives. In the case where noise is produced at the partly closed glottal orifice (instead of forcing the folds into vibration) it is termed *aspiration*. Aspiration is used as the source, in place of voicing, during whispered speech. The output is characterized by the random source, and formant patterning. In "breathy voice" both voicing and aspiration may be present.

Another class of sounds, the stop consonants, result from complete closure of the vocal tract. These sounds may or may not be accompanied by various phenomena. For example, phonation during closure (in voiced stops); the release of overpressure (resulting in transient excitation of the vocal tract); aspiration (voiceless stops in particular); or frication (production of incoherent noise) at the point of closure, as the closure is released. As there is relative silence during stop sounds, they are characterized almost entirely by the transient phenomena

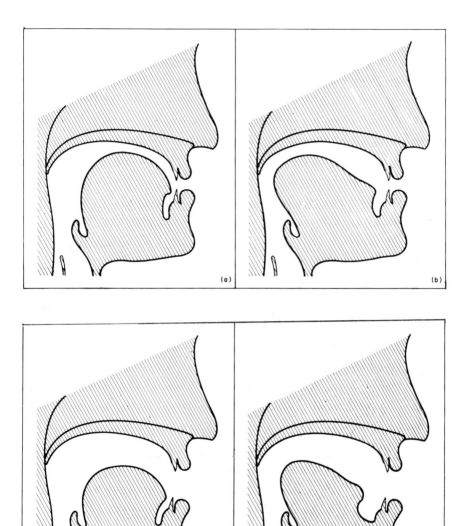

FIG. 5. Four relatively extreme vowel articulations: (a) high front vowel (similar to that in "heed"); (b) high back vowel (similar to that in "who'd"); (c) low front vowel (similar to that in "had"); (d) low back vowel (similar to that in "hard").

that are associated with them, including the rapid changes of formant frequencies preceding and/or following the silent interval. These formant transitions are important acoustic phenomena associated with many consonants, and are more rapid than the changes of formant frequency associated with, say, diphthongs, where a glide from one vowel configuration to another takes place. Voiced stops are distinguished from unvoiced stops, in the main, by the relative timing of phonation and closure. For example, an initial unvoiced stop such as /p/ in "pat" is distinguished from an initial voiced stop such as /b/ in "bat" mainly by the fact that in the latter case voicing starts before, or virtually coincident with the release of closure, whereas in the former case the start of voicing occurs some time after release of the closure, and the first part of the associated formant transitions are superimposed on aspiration noise.

Nasals constitute a further class of speech sounds. These depend on coupling the nasal cavity to the vocal tract by opening the velum. Additional formants appear in the radiated sound, and there is a reduction in the amplitude of the higher frequency components. If the oral cavity is relatively unobstructed, nasalized vowels are produced. If the oral cavity is closed, nasal consonants are produced; for example, in English, /m,n/.

Both stops and nasal consonants are commonly classified according to the place of closure of the vocal tract—in English, velar, alveolar, and bilabial, for example. Other sounds are (similarly) classified according to the place of maximum constriction of the tract. An orthogonal classification is according to *manner* of articulation—" how " as opposed to " where " the sound is articulated—e.g., voiced stop, and nasal.

Affricate sounds are somewhat like the stops, but involve a slower separation of the articulators during release, with a greatly extended period of frication. They are commonly represented by the symbol for the stop sound followed by the symbol for the appropriate fricative. The initial sound in English "chip" is an unvoiced palato-alveolar affricate, represented /tʃ/.

Finally, there are the four sounds /w/ as in "we," /j/ as the first sound in "you," /r/ as in "real," and /l/ as in "let." The sounds are vowel-like, in that they are characterized by formant values and are continuant. However, they are characterized also by the change of formant values, not unlike the diphthongs, together with a degree or type of constriction that places them away from vowels.

3.3 Phonemes

The number of distinguishably different sounds that may be produced by the human vocal apparatus, though not unlimited (due to the built-in constraints of the vocal apparatus) is very large. Nevertheless, these sounds may be grouped, for a given language, into a comparatively small number of categories—phoneme categories. Two sounds are placed within the same phoneme category if they never form the basis of a distinction between two words in the language. In representing the spoken form of a language, various marks and letters may be used to represent the various sounds. Each symbol may represent a phoneme, in which case the transcription is "broad" and the symbols are usually enclosed within virgules (/ . . . /); or the precision of the representation may be greater, so that a "narrow" transcription results, and the symbols are usually enclosed within square brackets. The greater precision of the narrow transcription allows different sounds from within the same phoneme category to be represented differently, and such a transcription is nonphonemic. The different sounds falling in one phoneme category are termed allophones of the phoneme. It is important to realize that the acoustic variation between different allophones of a given phoneme may be very great indeed. For doubters who need to be convinced, the section describing the detailed realization of the /r/ phoneme in R. P. English in Daniel Jones' classic [73] is worth reading. The whole book is an excellent, detailed reference, which will reveal some of the gross simplification involved in the outline of some speech sounds of English given in Section 3.2.

For a known language, since the different conditions under which different allophonic variations of a particular phoneme occur are known, the broad, or phonemic transcription usually suffices to transcribe the spoken utterance into a written equivalent, and native speakers are usually unaware of the extent of the variation.

Phonemes may be regarded as speech segments or units only in a descriptive sense, and considerable training is required to learn to "hear" the sounds of speech. In addition to segmental descriptors of speech such as phonetic value and stress, there are supra-segmental characteristics—those that extend over more than one segment—and these may affect the meaning of an utterance radically. Thus the intonation pattern, or rise and fall of pitch (voicing frequency) must be controlled as a vital part of the speech production process.

3.4 Speech Perception

The natural medium of speech is the acoustic waveform. Speech is first an acoustic phenomenon, acting on the auditory system comprising the pinna (the externally visible part of the ear); the external canal or meatus; the ear drum which vibrates three small bones or ossicles in the middle ear; the cochlea—a coiled chamber divided for almost its entire length into halves by an elastic partition, each half being filled with fluid; and a system of nerves, leading ultimately to the cortex, in particular the auditory cortex.

A schematic diagram of the uncoiled cochlea is shown in Fig. 6. The elastic partition is shown as a single wall, though it actually contains a duct comprising additional components—including the basilar membrane and the important "organ of Corti" in which are found hair cells, the ultimate end organs of hearing. These hair cells generate nerve pulses in response to disturbance of the basilar membrane.

Acoustic vibration is transformed into movement of the perilymph in the cochlea by the ossicles acting upon the oval window. At very low frequencies (below 20 Hz) this movement is a to and fro movement of fluid between the oval and round windows. Higher frequencies act to produce displacement of the basilar membrane so that the point

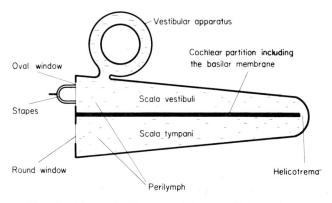

FIG. 6. Schematic diagram of the uncoiled cochlea.

of maximum displacement varies with frequency. The highest frequencies are quickly dispersed, and produce maximum displacement towards the oval window end of the membrane. The lowest frequencies produce the greatest effect towards the helicotrema. Thus the response of the basilar membrane and organ of Corti to incoming sound, in terms of frequency and phase, is rather like a continuum of overlapping bandpass filters of comparatively broad band-width. Frequency resolution is best at the low-frequency end, the "Q" being roughly constant [37]. Signals related to the displacement of the basilar membrane over its entire length are transmitted to the brain, which may be regarded as the seat of perception.

Interest in this system—from the point of view of perception—may take two forms. The classical approach of psychophysics may be used to determine the accuracy or resolution of the system in the discrimination of elementary sounds. On the other hand, the perception of speech, per se, may be investigated, for there is considerable evidence to support the view that the perception of multidimensional, temporally complex speech sounds is of a different character to the naive perception of simple sounds. Speech perception involves learning, and judgments are categorical. A tone frequency may be perceived as lying "somewhere" in between two reference tone frequencies. In the "speech mode" however, a sound will be heard as either this reference sound, or that reference sound. Stevens [140] has tentatively concluded that even vowels, in context, are subject to similar categorical judgments. This is at variance with earlier belief based on experiments with isolated vowels, which had suggested vowels were different from other speech sounds in this respect. There is a large body of knowledge derived from the psychophysical approach, but we know much less about speech perception. Most of the work in this latter category has consisted of identification experiments.

It is possible to generate synthetic speech in a variety of ways (see Section 4.2). Using synthetic speech, it is possible to produce systematic variation in cues believed important for certain speech discrimination judgments, and use these in psychophysical experiments to find out how perception changes. This was the approach adopted by workers at the Haskins Laboratory in New York and their work has given us considerable insight into the nature of speech cues, and experimental methods for investigating speech.

A summary of some of the Haskins' results [85] indicates the importance of the spectral properties of noise produced at constrictions; the importance of the formant transitions in the perception of fricatives, affricates, and stops; and shows the close relation between nasal and stop sounds, which may be classified according to place of articulation and manner (see above, Section 3.2). Lisker and Abramson [92] have shown the importance of relative time of onset of voicing in the perception of stops. Acoustic cues for the perception of /w,j,r,l/ have been investigated [108]. Important work has been carried out at other centers: M.I.T. Research Laboratory of Electronics, for example; and in Fant's Laboratory at the Royal Institute of Technology in Stockholm. Both these places produce quarterly reports of their work, in addition to papers in the literature. To attempt a comprehensive list of published work would be foolish, and do grave injustice to the work which would, of necessity, be omitted. Not all work depends on synthetic stimuli. Analysis of speech is also important. For example, Strevens, [144] data on fricatives has already been mentioned; Wells, at University College, London, has published data on the formants of pure vowels [166]; and Lehiste has published data on acoustical characteristics of selected English consonants [83]. It is, perhaps, worth mentioning a few other centers where the experimental study of speech is a primary concern. Among these are Bell Laboratories, Speech

Communication Research Laboratory (Santa Barbara, California), the Department of Linguistics, at University of California at Los Angeles, the Air Force Cambridge Research Laboratory (Bedford, Massachusetts), the Department of Phonetics and Linguistics of Edinburgh University, the Institute for Perception Research (Soesterberg, Netherlands), and the Department of Phonetics of the University of Bonn (Germany). That work carried out in industry generally tends to be directed more at the solution of particular engineering problems for automatic speech recognition, speech synthesis, or analysis–synthesis speech communication systems (vocoders, see Section 3.5).

It is exceedingly difficult to give an adequate summary in such a complex ongoing field as speech perception. It is perhaps best to leave the subject, while re-emphasizing that further information may be obtained from Flanagan's book [37], from Meetham's Encyclopaedia [102], and the literature. We return to the subject, from a different viewpoint, in Section 5. There is, as yet, no generally accepted theory of speech perception, though there is a growing feeling that it is an active, constructive process—learned during early childhood on the basis of more primitive perceptual ability. Knowledge is still fragmented among a number of disciplines. Many of the unanswered questions in speech perception constitute unsolved problems in automatic speech recognition. The dominating question at the present time seems to be concerned with the means whereby such widely varying stimuli as different allophones rendered by different people can be perceived as "the same sound" while fine distinctions can be drawn in other cases. This may be regarded as the question "How can one adequately characterize phonemes?"—though this implies that phonemes are the "units of speech" in some basic sense. *If* the implication is accepted, then the question arises as to whether phonemes are recognized by segmenting the continuous acoustic waveform or not. Stevens has described the segmentation problem as "the problem that you can't." [See also Section 5.2.2(b).]

The problems of automatic speech recognition (ASR) are considered in Section 5. However, it should be noted that *an ASR machine is an analog of the human perceptual mechanism. Insofar as such a machine models the human process, it can be a test of hypotheses about the human perceptual process for speech.* This author has never seen this given as a reason for ASR research, but believes that it is an important reason, and one which should be given greater recognition.

3.5 Vocoders

Vocoders are important, in the context of this section, for the impetus they have provided to speech research. A vocoder was originally conceived as a device to reduce the amount of information required in the transmission of speech messages over telephone circuits, and later (as radio frequency channels became filled) over radio channels. Vocoders are also valuable as a means of secure transmission of information for, say, military purposes. In information theory terms about 40,000 bits per second are required for transmission of the 300 Hz to 3.4 kHz bandwidth speech signal common in telephone circuits. High fidelity speech would require 100,000 bits per second, or more. A generous estimate of the amount of information contained in speech, based on the frequencies and rates of phoneme production, gives a figure of about 50 bits per second. The huge discrepancy suggests that a more efficient coding of speech would allow very many more conversations to be carried on a given telephone circuit, with a consequent saving in cost. Of course, this degree of reduction (to only 50 bits per second) would convey only the message. Some additional information would be required to transmit speaker-dependent cues. The original VOCODER (derived from VOice CODER), invented by Homer Dudley, was designed to achieve a significant reduction in the amount of information transmitted. Incoming speech was analyzed in terms of the amount of energy present at various frequencies (to derive the spectral envelope) and the pitch or form of excitation (to determine the spectral fine structure). This information could be transmitted over about one tenth the bandwidth required for full speech and then reconstituted at the other end. Such a scheme is shown, diagrammatically as Fig. 7. Because speech was analyzed into different frequency channels (typically fifteen) the device has been described as a "channel vocoder." The chief difficulty with the channel vocoder is in analyzing for "source," that is to say, in deciding whether

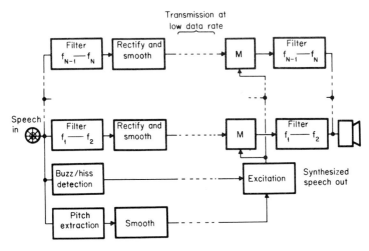

FIG. 7. Block schematic of a channel vocoder.

the source is voiced or not, and, if so, what the pitch frequency is. Schroeder [134] gives an excellent review of vocoders, and of attempts to solve the "pitch extraction" problem. Suffice it to say here that another type of vocoder—the resonance vocoder—was developed on the basis of a *resonance model* of speech. The channel vocoder was based on what may be termed an *acoustic model* of speech [see also Section 4.2.2(b)]; i.e., that speech may be regarded as a time series of spectra having defined shape and fine structure. The resonance model assumes knowledge of the constraints implied in the production process at the level of the vocal tract within the domain of an acoustic theory. Analysis is typically performed, therefore, in terms of the first three formant frequencies, the amplitude and frequency of voicing, the amplitude of aspiration, and the amplitude and frequency of the main incoherent noise spectral peak. The values of these eight parameters may be transmitted over quite a narrow band, and then reconstituted by means of a parametric synthesizer, e.g. [2, 81] [also see below, Section 4.2.2(b)]. Such a synthesizer, constituting the synthesizing half of a resonance (or formant) vocoder, is also commonly called a parametric synthesizer, although in theory synthesizers based on other parameters (e.g. physiological parameters) could be developed. The main problem, apart from "pitch extraction," is "formant tracking." The parametric synthesizer is important because it is simple to control, even compared to a channel synthesizer, and it reflects the speech production process much more directly. However, both are of value in producing talk-back from a machine, as well in vocoder systems.

4. Talk-Back

4.1 Introduction

A machine that "talks back" must be equipped with some equivalent of the human speech production mechanism. The degree of sophistication may be slight, as when, parrot-like, the machine simply regurgitates a previously recorded message, when it is deemed appropriate; or the degree of sophistication may be such as to allow unlimited spoken output, composed—without special methods of any kind—by users, or even by the machine itself, and output by the *vocal* equivalent of a line-printer or graphical display. This section examines and discusses some of the practical methods within this range.

4.2 Methods of Generating Speech by Machine

4.2.1 Recording

The output of a machine which generates speech is, clearly, an appropriate acoustic waveform. The waveform may be derived in a number of ways. The simplest method is to record a magnetic or other physical representation of the actual waveform of a desired utterance, and use this to recreate the acoustic waveform when required. This can be thought of as a *direct representation*. The physical representation need not be continuous, it may be discrete, and consist of amplitude samples (to the required accuracy) taken at a rate of at least twice the highest frequency component present in the waveform. If the samples are digitized, then such a discrete representation of the original analog waveform may be stored in conventional computer memory locations. Assuming 6-bit accuracy of amplitude samples, and a highest frequency of 3.4 kHz (to give telephone quality speech) leads to a storage requirement of about 40 kilobits for each second of speech. High-fidelity speech would require in excess of 100 kilobits of storage for each second of speech. Messages could be retrieved easily and replayed using a standard digital-to-analog converter into an audio-amplifier/loudspeaker system.

Conventional audio-recording techniques, such as magnetic drums, records, audio tape, or wire recorders, may be used to store and replay messages in the continuous direct representation. Such apparatus would constitute special peripheral equipment, and there could be problems of access time, and message synchronization. There is an interesting third alternative. Willshaw and Longuett-Higgins [168] have described a device called the *holophone*, which is analogous to the holograph, but operates in time rather than space. Such a device may store many waveforms, and if part of a stored waveform is played into the device, the continuation of the waveform emerges. It would be possible to start each waveform with a unique sound, the sound being one the computer could generate without special equipment, as a pulse stream perhaps. Messages could then be retrieved simply and precisely when required.

4.2.2 Synthesizing

(a) *General*   The alternative method of producing the required waveform for an utterance involves *synthesizing* the waveform using suitable ingredients and an appropriate recipe. The recipe is the set of rules implied in a particular way of describing, or modeling, speech. The ingredients are the particular values assumed by the units or parameters required for the model, in order to produce the required utterance.

Von Kempelen, the ubiquitous Baron, is generally credited with the first speaking machine of the synthesizer type [161]. It could, with the aid of a human operator, produce (synthesize) all Latin, French, and Italian words, except those containing about five sounds beyond the machine's capability. Like the synthesizer of a resonance vocoder, it simulated the resonance properties and source characteristics of human vocalization, but it did so mechanically. Another machine of

note, which also required a human operator, was Dudley's VODER—
demonstrated at the World's Fair in New York in 1939 [27]. Trained
operators (whose training took a year or more) could play this machine
to produce intelligible speech. Like von Kempelen's machine, it was
a resonance analog of the vocal apparatus, but was electrical rather than
mechanical. Synthesizers have been many and varied. Dunn and
Barney [29] provide a comprehensive review of synthesizers up to
1958. Flanagan [37] is again a most excellent reference. He devotes
some 125 pages to a comprehensive treatment of speech synthesis,
and the related topic of bandwidth reduction, tracing it from its earliest
history. Much of the work on synthesizers has been aimed at improving
speech communication and at attaining a better understanding of
speech, the synthesizer providing a flexible medium for testing hypotheses, and gathering data on the cues for different perceptual effects.
With the advent of computers, which are able to manipulate the
information needed to control synthesizers, they have assumed a
special importance as a means of speech output from machines.

(b) Models and Synthesis   The very simplest model of speech assumes a
series of concatenated units (phonemes?) and attempts to synthesize
new utterances by cutting and splicing the trace from a direct representation of other utterances. This model is too simple, principally because
of the variability of speech and the effect of interaction between neigh-
boring speech sounds, both of which lead to poor matching at the joins,
unnatural effects, conflicting cues, and the like. Nevertheless, useful
results have been obtained using this model in experiments on speech
perception ([47, 51, 54, 124], for example). To account for many
interaction effects between phonemes, segments which are not phonemic
are usually chosen. Wang and Peterson [165] suggest that as many
as 8500 segments may be required. A bandwidth compression scheme
was initiated at RCA Laboratory [110, 111] which identified segments
at the analyzing end, and transmitted only codes. Synthesis was then
achieved by retrieving prerecorded segments from a drum store.
There were problems of timing and in dealing with suprasegmental
features. More recently, a highly successful method of segmental
synthesis has been developed at IBM [26, 30] by Dixon and Maxey,
whose demonstration of synthetic speech was the most impressive
that was heard at the IEEE/AFCRL Boston meeting in 1967. Matching
(of amplitude envelope, formant frequencies, etc.) at segment boundaries is achieved by using a parametric (resonance analog) synthesizer
to produce the segments. The segments themselves are carefully chosen
to have boundaries where interaction effects are least, and they carefully adjust their segments on the basis of repeated listening trials

with naive listeners. This operation is made easier because the required parameter tracks are stored in discrete form in computer memory. They note, in this connection, the impossibility of one operator listening critically to very much synthetic speech, and part of their success undoubtedly stems from recognition of this fact, and the use of relays of fresh naive listeners, to highlight the inadequacies of their intermediate attempts. They estimate 1000 segments to be the basic minimum for highly stylized speech (as compared to about 40 phonemes required for a "synthesis-by-rule" approach, see below). The weakness of the scheme, as with any scheme producing speech by concatenating prerecorded segments—no matter how sophisticated the segments—is an inability to handle suprasegmental features economically. To produce real flexibility in these suprasegmental features would multiply a prerecorded segment inventory by a large number. The alternative is to handle the suprasegmental variation at the time the speech is synthesized, which would require an on-line parametric synthesizer (see below). Speech synthesis by segment assembly, of segments produced synthetically, is a two-tiered synthesis, in which the first stage could be replaced by the one-time use of a highly skilled, obedient, and completely standardized human being, if one existed. This fact is emphasized purely to clarify the distinction from approaches described in the next part of this section. The parametric synthesizer involved for two-tiered synthesis is used, in a sense, merely as a convenience.

Other forms of synthetic speech require a synthesizer which models more general aspects of speech, or speech production, and in this way embodies enough of the constraints or rules of speech (the recipe for synthesis) to simplify the ingredients (units or parameters). Ladefoged [77] has distinguished four approaches to speech synthesis: the use of an acoustic analog, the use of acoustic parameters, the use of a physiological analog, the use of physiological parameters. Each requires control information, suited to the form of the implied model.

The acoustic analog, which is the least restrained, requires the most arbitrary kind of control information. It models the acoustic domain of speech in terms of time–frequency–energy distribution. The input may be thought of as a two-dimensional distribution of points of varying intensity, specifying the amount of energy present at a given frequency and time. The Pattern Playback synthesizer [21], used in so many of the Haskins Laboratory experiments, and the channel vocoder synthesizer are both acoustic analogs, the latter being perhaps towards one extreme (the peak-picking vocoder, a variant of the channel vocoder, is in fact rather close to an acoustic parameter approach [134]). DECIPUS, a machine at University College Department of Phonetics in London, which allows a small number of spectral patterns of varying durations to be played in succession, also comes into this category. Control information for such synthesizers is, typically, derived from some form of continuous spectral analysis. A spectrogram is one such analysis, consisting of a two-dimensional pattern of variable intensity marking on special paper. The marks are made according to the output of an analyzing filter which is scanned over the frequency range of interest while the marking stylus moves along the frequency axis. By wrapping the paper around a drum, and rotating this in synchronism with a repeated recording of the utterance, the time axis is generated. Figure 8 shows a spectrogram of the word "zero."

Pattern Playback accepted its input in almost exactly this form, which allowed simplified spectrograms (embodying systematic variation of selected attributes) to be "played back" for the purposes of their experiments. There is a time-frequency tradeoff in spectrographic analysis. The more accurately the frequency is determined, the more the time structure is blurred, and vice versa. Figure 8 was obtained using an analyzing filter bandwidth of 300 Hz. Reducing the bandwidth would emphasize the harmonic structure at the expense of the spectral envelope. The original papers on the sound spectrograph appear in [117]. A paper by Presti [119] covers recent developments, including increased speed of operation, and the generation of intensity "contours" to clarify the marking.

An interesting, and virtually unexplored method of synthesis is that based on acoustic features, or events. This is a variant of acoustic analog synthesis in which speech is regarded as a mixture of events, the events being perceptually significant data groupings within the acoustic domain. Such an approach would handle transient phenomena as a single event, rather than a time series of changing spectra, and take specific account of a feature like "rapid onset." The approach involved in Schouten et al. [135] is certainly of this kind. Haggard has made some unpublished, related experiments in which, for example, using a parametric resonance analog synthesizer (see below, this section), the acoustic events associated with the initial fricative and stop of an utterance of the word "steel" were mixed with the acoustic events associated with the vowel and final lateral. The word "steel" was still heard (sic).

Synthesis in terms of acoustic parameters implies a model embodying all that is known of the constraints in the acoustic domain, and controlled by parameters directly representing the significant characteristics of the acoustic signal. Such a model is the resonance analog, the synthesizing device in a resonance vocoder system (see Section 3.5). Such a model should only generate noises within the range of a human vocal system, and indeed, this author's experience was that even

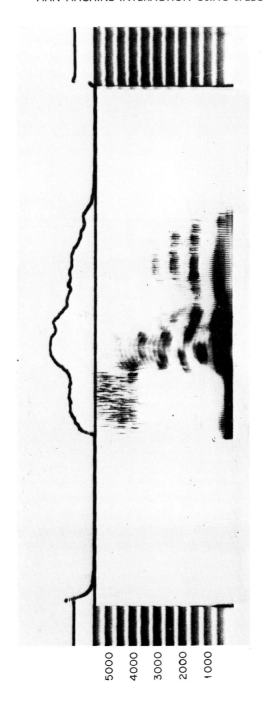

Fig. 8. Spectrogram of the word "zero."

uncontrolled variation of the parameters of one such synthesizer (PAT, see below) produced a very natural "belch." The original parametrically controlled resonance analog was the Parametric Artificial Talker, or PAT [81]. The original version used four parameters, but by 1958 it had six [143] and by 1962, eight [2]. The eight parameters control the frequencies of three cascaded formant filters (F_1, F_2, and F_3), the amplitude and frequency of voicing (A_x and F_x), the amplitude and frequency of frication (A_{H2} and F_{H2}), and the amplitude of aspiration (A_{H1}). An additional nasal branch has been used, though this does not appear in the simplified block diagram of PAT shown in Fig. 9.

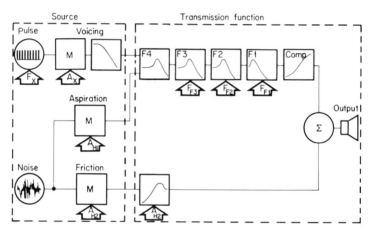

Fig. 9. Block schematic of the Parametric Artificial Talker (PAT).

Parallel connection of the formants is also possible (as in the synthesizer used by Holmes [64]), but such an arrangement requires additional parameters to control the formant amplitudes. There is, of course, a gain in flexibility. The control signals for such synthesizers consist of a small number (eight for PAT) of time-varying parameter values. The information may be extracted from various kinds of analyses of real speech, by hand (for example, the parameters controlling formant frequencies may be traced directly from spectrograms [153]), or automatically (as in the formant vocoder system). Alternatively, the required parameter variations may be calculated according to rules, using phonetic script as the only ingredient. This "speech-by-rule" can be quite intelligible, and is produced without direct reference to any real utterance (for example, [50, 64, 95]). The present limit seems to be not so much the synthesizers, as the rules for driving the synthesizers. With sufficient care, and using natural speech as a model, Holmes has synthesized a sentence which is of very high quality in terms of intelligibility and naturalness [63]. This author has hand-simulated the production of speech by rule (based on the Haskins findings [85, 86, 108], British vowel formant data published by Wells [166], and some departmental "rules-of-thumb" of the Phonetics Department at Edinburgh) and the parameter tracks produced appear as Fig. 10. The resulting speech is reasonably intelligible, but the intonation is poor, no rule having been used for the pitch parameter. Mattingly [95] has worked on problems of suprasegmental rules, and recently Iles [71] has achieved some success with adequate intonation, based on Halliday's theories of intonation for British English [53].

Lawrence's innovation of parametric control of a resonance analog synthesizer was important because it simplified the problem of control.

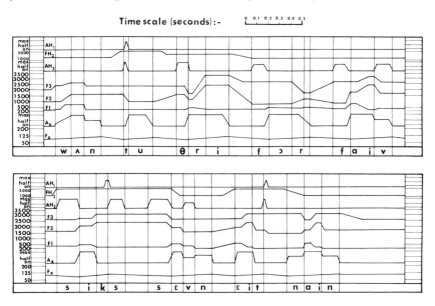

FIG. 10. PAT parameter tracks, generated by rule, for the synthesis of the nine digits "one" to "nine," inclusive.

A few meaningful and simply varying control signals suffice to determine the acoustic signal in such devices. The latest synthesizer of this type, in use at the Haskins Laboratory [96] uses nine parameters and three binary channels. A similar synthesizer (the one used by Dixon and Maxey) at IBM Laboratories, North Carolina, uses seven parameters and two binary channels. OVE III at Fant's laboratory at the Royal Institute of Technology in Stockholm [34, 88]—which includes a nasal resonator and control of the voicing spectrum—and the latest PAT represent developments of earlier versions, circuit and control improvements representing the main changes. All the latest machines or models have further simplified the control problem by allowing for digital control of the parameters, which has also reduced the practical difficulty of drift in the dc amplifiers required when using parameter-track control, and has simplified computer control of their behavior. Figure 11 illustrates the means of controlling PAT, from a PDP-8/I computer, as developed at The University of Calgary. Two modes of operation may be selected. One packs two 6-bit channel samples per computer word, and loads all channels sequentially, at each sample time. The other mode allows an individual channel to be changed, storing the channel address, and one 6-bit channel sample in a computer word.

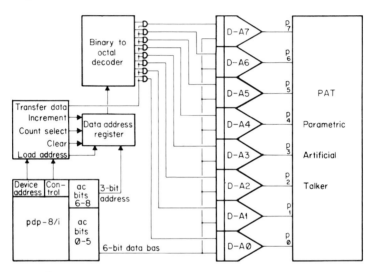

Fig. 11. Block schematic of the means of attaching a PAT to a PDP-8/I computer.

The third approach to synthesis, by means of a physiological analog, involves a controlling apparatus which represents the physiological aspects of vocalization. Such analogs generally take the form of an electrical network consisting of sections, each representing a short cylindrical section of the vocal tract, of variable cross section (see above Section 4.2). DAVO (Dynamic Analog of the Vocal Tract) at the Research Laboratory of Electronics, M.I.T., was one such analog. A nasal branch (DANA) was added later [56]. There are problems with dynamically variable hardware analogs in the form of a tendency to instability [79]. Another problem arises in the control. First, the control signals, though parameteric in form, are arbitrary, and reflect too little of the real constraints of the real vocal tract; second, data on the area functions required is very difficult to obtain, and to date no satisfactory method has been invented for obtaining vocal tract area data, though various methods, including that of filling the mouth cavity with moulding compound, have been tried. Height, in saggittal-section X-ray data, is usefully related to the required data, but there seems little progress of immediate practical importance in this area, partly because of this lack of data, partly because of the difficulties experienced with dynamic analogs, and partly because parametric resonance analog approaches have proved so simple, practical, and economical.

The fourth approach to synthesis would require parameterization of the physiological aspects of vocalization, to give a few slowly varying signals related to the important features of physiological variation. This could be supplied by an articulatory model, requiring parameters such as "position of tongue hump." Even less progress has been made in this area, which has important implications for our understanding of the speech process. Work in the Department of Linguistics at the University of California, Los Angeles, is specifically directed toward obtaining the data needed for the required character-ization of speech in terms of physiological parameters [77, 79] and a more fundamental understanding of the whole speech production process.

4.3 Discussion

Synthesis-by-rule, using a parametric resonance analog synthesizer, seems to offer the best prospect for talk-back from machines, at present. Such an approach, besides being immediately practical, seems to offer clear advantages in terms of the amount of information to be stored (at the most, say 250 bits per second instead of 40,000 to 100,000 bits per second required for direct representation) and in terms of flexibility; by changing the rules one could, perhaps, change the "accent" of the machine. In practice, however, the techniques for handling speech information may be combined in almost any propor-tion. One may store a representation of the low information rate signals required to drive a parametric resonance analog synthesizer giving a bit rate of perhaps 2400 bits per second; or one may "vocode" the original speech, and store the vocoder channel symbols. These symbols, it may be remembered, are typically binary codes which represent the varying energy levels in various frequency bands, to-gether with some additional information about the presence/absence of voicing and pitch. Such vocoding may again reduce the bit rate to about 2400 bits per second, though this figure represents the state-of-the-art on channel vocoders, and the quality is poor. It may be seen that the two methods—recording or synthesizing—are not so far apart as might be imagined. They are, perhaps, closest when an utterance is synthesized by copying the control signals from a real utterance. This is essentially what is done by using a channel vocoder synthesizer in the manner suggested. The control signals for a para-metric synthesizer may also be extracted automatically from real speech as in the resonance vocoder, though, so far, with less success. In general, one should distinguish what is recorded, and what is synthe-sized. Storing vocoder samples is more economical than storing the original waveform, but a synthesizer is required to reconstitute the speech. Of course the synthesizer may be simulated, but this takes a lot of computing power and real-time operation, and becomes imprac-tical if not impossible. Whatever form is used, storage in normal computer memory simplifies the data access problem prior to synthesis.

If direct representation is used, then the recording may be either continuous (which is familiar to most people) or discrete (digital), which requires analog-to-digital conversion during recording, and digital-to-analog conversion during play-back. Digital recording again offers the advantage of being able to store the waveforms in ordinary computer memory from whence they may be retrieved at will and replayed. However, in the departure from straightforward record-ing, it has again been necessary to introduce a rudimentary analysis (A–D conversion) and synthesis (D–A conversion).

Problems of random access to large numbers of stored messages in *analog* form make it seem rather unlikely that straight recording will ever be of any great importance, except in situations where fidelity or other special considerations are paramount, or where the vocabulary is so small that analog drum storage, or something similar, is economic. An attractive, but unexploited, method of storing and replaying direct recordings of isolated words, or short phrases, would use the principle of the Mellotron organ, pulling spring loaded strips of ordinary one-quarter inch magnetic recording tape past replay heads, by means of solenoids. Such a system offers immediate, random access, inter-changeability, ease of expansion, and parallel capability.

At present, IBM offers several versions of a basic drum talk-back system (the 7770 Audio Response Unit [70]) which, for example, deals with forty-eight outgoing lines, and stores one word per drum track; also a channel-vocoder based system (the 7772 ARU [69]), which is able to deal with eight lines per synthesizer, and up to four synthesizers. The quality of this low-bit rate (2400 bits per second) vocoded speech is considerably improved since it is not analyzed in real time, and arbitrary adjustments may be made to improve quality and intelligibility [*11, 12*]. These two audio response units allow spoken messages to be generated by suitably equipped computers. Stock quotations have been generated using such a system in New York. An advantage of talk-back is that an ordinary telephone may be used as a remote enquiry terminal (above). At present the query must be keyed or dialed in, but a recognition input would allow a true speech interface. Speaking clocks often use the drum method of "speaking."

On long-term considerations, speech output by rule synthesis from a phonetic, or similar low bit-rate, storage format seems to offer many advantages. A prime advantage is that the spoken output can be completely unrestricted, at least in a better sense than the sense that a present line-printer output is unrestricted. There would not be "characters" which were unprintable. Indeed, instead of being restricted to one type font, many different accents could be produced, the equivalent of an infinitely variable font, by suitable rule changes. Only a small amount of information need be stored for each message. The output rate would be greater than that for the printed output from a Teletype. Faster output still could be achieved by increasing the output rate, and using normal rate playback later, but it would, of course, involve recording. It is not foreseeable that printed output can be done away with, *indeed one must avoid the suggestion that speech output (or input) is a panacea*, but one can foresee that edited recordings could be "typed up" by a special purpose recognition machine, whose recognition task would be considerably simplified because of the formalized nature of the machine-produced speech. Such a system might offer advantages for some secretarial work.

At present, offline synthesis and online assembly of diphone segments is a good approach, but this author believes it is not sufficiently general and will be displaced by rule synthesis as soon as the techniques are perfected. It is likely, however, that the diphone will replace the phoneme as the basic unit for synthesis by rule, since considerable saving in the required complexity of rules, and hence computing time needed for synthesis, could result.

4.4 Cost

To give an idea of the cost—it is now certain that speech parameters may be synthesized for a parametric resonance analog synthesizer in at least real time, and soon (using new techniques such as diphone-based rules, and faster computers) in better than real time. This will be CPU time. Being rather pessimistic about the size of computer required one might suppose that speech output would cost $600 per hour at present, or about fifteen times the cost of a university lecturer.

Being optimistic, however, such output means are likely to be used in interactive situations, when the computer will only be talking half the time. Furthermore, in a multi-access environment, the computer may be "i/o bound" and the central processing unit (CPU), say, 50% idle. In such a case, the rule synthesis might simply mop-up available CPU time and "cost" nothing. These represent extremes. In these days of parallel processing, it could be worth having a second CPU in such a system, simply for speech synthesis. There is also the cost of the synthesizer hardware—a few hundred dollars.

A final word on the economics with regard to a particular application. With a multi-access system, the old choice of "store-versus-compute" comes up quite clearly. Many common words probably should not be completely resynthesized each time needed, and very common messages may be stored in parametric form for multi-access. For a Computer-Aided Instruction situation, messages may be synthesized when first needed, and then kept until the slowest student has passed the region in the course where the message may be used. Whatever view is taken, speech output is unlikely to be ruled out on economic grounds.

4.5 Conclusion

The practical steps taken towards speech output for machines are thus seen to be many, varied, and effective. At present, voice output is available by the expedient of partial or complete storage of speech originally generated by a human. In general the less the information stored for messages, the more the information required as a supplement, either in terms of hardware which embodies "rules" of some sort, or extra computer program which again embodies "rules." With larger message sets, the reduced storage achieved by more sophisticated approaches becomes increasingly attractive. A particular advantage of *parametric* synthesis is the potential ease and economy in dealing with the intonation and rhythm of speech. For connected speech, this advantage would be an overwhelming one. For many practical purposes in the future, it is likely that speech output will be generated by rule from a diphone representation, using an on-line, parametric resonance analog synthesizer.

5. Speech Recognition

5.1 Introduction

We now turn our attention to recognition. In his report on establishing voice communication with computers, Lea [82] dismisses consideration of the synthesis problem on the grounds that recognition is a more difficult problem. He states that work must concentrate on recognition, since the "lead" time required to get an operational recognizer exceeds very considerably the lead time needed for adequate synthetic output. The previous section draws a picture supporting Lea's view. It is important, however, to define what is meant by an operational recognizer, and to what end is research in recognition most effectively pursued. Some reasons for the greater difficulty of recognition have already been discussed. The basic problem is the involvement in "perception." The higher level processes associated with perception are not so well understood as the acoustics of speech production. Thus the problem is one of representation, or how we specify the task of recognition, and the input to the machine, in such a way that words which are the "same" (defined as the "same" by a panel of listeners who speak the appropriate language) produce sufficiently similar representations within the machine to be judged the same, by the machine; while, at the same time, allowing the machine to discriminate between words that are different. The requirements for the representation prior to *synthesis* are not only better understood, but are also much less severe, because there is no strong requirement for generality. This probably explains the "synthetic" quality of all machine-produced speech to date, as well as explaining the fact that it has been possible at all.

In Flanagan's book [*37*] the topic of Automatic Speech Recognition (ASR) and the related topic of automatic speaker recognition, receive cursory attention—eight pages. This perhaps reflects to some extent the smaller amount of progress, but probably also represents the reputation of such work at the time the book was written. Nevertheless the whole book is a handbook on ASR. However, it cannot and does not treat certain important experiments in neural processing of sensory input data in animals [*42, 65, 84, 97, 167*] which tend to support ideas of relative measures and feature extraction as mechanisms in neural processing; general problems of pattern recognition; the huge subject of generative grammars, and other linguistic topics of importance; nor the equally huge topic of decision theory. It is concerned with speech research *per se*, not language, decision-taking, pattern recognition research, or neurophysiology. It is worth noting that Lindgren [*89*], writing in the year of the book's publication, says the engineer who attempts to build a speech recognizer must "drink deep of the linguistic mysteries." This may be amplified. He must become well versed in such diverse topics as the visual perception of frogs, and the resonant properties of organ pipes; the study of phonetics, and the study of decision strategies; the physiology of the human ear, and problems of generative grammars; the meaning of meaning, and frequency analysis. What is, perhaps, worse—he must continue to be well versed! Lindgren also notes that ". . . the question, 'What is the present state of automatic speech recognition?,' transforms itself into the question, 'What is the present state of speech research?','' which is the subject of Flanagan's book. There is, however, no "neural theory of speech perception" to complement Fant's work on speech production, nor are there any clear divisions by which the field of automatic speech recognition may be partitioned for study. Much of this section, therefore, will rely on particular examples, and citation, rather than any clear signposting of the field. Otten [113] has reviewed some of the problems in automatic speech recognition, from a traditional standpoint. Hyde [68] has also surveyed work on automatic speech recognition up to 1967. There is an excellent and wide-ranging collection of earlier papers relevant to automatic speech recognition available as two volumes used for the University of Michigan summer course in 1963 [156], and Hill [58] describes a hypothetical recognition machine which constitutes a review of the problems. Hyde's report includes a bibliography. Other recent ASR bibliographies include Hill [57] (noted above) and Paulus [114], the latter including a second section covering linguistically oriented material.

5.2 Approaches to Machine Perception of Speech

5.2.1. Waveform Matching

The input to a machine which recognizes speech is most conveniently thought of as an electrical representation of an acoustic waveform. The transformation involves the familiar microphone, and the only word of caution needed is to remark that some microphones do not produce very precise electrical copies of the original. In particular, the carbon microphone (used, for example, in British telephone handsets) produces an electrical waveform which is approximately the time derivative of the original acoustic waveform, and of restricted bandwidth. An "obvious" mechanism, to allow machine response to selected words, would be to match the incoming waveform with a stored set, in either continuous or discrete representation, and assign a response or label to the incoming waveform according to the stored waveform which most nearly resembled it. Although this approach, on the face of it, is straightforward, and of guaranteed effectiveness, it is completely useless in practice because of the variability of speech. Even one speaker, trying hard, cannot reproduce a waveform with sufficient precision, for a given word. A particular waveform version of an utterance is satisfactory for machine-generated speech; it is not nearly general enough for purposes of machine perception. Storing many versions of the waveform for each utterance offers little hope either since, to maintain discrimination between utterances that were different, a match would need to be quite precise to allow "same" judgment, and the machine would spend more time storing new waveforms than in producing responses.

5.2.2. Analysis, Segmentation, and Pattern Recognition

(a) General Analysis is the converse of synthesis, and just like synthesis it assumes some underlying structure for the object being analyzed. The more complete the model in terms of which the analysis is performed, the simpler (for example, in terms of bits of information) the results of the analysis. This fact is entirely analogous to the fact that the more complete our model of speech, the simpler the ingredients required for synthesis—as in synthesis by rule, where only about fifty bits per second suffice to specify intelligible speech. There is one important qualification. Models for speech synthesis need account for nothing beyond the acoustics of speech to make noises that are meaningful to humans. Synthesis need not be concerned with meaning, at least at this stage. On the other hand, a voice responsive machine is inevitably concerned with meaning, in that it must associate a meaningful response with a given meaningful input. Even a phoneme recognizer is responding on the level of meaning, rather than mere identity, for assignment of phonemic identity to speech sounds *must* involve meaning (see above, Section 3.3—this is the underlying problem in the need for generality). Unless a voice-responsive machine is simply to produce a phonetic transcription of the input, then it must produce responses at a higher level of meaning than phonemes—it must *do* something appropriate to the meaning of the input (for example, stop when told to "stop").

(b) Segmentation Speech is a continuous waveform punctuated by pauses (to allow breathing, thinking, or reply) and sprinkled with short gaps, representing some stop sounds (voiced stops may exhibit voicing all through the "gap"). No simple way has yet been devised to place boundaries consistently at all phoneme boundaries (see below, Sitton [139]). The reason is simple—the latter boundaries do not, in general, exist. One part of the rules needed for synthesis-by-rule, on a phonetic basis, is concerned to calculate how to merge individual phonemes smoothly into each other. Boundaries are purely conceptual, and as such can only represent the "midpoint" of the transition from one phoneme to the next. Truby highlighted this fact as long ago as 1958 [151]. The desire to put in segment boundaries where any distinction can only be based on compromise, has led to what is variously called "the segmentation problem"—which, as noted above, Stevens suggests "is the problem that you can't"—or to the "time normalization problem," which arises from an inability to segment, or from attempts to segment which do not succeed. This author believes that it is only *necessary* to segment at the level of meaning, and that up to this level as many possible relevant clues as can be handled should be preserved, relying on the excellence of the model used to ensure economy. A phoneme recognizer is only necessary insofar as phonemes have meaning to some system. It may not be necessary to make a phonetic inventory of an utterance before ascribing meaning at a higher level. To draw an analogy with reading—it is possible to read by identifying letters, and hence deducing words, but an efficient reader recognizes (and relates to meaning) whole words. He even skips large numbers of words. If letters are in doubt—as they might be in a handwritten message—it may be necessary to determine the word, and the letters composing the word, by parallel processing, using context, yet for common words, a squiggle will suffice.

Machines intended to produce unique responses to words must segment into words at some stage, it would seem, at least in the sense of producing a unique output for each. Otten [*113*] distinguishes two varieties of segmentation: direct segmentation, in which an explicit segmentation procedure cuts the continuous speech into segments which are then classified; and indirect segmentation which requires continuous classification of the waveform input, with segmentation partly implicit in the classification, and partly in *post hoc* procedures operating on the (tentative) segments produced. Sitton [*139*] has recently developed a new approach to direct segmentation, at the phonemic level, which looks promising. Much current work on voice responsive machines assumes that segmentation into phonemes, at some stage, is necessary, or desirable, or both. One common argument suggests that only a small alphabet is then required to represent any word in a language. However, to produce a unique response (other than a spelled output) still requires a unique output line for the response, and a further stage of pattern recognition. To make the step to word or phrase recognition, in terms of a unique output for each, from *unsegmented, noisy* phoneme strings is decidedly nontrivial. Newcomb [*105*], Petrick [*115*], Morgan [*104*], Alter [*1*], and Vicens [*158*] are among those who have worked on some of the problems. Work by McElwain and Evens [*100*] on a degarbler of machine-transcribed Morse code is also relevant. Even spelled speech, if it involves transforming phoneme strings directly into correctly spelled words without identifying the words, is less than straightforward, since this assumes that people all speak as they should, in terms of the phoneme strings they utter for a given word—which they do not; or it assumes some rather sophisticated error correction procedure operating on the phoneme strings; and finally, a phoneme-to-spelled-speech conversion is required

In conclusion to the topic of segmentation, it may be said that the rules used in speech synthesis by rule, and implied in the speech production process, effectively scramble the egg that is speech. Segmentation is a procedure to help in unscrambling the egg—if it works. The most widespread strategy to assist in this unscrambling process, adopted by nearly every worker to date, has been to require speakers to speak the words or phrases (meaningful units), which their machines were designed to recognize, in isolation, thus *imposing* cues for direct segmentation at the level of meaning. One strategy which does not seem to have been considered at all is to aim at diphone segmentation akin to that used for synthesis by Dixon and Maxey. Fant has suggested that segmentation should be imposed at places where the time derivative of spectral measures is greatest. Perhaps an approach based on the opposite idea, segmenting only where the rate of spectral change was minimum, would lead to more readily identifiable segments of a "di-phonemic" kind. This author favors indirect segmentation at the word or phrase level for current work on voice-responsive machines. However, in order to recognize any segment, the segment must first be described, and this is another great problem.

(c) *Description and the Problem of Feature Selection*   Description of an object implies an analysis in terms of the important features of the object. The important features of an object may be its function, its composition, or any number of attributes. If two objects differ in terms of an important feature, then presumably the two objects are not the same. Conversely, if two objects are the same, then presumably they do not differ in any important feature. The problem in deciding whether two speech utterances are the same is that acoustical descriptions refer to the composition of the utterance, while they are judged the same on the same functional basis that serves to define phonemes (see Section 3.3). The problem of choosing acoustically derived features to represent what is, at least in part, a functional equivalence leads to what has been called "the feature extraction problem." The possibility of success in solving this problem is presumed, on the basis that every listener must solve it; but, clearly, the analysis must be carried out in terms of a model that includes parts at a higher level than the acoustic level. One is concerned not with machine classification, so much as machine perception; a process by which acoustic evidence is interpreted and evaluated in terms of a total model. Perception seems to be a constructive, organizing process, which requires a period of learning at a level above that of the raw data. This is why people confronted by an utterance in a new language cannot even hear the words, which would at least allow them to ask a bilingual companion "What do —— and —— and —— mean?" There is parallel evidence in visual perception. Persons, blind from birth, given sight by an operation, have been appalled by the confusing, disorganized patches of light and color confronting them, on removal of the bandages, and some return completely to the security of their world of touch and sound by wearing opaque glasses [162]. Current psychological theory of perception assumes an active process, which consists largely of rules—for organizing the data input—learned from experience [145]. This need for an active component in speech perception has led in the past to "the motor theory of speech perception" (for example, [87]). Halle and Stevens [52] and Stevens [141] proposed "analysis-by-synthesis" approaches to automatic speech recognition on this basis. Hill and Wacker [60] reveal a scheme studied in 1963 which used a learning machine as part of the active process. Denes [23] attempted to obtain direct confirmation of the motor theory of speech perception by psychophysical experiments, using a speech distorting system. The control group learned the distorted auditory patterns related to printed text; the experimental group had the same task, but could hear their own voices after being through the same distorting system. Little confirmation of the motor theory was obtained.

An analysis-by-synthesis approach to speech recognition may be necessary, but it does not solve the problem of feature extraction, or for that matter the problem of segmentation/time-normalization. Speech still has to be described in terms of the important features in order to judge whether or not the internally generated construct matches the incoming acoustic stimulus. To try to carry out this matching process in the acoustic domain merely consigns the two major problems to the comparison machine. It seems likely that the constructive process must be directed upward, from acoustic primitives to recognizable pattern descriptions, rather than outward, from abstracted acoustic descriptions to an acoustically matching response. This is where the requirement for information at a higher level than the acoustic level arises, for out of all the pattern groupings that could be learned, only those that are *meaningful* are learned. Sutherland [145] argues the points involved in such a model of perception very cogently, for the visual case. We do not, at present, know enough about the process of speech perception to duplicate the feat. Sutherland's model for visual perception, which is still highly general at present, arose because, as a psychologist obtaining results from experiments on visual perception, he found that information from work on the neurophysiology of vision and on machine procedures for automatic pattern recognition (particularly Clowes [18, 19], but also well exemplified by Guzman [48, 49]) could be combined into a model of visual pattern recognition which offered great explanatory power in terms of the results he obtained. A start on the explanation of speech perception may very well involve a similar interdisciplinary approach, based on the same combination of psychology, machine methods, and neurophysiology. An appreciation of the need for such an explanation, on the part of those attempting machine perception of speech, and an appreciation of the source of relevant information, including related work in the field of visual pattern recognition, is probably essential to real progress in machine descriptions of speech patterns, of which the feature extraction problem is but part.

(d) Models and Analysis   The development within this subsection will follow, as far as possible, the lines of the section on models and synthesis [Section 4.2.2(b)] in an attempt to show the relationships, and illustrate more clearly some of the unexplored areas. The picture is complicated somewhat by the need to account for a time scale which can no longer be chosen arbitrarily, and which varies considerably; by the ingenious variations that have proved possible, in describing components of the models involved, in specific realizations; and by the fact that, whatever model is adopted, there ultimately must be some form of segmentation, which interferes with any attempt at clear distinctions between the approaches, in the former terms. Also physiologically based approaches are almost unrepresented.

The very simplest model of speech, then, assumes a series of concatenated units. In the analysis case these may be interpreted as segments of the waveform which can be identified. Since segmentation at some stage is inevitable, this approach hardly differs from that of waveform matching, except that by trying to match shorter sections, the process should presumably be somewhat easier. An approach which identified phonemes on the basis of autocorrelation analysis of waveform segments would be in this category, but no significant devices appear in the literature. Such an approach would almost certainly require reliable direct segmentation.

Other approaches to analysis attempt to retrieve the ingredients that would need to be used, by some particular model, in producing the unknown utterance. These ingredients may be used as descriptors of segments at particular levels in order to classify them. Almost always, segments compatible with phonemic analysis are used at some stage, although for convenience in computer analysis the raw data may initially consist of shorter segments arising from some fixed sampling scheme. Early approaches to automatic speech recognition worked almost entirely in the domain of the acoustic analog, and the simplest version thereof. The approach is characterized by some form of spectrographic analysis, giving a two-dimensional array of data points representing energy intensity at some time and frequency. Time, frequency, and intensity are usually quantized to have a small number of discrete values—usually two for intensity, energy present or absent. Thus analysis produced a binary pattern which could be matched against stored patterns derived from known words, and a decision made as to which of the stored patterns most nearly resembled the unknown input, hence naming the input. This was the method of Sebesteyen [136], Uhr and Vossler [154, 155], Purton [120]—who actually uses multitap autocorrelation analysis rather than filter analysis, Shearme [137], Balandis [3]—who actually uses a *mechanical* filter system, and Denes and Matthews [24], as well as others. A rather similar kind of analysis may be obtained in terms of zero-crossing interval density or reciprocal zero-crossing interval density, the latter being closely related to frequency analysis [127, 128, 132, 139]. The major difficulties with either analysis lie in the time and frequency variability of speech cues. Time-normalization on a global basis (squashing or stretching the time scale to fit a standard measure) assumes, for example, that a longer utterance has parts that are all longer by the same percentage, which is not true. One simple way around the difficulty was adopted by Dudley and Balashek [28]. They integrated with respect to time for each of ten selected spectral patterns, and based their word decision on matching the ten element "duration-of-occurrence" pattern, for an unknown input, against a master set. The more usual approach adopted has been to "segment" the input in some way, usually into phonemic segments, so that a series of (supposedly significant) spectral patterns, or spectrally based phonetic elements, results.

Segmentation is either indirect—segments beginning when a named pattern is first detected and ending when it is no longer detected—or it is based on significant spectral change, much as suggested by Fant [see Section 5.2.2(b)]. Segmentation is frequently two-stage in computer-based approaches, the short (10 msec) raw data segments due to the sampling procedure being lumped to give the larger segments required. Vicens [158] describes one such scheme of great significance, using three stages, followed by "synchronization" of the input segments detected with the segments of "candidate" recognition possibilities stored in memory. His approach may be considered a "head-on" attack on the related problems of segmentation and time normalization and is the only scheme with a *demonstrated* ability to handle words in connected speech. The work is important for other reasons, as well.

Other examples of the indirect approach include Olson and Belar [*109*], Bezdel [*5*], Fry [*43*], and Denes [*22*]—who also built in specific linguistic knowledge for error correction, and Scarr [*133*]—who incorporates an interesting scheme for amplitude normalization of the input speech. Examples of the direct approach include Gold [*45*]—who included other segmentation clues as well, Ross [*125*]—who included some adaptation, Traum and Torre [*150*], and Sakai and Doshita [*128*]. Needless to say, either approach requires a further stage of recognition, to recognize words. Sakai and Doshita, and Bezdel used mainly zero-crossing measurements in their schemes. This may be significant in building machines entirely from digital components.

At this stage, the different approaches become harder to disentangle. Individual segments, usually phonemic in character, may be described partly in terms of the kind of parameters used by a parametric resonance analog synthesizer, and partly in terms of measures derived from these parameters, or from spectral attributes. Otten [*112*] and Meeker [*101*] both proposed that the parameters in a formant vocoder system should be adequate for recognition, but the results of any such approach are not generally available. Forgie and Forgie approached vowel and fricative recognition on the basis of formant values, fricative spectra, and transient cues, which are related to such parameters, and were quite successful [*39, 40*]. They reported up to 93% correct on vowel recognition, and "equal to humans" on fricative recognition. Frick [*42*] pointed out the advisability of "not putting all the eggs in one basket," stating the M.I.T. Lincoln Laboratory aim at that time as being to define a set of cues which might be individually unreliable but, in combination, could lead to a reliable decision. This really indicates the general feeling for the decade that followed. Such a philosophy clearly leads to combined approaches, which are still in vogue. Here, really, is the nub of the "feature extraction problem," which now centers around the question of which particular blend of which features is best suited to describing individual segments. The not too surprising conclusion, according to Reddy, is that it depends on what particular kind of segment one is trying to classify. Thus in Reddy's scheme [*121*], segments are broadly classified on the basis of intensity and zero-crossing data, and finer discrimination within categories is accomplished on the basis of relevant cues. This seems an important idea, spilling over from research on the problems of search in artificial intelligence (and is the one developed by Vicens). He emphasizes the point that much automatic speech recognition research has been directed at seeking a structure, in terms of which the problems might be formulated, rather than seeking the refutation of a model or hypothesis. He further remarks that lack of adequate means for collecting and interacting with suitable data has held up this aspect of the work.

In 1951 Jakobson, Fant, and Halle published their *Preliminaries to Speech Analysis*. This work, recently reprinted for the eighth time [72], has a continuing importance for those working in fields of speech communication. The idea of distinctive features is based on the idea of "minimal distinctions," a term coined by Daniel Jones [74] to indicate that any lesser distinction (between two sound sequences in a language) would be inadequate to distinguish the sequences clearly. Distinctive features are thus tarred with the same brush as phonemes; they are functionally defined. In *Preliminaries to Speech Analysis* it is suggested that a minimal distinction faces a listener with a two-choice situation between polar values of a given attribute, or presence versus absence of some quality. There may be double, or triple differences between some sound sequences. But the fact that there are interactions between adjacent phonetic elements in speech means that in practice a "minimal distinction" may not be confined to one phoneme. For example English "keel" and "call" are distinguished by more than the distinctions between the medial vowel sounds; for instance, the initial velar stops are markedly different, but the difference is not phonemically significant in English (though it is in some languages). However, distinctive features form a ready-made set of binary descriptors for phonemes, which fact has had practical and psychological effects on those working towards machine recognition.

In their book, Jakobson, Fant and Halle describe the acoustic and articulatory correlates of their distinctive features, but in qualitative terms. They remark that use of distinctive features for acoustic analysis would make the analysis easier, and supply the most instructive (acoustic) correlates. The search for acoustic correlates is not yet ended, for rather the same reasons that phonemes have resisted description. Daniel Jones' discussion of minimal distinctions in [74] reveals some of the difficulties. Nevertheless, approaches in terms of "distinctive features," whether following the original set, or merely using the concept, but instrumenting features more easily detected by machine, have been made, and the concept has had a systematizing effect. One noteworthy scheme, which follows the original distinctive feature set closely is that of Hughes and Hemdal [67]. Vowel recognition scores of 92% and consonant recognition scores of 59%, giving over-all recognition scores for words comparable with those of listeners, are reported for a single speaker. Their results indicated that hopes of a nonadaptive recognition scheme for more than one speaker are ruled out. An earlier approach, based on the original distinctive features, was that due to Wiren and Stubbs [169].

Work by Bobrow and his colleagues [7, 8] is the only reported truly parametric approach, though using rather different parameters from those required for a resonance analog synthesizer. Various binary features are detected, on the basis of the outputs of a nineteen-channel spectrum analyzer, and these are then treated independently, as binary parameters of individual utterances. For each feature (which at any given time may be "1" or "0") the time dimension resulting from fixed sampling is collapsed, to give a sequence of single 1's and 0's (i.e., 101 rather than 11100011). Each feature sequence present votes for any recognition possibility in which it has appeared, the output comprising the most popular possibility. Two sets of features were used, a linguistically oriented set and an arbitrary set. Both performed comparably, but the latter set degraded more when the parameter patterns for one speaker were tried on another. Single speaker recognition scores of 95% were achieved for single speakers on a fifty-four word vocabulary. The developments reported in the second paper were concerned with the testing of some new features in conjunction with an increased vocabulary size to 109 words. Recognition scores of 91–94% were achieved. This approach is a departure from the conventional approach of segmenting into phonemes, classifying the phonemes on some basis, and then recognizing words on the basis of phoneme strings. However, it throws away a certain amount of information about the relative timing of events.

Vicens' scheme carried out segmentation, primary classification, and detailed matching in terms of six parameters based on the amplitude and zero-crossing rates of the signals derived in three frequency bands related to vowel formant domains. It is thus, in a sense, a parametric approach, but is concerned with *segments as descriptors* (of units of meaning), so is not truly parametric. Recognition performance for isolated words and single speaker (98% on a fifty-four word vocabulary in English, 97% on a seventy word vocabulary in French, and 92% on a 561 word vocabulary in English) and for words embedded in the connected utterances of strings of words in simple command language statements (96% on words, 85% for complete commands) is impressive. He makes a number of important points concerning ASR machines; that the features or parameters used are less important than the subsequent processing used; that accurate phoneme-like classification may be unnecessary in practical applications using a suitably restricted language; and that the techniques of artificial intelligence are important in ASR research. He also points out that Bobrow and his colleagues [7, 8] have an approach which does not extend easily to longer connected utterances in which a division into smaller segments (words or phonemes) is necessary, though this is clearly understood by those authors, who called their machine "LISPER" (LImited SPEech Recognizer). One reason is that information concerning relative timing of feature sequences is not preserved.

Another new approach to the handling of the kind of information derived from binary feature extractors is described by this author in earlier papers [*59, 60*]. The approach is based on the notion of treating the start and end of binary feature occurrences as events. The input may then be described in terms of the occurrence and non-occurrence of various subsequences of these events, which provides a binary pattern output for decision taking. There are means of applying various constraints on what events are allowed, and what events are not allowed in the sub-sequences. The scheme has certain general properties in common with that of Bobrow and his colleagues, but it specifically includes information about relative timing of individual features. In this respect, it perhaps has something in common with the model of speech which regards speech as a mixture of events [see Section 4.2.2(b)]. It assumes the necessity of analyzing speech *explicitly* in terms of both content (events) and order, a distinction noted by Huggins [*66*] as long ago as 1953. The scheme (at time of writing) has had no testing with a reasonable set of features. Experiments on an early prototype hardware version, using a feature set consisting of just the two features "presence of high frequency" and "presence of low frequency," gave recognition scores of 78% correct, 10% reject, and 12% misrecognized, for a sixteen-word vocabulary of special words (chosen with the feature limitations in mind) and twelve unknown speakers [*59*]. In the new machine [*60*] the determination of subsequences is independent of any absolute time scale. As a consequence of the strategy used to achieve this time independence, the machine may be able to say *what* has occurred at some level of analysis, but it may be unable to say at all precisely *when* it occurred, since the irrelevant aspects of absolute time are discarded at an early stage in the processing. This failing it seems to share with the human [*78*]. The detection of subsequences is carried out by a "sequence detector." This is essentially an implementation of a simple grammar-based description machine, and operates in the dimensions of time and auditory primitives in a manner entirely analogous to the way, say, Guzman's figure description language operates in the dimensions of space and visual primitives (see below, Section 5.3). The bit pattern output provides a staticized commentary on the history of the input. By arranging for deactivation of those binary outputs from the sequence detector which lead to a particular decision at some level of meaning (initially words), or which are too long past to be relevant to the current situation, the system is readily extended to dealing with the recognition of successive parts of connected utterances.

Other approaches, each of interest in its own way, can be listed. An exhaustive survey is out of the question. Dersch [25] described a recognizer based on waveform asymmetry, as a measure of voicing, and a crude vowel discriminant. Recognition depended on identification of a voiced segment, which was crudely classified and which could be preceded and/or followed by friction. A recognition rate of 90% for the ten digits is quoted, using both male and female speakers. Scores could be improved with practice. Martin et al. [94] describe a feature-based system using neural logic operating on spectral information. Following recognition of phoneme segments, words are recognized on the basis of particular phoneme sequence occurrences. Teacher et al. [147] describe a system aimed at economy. Segments are classified according to the quantized values of only three parameters—the Single Equivalent Formant (SEF), voicing, and amplitude. The SEF is reported as a unidimensional measure of vowel quality based on the zero-crossing interval under the first peak of the waveform segment in a pitch-synchronous analysis. This is similar to work by Scarr [132]. Tillman et al. [149] describe an approach based on features convenient to machine analysis, but linguistically oriented. There are five features, and (due to redundancy) seven possible combinations of these, which lead to segments by indirect segmentation. Recognition is based on the occurrence of sequences of segments. Von Keller [159, 160] reports an approach which involves formant tracking as one of the required operations. Initial segmentation into voiced fricative, unvoiced fricative, plosive, nasal, and vowel-like is achieved on the basis of two spectral slope measures (over-all slope, and slope below 1 kHz), amplitude, rate of change in amplitude, and a nasal indicator. Part of the decision pattern consists of discrete features, referring to the segment pattern (somewhat like Dersch's machine) and part is continuous, based on key values of F1 and F2. Recognition rates around 95% are reported. Velichko and Zagoruyko [157] describe a scheme which recognizes segments on the basis of five frequency band parameters, and uses another form of segment synchronization (cf. Vicens, above) in the decision process. Single-speaker recognition scores of around 95%, for a 203-word vocabulary are reported.

There is one final study that falls in a class almost by itself. Hillix and his colleagues [61, 62] report the use of six nonacoustic measures in a speech recognizer. These measures were designed to reflect physiological descriptions of speech, and used special instrumentation. Single-speaker recognition rates were reported as 97%. Recognition of one speaker, on the basis of data obtained from three others, gave recognition scores of 78–86%. Approaches based on physiological models of any kind are rare. It is difficult to manage the required characterization, or the alternative of direct measurement. Analysis, at the physiological model level has been confined to basic speech research. As Jakobson, Fant, and Halle remark in their book, there is a hierarchy of relevance in speech transmission: perceptual, aural, acoustical, and articulatory. The last level is least relevant to identification of sounds. There may, in fact, be more than one way of operating at the articulatory level to produce the aural or perceptual effect. A good example of this is the perceptual similarity of the effect of lip rounding and pharyngealization.

5.3 Discussion

Richard Fatehchand [35] was able to write that there was, in 1960, no machine capable of dealing with continuous speech. Lindgren [89] five years later was able to say the same. It is not possible to repeat the statement a third time. The scheme developed at Stanford by Vicens [158] based on earlier work by Reddy [121–123] undoubtedly deals with connected speech and has been used for connected utterances forming commands to a robot arm, and to a desk calculator program [158, 99] in both of which individual words had to be recognized in order to "understand" the command. The acoustic task is eased by using tightly defined simple language syntax and easily segmented "key-words," such as "block." Vicens notes one of the major subproblems to be *error recovery* following failure to find a word boundary. A film (*Hear, Here* available from Cine-Chrome Laboratories Inc., 4075 Transport Avenue, Palo Alto, California) shows a speaker telling a computer equipped with an eye and an arm to pick up blocks (the "robot arm" referred to above).

The progress is more in terms of *excellence* than in terms of a radical new approach, though "segment synchronization" is both novel and effective. Perhaps our definitions are progressing. A short utterance is different only in a small degree from the utterance of a long word, and a number of recognizers have been constructed which essentially recognize phoneme strings rather than, or as well as, words. The extended version of AUDREY [28] recognized a small number of continuant phonemes, though the output was in terms of words. Sakai and Doshita's [128] system was intended to accept "conversational" speech using unlimited vocabulary, and designed to type a phonetic representation, thus segmenting into ·phonemes. This machine has subsequently led to a digit recognizer [15]. Vicens dismisses the segmentation controversy saying that, rather than arguing as to whether phonemes, syllables, or words should be chosen, he uses all of these at various stages of the recognition process. The present author suggests that the only *essential* "segmentation" is into a unit of meaning, be it a word, phrase, or (for some purposes) a phoneme.

It is difficult to show evidence of consistent progress in automatic speech recognition comparable to that in automatic speech generation. There is a lack of unity still, 10 years after Fatehchand [35] first noted it. The practical steps are best implied in terms of a "then and now" comparison, and sometimes it is hard to see that the steps have been forward, or even very practical. Real progress has been, and largely still is, confined to fundamental speech studies, which often have no direct, immediate significance to the engineer's goal of building a *viable* ASR machine. McLucas, President of the Mitre Corporation, speaking at the IEEE Systems Science and Cybernetics Dinner, 1967, remarked that an engineer is "driven by a desire to see something work." A friend of mine has an equally apt definition, "an engineer is someone who can do for a quarter what any fool can do for a buck." Machines may or may not work, but few are engineered in the sense that my friend implies they should be. Industrial organizations have become very wary of speech recognition as a profitable exercise. Dreaming of profits, or at least product lines, within a few years, they feel hurt when their investment in research fails to turn up the final answer, and hurriedly stop work, trying to forget it was ever started. When they succeed in forgetting, they start again, and have to start again at the beginning. Surprisingly few workers concern themselves with practical economics on top of all their other problems. Vicens suggests a figure of $50,000 as a goal for a speech input terminal. One machine already mentioned [Sections 5.2.2(d)], that has repeatedly been overlooked in the literature, deserves mention in this connection. DAWID I, built in 1 year—1963—at the University of Bonn [149] represented a significant advance in terms of practicality versus performance. This machine, consisting of a surprisingly small amount of hardware, could recognize twenty Italian words—ten digits and ten commands. Recognition scores are unpublished, it seems, but even a nonspeaker of Italian could achieve a satisfying 90% or more on first acquaintance with the machine.

Probably the most important recent step has been not in ASR, as such, but in the related field of visual pattern recognition, typified by the work of Bloom and Marril [6], Guzman [48, 49], Clowes [18, 19], and Evans [31, 32]. Their contribution to pattern recognition in general terms is important, because it is aimed at the problem of representation; and it is certainly practical because it works. They have approached the problem of describing visual fields, and visual patterns to be recognized, in terms of a common "figure description language." Such a language is able to describe scenes and objects in a general way by identifying primitives (the basic visual features, analogous to the features that may be extracted by neural systems), and expressing relationships between these primitives in a hierarchical manner. Such a hierarchical system allows any desired complexity to be described, as required by the recognition task, in terms of a small set of rules. We have already noted the generative power of rules in speech synthesis. This approach is used for the *visual pattern recognition* (of blocks), in the Stanford Hand–Eye project noted above [*99*], and is now starting to be used in ASR [*59, 60*], as well as in psychological modeling of human pattern recognition processes [*145*].

One final problem has been touched on above, and was strongly underlined by Lindgren in his admirable (though somewhat American) survey of the machine recognition of human language [*89*]. Quoting Sayre [*131*], he refers to a deep obscurity,

> ... an unclarity about the nature of the human behavior we are trying to simulate. We simply do not understand what recognition is. And if we do not understand the behavior we are trying to simulate, we cannot reasonably hold high hopes of being successful in our attempts to simulate it.

Recognition implies some degree of understanding, or at least some specific response related to the identity of the spoken input. If we build a phoneme recognizer, we are building an automatic phonetician, or at the very best, a typist who cannot spell. Phoneticians require a considerable training, in addition to that required to recognize and generate speech. If the machine is to *do* something, as a result of our speaking to it (other than to make a representation of the noises we made), it must, at the very least, recognize words. In practice it will need to recognize phrases, sentences, and ultimately, if Licklider's "chemical thing" is to fulfill its intended function, whole conversations. The latter surely implies real understanding—a process far deeper than mere identification of words or phrases. Understanding is an active process of reconciling objects, ideas, and relations in the real world with the objects, relations, and ideas implied by the denotations of the words and phrases. The difference between what we may term "identification-type recognition" and "understanding-type recognition" is similar to the difference between provability and truth. Understanding and truth both require an appropriate representation of the real world, and the ability to test it against reality. This is the monumental problem we must ultimately face.

5.4 Conclusions

Although it is difficult to show evidence of consistent progress comparable to that in machine-generated speech, a "then and now" comparison reveals that progress has actually occurred. In 1961

Marril [*93*] suggested four main problem areas in "speech recognition": segmentation, choice of measurements, choice of decision procedures, and handling large amounts of data. It is perhaps in the last area that least progress has occurred, despite the upsurge of computer processing, since, in order to automate data handling, one must know precisely what must be done with the data—which is just the whole point of the research; we are not sure. However, recent machines have been more thoroughly tested, perhaps, than their predecessors. Decision procedure problems seem to have lost their sting, perhaps partly because decision theory has advanced in the period, and in any case many schemes use decision procedures tailored to their special conditions that are simple yet effective. Simple voting schemes have been found very useful. Adequate segmentation has been demonstrated, and other schemes have managed to bypass conventional segmentation. This latter looks a promising approach. The variety of features researched is impressive—every scheme having its own set. The performance of linguistically oriented and arbitrary features has been compared, and the difference found to be slight, for single speaker recognition. Perhaps this indicates that we have not yet solved the problem of measurement, reinterpreted as the problem of feature selection. We do, however, have usable means of controlling machines by human voice, though cost reduction will prove an important problem for the immediate future in some approaches.

Perhaps the most significant progress has been not so much a step forward, as a change of direction allowing new attitudes and definitions. Instead of talking about "measurement" and "decision procedures" we now talk about "features" and "problems of representation." It is here, in the area of information handling, and data representation (including the use of interactive systems), that the next major set of problems lies, and progress will have a more *general* significance than in the past. Progress in speech recognition procedures is of importance in its own right, but problems are now being faced which are common to larger areas of computer science.

6. Progress toward Man–Machine Interaction Using Speech at the University of Calgary

6.1 Introduction

There are three projects at The University of Calgary directly related to the development of a man–machine interface using speech. Two of these are ASR research projects, and the third a Computer-Aided Instruction (CAI) project. One ASR project is aimed at two goals: the investigation of basic procedures for use in ASR machines, and the production of a limited objective voice-operated controller [see Section 5.2.2(d)], also Hill [59], Hill and Wacker [60]). The project is presently concerned with developing computer-based methods for speech analysis, using a PDP8/I computer; with the construction of a simple voice-operated controller, ESOTerIC II (*E*xperimental *S*peech *O*perated *Ter*minal for *I*nput to *C*omputers II), which represents a linear and digital microcircuit hardware embodiment of the theoretical developments arising from ESOTerIC I; and with synthesis of speech. The second ASR project is presently concerned with establishing a theoretical basis for, and extending the application of, the phase-dependent asymmetry measure, first used in SHOEBOX as an indication of voicing, and found to have value as a vowel discriminant [20]. Recent results of this work are available as a thesis [13], and represent a theoretical advance which so far has not been put into practice. The third project, Computer-Aided Instruction, under Hallworth, is a practical applications project, with one speech-related aim—the use and development of a practical man–machine interface using speech. Clearly, there is an intimate relationship among the three projects, but this section will naturally emphasize the third.

6.2 The Computer-Assisted Instruction (CAI) System

The requirement for speech output at a CAI terminal raises many problems general to speech output. Such a terminal must be inexpensive; it is only one among perhaps fifty terminals serviced by the same computer; it requires random access to a large number of messages, preferably composed of connected speech; it must work in real time; and it must be as natural as possible. A random access tape recorder was considered, but there are disadvantages associated with such a solution. The message set is limited; the correct tape must be mounted and indexed prior to a lesson; access may be delayed during rewind—an uncontrolled factor in the learning situation; and, although the capital cost could, perhaps, be kept down (but a comparison of the cost of random access slide projectors with standard slide projectors suggests it could not), there is the considerable reliability/maintenance problem common to most electromechanical devices. These disadvantages are multiplied by any increase in the number of terminals. For this reason it has been decided to experiment, from the start, with messages synthesized from information stored within the computer system. Ultimately speech messages will be synthesized entirely by rule, at or just before the time they are needed. Initially, however, speech will be synthesized in a manner similar to that used for the IBM 7772 Audio Response Unit; i.e., using stored control signals and a similar bit rate, but using a parametric resonance analog synthesizer instead of a channel vocoder synthesizer. The synthesizer to be used is the latest PAT, built in linear and digital microcircuits and driven digitally. The means of connecting PAT to the PDP8/I computer has appeared above [Fig. 11, Section 4.2.2(b)]. The use of such a means of speech output overcomes all the disadvantages listed above for the tape recorder approach. A number of important advantages also accrue. The same basic information may be used to generate messages in which the intonation pattern varies. Since the intonation pattern is an essential component of the meaning of an utterance, this advantage is important—quite apart from the improvement in naturalness. Furthermore, the speech is held in digital form like the rest of the CAI program, so that the distribution and exchange of CAI programs between different centers is simplified—cards or digital tapes alone will suffice. Clearly, some national, or better still international, agreement on synthesizer standards is economically important for this advantage to be fully realized. (In this connection, it should be mentioned that there is a user group for the Glace–Holmes resonance analog synthesizer. Details are available from Weiant Wathen-Dunn at the Air Force Cambridge Research Laboratory, Bedford, Massachusetts.)

The present CAI setup at Calgary is a pilot system to be used for research into some unsolved problems of computer-aided education and man–machine interaction, many of which arise from our lack of knowledge concerning the educational process in general; to gain experience and gather data, which will be invaluable when a larger, operational, system is built; to discover problems which have not yet been thought of; and to show what can be done with present techniques. The system consists of a PDP8/I, in time-shared configuration, driving four terminals each having a Teletype keyboard/page-printer and a random access slide projector. Initially, a separate PDP8/I has been set up with a PAT synthesizer for experimental purposes, though others will be incorporated into the main system by the end of this year. Speech may be generated locally (at the computer) and, if required for a remote location, can be transmitted over the telephone lines being used for the data connection, preceded and followed by suitable control characters, for output control. Some work on speech by rule has already been carried out [see above, Section 4.2.2(b), especially Fig. 10]. Development of software for the new work is now in progress.

Speech *input* for the CAI system is already in pilot operation on the separate PDP8/I using an ESOTerIC II. In later work, an ESOTerIC II device may be placed at each terminal (whether remote, or local) and unique eight-bit codes assigned to each recognition possibility, allowing voice input data to be handled in the same way as Teletype response codes. Many problems are anticipated, but it is expected that the existence of an established teaching situation, with adequate feedback, will allow problems such as imperfect recognition, lack of understanding on the part of the student concerning the operation of the system, and other similar problems, to be overcome. Some pilot experiments on recognizing unknown speakers, and training non-technical staff [59] have been encouraging. With a CAI system, and a true speech interface, more extensive and more representative experiments may be carried out. The only unexpected result of this work would be no unexpected results! Figure 12 shows ESOTerIC I being

FIG. 12. Voice control of the PDP-7 text editor program.

used for voice control of a text-editing program based on the PDP7 and graphic display at Cambridge University Mathematical Laboratory. The figure shows a hand-held microphone, though a boom microphone was normally used. The component cost of ESOTerIC II is of the order of $1000, but this could be reduced for nonresearch applications.

6.3 Conclusion

The foregoing remarks briefly recount the practical steps that are being taken towards a man–machine interface using speech, at The University of Calgary. Work on both recognition and synthesis of speech is being carried out. The results of this work are being applied, in a practical way, to a man–machine interface using speech for CAI work. In a CAI situation the shortcomings of such an interface, using our present speech capability, are most likely to be overcome. The human factors experience gained in this early system should prove invaluable in designing applications which place a greater demand on the speech interface.

7. Applications

7.1 Introduction

The previous section has preempted one major potential application of the man–machine interface using speech—namely in automated audiovisual display systems. Such systems themselves may be applied in a wide variety of ways [107]: to teaching, to mass screening (census taking and medical screening for example), to interaction with computers, to Air Traffic Control (controllers must speak to aircraft, and such an interface would allow this speech to be a means of data entry to the ATC computer, reducing the over-all load on the controllers), and to therapy or prosthesis for various forms of disability or injury. This is a good reason for conducting research in the context of such a system. Some general advantages and disadvantages of a speech interface have been covered in Section 2 of this article. Some particular advantages of using a speech interface in such audiovisual systems have been covered elsewhere [59] and also, in the context of a CAI situation, in the preceding section.

7.2 Specific Examples

7.2.1 Speech Input

A "speech-recognizer," or "voice-operated controller" is a more or less sophisticated version of an acoustically operated controller. Probably the first application of acoustical control was to switch a tape recorder on or off, depending on whether there was a signal to record or not. The difference between "something" and "nothing" was decided on the plausible basis of short-term mean power. Some forms of burglar alarm are operated by a similar device, on the grounds that noises in an empty factory, at night, need investigating. These are not really different from Paget's toy dog Rex, which responded to its name, because a sensor "recognized" the high frequency at the end of "Rex."

Two acoustically controlled telephone answering machines in the

United Kingdom use the human voice as a signal source. One, by Shipton Automation, is called the Telstor, and responds in much the same way as the noise switches mentioned above, except that a counter is incorporated. The correct code (three separate counts) allows messages to be replayed, and then erased, from a remote telephone. A device by Robophone is similar, but measures the duration of "silence" (as the operator counts under his/her breath) to obtain different numbers for use in the code. Some telephone-answering machines may be remotely operated by tones, but (in the absence of a TOUCH-TONE® phone) the operator, out on his travels, must carry a tone generator. Machines which allow the voice to be used offer a clear advantage for the present.

In *Electronics* for May 15, 1967, Dorset Industries Inc., of Norman, Oklahoma, were reported to be offering a teaching machine for $350, together with an optional voice input costing a further $100, which allows the eight inputs to be stimulated by eight different sounds. Chiba [15] reports that the phonetic typewriter, developed at the Nippon Electric Company, has led to a digit recognizer, which is now being used for voice dialing on a small telephone exchange. SHOEBOX (Dersch's machine [25]), when demonstrated at the New York World's Fair in 1962, was used to operate a calculating machine. Dersch, who left IBM—after working on SHOEBOX—to form his own company, offered a voice-sensitive switch, which would respond to a human voice, even when the voice was 95 dB below the ambient noise. A device called VOTEM (Newell [106]) at Standard Telecommunication Laboratories, in the United Kingdom, is a Morse-code operated typewriter which uses the human voice as a signal source. Use of Morse-code makes the device cheap and universal. Though somewhat slow (about two-thirds the speed of a good typist) it could allow a seriously disabled person to type personal correspondence and perhaps even do useful work—both of these activities contributing immeasurably to the person's confidence and self-respect. Vicens applied his recognition procedure to providing input for the robot arm, and a desk calculator. Lavoie [80] refers to an RCA voice operated "stockbroker" which learns 28 command words for each new speaker, and then allows him to use the words to carry out stock transactions by phone. Another RCA device for recognizing the digits of zip codes has just completed field trials in Philadelphia, in a parcel-sorting task.

These are some of the ways in which voice-operated acoustical controllers have been *applied*. It will be noted that the earliest devices are analogous to the first light-operated devices, which responded to the presence–absence of light; such devices subsequently progressed to counting and then coding. The analogous progression may now be observed in the development of sound-operated devices designed for speech. The analogy is incomplete because there is no general requirement to recognize machine-generated speech (the acoustic equivalent to printed words). Instead, sound-operated devices are in the process of jumping a logical gap, by going straight to the recognition of humanly generated symbols, without the benefit of experience gained on machines designed to recognize machine-produced symbols (synthetic speech). This phase of recognizing humanly generated symbols has only just begun for light-operated devices, even though they must have enjoyed a greater investment than ASR devices because of their success in the previous phase.

7.2.2 Speech Output

On the synthesis side, some devices have found more general application. The two IBM audio response units have been mentioned above. Speaking clocks, which may be dialed from any telephone and then generate a message such as, "At the next tone the time will be exactly three twenty-seven . . . (peep)," have been widely used for years; the principle is exactly the same as that of the IBM 7770 ARU—namely the assemblage of prerecorded words. There was, on the London (United Kingdom) underground railway, a recorded message warning passengers to "Stand clear of the doors, please." An unconfirmed report concerns a device in the United States of America which incorporates a voice output, printed display, and a typewriter. Apparently this device has been used with some success in helping autistic children to communicate at a very simple level. It produces a story, one letter at a time, chanting each letter until the appropriate key on the typewriter is struck.

7.3 Discussion

As we look to the immediate future, the requirement for *communication*, and hence two-way operation, looms large. The doors in the underground system still closed, even if a passenger shrieked. Mechanical sensors were used to avoid the obvious consequences of such lack of feeling, and perhaps the equivalent will always be necessary, as a fail-safe mechanism for most devices. In the future, however, in many applications of either synthesis, or recognition of speech, the use of either one will require the other. Anyone who has tried using a TOUCH-TONE ® phone to pass information will appreciate the difficulty of remembering to what point, in a desired sequence, keypressing has progressed; the uncertainty about what question elicited the present answer; and the annoyance of being able to hear the answers in a replay of a recorded transaction, without being able to identify the sounds generated at the TOUCH-TONE® end. No doubt these problems diminish with practice.

One interesting class of applications for speech-operated and speech-generating devices is in prosthetic aid for various disabilities. Speech output would be of obvious advantage to a blind person, whether as a computer-programmer, or as a "listener" in the audio-output section of a computerized library of the future. Speech recognizers are highly relevant to the deaf. It is a sad comment on the profit motive that so little of real value to the deaf has been produced in hardware, though instruments used in ASR research would at least be better than the present aids used in teaching the profoundly deaf. Two devices have been produced with the deaf in mind in Fant's laboratory in Stockholm. One gives a simple display of the varying energy spectrum of speech and may be "frozen" at any moment to give a section for study. The other gives a measure of pitch variation—of particular importance to deaf persons whose poor intonation conveys an impression of stupidity to uninformed listeners. These are indirect applications of ASR work. Cues, found important in recognition by machine, may be useful information for deaf persons learning to speak. As a more direct application, consider the utility of a device which responded to a deaf person's name. It could respond slightly to any sudden change in the acoustic environment, and much more to a sound like the deaf person's name—and perhaps to a motor horn as well. Coupled to a tactile communicator, worn round the waist like a belt, and designed to give indication of the direction of the sound, it would prove an immense boon to the deaf. Acoustic controls for severely disabled persons have already been mentioned, in connection with VOTEM (Section 7.2.1).

It is possible to summarize all applications of a man–machine interface using speech as being to "make machines more intelligent." An acceptable definition of intelligence is "the ability to handle information effectively." This implies goals, in order that effectiveness may be gauged in terms of goal achievement. It also implies gathering, sorting, selecting, structuring/storing (representing), and communicating information—these comprise "handling." This definition admits that any system having a goal, and the ability to handle information in a manner suitable for attaining that goal, is intelligent. Presumably handling more information to achieve more goals, or handling less information to achieve the same goal(s), or handling the same information to achieve more goals, would each count as demonstrating greater intelligence. However, a machine which was able to communicate more effectively would, by the above definition, be more intelligent. The main purpose of a man–machine interface using speech is to allow more effective communication. In thus making machines more intelligent, we are making them more useful. Perhaps, in the process, we shall make them more like ourselves, despite the opposing view expressed by Pierce [116].

7.4 Conclusions

It seems that a small number of applications of limited usefulness have been tried with ASR equipment; applications of machine-generated speech have been wider and more successful, but such output means are not yet in general use. One significant reason for the lack of speech interface hardware is probably lack of demand, due to lack of awareness. A kind of "credibility gap" which causes potential users to dismiss the subject as too fanciful. The idea that machines have switches, knobs, keys, and means for printing or even plotting is generally accepted; the idea that machines might draw, or recognize pictures is gaining credence; the idea that machines might speak and obey commands is sufficiently new that it is seldom considered as a practical proposition. We are now in a position to experiment with prototype speech interfaces, say for CAI work, and attack the credibility gap.

8. Concluding Remarks

An attempt has been made to keep the various sections of this report fairly self-contained, and there is little that can be added by way of further specific conclusions. An optimistic picture has been painted, based upon a total range of progress, in areas relevant to the subject of the report, that is impressive. There remain serious obstacles to the kind of speech interface that would really facilitate communication between men and machines. Providing computers with adequate means of speech production and perception is a small part of the total problem. This is well illustrated by considering the situation where all computers were provided with speech output and with expert, incredibly fast typists, who could enter a perfect written copy of any utterance as it was made. There are still the problems of natural language processing, of techniques for computer-aided learning, and of information retrieval, to mention only the first that spring to mind. The really serious problems are now problems of information handling, even though we have not completely solved the problems at the acoustic level. In fact a solution of some of the problems at the higher levels is almost certainly essential to what might appear, superficially, as acoustic recognition of speech, since speech perception ultimately involves the whole of language. However, we must use the equipment we now have, for in some restricted situations we may already reap benefits. At the same time we shall gain an appreciation of the real restrictions on present techniques, and be able to formulate more pertinent questions on which to base further research.

ACKNOWLEDGMENTS

The author can only claim the errors and omissions as his own. Many people, knowingly and unknowingly, have contributed ideas and information, by publication and discussion, too many for individual recognition, but the author is deeply grateful to those concerned. The author wishes to thank especially Professor Abercrombie and the members of the Edinburgh University Phonetics Department (as it was then) for providing the facilities and experience necessary to the author's work on synthesis. The author also gratefully acknowledges the financial support given to his research by the National Research Council of Canada.

REFERENCES

1. Alter, R., Utilization of contextual constraints in automatic speech recognition. *IEEE Trans. Audio Electroacoustics* **AU-16**, 6–11 (1968).
2. Antony, J., and Lawrence, W., A resonance analogue speech synthesiser, *Proc. 4th Int. Cong. Acoust., Copenhagen, 1962*, G.43.
3. Balandis, L. S., Sceptron: a sound operated fiber-optic "Brain cell." *Electron. World* **69** (1963).
4. Bar-Hillel, Y., *Language and Information: Selecteds Esays and their Theory and Application*. Addison-Wesley, Reading, Massachusetts, 1964.
5. Bezdel, W., and Bridle, J. S., Speech recognition using zero-crossing measurements and sequence information. *Proc. Inst. Elect. Eng.* **116**, 617–624 (1969).
6. Bloom, B. H., and Marril, T., The Cyclops-2 system. Tech. Rept. TR65-RD1, Computer Corp. of Amer., Cambridge, Massachusetts, 1965.
7. Bobrow, D. G., and Klatt, D. H., A limited speech recognition system. *Proc. AFIPS Fall Joint Computer Conf., San Francisco, 1968* **33**, Part 1, pp. 305–318. Thompson, Washington, D.C., 1968.
8. Bobrow, D. G., Hartley, A. K., and Klatt, D. H., A limited speech recognition system II. Bolt, Beranek, & Newman Rept. No. 1819, Job No. 11254, under Contract NAS 12-138, Cambridge, Massachusetts, 1969.
9. Borko, H. (ed.), *Automated Language Processing—The State of the Art*. Wiley, New York, 1967.
10. Broadbent, D. E., *Perception and Communication*. Pergamon, Oxford, 1958; also Scientific Book Guild (Beaverbrook Newspapers), London, 1961.
11. Buron, R. H., Generation of a 1000-word vocabulary for a pulse-excited vocoder operating as an audio response unit. *IEEE Trans. Audio Electroacoustics* **AU-16**, 21–25 (1968).
12. Buron, R. H., Audio response unit connected to a digital computer. Div. I.I/1. *Nat. Ass. Telecommun. Engrs. Conf., Madrid, 1965*, pp. 1–13.
13. Bryden, B., Speech recognition by machine. M.Sc. Thesis, Dept. of Electrical Engineering, The Univ. of Calgary, Alberta, Canada, February, 1970.

14. Cherry, C., *On Human Communication*. M.I.T. Press, Cambridge, Massachusetts, and Wiley (Studies in Communication Series), New York, 1957; also Science Edition, Inc., New York, 1961.

15. Chiba, S., Machines that "hear" the spoken word. *New Scientist* **37** (552), 706–708 (1967).

16. Chomsky, N., *Syntactic Structures*. Mouton, 's-Gravenhage, The Netherlands, seventh printing 1968.

17. Chomsky, N., and Halle, M., *The Sound Pattern of English*. Harper, New York, 1968.

18. Clowes, M. B., Pictorial relationships—a syntactic approach, in *Machine Intelligence* (B. Meltzer and D. Michie, eds.), Vol. 4, pp. 361–383. Edinburgh Univ. Press, Edinburgh, Scotland, 1969.

19. Clowes, M. B., Perception, picture processing and computers, in *Machine Intelligence* (N. L. Collins and D. Michie, eds.), Vol. 1, pp. 181–197, Oliver & Boyd, Edinburgh, Scotland, 1967.

20. Comer, D., The use of waveform asymmetry to identify voiced sounds. *IEEE Trans. Audio Electroacoustics* **AU-16**, 500–506 (1968).

21. Cooper, F. S., Liberman, A. M., and Borst, J. M., The interconversion of audible and visible patterns as a basis for research in the perception of speech. *Proc. Nat. Acad. Sci. U.S.A.* **37**, 318–325 (1951).

22. Denes, P., The design and operation of the mechanical speech recogniser at University College, London. *J. Brit. Inst. Radio Eng.* **19**, 219–234 (1959).

23. Denes, P., On the motor theory of speech perception, in *Proc. Int. Cong. Phon. Sci.* (E. Zwirner and W. Bettige, eds.), pp. 252–258. S. Karger, Basle, Switzerland, 1965.

24. Denes, P., and Mathews, M. V., Spoken digit recognition using time frequency pattern matching. *J. Acoust. Soc. Amer.* **32**, 1450–1455 (1960).

25. Dersch, W. C., Decision logic for speech recognition. IBM Tech. Rept. 16.01.106.018, San José, California 1961.

26. Dixon, N. R., and Maxey, H. D., Terminal analog synthesis of continuous speech using the diphone method of segment assembly. *IEEE Trans. Audio Electroacoustics* **AU-16**, 40–50 (1968).

27. Dudley, H., Riesz, R. R., and Watkins, S. A., A synthetic speaker. *J. Franklin Inst.* **227**, 739–764 (1939).

28. Dudley, H., and Balashek, S., Automatic recognition of phonetic patterns in speech. *J. Acoust. Soc. Amer.* **30**, 721–732 (1958).

29. Dunn, H. K., and Barney, H. L., Artificial speech in phonetics and communications. *J. Speech Hearing Res.* **1**, 23–39 (1958).

30. Estes, S. E., Kerby, H. R., Maxey, H. D., and Walker, R. M., Speech synthesis from stored data. *IBM J. Res. Dev.* **8**, 2–12 (1964).

31. Evans, T. G., A heuristic program to solve geometric analogy problems. *Proc. AFIPS Spring Joint Computer Conf., 1964* **25**, 327–338. Spartan, New York, 1964.

32. Evans, T. G., A grammar based pattern analysing procedure. *Proc. IFIP Conf., Edinburgh, Scotland, 1968*. Preprints H152-H157, August (1968).

33. Fant, C. G. M., *Acoustic Theory of Speech Production*. Mouton, 's-Gravenhage, The Netherlands, 1960.

34. Fant, C. G. M., Martony, J., and Rengman, U., OVE II synthesis strategy. *Proc. Stockholm Speech Commun. Seminar* **II**, F5. Speech Transmission Lab., Royal Inst. Technol., Stockholm, 1962.

35. Fatehchand, R., Machine recognition of spoken words. *Advan. Computers* **1**, 193–229 (1960).

36. Feigenbaum, E. A., Artificial Intelligence: themes in the second decade. Stanford Univ. Artificial Intelligence Res. Proj. Mem. No. 67 (1968).

37. Flanagan, J. L., *Speech Analysis, Synthesis, and Perception.* Springer, New York, 1965.

38. Fodor, J. A., and Katz, J. J., *Structure of Language: Readings in the Philosophy of Language.* Prentice-Hall, Englewood Cliffs, New Jersey, 1964.

39. Forgie, J. W., and Forgie, C. D., A computer program for recognising the English fricative consonants /f/ & /θ/, *Proc. 4th Int. Cong. Acoust., Copenhagen, 1962.*

40. Forgie, J. W., and Forgie, C. D., Results obtained from a vowel recognition computer program. *J. Acoust. Soc. Amer.* **31**, 1480–1489 (1959).

41. Foster, J. M., *Automatic Syntactic Analysis.* Macdonald, London, 1970.

42. Frick, F. C., Research on speech recognition at Lincoln Laboratory, *Proc. Seminar on Speech Compression and Coding.* PB 146624, Air Force Cambridge, Res. Lab., LG Hanscom Field, Bedford, Massachusetts, 1959.

43. Fry, D. B., Theoretical aspects of mechanical speech recognition. *J. Brit. Inst. Radio Eng.* **19**, 211–218 (1959).

44. Giuliano, V. E., Analog networks for word association. *IEEE Trans. Mil. Electron.* **MIL-7**, 221–234 (1963).

45. Gold, B., Word recognition computer program. Tech. Rept. 452, Mass. Inst. Technol., Cambridge, Massachusetts, 1966.

46. Green, B. F., Wolf, A. K., Chomsky, C., and Laughery, K., BASEBALL: an automatic question answerer. *Proc. Western Joint Computer Conf.* **19**, 219–224 (1961); also in *Computers and Thought* (E. A. Feigenbaum and J. Feldman, eds.), pp. 207–216. McGraw-Hill, New York, 1963.

47. Guelke, R. W., and Smith, E. D., Distribution of information in stop consonants. *Proc. Inst. Elec. Eng.* **110**, 680–689 (1963).

48. Guzman, A., Scene analysis using the concept of model. Sci. Rept. No. 1, Computer Corp. of Amer. Contract (to AFCRL) AF 19 (628)–5914, 1967.

49. Guzman, A., Decomposition of a visual scene into three-dimensional bodies. *Proc. 1968 AFIPS Fall Joint Computer Conf.* **33**, Part 1, pp. 291–304. Thompson, Washington, D.C., 1968.

50. Haggard, M. P., and Mattingly, I. G., A simple program for synthesising British English. *IEEE Trans. Audio Electroacoustics* **AU-16**, 95–99 (1968).

51. Halle, M., Hughes, G. W., and Radley, J-P. A., Acoustic properties of stop consonants. *J. Acoust. Soc. Amer.* **29**, 107–116 (1957).

52. Halle, M., Stevens, K., Speech recognition: A model and a program for research. *IRE Trans. Inform. Theory* **IT-8**, 155–159 (1962).

53. Halliday, M. A. K., *Intonation and Grammar in British English.* Mouton, 's-Gravenhage, The Netherlands, 1967.

54. Harris, K. S., Cues for the discrimination of American English fricatives in spoken syllables. *Language Speech* **1**, Part 1, 1–6 (1958).

55. Hayes, D. G. (ed.), *Readings in Automatic Language Parsing.* American Elsevier, New York, 1966.

56. Hecker, M. H. L., Studies of nasal consonants with an articulatory speech synthesizer. *J. Acoust. Soc. Amer.* **34**, 179–188 (1962).

57. Hill, D. R., An abstracted bibliography of some papers relative to automatic speech recognition. Standard Telecommun. Labs., Harlow, England. Tech. Memo. 522, 1967.

58. Hill, D. R., Automatic speech recognition—a problem for machine intelligence, in *Machine Intelligence* (N. L. Collins and D. Michie, eds.), Vol. 1, pp. 199–266. Oliver & Boyd, Edinburgh, 1967.

59. Hill, D. R., An ESOTerIC approach to some problems in automatic speech recognition. *Int. J. Man–Machine Studies* **1**, 101–121 (1969).

60. Hill, D. R., and Wacker, E. B., ESOTerIC II—An approach to practical voice control: progress report 69, in *Machine Intelligence* (B. Meltzer and D. Michie, eds.), Vol. 5, pp. 463–493. Edinburgh Univ. Press, Edinburgh, 1969.

61. Hillix, W. A., Use of two non-acoustic measures in computer recognition of spoken digits. *J. Acoust. Soc. Amer.* **35**, 1978–1984 (1963).

62. Hillix, W. A., Fry, M. N., and Hershman, R. L. Computer recognition of spoken digits based on six non-acoustic measures. *J. Acoust. Soc. Amer.* **38**, 790–797 (1965).

63. Holmes, J. N., Research on speech synthesis carried out during a visit to the Royal Institute of Technology Stockholm November 1960 to March 1961. Post Office Eng. Dept., England, Rept. No. 20739 (1961).

64. Holmes, J. N., Mattingly, I. G., and Shearme, J. N., Speech synthesis by rule. *Language Speech* **7**, Part 3, 127–143 (1965).

65. Hubel, D. H., and Wiesel, T. N., Receptive fields, binocular interaction, and functional architecture in the cat's visual cortex. *J. Physiol.* **160**, 106–154 (1962).

66. Huggins, W., A theory of hearing, in *Communication Theory* (W. Jackson, ed.), pp. 363–380. Butterworth's, London, 1953.

67. Hughes, G. W., and Hemdal, J. F., Speech analysis. Purdue Research Foundation, Lafayette, Indiana, Tech. Rept. TR-EE65-9, 1965.

68. Hyde, S. R., Automatic speech recognition literature survey and discussion. Res. Dept. Rept. No. 45, Post Office Res. Dept., Dollis Hill, London, 1968.

69. IBM, IBM 7772 Audio Response Unit. Form A27-2711-0 IBM Systems Library.

70. IBM, IBM 7770 Audio Response Unit Models 1, 2, and 3. Form A27-2712-0 IBM Systems Library.

71. Iles, L. A., Speech synthesis by rule. Use of Holmes, Mattingly, and Shearme rules on PAT. *Work in Prog. No. 3* (E. Uldall and A. Kemp, eds.), pp. 23–25. Dept. of Phonetics and Linguistics, Univ. of Edinburgh, Scotland, 1969.

72. Jakobson, R., Fant, C. G. M., and Halle, M., *Preliminaries to Speech Analysis.* M.I.T. Press, Cambridge, Massachusetts, 1951; eighth printing, 1969.

73. Jones, D., *An Outline of English Phonetics.* W. Heffer, Cambridge, England, 1918; ninth edition, 1960.

74. Jones, D., *The Phoneme: Its Nature and Use.* W. Heffer, Cambridge, England, 1959; second edition, 1962.

75. Kiss, G. R., Networks as models of word storage, in *Machine Intelligence* (N. L. Collins and D. Michie, eds.), Vol. 1, pp. 155–167. Oliver & Boyd, Edinburgh, 1967.

76. Kiss, G. R., Steps towards a model of word selection, in *Machine Intelligence* (B. Meltzer and D. Michie. eds.), Vol. 5, pp. 315–336. Edinburgh Univ. Press, Edinburgh, 1969.

77. Ladefoged, P., Some possibilities in speech synthesis. *Language Speech* **7**, Part 4, 205–214 (1964).

78. Ladefoged, P., and Broadbent, D. E., Perception of sequence in auditory events. *Quart. J. Exptl. Psychol.* **12**, Part 3, 162–170 (1960).

79. Ladefoged, P., Private communication 1969.

80. Lavoie, F. J., Voice actuated controls. *Mach. Des.* **42**, 135–139 (January 22, 1970).

81. Lawrence, W., The synthesis of speech from signals which have a low information rate, in *Communication Theory* (W. Jackson, ed.), pp. 460–471. Butterworth's, London, 1953.

82. Lea, W. A., Establishing the value of voice communication with computers. *IEEE Trans. Audio Electroacoustics* **AU-16**, 184–197 (1968).

83. Lehiste, I., Acoustical characteristics of selected English consonants. AD 282 765, Armed Services Tech. Inform. Agency, 1962.

84. Lettvin, J. Y., Maturana, H. R., McCulloch, W. S., and Pitts, W. H., What the frog's eye tells the frog's brain. *Proc. Inst. Radio Eng.* **47**, 1940–1951 (1969); also in *Embodiments of Mind* (collected works of W. S. McCulloch), pp. 230–255, M.I.T. Press, Cambridge, Massachusetts, 1965.

85. Liberman, A. M., Some results of research on speech perception. *J. Acoust. Soc. Amer.* **29**, 117–123 (1957).

86. Liberman, A. M., Ingemann, F., Lisker, L., Delattre, P., and Cooper F. S., Minimal rules for synthesising speech. *J. Acoust. Soc. Amer.* **31**, 1490–1499 (1960).

87. Liberman, A. M., Cooper, F. S., Harris, K. S., and MacNeilage, P. F., A motor theory of speech perception. *Proc. Stockholm Speech Commun. Seminar* **II**, D3, Speech Transmission Lab., Roy. Inst. Technol., Stockholm, 1962

88. Liljencrants, J. C. W. A., The OVE III speech synthesiser. *IEEE Trans. Audio Electroacoustics* **AU-16**, 137–140 (1968).

89. Lindgren, N., Machine recognition of human language; Part I: Automatic Speech Recognition; Part II: Theoretical models of speech perception and language; Part III: Cursive script recognition. *IEEE Spectrum* **2**, No. 3, 114–136 (1965); No. 4, 44–59 (1965), No. 5, 104–116 (1965).

90. Lindgren, N., Speech—man's natural communication. *IEEE Spectrum* **4**, No. 6, 75–86 (1967).

91. Lindsay, R. K., Inferential memory as the basis of machines which understand natural language, in *Computers and Thought* (E. A. Feigenbaum and J. Feldman, eds.), pp. 217–233. McGraw-Hill, New York, 1963.

92. Lisker, L., and Abramson, A. S., Stop categorization and voice onset time, in *Proc. 5th Int. Congr. Phon. Sci.* (E. Zwirner and W. Bettige, eds.), pp. 389–391. S. Karger, Basle, 1964.

93. Marril, T., Automatic recognition of speech. *IRE Trans. Human Factors Electron.* **HFE-2**, 35–38 (1961).

94. Martin, T. B., Zadell, H. J., Nelson, A. L., and Cox, R. B., Recognition of continuous speech by feature abstraction. Tech. Rept. TR-66-189, Advanced Technol. Lab., Defense Electron. Prod., RCA, Camden, New Jersey, 1966.

95. Mattingly, I. G., Synthesis by rule of prosodic features. *Language Speech* **9**, No. 1, 1–13 (1966).

96. Mattingly, I. G., Experimental methods for speech synthesis by rule. *IEEE Trans. Audio Electroacoustics* **AU-16**, 198–202 (1968).

97. Maturana, H. R., Uribe, G., and Frenk, S., A biological theory of relativistic colour coding in the primate retina. *Arch. Biol. Med. Exptl. Suppl.* **1**, 1968.

98. McConologue, K., and Simmons, R. F., Analysing English syntax with a pattern-learning parser. *Commun. Ass. Comput. Machinery* **8**, 687–698 (1965).

99. McCarthy, J. Earnest, L. D., Reddy, D. R., and Vicens, P. J., A computer with hands, eyes, and ears. *Proc. Fall Joint Computer Conf., San Francisco, 1968*, pp. 329–338. Thompson, Washington, D.C., 1968.

100. McElwain, C. K., and Evens, M. B., The degarbler—a programme for correcting machine-read morse code. *Inform. Control* **5**, 368–384 (1962).

101. Meeker, W. F., Parametric recognition of speech sounds. *Proc. Seminar Speech Compression Coding.* PB146624, Air Force Cambridge Res. Lab., LG Hanscom Field, Bedford, Massachusetts, 1959.

102. Meetham, A. R., and Hudson, R. A. (eds.), *Encyclopaedia of Information, Linguistics, and Control.* Pergamon, Oxford, 1969.

103. Miller, G. A., *Language and Communication.* McGraw-Hill, New York, 1951.

104. Morgan, O. E., Private communication, 1969.

105. Newcomb, W. B., A dictionary programme for speech recognition, Unpublished, private communication, July 30, 1964.

106. Newell, A. F., VOTEM—A voice operated typewriter. 53rd Exhibition, The Institute of Physics and the Physical Society, London, 1969.

107. Newman, E. A., and Scantlebury, R., Teaching machines as intelligence amplifiers. Rept. Auto 31, Nat. Phys. Lab. Teddington, England, 1967.

108. O'Connor, J. D., Gerstman, L. J., Liberman, A. M., Delattre, P. C., and Cooper, F. S., Acoustic cues for the perception of initial /w, j, r, l/ in English. *Word* **13**, 24–43 (1957).

109. Olson, H. F., and Belar, H., Phonetic typewriter III. *J. Acoust. Soc. Amer.* **33**, 1610–1615 (1961).

110. Olson, H. F., and Belar, H., Syllable analyzer, coder, and synthesiser for the transmission of speech. *IRE Trans. Audio* **AU-10**, 11–17 (1962).

111. Olson, H. F., and Belar, H., Performance of a code operated speech synthesiser. *Proc. 16 Ann. Meeting Audio Eng. Soc., October, 1964.*

112. Otten, K. W., The formant vecoder and its use for automatic speech recognition. *Proc. 3rd Int. Conf. Acoust.* (L. Cremer, ed.), Elsevier, Amsterdam, 1961.

113. Otten, K. W., Approaches to the machine recognition of conversational speech. *Advan. Computers* **11**, 127 (1971). (this volume)

114. Paulus, E., Bibliography on automatic speech recognition. Tech. Rept. TR 25.064, IBM Lab., Vienna, 1966.

115. Petrick, S. R., and Griffiths, T. V., On the relative efficiencies on context free grammar recognisers. *Commun. Ass. Comput. Machinery* **8**, 289–299 (1965).

116. Pierce, J. R., Men, machines, and languages. *IEEE Spectrum* **5**, No. 7, 44–49 (1968).

117. Potter, R. K., The technical aspects of visible speech. *J. Acoust. Soc. Amer.* **17**, 1–89 (1946), also Bell Monograph 1415, Bell Telephone Labs., Murray Hill, New Jersey, 1946.

118. Potter, R. K., Kopp, G. A., and Kopp, H. G., *Visible Speech.* Dover, New York, 1966.

119. Presti, A. J., High Speed sound spectrograph. *J. Acoust. Soc. Amer.* **40**, 628–634 (1966).

120. Purton, R. F., An automatic word recogniser based on autocorrelation analysis. *Colloq. Some Aspects Speech Recognition Man-Machine Commun.* Reprint, Inst. of Elec. Eng., London, England, 1968.

121. Reddy, D. R., An approach to computer speech recognition by direct analysis of the speech wave. Ph.D. dissertation, Tech. Rept. CS49, Stanford University, Stanford, California, 1966.

122. Reddy, D. R., Computer recognition of connected speech. *J. Acoust. Soc. Amer.* **42**, 329–347 (1967).

123. Reddy, D. R., and Vicens, P. J., A procedure for the segmentation of connected speech. *J. Audio Eng. Soc.* **16**, 404–411 (1968).

124. Reeds, J. A., and Wang, W. S. Y., The perception of stops after s. *Phonetica* **6**, 78–81 (1961).

125. Ross, P. W., A limited-vocabulary adaptive speech-recognition system. *J. Audio Eng. Soc.* **15**, 415–418 (1967).

126. Sager, N., Syntactic analysis of natural language. *Advan. Computers* **8**, 153–188 (1967).

127. Sakai, T., and Inoue, S. I., New instruments and methods for speech analysis. *J. Acoust. Soc. Amer.* **32**, 441–450 (1960).

128. Sakai, T., and Doshita, S., The automatic speech recognition system for conversational sound. *IEEE Trans. Electron. Comput.* **EC-12**, 835–846 (1963).

129. Salton, G., *Automatic Information Organization and Retrieval.* McGraw-Hill, New York, 1968.

130. Salton, G. A., Ph.D. program in Information Retrieval. *Commun. Ass. Comput. Machinery* **12**, 110–117 (1969).

131. Sayre, K. M., *Recognition: A Study in the Philosophy of Artificial Intelligence.* Notre Dame Univ. Press, Notre Dame, Indiana, 1965.

132. Scarr, R. W. A., Zero-crossings as a means of obtaining spectral information in speech analysis. *IEEE Trans. Audio Electroacoustics* **AU-16**, 247–255 (1968).

133. Scarr, R. W. A., Normalization and adaption of speech data for automatic speech recognition. *Int. J. Man–Machine Studies* **2**, 41–59 (1970).

134. Schroeder, M. R., Vocoders: analysis and synthesis of speech. *Proc. IEEE* **54**, 720–734 (1966).

135. Schouten, J. F., Cohen, A., and 't Hart, J., Study of time cues in speech perception. *J. Acoust. Soc. Amer.* **34**, 517–518 (1963).

136. Sebesteyen, G., Automatic recognition of spoken numerals. *J. Acoust. Soc. Amer.* **32**, 1516 (1960).

137. Shearme, J. N., and Leach, P. F., Some experiments with a simple word recognition system. *IEEE Trans. Audio Electroacoustics* **AU-16**, 256–261 (1968).

138. Simmons, R. F., Burger, J. F., and Schwarcz, R. M., A computational model of verbal understanding. *Proc. AFIPS Fall Joint Computer Conf., San Francisco, 1968* **33**, 411–456. Thompson, Washington, D.C., 1968.

139. Sitton, G., Acoustic segmentation of speech. *Int. J. Man–Machine Studies* **2**, 61–102 (1970).

140. Stevens, K. N., On the relations between speech movements and speech perception. *Z. Phonetik, Sprachwissenschaft und Kommunikationsforschung* **21**, 102–106 (1968). Presented by invitation at seminar on speech production and perception, Pavlov Inst. of Physiol., Leningrad, 1966.

141. Stevens, K. N., Toward a model for speech recognition. *J. Acoust. Soc. Amer.* **32**, 47–55 (1960).

142. Stevens, S. S., *Handbook of Experimental Psychology.* Wiley, New York, 1951; eighth printing, 1966.

143. Strevens, P. D., and Antony, J., The performance of a 6-parameter speech synthesiser (a lecture demonstration). *Proc. 8th Intern. Cong. Linguists*, pp. 214–215, Oslo Univ. Press, Oslo, Sweden, 1958.

144. Strevens, P. D., Spectra of fricative noises in human speech. *Language Speech* **3**, Part 1, 32–49 (1960).

145. Sutherland, N. S., Outlines of a theory of visual pattern recognition in animals and man. *Proc. Roy. Soc. (London)* **B171**, 297–317 (1968).

146. Taylor, E. F., A skimmable report on ELIZA. Educ. Res. Center Rept., Mass. Inst. Tech., Cambridge, Massachusetts, 1968.

147. Teacher, C. F., Kellet, H. G., and Focht, L. R., Experimental, limited vocabulary speech recognizer. *IEEE Trans. Audio Electroacoustics* **AU-15**, 127–130 (1967).

148. Thorne, J. P., Bratley, P., and Dewar, H., The syntactic analysis of English by machine, in *Machine Intelligence* (B. Meltzer and D. Michie, eds.) Vol. 3, pp. 281–297. Edinburgh Univ. Press, Edinburgh, Scotland, 1968.

149. Tillman, H. G., Heike, G., Schnelle, H., and Ungeheuer, G., DAWID I— ein Betrag zur automatischen "Spracherkennung," *Proc. 5th Int. Cong. Acoust.*, Liege, 1965.

150. Traum, M. M., and Torre, E. D., An electronic speech recognition system. *Proc. 1967 Spring Symp. Digital Equipment Corporation User Soc.*, *The State University, New Brunswick, New Jersey*, pp. 89–92. Digital Equipment Corporation User Society. Maynard, Massachusetts,

151. Truby, H. M., A note on invisible and indivisible speech. *Proc. 8th. Int. Cong. Linguists*, pp. 393–400, Oslo Univ. Press, Oslo, Sweden, 1958.

152. Turing, A. M., Computing machinery and intelligence. *Mind* **59**, 433–460 (1950), also in *Computers and Thought* (E. A. Feigenbaum and J. Feldman, eds.), pp. 11–35. McGraw-Hill, New York, 1963.

153. Uldall, E., and Antony, J. K., The synthesis of a long piece of connected speech on PAT. *Proc. Stockholm Speech Commun. Seminar* **II** F8, Speech Transmission Lab., Roy. Inst. Technol., Stockholm, 1962.

154. Uhr, L., and Vossler, C., Recognition of speech by a computer program that was written to simulate a model for human visual pattern perception. *J. Acoust. Soc. Amer.* **33**, 1426 (1961).

155. Uhr, L., and Vossler, C., A pattern recognition program that generates, evaluates, and adjusts its own operators. *Proc. Western Joint Computer Conf.* **19**, 555–570 (1961), also in *Computers and Thought* (E. A. Feigenbaum and J. Feldman, eds.), pp. 251–268, McGraw-Hill, New York, 1963.

156. University of Michigan, Automatic Speech Recognition. Univ. of Michigan Eng. Summer Conf. Automatic Speech Recognition, Serial 6310, Vols. I and II (1963).

157. Velichko, V. M., and Zagoruyko, N. G., Automatic recognition of 200 words. *Int. J. Man–Machine Studies* **2**, pp. 223–234 (1970)

158. Vicens, P., Aspects of speech recognition by computer, Ph.D. Dissertation, CS 127, Dept. of Computer Sci., Stanford Univ., Stanford, California, 1969.

159. von Keller, T. G., An on-line system for spoken digits. *J. Acoust. Soc. Amer.* **44**, 385 (1970).

160. von Keller, T. G., Automatic recognition of spoken words. *75th Meeting Acoust. Soc. Amer., Ottawa, 1968.*

161. von Kempelen, W., Speaking Machine, *Philips Tech. Rev.* **25**, 48–50 (1963/ 1964).

162. von Senden, M., *Space and Sight: The Perception of Space and Shape in the Congenitally Blind Before and After Operation.* Free Press, Glencoe, Illinois, 1960.

163. Walker, D. E., English pre-processor manual (revised). Rept. SR-132, Inform. System Language Studies No. 7, MITRE Corp., Bedford, Massachusetts, 1965.

164. Walker, D. E., Chapin, P. G., Geis, M. L., and Gross, L. N., Recent developments in the MITRE syntactic analysis procedure. Rept. MTP-11, Inform.

Systems Language Studies No. 11, MITRE Corp., Bedford, Massachusetts, 1966.

165. Wang, S-Y., and Peterson, G. E., Segment inventory for speech synthesis. *J. Acoust. Soc. Amer.* **30**, 1035–1041 (1958).

166. Wells, J. C., A study of the formants of the pure vowels of British English. Dept. of Phonetics Progress Rept., under Contract AF EOAR 62-116 USAF European Office OAR, Univ. College, London, 1963.

167. Whitfield, I. C., and Evans, E. F., Responses of auditory cortical neurones to stimuli of changing frequency, *J. Neurophysiol.* **28**, 655–672 (1965).

168. Willshaw, D. J., and Longuett-Higgins, H. C., The Holophone—recent developments, in *Machine Intelligence* (B. Meltzer and D. Michie, eds.), Vol. 4, pp. 349–357. Edinburgh Univ. Press, Edinburgh, 1969.

169. Wiren, J., and Stubbs, H. L., Electronic binary selection system for phoneme classification. *J. Acoust. Soc. Amer.* **28**, 1081–1091 (1956).

170. Woods, W. A., Procedural semantics for a question answering machine. *Proc. AFIPS Fall Joint Computer Conf., San Francisco, 1968*, **33**, Part 1, 457–471. Thompson, Washington, D.C., 1968.

Balanced Magnetic Circuits for Logic and Memory Devices

R. B. KIEBURTZ AND E. E. NEWHALL[*]

Bell Telephone Laboratories
Holmdel, New Jersey

[*] Present address: Department of Electrical Engineering, University of Toronto, Toronto, Canada.

1. Introduction

One of the early applications of magnetics to digital computation was the coincident current core memory, about 1952 [1]. Multiaperture ferrite devices were introduced about 1955 [2], and they potentially extended the capability of magnetic devices from memory to logic operations. Transfluxors, as they were called, were made in the form of ferrite discs with several holes or apertures punched through the disk, and depended for their operation on local flux switching around the apertures, caused by current flowing in wires threaded through them. Other ideas included the Biax logical element discussed by Wanlass [3], Laddic reported by Gianola and Crowley [4, 5], the multiaperture device (MAD) reported by Crane [6–8] and a guided flux device using Permalloy sheets described by Carbonel et al. [9]. Widespread utilization of multiaperture ferrites has been limited because although the basic concept is simple and attractive, certain second-order effects have seriously limited practical circuits. Research at Bell Telephone Laboratories in the period 1961–1966 [10–13] resulted in the description of one circuit configuration, called the "balanced magnetic circuit," which effectively overcame the second-order problems of back transfer and zero buildup. However, the power supply current required by large arrays of balanced magnetic circuits was high, and also at this time the costs of semiconductor logic circuits were dropping substantially. The net result was that no economic advantage over a broad range of logic applications was obtained.

Magnetic core memories have been successful because they have been cheap and easy to build, and have been capable of constant improvement over the years. Loss of energy between input and output of the magnetic circuit is compensated for by gain in the selection and buffer circuits. Furthermore, the nonmagnetic part of the circuit can be shared over many cells of the magnetic portion because of the regularity of the array. The situation changes when the requirements are expanded from memory to logic because now each stage must provide gain and have interface compatibility with the next stage.

The unique features of balanced magnetic circuits are that they have two natural stable states, and gain is achieved where it is easiest to get, at low signal levels. Element saturation is used to get each of the stable states in a symmetrical manner. This leads naturally to the idea of bipolar signal representation and the notion of flux tipping about an aperture. These ideas are brought out in more detail in the discussion of Section 2. The important issue of gain is treated in Section 4 from a theoretical point of view, and in Sections 7 and 11 from an experimental point of view.

The basic balanced magnetic unit is an amplifier stage consisting of six apertures, interconnected by three coupling loops, and driven by a 3-phase clock. Units can be combined to form shift registers or logic circuits. While the complete discussion is in Section 5, the basic features are that this circuit organization successfully controls back transfer and zero buildup, the two second-order effects which were serious problems in unipolar organizations. Back transfer is controlled by clocking and the arrangement of storage and buffering elements. Zero buildup is controlled by means of bipolar signal representation. Section 5 also includes a comparison between unipolar and bipolar circuits.

The next two Sections, 6 and 7, describe two ways of realizing logical functions with balanced magnetic circuits and include examples of some importance in the experimental work which was done.

Up to Section 8 the nature of the paper is largely review and tutorial. Section 8 describes the most complex utilization of balanced magnetic circuits to date, the design and construction of an automatic wiring machine capable of interconnecting balanced circuit subassemblies. The control portion of the machine used the ferrite structures under study.

Section 9 presents alternate clocking arrangements including some modified 3- and 4-phase clocks. Section 10 discusses flux pattern regeneration in sheets. Section 11 describes a balanced magnetic storage element which can be used for either destructive or nondestructive readout, and is compatible directly with other balanced magnetic circuits. The final section describes measurements of circuit gain and the sensitivity of gain to material composition.

In summary, balanced magnetic circuits have been the object of system and device research for several years. A circuit organization has been described which effectively overcomes some previously severe problems. The future application of balanced magnetic circuits depends on the trends of relative cost of semiconductors and ceramic ferrites, the availability of cheap pulsed power supplies, and emergence of a system requirement which matches the unique capabilities and limitations of balanced magnetic circuits.

Physical Properties of Ferrites

To model square loop magnetic circuits two basic relationships relating applied currents and voltages to internal fields and flux changes should be recalled: Ampere's law and Faraday's law. In addition, the behavior of square loop material in the presence of a pulse of field must be known. It will be assumed that switching is primarily by domain wall motion.

A dynamic form of Ampere's law is readily obtained from Maxwell's equation

$$\nabla \times \mathbf{H} = j + (\partial D / \partial t). \tag{1}$$

Taking the scalar product of both sides with da and integrating yield

$$\int \nabla \times \mathbf{H} \cdot da = \int j \cdot da + (\partial / \partial t) \int D \cdot da. \tag{2}$$

In almost all magnetic logic circuits the second term on the right is small compared with the first. If the second term were large, switching using displacement current would be practical, and memories could be constructed without feeding wires through holes. Thin film geometries and coercivities may eventually reach the state where this is practical. Neglecting displacement currents, Stokes theorem can be applied to the left side of the above in which case the following relationship results

$$\int \mathbf{H} \cdot dl = i. \tag{3}$$

The above is a familiar form of Ampere's law, arrived at by starting with Maxwell's equations and arguing that the displacement current term is small compared with the conduction current term. We can then regard the above relationship as a dynamic form of Ampere's law which applies even though switching times may be in the microsecond range (Ampere's law is usually regarded as a magnetostatic relationship). In applying this relationship to circuits in which square loop material is present, the instantaneous value of the input current can be observed and the value of H calculated provided we can find a contour within the square loop material around which H is constant or known. In this case the integral may be replaced by the product of H times the path length and the instantaneous value of H estimated from a direct observation of the instantaneous current. If the material geometry varies so that H is not constant, then we are forced to estimate H from a knowledge of the initial internal condition of the material, wall areas, and wall velocities. These techniques have not yet reached a stage where they can be applied easily, or accurately, to arbitrary geometries. They can, however, very often be applied in a qualitative way to explain observed terminal characteristics. If H is in oersteds, i is in amperes, and l is in centimeters then Ampere's law takes the following form

$$\int \mathbf{H} \cdot dl = 0.4\pi i. \tag{4}$$

The second relationship to be recalled is Faraday's law

$$e = N(d\phi/dt) \times 10^{-8}. \tag{5}$$

Here e is in volts, ϕ is in lines or maxwells. The form of this relationship which is most often used is obtained by integrating the above:

$$\int e \, dt = NA(\Delta B)10^{-8}. \tag{6}$$

Here A is the cross-sectional area in square centimeters, and ΔB is the change in flux density in maxwells per square centimeter or gauss. The circuit quantity which can be observed is the actual wave shape of the voltage. From the integrated value of e the total change in the internal flux condition can be estimated.

Consider next how the applied internal field acts upon the square loop material to cause flux reversal. The type of behavior actually observed is shown in Fig. 1. Here a square pulse of current is applied

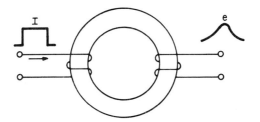

FIG. 1. Typical core response

to a toroid which tends to cause flux reversal from a saturated counter-clockwise state to a saturated clockwise state. The voltage wave shape observed is shown at the output terminals. We seek to relate the wave shape we see to the internal physics of the material at least in a qualitative fashion. Once this is done it becomes a fairly simple matter to explain some of the wave shapes which exist in a reasonably complicated magnetic circuit [14–16].

The material shown in the circuit in Fig. 1 is polycrystalline ferrite. To appreciate its behavior first consider a simpler material, a single crystal. A simplified view of a single crystal is shown in Fig. 2 [14]. Suppose the crystal is magnetized so that the inside periphery is set clockwise and the outside periphery is set counterclockwise as shown in Fig. 2. Between the inner and outer periphery there will be a transition region in which the magnetization vector must go from down to up. This transition region is termed a wall and in Fig. 2 an attempt has been made to show how the magnetization vectors appear within

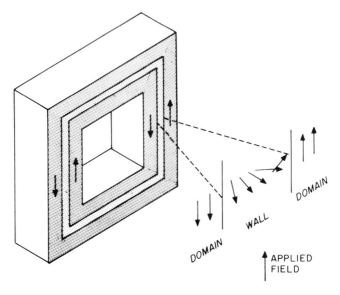

FIG. 2. Switching a single crystal with a single wall.

the wall. Suppose the wall is in the position shown and we apply a
field in the direction shown. It is not unreasonable to believe that the
magnetization vectors within the wall are less stable than those within
the domains. With this in mind we can expect the field to cause the
magnetization on the right-hand side of the wall to align itself with the
domain on the right-hand side of the figure. Furthermore, we will
expect the magnetization on the left-hand side of the wall to misalign
itself from the adjacent domain. Under these circumstances the entire
transition region moves and it is said the wall moves. By direct observation of a single wall it has been shown that the velocity with which
this wall moves is proportional to the difference between the applied
field and the coercive field [14]. The experimentally determined
relationship is:

$$v \propto H - H_c.$$

If the applied field is less than the coercive field of the material, H_c,
then nothing happens. On the other hand, if the applied field is slightly
greater than the coercive field, then a wall moves across the single
crystal with a velocity determined by the above relationship. As the
wall sweeps across the cross section the flux is reversed and an associated constant voltage is seen on a sense winding which links the
cross section.

If we increase the field, the wall velocity will go up and the output voltage will go up. A point is finally reached where the applied field will nucleate a second wall at some point in the crystal cross section. This second wall will also sweep across a section of the crystal reversing the magnetization. The first wall will stop when it comes to the region which has been reversed by the second wall; the switching time is decreased, and the output voltage increased. From these observations it is not unreasonable to believe that the output voltage at any instant of time is proportional to the product of the wall area and wall velocity

$$e \propto (\text{wall area})(\text{wall velocity}).$$

Consider now the behavior of the polycrystal of Fig. 1 when a step of field is applied.[1] The behavior is summarized in Fig. 3. When we apply a constant field to reverse the polycrystal many walls initially move out from nucleation sites with a constant wall velocity. In an oversimplified model we can imagine small cross-section flux tubes extending around the toroid. The magnetization inside the tubes is reversed and that outside the tubes is about to reverse. As the walls move away from the nucleation sites the wall area grows, increasing the flux reversed per unit time, hence increasing the output voltage.

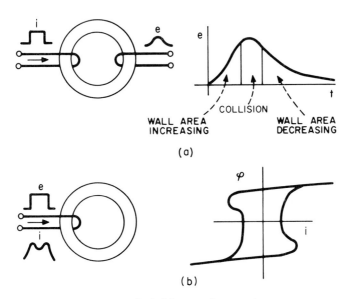

FIG. 3. Switching a polycrystal.

---

[1] The discussion in the remaining portion of this section is based primarily on material contained in [14–16]. Wall motion, rather than rotation, is assumed to be dominant. This is a simplified view of a complex internal process.

This process continues until the walls start interacting with one another at which time the net magnetization swept out in unit time begins to decrease. The actual wave shapes observed together with an estimate of the internal behavior is shown in Fig. 3(a).

It is interesting to ask what occurs when we apply something different from a step of current. Suppose instead a step of voltage is applied. Switching in the toroid must generate a back voltage to balance this applied voltage. The current wave shape observed is then that shown in Fig. 3(b). When the step of voltage is initially applied, the wall area will be extremely small and the necessary back voltage can only be developed by a very high wall velocity. This high wall velocity can only be sustained by a high field and hence initially we have a large surge of current. As the wall area grows the necessary back voltage can be sustained by a lower wall velocity hence a lower field and hence a lower input current. Toward the end of the switching process the wall area begins to decrease so that the necessary back voltage can only be generated by a higher wall velocity and hence an increased input current. If the flux reversed is plotted versus input current a reentrant type of hysteresis loop shown in Fig. 3(b) results. Such "reentrant hysteresis loops" have been observed by the authors using appropriate driving circuits (voltage source).

There is one other phenomenon which is very important in influencing the behavior of multiaperture circuits as well as cores. Consider performing the following simple experiment on a single core. Suppose the core is initially saturated and then driven from negative saturation part way to positive saturation. Suppose this switching is allowed to take place slowly by means of a ramp of current. Further suppose the response of the partially set core is subsequently measured using a slowly varying current. Characteristics of the type shown in Fig. 4(a) result [12]. This shows the behavior of a single core when set to various initial levels the setting operation taking place in approximately 80 μs. In Fig. 4(b) the same experiment was performed. However, the partial setting operation was performed using a time-limited pulse and the total switching time was approximately 1 μs. It is clear in this case that the threshold of the partially set core is not nearly as distinct as it was in the slow setting case. This lack of sharpness in the threshold field of a partially set core is termed the "soft threshold effect."

The reasons for this behavior are not clearly understood. Magnesium–zinc ferrite exhibits the greatest reduction in coercive field with partial setting, manganese–magnesium–cadmium ferrite exhibits somewhat less, and manganese–magnesium the least. Although this experiment was done on a simple core there are considerable implications as to the behavior of multiaperture magnetic circuits. It is clear that if a

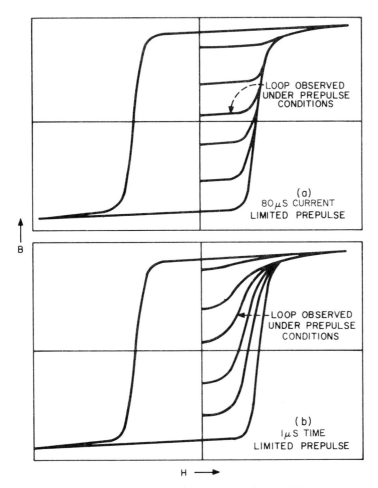

Fig. 4. Soft threshold behavior of a toroid.

leg is not initially saturated then merely knowing its flux level is not sufficient to predict its future behavior. We must know as well the rate at which that flux level was achieved. This fact makes it very difficult to predict the behavior of multiaperture circuits unless we start from a saturated condition [17].

2. Multiaperture Elements Regarded as Circuits

2.1 Mapping between Core and Sheet Circuits [18]

Under certain circumstances an arrangement of cores with inter-connecting coupling windings may be replaced by a simple magnetic circuit. A simple series magnetic circuit and a simple parallel magnetic circuit are considered, and their core equivalents established. Adopting a circuit point of view it is shown that a two core per bit scheme, a balanced circuit, and a simple parallel circuit are all identical.

Consider the pair of coupled cores shown in Fig. 5(a). If we apply

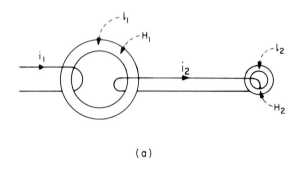

(a)

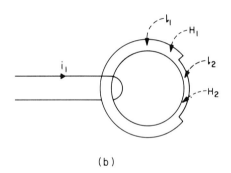

(b)

Fig. 5. Series circuit and its core equivalent.

Ampere's law to the large core, we obtain

$$H_1 l_1 = i_1 - i_2. \tag{7}$$

Applying Ampere's law to the small core yields

$$H_2 l_2 = i_2. \tag{8}$$

If we substitute the second relationship into the first, we obtain

$$H_1 l_1 + H_2 l_2 = i_1. \tag{9}$$

Consider the circuit interpretation of Eq. 9. We have a drive magneto-motive force and two magnetomotive force drops. It is clear that if we apply Ampere's law to the slotted toroid shown in Fig. 5(b) then again Eq. 9 will result. We then have the beginning of an equivalence between the circuit shown in Fig. 5(a) and the circuit of Fig. 5(b). In addition to the relationships stated so far, we need two additional constraints to achieve equivalent behavior as a function of time. First of all we must be sure that the initial conditions in both circuits are the same: the initial condition of the material in the small core in Fig. 5(a) must be the same as the material in the slotted region in Fig. 5(b). Not only must the flux levels in these regions be identical, but if the levels are different from saturation, the rate at which these levels were established must be identical. This restriction follows from observations made on partially set cores. The threshold and subsequent switching behavior is strongly dependent on the rate at which the partial set is established. Having insisted on the same initial conditions in both circuits, it is clear we must also require that the total allowed flux excursions be the same in both cases. This implies that the areas are equal. We can then summarize the criteria for equivalence as follows:

(a) Each core in the core circuit is replaced by a leg in the sheet circuit of the same length and same cross-sectional area.

(b) The initial flux levels in the circuits must be adjusted so that the levels are the same and if the levels are different from saturation, then the rates at which these levels are established should be identical.

Under the circumstances described above, every microscopic volume in Fig. 5(a) will have a corresponding microscopic volume in Fig. 5(b) whose initial condition is the same and which sees the same field. Ideally we should map inside and outside diameters, as well, to maintain identical field conditions. Under these circumstances we can expect the time behavior of both circuits to be identical. Corresponding to every flux and every dynamic magnetomotive force in Fig. 5(a) there will be a corresponding flux and dynamic magnetomotive force in Fig. 5(b) with the same time behavior. Furthermore, looking in the input terminals we will see exactly the same relationships between input current wave shape and back voltage in both cases. This argument can be extended to show that cores coupled to other separate and distinct coupling loops map into other slots.

Consider applying the circuit ideas discussed in the last section to obtain a quantitative estimate of the dynamic magnetomotive force across leg l_2 in Fig. 5(b). If leg l_2 is initially saturated then from flux continuity considerations leg l_1 must be in some state different from saturation. When a constant current is applied to reverse the core the rate of change of flux in legs l_1 and l_2 must be equal if we neglect leakage. However, l_1 has a much higher initial wall area than l_2; consequently a high initial field must exist across l_2, to cause a high wall velocity, such that flux reversal in l_1 and l_2 are equal. As the wall area in l_2 builds up the field can decrease and still maintain equal rates of flux reversal in l_1 and l_2. However as l_2 approaches saturation the field must again go up to maintain the necessary wall velocity. At the termination of switching almost all the applied magnetomotive force is absorbed by region l_2. This dynamic magnetomotive force, which decreases and increases again, can be observed using a probe of the type shown in [12]. Arguments of this kind can often be used to explain apparently peculiar behavior of complicated arrays. These observations are of course often complicated by a lack of knowledge as to the rate at which the initial conditions were established.

Next consider a core to which two other cores are coupled; suppose these cores have the same magnetic path length. The same approach leads to the conclusion that the two cores coupled to the same winding map into parallel paths as shown in Fig. 6. The relationships between length and areas are shown. In this case we can also argue that corresponding to every unit volume in Fig. 6(a) there is a corresponding unit volume in Fig. 6(b) which has the same initial state and is subjected to the same field and has the same time behavior. Then, corresponding to every flux and every dynamic magnetomotive force in Fig. 6(a) there is a corresponding flux and magnetomotive force in Fig. 6(b) with the same time behavior. If the two cores are made

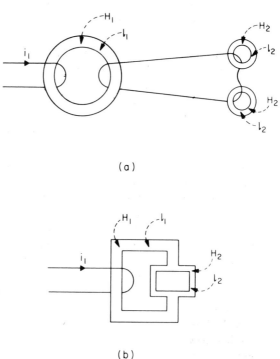

(a)

(b)

FIG. 6. Parallel circuit and its core equivalent.

different in length the two parallel paths become different in length. Furthermore, if we have three equal length cores on the same coupling loop then the sheet version consists of three equal length parallel paths. In these equivalences the response of the core and sheet circuits are identical looking in the input terminals provided initial conditions are matched. In other words, a particular wave shape of applied current will generate the same back voltage wave shape in both cases.

2.2 Simple Balanced Circuit and Its Core Equivalent

It is clear from the above discussion that reasonably complicated mappings may be performed if one recognizes the core equivalent of a simple series circuit and a simple parallel circuit. For example, consider the simple balanced circuit shown in Fig. 7(a): this is just a simple parallel circuit in which a portion has been modified so as to provide a flux source capable of delivering a fixed amount of flux to the circuit. Initially the clear winding saturates all paths. This saturated condition is illustrated by the use of arrows shown in Fig. 7(a). The sum of the arrows in any leg is equal to the total flux capacity of that leg. An arrow of unit length represents an amount of magnetization which will just saturate the smallest leg: in the diagram the smallest saturated leg has one arrow; the saturated leg of double thickness, two arrows. At any junction point, provided there is no leakage, the sum of the incoming arrows must be equal to the sum of the outgoing arrows.

If we next energize the pump winding, the magnetization in leg 1 will reverse and leg 2 will not change as leg 2 is already saturated in the direction of the applied field. The flux which switches in leg 1 will also switch in legs 3 and 4 and will split equally between legs 5 and 6 if the structure is symmetric. The resulting flux pattern is shown in Fig. 7(b). The total flux which switches in leg 1 is only sufficient to carry legs 3 and 4 from saturation to a state of zero magnetization or neutral. This is represented by two equal but opposite arrows in legs 3 and 4. The same is true of legs 5 and 6: each goes to a neutral state.

Consider the core equivalent of the circuit shown in Fig. 7(a). The steps in taking the core equivalent are shown in Fig. 8. First the two parallel paths, 5 and 6, are replaced by two cores as shown in Fig. 8(a). Next the flux source, which is also composed of two parallel paths, is replaced by two cores. Finally it is noted that core 2 never switches so it may be discarded; in addition, it is observed that core 3-4 acts as a transformer coupling core 1 to cores 5 and 6 with a 1-to-1 turns ratio. This transformer may then be replaced by a direct connection. The result is shown in Fig. 8(c). Although core 2 is not necessary in Fig. 8(c), it is necessary in the sheet version to satisfy flux continuity

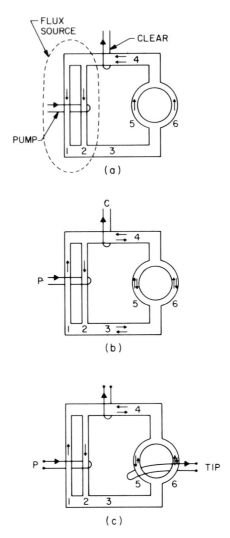

Fig. 7. Simple balanced circuit.

requirements at each junction. It is clear from this example that although the mapping from sheet circuits to core circuits is straightforward and unique, the reverse is not necessarily the case.

The circuit shown in Fig. 8(c) is used in two core per bit memory schemes. The operation of this memory element first involves saturating elements 1, 5, and 6 as shown in Fig. 8(c). Next, core 1 is switched from negative to positive remanence. If Kirchoff's law and Faraday's law

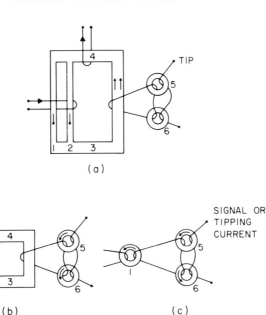

(a)

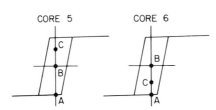

(b)   (c)

CORE 5   CORE 6

A- STARTING POINT
B- TERMINATING POINT- NO SIGNAL APPLIED
C- TERMINATING POINT- CORE 5 PREFERRED OVER CORE 6

(d)

FIG. 8. Core equivalent of a simple balanced circuit.

are applied to the coupling loop linking cores 1, 5, and 6, and coupling
loop resistance is neglected, then after integration we obtain:

$$2\phi_s = \phi_1 + \phi_2 \tag{10}$$

where ϕ_s is the saturation flux of core 1; ϕ_1 and ϕ_2 are the flux changes
in cores 5 and 6. We can then regard core 1 as a flux source which
delivers $2\phi_s$ units to cores 5 and 6. In the absence of a signal current,
cores 5 and 6 will terminate in a neutral state as did legs 5 and 6 in
Fig. 7(a). However, if a signal or tipping current is applied in coincidence with the pump current, switching will be aided in one core

and inhibited in the other. The total flux delivered will still be the same, however; one core will go past neutral while the other core will stop short of neutral as shown in Fig. 8(d). Information is then stored as a flux difference in cores 5 and 6 and may be read out by saturating cores 5 and 6. The output signal will be positive or negative depending on which of cores 5 or 6 is set to the greater extent.

The circuit shown in Fig. 7(c) operates in the same manner. If a signal is applied in coincidence with the pump current in the sense shown in Fig. 7(c), leg 5 will be preferred over leg 6. The various flux states which can result are shown in Fig. 9. In the saturated state no

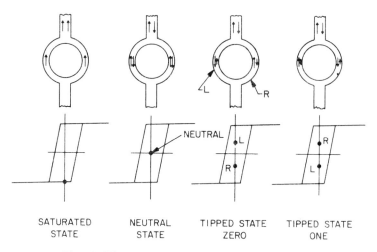

SATURATED   NEUTRAL   TIPPED STATE   TIPPED STATE
STATE   STATE   ZERO   ONE

Fig. 9. Flux states in a simple balanced circuit.

information can be stored in the aperture. The saturated state is reached after application of a pulse to the clear winding. The neutral state is reached from the saturated state by application of the pulse to the pump winding only. The tipped state is reached upon simultaneous application of a current to the pump winding and the tipping winding. Various degrees of tipping are possible, these being measured from the zero tip or neutral state. A 100% tip results when all the flux switched at the time of pump is forced down one of the parallel paths and none down the other. The percent tip is expressed as:

$$\text{percent tip} = \frac{\Delta\phi_5 - \Delta\phi_6}{\Delta\phi_5 + \Delta\phi_6} \times 100 = \frac{\Delta\phi}{\Delta\phi_5 + \Delta\phi_6} \times 100 \qquad (11)$$

where $\Delta\phi_5$ is the flux which switches in leg 5 at the time of pump and $\Delta\phi_6$ is the flux which switches in leg 6 at the time of pump. The difference flux $\Delta\phi$ can easily be measured by integrating the voltage which appears on the tipping winding.

As in a two core per bit scheme, the stored information may be read out by clearing the element; the sense of the output voltage again depends on the relative flux levels in legs 5 and 6. The amount of signal output obtained at the time of clear will depend upon the value of the signal current tipping the balanced circuit at the time of pump.

The balanced circuit of Fig. 7 was introduced by connecting a specific flux source to a simple parallel circuit. It is useful to consider flux sources in their own right.

2.3 Flux Sources

The flux source used in Fig. 7 is shown in Fig. 10. The flux state after clear is shown in Fig. 10(a) and the state after pump in Fig. 10(b). In this and other diagrams, the sum of the arrows into any junction point must always equal the sum of the arrows leaving the junction point, representing the continuity of flux and the absence of leakage. The basic unit of flux chosen in Fig. 10 is that required to saturate the smallest leg. This is not always the most convenient unit. For

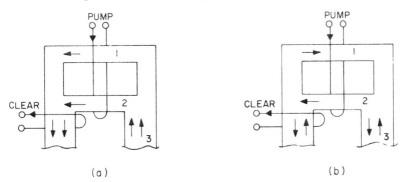

(a)   (b)

Fig. 10. Flux source.

example, a slightly different flux source is shown in Fig. 11. After several cycles, the pattern shown in Fig. 11(a) will be established.[2] Energization of the pump winding will now reverse one unit of flux in the leg 1. If the leakage is zero, an equivalent amount of flux must reverse in leg 3. Switching is impossible in leg 2 as the sense of the applied magnetomotive force tends to saturate leg 2 and it is already saturated (all arrows in one direction). Switching ceases when leg 1

---

[2] This follows if the circuit ideas discussed in Section 1 are applied.

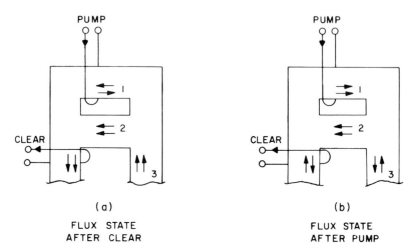

(a)

FLUX STATE
AFTER CLEAR

(b)

FLUX STATE
AFTER PUMP

Fig. 11. Modified flux source.

reaches saturation and the field generated by the pump winding cannot cause further reversal of magnetization. This leaves leg 3 in a neutral state. If we now reenergize the clear winding, it is easy to see that the state that results is that shown in Fig. 11(a). Thus successive energization of pump and clear windings generate the patterns shown in Fig. 11. Now, in both Figs. 10 and 11, the connected circuits will go from saturation to neutral and return, so that both of these flux sources establish the same flux condition in connected circuits.

Both flux sources deliver a constant amount of flux without requiring time-limited drive: the structure geometries establish the amount of flux delivered. In both circuits leg 2 never switches; however, leg 1 in Fig. 10 goes from negative to positive remanence, while leg 1 in Fig. 11 goes from neutral to saturation. At high switching rates heating will be less in the element shown in Fig. 11, as the internal heat generated in both will be almost the same but the cooling area is greater in the element of Fig. 11. The aperture shown in Fig. 11 is also easier to construct than that shown in Fig. 10, particularly when the dimensions become very small. Thus the structure shown in Fig. 11 allows one to use less than the full amount of flux in the structure, permitting partial switching operations, without requiring a corresponding reduction in critical dimensions. The limit to this procedure is established in practice by reversible switching (elastic switching) of supposedly saturated legs.

We can extend the flux source shown in Fig. 11 further to that shown in Fig. 12(a) and 12(b). The size of leg 1 has been reduced to one half that shown in Fig. 11. Under these circumstances the flux source will

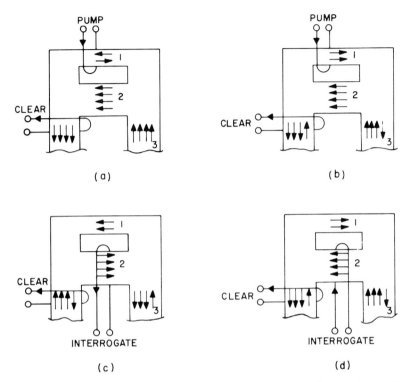

FIG. 12. Flux source suitable for reading, writing, and nondestructive readout (NDRO).

deliver an amount of flux sufficient to send the connected structure one quarter the distance from negative to positive remanence. This partially switches the connected circuits without requiring time limits on the applied drive. The operation is as before: if the state is as shown in Fig. 12(a) and the pump is applied, then the unit of flux reversed by the pump will not switch in leg 2 as leg 2 is already saturated, but will reverse one unit of flux in leg 3, leaving leg 3 in the condition shown. Thus leg 3 is switched one quarter the distance from negative to positive remanence.[3] Subsequent energization of the clear winding will return leg 3 to saturation and leg 1 to neutral, preparing leg 1 for the next energization of the pump winding.

The flux source of Fig. 12(a) may be operated in another manner as shown in Fig. 12(c) and 12(d). This mode of operation is intended to provide three final flux levels in the associated structure: saturation,

[3] This is modified somewhat if reversible switching in leg 2 is considered.

one quarter the distance from negative to positive remanence, and three quarters the distance from negative to positive remanence. These states are used in the nondestructive interrogation of balanced circuits. It has been shown that when a balanced element is tipped, and subsequently an amount of flux, insufficient to saturate the structure, is oscillated back and forth through the element, the leg preferred will be the leg preferred when the element was first tipped, even though the tipping signal is removed [12]. This process provides large nondestructive readout signals as considerable irreversible switching takes place.

Assume the structure has been pumped and tipped, establishing the flux source pattern shown in Fig. 12(b) and establishing information in a connected balanced circuit. The connected circuit will be one quarter the distance from negative to positive saturation. Nondestructive readout can be accomplished by energizing the interrogate winding shown in Fig. 12(c). Since leg 1 is shorter than leg 3, two units of flux will reverse in leg 1 and two units will switch in leg 3, leaving leg 3 three quarters of the distance from negative to positive saturation. In the associated balanced circuit, the leg preferred when the structure was first tipped will again be preferred. The structure can be returned to a state one quarter the distance from negative to positive saturation by energizing the interrogate winding in the sense shown in Fig. 12(d). Thus oscillation between one quarter and three quarters positive saturation can be accomplished by energizing the interrogate winding of Fig. 12(c) and 12(d) in opposite directions, allowing nondestructive readout of the connected elements. Clearing and rewriting can be accomplished by using the windings shown in Fig. 12(a) and 12(b). Experimental results using this method of operation are described in the next section.

From the above discussion the following is clear: Flux sources may be configured to cause the connected magnetic circuit to switch between any two arbitrary flux levels; with suitable geometries different windings may be connected to the same source and used to switch the connected circuit between different pairs of flux levels.

3. Element Characteristics

A typical balanced circuit is shown in Fig. 13. Here a flux source is placed at either end and six balanced elements connected in series. The flux source is split into two parts to minimize leakage. As in conventional circuits the two flux sources may be regarded as generating a series magnetomotive force to drive the series-connected balanced

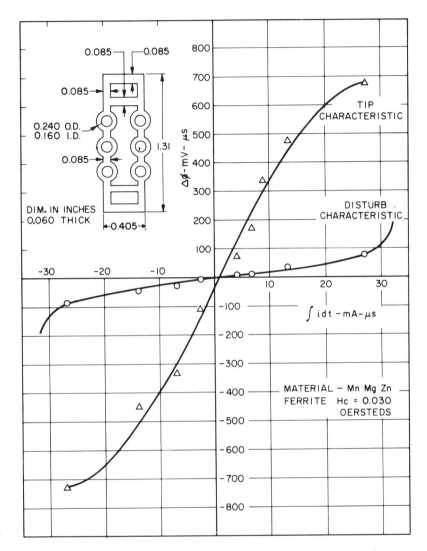

FIG. 13. Typical balanced element tip and disturb characteristics.

elements. The response of a hole to a tipping current applied at the time of pump is shown in Fig. 13. Here the difference flux $\Delta\phi$ is plotted as a function of the integral of the tipping current. This is a convenient choice of variables for use in the circuit model to be discussed. The pump and clear windings were wound as shown in Fig. 11.

In a two core per bit memory scheme, once information has been stored in the core its susceptibility to disturbing currents becomes important. The same is true when an element of this kind is used to amplify signals. The susceptibility of a balanced circuit to a disturbing current is also shown in Fig. 13. Here the flux switched around the periphery of the hole is plotted versus the integral of the disturbing current. The element was first pumped and tipped, the pump removed and a disturb current applied to the tip winding. Note that even for small currents some disturbing exists, because the core, composed of legs 5 and 6 has a so-called soft threshold in the tipped state. This implies an almost indistinguishable threshold as well as many walls ready and willing to move. The control of this soft threshold is extremely important for both memory and logic applications. Experiments on grain structure, aimed at achieving adequate control of disturb characteristics, are described in a subsequent section (see Section 12).

For memory and logic applications the offset or unbalance of the balanced elements is important. Measurements on 85 elements or 510 holes from several batches are shown in Fig. 14. The element dimensions

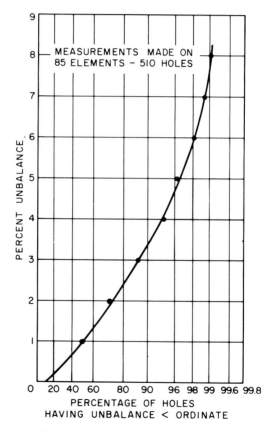

FIG. 14. Unbalance measurements.

are given in Fig. 13. Percent unbalance is determined by measuring the difference flux at the time of pump and expressing it as a fraction of the total flux switched at the time of pump. The stable operating level of the amplifier to be described is usually greater than a 50 percent tip so that a 5 percent unbalance is quite acceptable. Under these circumstances it is clear from Fig. 14 that 96% of the structures measured are acceptable.

Nondestructive readout of a single element is shown in Fig. 16. The actual element and its wiring arrangement are shown in Fig. 15.

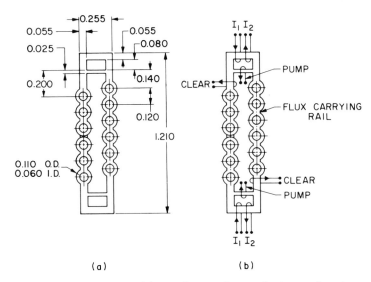

(a)   (b)

Fig. 15. Element used in nondestructive readout experiment.

The operation is similar to that discussed in connection with Fig. 12. The material is Mn, Mg, Zn ferrite with a coercive force of 0.30 oersteds. Similar behavior has been observed in other materials including standard Mn, Mg ferrite.

The clear winding was energized followed by tipping at the time of pump followed by nine interrogate cycles (I_1 and I_2). The cycle was then repeated. Energization of the pump switches the flux carrying rail (Fig. 15) from negative saturation to point B in Fig. 16(b). Calculation from the structure dimensions shows that this point is 60% of the distance from N to A. Energization of I_1 sends the flux rail from point B to point C. The duration of I_2 was set so that energization of I_2 sent the flux carrying rail back to point N. If I_2 is not limited in time point B will be reached. I_1 and I_2 oscillate the flux rail between points N and C. The structure remembers the initial direction in which it was tipped: the amount of nondestructive output is shown in

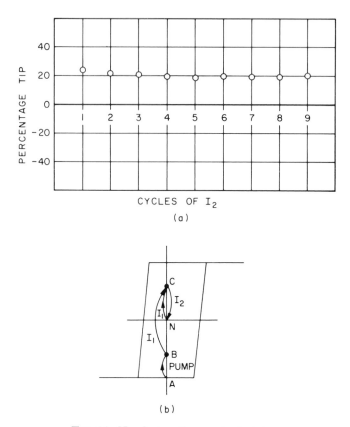

(a)

(b)

FIG. 16. Nondestructive readout states.

Fig. 16(a). Here 100% tip is taken to be the amount of flux which switches when the flux rail is switched from A to N. The level degenerates slightly from that at the first interrogation and remains stable thereafter. The difference flux was read at the time of I_2.

The wave shape of the voltage seen across the sense winding at I_2 time is shown in Fig. 17(a). This is the wave shape seen when I_2 just drives the flux rail to neutral. However, if I_2 is not time-limited then point B (Fig. 16) is reached. In this case the wave shape is as shown in Fig. 17(b). Some hypotheses may be made of the mechanism involved from these and other observations. It is assumed that the leg in the balanced circuit preferred during pump is left in a state with many low coercive force walls which are the easiest walls to switch during I_1 and I_2. If the flux carrying rail is sent from C to N during I_2 it is assumed that the many low coercive force walls in the preferred leg contribute a greater amount to flux switching than its counterpart,

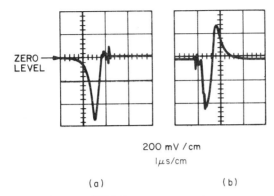

200 mV / cm

1μs/cm

(a)   (b)

Fig. 17. NDRO output waveshapes.

giving a net sense to the difference flux output. However, if I_2 carries the flux rail past neutral the leg preferred will approach negative saturation first, and must therefore have its low coercive force walls removed as it approaches saturation. The leg not preferred is further from saturation and it now becomes the preferred leg, reversing the sense of the nondestructive readout signal. Nondestructive readout is still accomplished but the sense winding shows a pulse of the type shown in Fig. 17(b) at both I_1 and I_2 times.

4. Circuit Characteristics

4.1 Information Transfer between Apertures

This section discusses information transfer from one aperture to another, the theoretical and practical limits on energy gain per transfer, and the basic circuit functions sufficient to construct bistable magnetic circuits.

Consider the circuit arrangement shown in Fig. 18(a). Three interconnected apertures are shown with an input circuit, a coupling loop linking all three structures, and an output circuit. All three structures are connected to pump and clear windings which are energized in a definite repeated sequence. It will be argued that energy gain is present in this circuit: the output signal is a higher energy level than the input signal [10, 11, 19].

When quiescent, the aperture shown in Fig. 18(a) will assume one of two states: the saturated state after application of a clear pulse, the tipped state after application of a pump pulse. Now it was convenient in Fig. 9 to imagine a single unique neutral state separating the set of flux states representing a "0" from the set of flux states

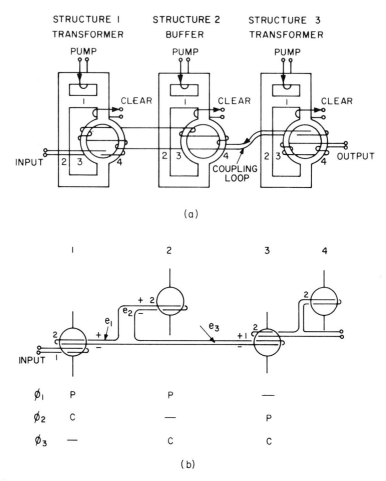

FIG. 18. Three elements connected so as to amplify. (a) Physical arrangement; (b) line drawing representation.

representing a "1". In practice, in the absence of signal input, perfect flux splitting does not occur and the resultant pattern will tend to be a "1" or tend to be a "0". The term "tipped state" will then be used to include the state which exists after the element has been pumped in the absence of signal current.

First consider the response of an aperture to coupling-loop current when it is in the saturated state. Suppose structure 3 (Fig. 18) has been cleared leaving legs 3 and 4 saturated up. Under these circumstances a coupling loop current flowing in the sense shown cannot switch leg 4 further into saturation but can reverse the flux in leg 3 by switching around the loop composed of legs 3, 1, and 2. In practice the coupling loop currents which flow are usually much smaller than this threshold; even if sufficiently large, switching can be prevented by energizing the clear winding which will hold the element saturated. Thus, the flow of coupling loop current does not generate an output voltage or a back voltage. The same is true for a flow of output current. The coupling loop and output circuit are very effectively isolated. In addition, the isolator appears to the coupling loop current and the output current as a short circuit.

Next consider the response of an aperture to coupling loop current when in the tipped state. Suppose structure 2 in Fig. 18 is in the tipped state. A current flowing in the coupling loop can then cause flux reversal around the aperture composed of legs 3 and 4. Furthermore, this aperture will not usually be fully set and consequently will not have a well-defined switching threshold (soft threshold). It will be shown that the behavior of this aperture sets an upper limit to the energy which can be taken from the circuit. A typical curve relating flux switched to the integral of the disturb current is shown in Fig. 13 (disturb characteristic).

The details of a basic transfer as well as energy gain calculations will be discussed using the line diagram shown in Fig. 18(b). This line drawing, without the flux sources, is analogous to showing only the signal path of an ac amplifier, and not the dc supply, when calculating amplification. The clock sequence is also shown. During phase 1, aperture 3 is saturated and isolates, hence we need only consider the coupling loop as connecting, via a low resistance loop, structures 1 and 2. These structures are pumped together as shown in the timing diagram of Fig. 18(b) and respond to an input tipping current. Applying Faraday's law and Kirchoff's law to the coupling loop, neglecting the resistance losses and integrating yields:

$$\Delta \phi_1{}^1 = \Delta \phi_2{}^1. \tag{12}$$

Here $\Delta \phi_1{}^1$ is the difference flux in element 1 at the end of phase 1 and $\Delta \phi_2{}^1$ is the difference flux in element 2 at the end of phase 1. The total energy input is that required to tip apertures 1 and 2, and is small if each of these responds easily to a tipping current. Note that if aperture 2 were not present, the coupling loop connected to aperture 1 would cause it to act as a shorted transformer, requiring considerable energy for tipping, dependent on the nature of the short. Ideally aperture 2 acts as an open circuit at this time. If this were the case, the only energy input would be that required to tip element 1. During phase 2, aperture 1 is cleared and returns to its original saturated state. The difference flux output must then be $\Delta \phi_1{}^1$. This flux causes positive or negative current to flow dependent on the sense of $\Delta\phi_1{}^1$. It is convenient to regard aperture 1 as a voltage or flux source with aperture 2 regarded as an internal impedance and aperture 3 a load. Aperture 3 and its associated load, aperture 4, are pumped at this time and hence respond easily to a tipping current. They behave at this time just as apertures 1 and 2 behaved during phase 1. Some voltage will be lost across the terminals of aperture 2. However, this loss will be small as element 2 idles (aperture is in the tipped state and the clock windings are not energized) at this time and is much less responsive to a tipping current than the pumped load. (Fig. 13 shows the response of a single element in the pumped and idle state.) Ideally, aperture 2 acts as a very low impedance at this time, and the energy delivered is only limited by the resistance loss in the coupling loop. Considerably more energy can be delivered to the output than was required to initially tip the input, hence, energy gain is possible. Again applying Kirchoff's law, Faraday's law (using a turns ratio of 2 : 1), and recalling that $\Delta\phi_1{}^1 = \Delta\phi_1{}^2$ we have

$$\Delta\phi_3{}^2 = 2(\Delta\phi_1{}^1 - \delta\phi_2{}^2) \tag{13}$$

where $\delta\phi_2{}^2$ is the flux loss in aperture 2 during phase 2. If proper attention is given to reference positive directions, it is clear that the difference flux in aperture 2 is reduced by $\delta\phi_2{}^2$ at the end of phase 2 and so is given by:

$$\Delta\phi_2{}^2 = \Delta\phi_1{}^1 - \delta\phi_2{}^2 \tag{14}$$

therefore:

$$\Delta\phi_3{}^2 = 2\Delta\phi_2{}^2 \tag{15}$$

that is to say, the tip in aperture 3 at the end of phase 2 is exactly twice the tip in aperture 2, *regardless of the flux loss in aperture 2 during phase 2.*

It is important to note that in the zero signal input case $\Delta\phi_1{}^1$ and hence $\Delta\phi_1{}^2$ will be very small (limited by aperture unbalance). Ideally, no current will flow during phase 2. If $\Delta\phi_1{}^1$ is slightly positive, then a corresponding small current will flow during phase 2. If $\Delta\phi_1{}^1$ is slightly negative, then an opposite polarity current will flow during phase 2. Now ideally for small currents at phase 2 time, aperture 2 will be disturbed a negligible amount, hence if

$$\delta\phi_2{}^2 = 0 \tag{16}$$

$$\Delta\phi_3{}^2 = 2\Delta\phi_1{}^1. \tag{17}$$

Thus small positive difference fluxes will, in a chain of elements of this kind, build up to large positive difference fluxes. The same is true for large negative difference fluxes: the circuit has two natural stable states. Buildup ceases when the flux loss in aperture 2 exactly balances the flux gain (still neglecting resistance losses). This loss is small for small $\Delta\phi_1{}^1$, but will increase with larger $\Delta\phi_1{}^1$ as larger coupling loop currents will flow during phase 2.

During phase 3, aperture 3 acts as a generator just as aperture 1 did during phase 2. It delivers energy to a connected load, aperture 4 acting as a low impedance. It remains to consider what happens in the coupling loop connecting apertures 1, 2, and 3. We first observe that element 1 is in the saturated state and hence isolates in the back direction. Now during phase 3, aperture 3 is switching, generating a voltage in both loop 1 and loop 2. However, aperture 2 can be cleared at this time, generating a voltage in loop 1 which, ideally, will exactly cancel that of aperture 3, if we recall from Eq. (15) that

$$\Delta\phi_3{}^2 = 2\phi_2{}^2. \tag{15}$$

Apertures 1 and 2 are returned to the saturated state, and we can again apply phase 1, repeating the sequence, and amplifying another input signal.

The action of the transformer and buffer shown in Fig. 18 may be summarized as follows:

Transformer: When saturated the element acts to isolate input and output windings presenting a low impedance to signals at either terminals; when pumped it acts as a low loss gate, between input and output windings.

Buffer: This element when pumped should act as a high impedance to the flow of signal current; when in the idle state it should present a low impedance to signal current.

4.2 Theoretical and Practical Limits on Gain

In the case of polycrystalline ferrite it is extremely difficult to obtain good circuit models directly from considerations of internal physics as discussed in Section I. With this in mind consider measuring the characteristics of a balanced element using wave shapes of the type to which it will be subjected in actual circuits. These measurements must include the effect of soft threshold. The circuit shown in Fig. 18 has been used for this purpose. Here elements 1 and 2 serve to generate a representative wave shape which is applied to element 3. As usual, 1 and 2 are first tipped, then 1 is cleared, tipping element 3. The current tending to tip 3, during the second transfer, is determined by the level which is set into 1 during the first transfer.

We seek an expression for the energy gain of the system, where this is defined as the ratio of the signal energy into aperture 3 during the second transfer, divided by the energy into the input terminals of aperture 1 during the first transfer.

The energy input during the first transfer must be sufficient to set element 1 and 2. Consider setting element 1 with two distinct difference flux inputs, and consider the coupling loop current which flows during the second transfer corresponding to each of these inputs. Two such measured currents are shown in Fig. 19(a) and are labeled i and i'.

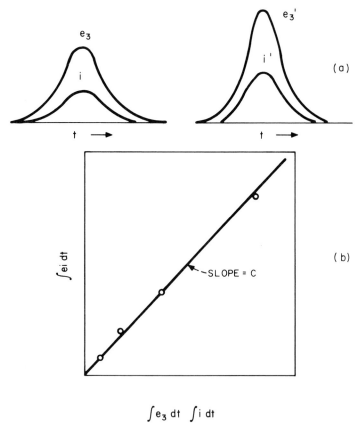

$$\int e_3 \, dt \quad \int i \, dt$$

FIG. 19. Experimental results showing the relationship between $\int ei \, dt$ and $\int e \, dt \int i \, dt$.

The voltage generated by i across the input of element 3 is labeled e_3 and that generated by i' labled e_3'. It is apparent from the wave shapes that it is not unreasonable to assume

$$e_3'(t) = k_1 e_3(t) \tag{18}$$

$$i'(t) = k_2 i(t). \tag{19}$$

These relationships imply that some basic wave shape exists and all others are scaled versions of these wave shapes. Now the energy into element 3 corresponding to e_3' and i' is

$$\int_0^T e_3' i' dt \tag{20}$$

where T is the transfer time. From relationships (18)–(20) we can then write

$$\int_0^T e_3' i' dt = k_1 k_2 \int_0^T e_3 i \, dt. \tag{21}$$

Now if we consider the product,

$$\int_0^T e_3' \, dt \int_0^T i' dt \tag{22}$$

it is clear this can be written

$$\int_0^T e_3' \, dt \int_0^T i' dt = k_1 k_2 \int_0^T e_3 \, dt \int_0^T i \, dt. \tag{23}$$

Dividing (21) by (23) we obtain

$$\frac{\displaystyle\int_0^T e_3' i' dt}{\displaystyle\int_0^T e_3' \, dt \int_0^T i_3' \, dt} = \frac{\displaystyle\int_0^T e_3 i \, dt}{\displaystyle\int_0^T e_3 \, dt \int_0^T i \, dt}. \tag{24}$$

Now e_3' and e_3 were wave shapes of two arbitrary amplitudes. If (24) holds for all pairs of wave shapes this implies that for any value of e_3 and i

$$\int_0^T e_3 i \, dt \bigg/ \left(\int_0^T e_3 \, dt \int_0^T i \, dt \right) = C. \tag{25}$$

The above relationship was tested experimentally by direct observation of the coupling loop current and difference flux into element 3 for a variety of coupling loop currents. The results are shown in Fig. 19(b). The highest point on this curve corresponds to a difference flux of 75%, which is as large a tip as usually occurs in operating circuits. We can regard this experimental result as a starting point and although eqs. (18) and (19) may be true, generally they may be stronger relationships than we need. With these results in mind it is clear that the energy into element 3 may be expressed as

$$E_3 = \int e_3 i \, dt$$

$$E_3 = C \int e_3 \, dt \int i \, dt \tag{26}$$

$$E_3 = C N_3 \Delta\phi_3{}^2 I$$

where $\Delta\phi_3{}^2$ is the difference flux into element 3 during phase 2, N_3 is the number of turns on element 3 in the coupling loop, and I is the integral of the coupling loop current.

The above relationship implies that the energy required to tip an element may be determined from a control curve of the type shown in Fig. 13. This control curve was measured in the manner described above: Elements 1 and 2 acted as a signal generator to supply representative signals to an aperture of the dimensions shown in Fig. 13. The volt-second area across the input terminals is plotted versus the integral of the coupling loop current. The energy input is proportional to the product of the ordinate and the abscissa in this control curve. Some reflection also shows that this curve may be scaled to provide the control curve for a larger or smaller hole. The abscissa is scaled in direct proportion to the length of the balanced element and the ordinate in direct proportion to the area. The control energy input is then directly proportional to the volume. Ideally inside and outside diameters of the balanced element should be scaled as well.

We seek to maximize the energy gain of the circuit shown in Fig. 18. First observe that the energy input during phase 1 is independent of aperture 3 as this aperture isolates at that time. Therefore we first try to maximize the transfer of energy during phase 2 by imagining elements 1 and 2 are fixed in size and imagine varying the length of element 3. This will show us how, for any combination of elements 1 and 2, element 3 may be shaped for maximum energy transfer. This is analogous to the conventional problem of a generator with a fixed internal impedance. We seek to find the load which will maximize the energy transfer.

The expression for the energy into element 3, during the second transfer, may be set up so that differentiation with respect to I corresponds to varying the length of element 3 relative to 1 and 2. From this the control curve of the load may be determined so that the energy transfer from 1 and 2 into the load is maximized. Having maximized the output during phase 2 this output may be divided by the input during phase 1 to maximize the energy gain. The determination of maximum gain may be handled in this two-step process since the energy required to set up 1 and 2 during phase 1 is independent of the length of element 3. The details of this analysis are carried out below.

The energy into the load during phase 2 is given by

$$E_{\text{out}} = CN_3 \Delta\phi_3^2 I. \tag{27}$$

Varying the length of element 3 will vary I and also $\Delta\phi_3^2$. Regarding $\Delta\phi_3^2$ as a function of I, differentiating the above and equating to zero yields

$$N_3 \Delta\phi_3^2 = -I(d/dI)(N_3 \Delta\phi_3^2). \tag{28}$$

Now $\Delta\phi_3^2$ may be expressed as a function of $\delta\phi_2^2$ and $\Delta\phi_1^2$ by writing Kirchoff's law for the coupling loop during the second transfer, and then integrating. This expression may be substituted into the right side of the above. Recalling also that $\Delta\phi_1^2$ is not a function of I, Eq. (28) becomes

$$N_3 \Delta\phi_3^2 = I(d/dI) \int e_2 \, dt + IR \tag{29}$$

where e_2 is the voltage at the terminals of element 2 during phase 2. The first term on the right may be evaluated from the disturb curve of an element. For example, Fig. 13 shows the integral of the voltage across element 2 as a function of I. If such a curve is measured using N_2 turns on element 2 then normalization for turns requires dividing the vertical axis by N_2 and multiplying the horizontal axes by N_2. Thus if K_B is the slope at the origin of the disturb curve of element 2 referred to one turn, Eq. (29) may be approximated by

$$N_3 \Delta\phi_3^2 = I(R + (N_2)^2 K_B). \tag{30}$$

Now the control curve of the load is merely a relationship between $\Delta\phi_3^2$ and I. The above then tells us what the control curve of the load should be for maximum energy transfer. It is apparent that the control curve of the load depends upon the coupling loop resistance and K_B. If we construct a load with this control curve and analyze the resultant circuit during phase 2 by applying Kirchoff's law and integrating, it is very easy to show that half the volt-second area delivered by aperture 1 arrives in the load and the other half appears across the combination of aperture 2 and the loop resistance R. This is exactly analogous to the matched generator problem where half the energy from the source is dissipated in the internal impedance and the other half is delivered to the load. Thus under conditions of maximum energy transfer

$$N_3 \Delta\phi_3{}^2 = \tfrac{1}{2}N_1 \Delta\phi_1{}^2 = \tfrac{1}{2}N_1\Delta\phi_1{}^1.$$ (31)

The energy output during phase 2 can then be expressed in terms of the difference flux input during phase 1 by substituting Eqs. (31) and (30) into (27).

$$E_{\max} = \{C(N_1\Delta\phi_1{}^1)^2/4(R + (N_2)^2 K_B)\}$$ (32)

It is clear from the above that the energy output depends on the size of element 2 as K_B is a function of element size.

The energy input during phase 1 is given by

$$E_{\text{in}} = E_1 + E_2$$ (33)

where E_1 is the energy required to tip element 1 and E_2 that required to tip element 2. Here we neglect coupling-loop loss as the current which flows during phase 1 in the loop connecting elements 1, 2, and 3 is usually small.

The energy required to tip these elements may be estimated from the control curve of the elements as the product of the ordinate and the abscissa. If the slope of the control curve for element 2 at the origin is K, referred to one turn the energy input may be approximated by

$$E_2 = \{C(N_2 \Delta\phi_2{}^1)^2/(N_2)^2 K\}.$$ (34)

Similarly

$$E_1 = \{C(N_1\Delta\phi_1{}^1)^2/(N_1)^2 K'\}$$ (35)

where K' is the slope of the control curve of element 1 referred to one turn. From Kirchoff's law applied during phase 1, it is also clear that

$$N_1\Delta\phi_1{}^1 = N_2 \Delta\phi_2{}^1.$$ (36)

Hence (34) becomes

$$E_2 = \{C(N_1\Delta\phi_1{}^1)^2/(N_2)^2 K\}.$$ (37)

The expression for the energy gain (E.G.) is obtained using Eqs. (35), (37), and (32)

$$\text{E.G.} = \frac{1}{4(R + N_2{}^2 K_B)} \bigg/ \left(\frac{1}{N_2{}^2 K'} + \frac{1}{N_2{}^2 K} \right).$$ (38)

Now K and K_B are both dependent on the size of element 2. However K' is dependent only on the size of element 1. The gain will be maximized if element 1 is made small compared to element 2 so that K' is large compared to K. In other words the input energy during phase 1 is used primarily in element 2 and not in element 1. The energy gain then becomes

$$\text{E.G.} = K \Big/ 4\Big(\frac{R}{N_2{}^2} + K_B\Big). \tag{39}$$

N_2 may be made large to minimize the effect of resistance losses. If these losses can be neglected the gain becomes

$$\text{Max E.G.} = K/4K_B. \tag{40}$$

From the above it is clear that the maximum available gain is dependent only on the characteristics of element 2. K is the slope of the control curve for element 2, and K_B is the slope of the disturb curve. If K is large element 2 will be tipped with very little current during phase 1. Ideally it will act as a very high impedance. During phase 2 if K_B is small it acts as a very low impedance. Equation (40) is extremely useful in comparing materials for logic applications. These same characteristics are also important in memory applications.

Equation (40) will give an accurate estimate of the gain provided

(a) Element 1 is made small compared to element 2.

(b) The resistance losses during phase 1 and phase 2 may be neglected.

(c) The control curve of element 3 is matched to the internal impedance of the source as given by equation (30).

The analysis above suggests a semiconductor magnetic circuit with two natural stable states in which all the amplifying capability is put into the semiconductors and all the storage in the magnetic elements. This circuit is shown in Fig. 20. Here aperture 2 has been

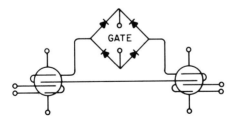

Fig. 20. A core semiconductor arrangement with memory in the magnetic elements and gain capability in the semiconductor.

replaced by a diode bridge which if clocked properly will act as a high impedance during phase 1 and a low impedance during phase 2. A high ratio of K/K_B will be realized. This kind of arrangement does not require standby power but will have the amplifying capability of semiconductor circuits together with the isolation and memory capability of magnetic circuit. In addition it will have two natural stable states. Furthermore a series arrangement of these elements requires only two clock phases for its operation rather than three in the completely magnetic case.

5. 3-Phase Circuits

5.1 Characteristics of Operating Circuits

In Section 4 (Fig. 18) it was shown how directivity, isolation, amplification, and two natural stable states were obtained when four elements were connected together. In order to construct a reentrant amplifier or shift register, 6 holes and three phases are required as shown in Fig. 21. Each of the phases performs the same basic operation but each is shifted one spatial position. The basic operation of phases 1 and 2 was discussed in Section 4.1 and is summarized in Fig. 21 together with the operation of phase 3. Here the buffers are shown large compared to the transformers to maximize the energy gain as discussed in Section 4.2. Although this is desirable whenever significant fan out is required, it is unnecessary for shift register construction [20]. For that purpose only the small balanced elements need be used. Element sizes used in practical circuits are shown in Fig. 22.

In Fig. 21(a) a row of 6 holes from structures 1 through 6 were wired together to form a bit, or amplifier, as shown in detail in Fig. 21(b). To construct a serial shift register the output of the first row of holes is fed back to the second row. A 6-bit shift register may be constructed using the six elements shown. The action of each of the elements is summarized below.

Phase 1:   Element 1 is pumped and receives information; element 5 is cleared and transmits information; element 3 isolates; elements 4 and 5 transmit together, their voltages cancelling in the common coupling loop; element 2 is pumped providing a high impedance in loop 1.

Phase 2:   Element 3 is pumped and receives information; element 1 is cleared and transmits information; element 5 isolates; elements 1 and 6' (or 6 if feedback is used) transmit together, their voltages cancelling in the common coupling loop; element 4 is pumped providing a high impedance in loop 2.

Phase 3:   Element 5 is pumped and receives information; element 3 is cleared and transmits information; element 1 isolates; elements 3 and 2 transmit together, their voltages cancelling in the common coupling loop; 6 is pumped providing a high impedance in loop 3. The system is now in a position to reapply phase 1.

The logical symbols used to represent an amplifier are shown in Fig. 21(c) and (d). Fig. 21(c) represents a complete amplifier made

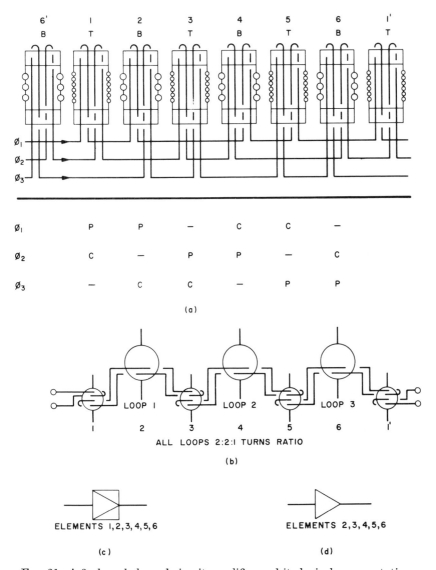

FIG. 21. A 3-phase balanced circuit amplifier and its logical representation.

from six holes. Fig. 21(d) represents an amplifier made with transformer 1 missing. In logic circuits this transformer is replaced by a logic element to be described.

The amplification of an amplifier stage using the elements shown in Fig. 22(a) and (b) is shown in Fig. 23(a). The difference flux output

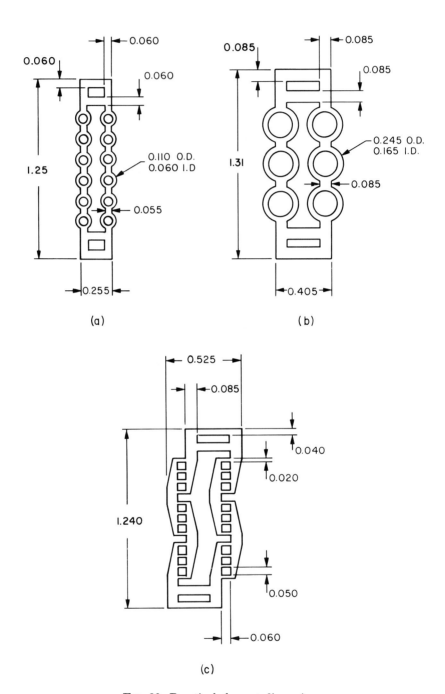

FIG. 22. Practical element dimensions.

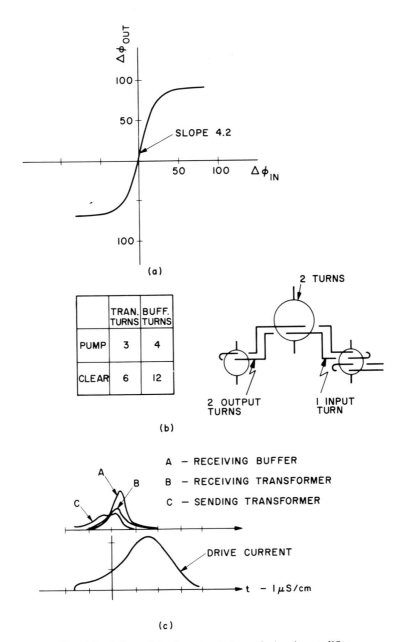

FIG. 23. Gain and timing of a balanced circuit amplifier.

from transformer 1 (Fig. 21) is plotted against the difference flux input to transformer 1. The output transformer was loaded with the next stage. Each transformer had 1 figure-eight input turn and 2 output turns. Each buffer had 2 figure-eight turns.

The relative timing of transformers and buffers influences the gain curve considerably. For the measurement shown in Fig. 23(a) the pump and clear turns on transformers and buffers were wound as shown in Fig. 23(b). The relative switching times of a transformer and buffers are shown in Fig. 23(c). It is important that the receiving transformer and buffer switch at least as long as the sending transformer, otherwise the tipping current is ineffective during a portion of its period. This is accomplished using the numbers of turns shown in Fig. 23(b). With these turns the circuit is relatively insensitive to the wave shape of the driving current. In this case the drive current was supplied by a capacitor–silicon-controlled rectifier combination which acted as a variable voltage source. When driven from a current source the gain curve was not significantly altered.

5.2 A Comparison of Unipolar and Bipolar Circuits

The unipolar circuit shown in Fig. 24 operates in a manner analogous to the balanced circuit shown in Fig. 21. In fact the clocking arrangement for the balanced circuit of Fig. 21 was arrived at by direct analogy with the circuit of Fig. 24. However, in the unipolar circuit a "1" is represented by a set core and a "0" by a reset core [21].

During phase 1 in Fig. 24(a), elements 1 and 2 are biased almost to the threshold for switching; element 3 isolates. If a "1" is applied to the input, elements 1 and 2 will switch from a reset to a set condition. Ideally, in the case of a "0" no input current appears, and the cores remain in the reset state. During phase 2 element 1 is pulsed so as to send it to a reset state: elements 3 and 4 are biased to the threshold for switching. If element 1 has previously been set, it is reset at this time generating a current to set elements 3 and 4. If it has not been previously set, ideally no current flows and elements 3 and 4 are left in a reset state.

There are two fundamental difficulties with this arrangement:

(1) Soft threshold effects make practical biasing extremely difficult.

(2) The system as described does not have two natural stable states.

During transfer of a full "1" from element 1 to elements 3 and 4 a large coupling loop current flows tending to switch element 2, which causes a loss in flux transferred. However, if element 1 has only been partially set the coupling loop current generated is less, and the tendency to lose flux in element 7 reduced. If a gain curve is measured by measuring the flux output from 1 and the flux input to 7, it will

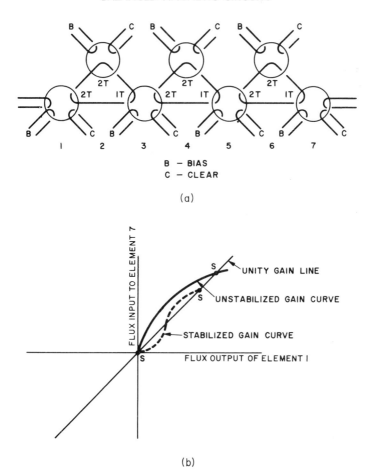

(a)

(b)

FIG. 24. Characteristics of a unipolar system.

appear as shown in Fig. 24(b). This implies that small noise signals will build up to the stable point shown and that indeed is what occurs. The system goes to a state where the register is loaded with "1"s. This may be overcome by adding a small core to absorb the small flux levels or adding coupling-loop resistance. Both of these usually lower the entire gain curve. However, two stable states can be created as shown in Fig. 24(b). Under these circumstances a two stable state system has been created by suppressing the small signals, which have the highest intrinsic gain, and insisting on amplifying the large signals which are the most difficult to amplify. By contrast the balanced circuit of Fig. 21 easily achieves two natural stable states by amplifying the small signals and allowing the limitation in gain for large signals to establish the operating levels. This fundamental difference manifests itself in almost inoperable margins in Fig. 24 compared to at least a 6 : 1 allowable switching time variations in the circuit of Fig. 21. With this comparison in mind it is sometimes convenient to regard the balanced element of Fig. 21 as a core to which a dynamic bias can be applied (the pump) without requiring tight margins on this bias.

6. Multiple Path Parallel Circuit—Logic Element

6.1 Interconnection of Logic Elements and Amplifiers

A basic structure containing six logic elements is shown in Fig. 22(c). Each of these elements has four parallel paths rather than two, and the structure has been shaped, with due regard for internal fields, so that flux will tend to split equally between all four legs in the absence of tipping current. The flux sources at the end have been chosen so that if all the flux at pump time is diverted into one of the four parallel paths, it will just saturate that path. A circuit using a logic element is shown in Fig. 25(a). An element with four parallel paths has been substituted in transformer position 1 and the clocking remains that of the usual three phase system; however, two logic inputs X and Y are now possible. Suppose the legs of this logic element have been saturated from right to left in Fig. 25(a). Then, at pump time (phase 1), flux will enter at the top. If X is "1", current will flow in the reference direction shown, tending to inhibit legs 1 and 2 and enhance switching in legs 3 and 4. Similarly, if Y is a "1", legs 1 and 3 will be inhibited and switching in leg 4 enhanced. The net effect is to select leg 4. Some reflection shows that each input combination is associated with a unique output leg. The legs selected are shown in Fig. 25(b). This type of function decomposition makes it possible to generate any function of two variables by linking the output legs selectively. For example, the sum and carry outputs for a binary counter are shown in Fig. 25(b). Now whereas inputs occur at the time of pump, outputs are usually taken at the time of clear. Therefore, if the output is a "1", it will cause current flow in the reference positive direction at the time of clear. This is easily verified for the sum and carry windings in Fig. 25(a). Whenever logic elements are cascaded without intervening stages the complement of the function must be generated, as the output at pump time is the complement of the output at clear time.

The symbol for a logic element together with the symbol for the five elements in the amplifier is shown in Fig. 25(c). The decimal numbers appearing in the symbol for the logic element are obtained directly from Fig. 25(b) by interpreting the columns as binary numbers with the least significant bit at the bottom of the column. For example,

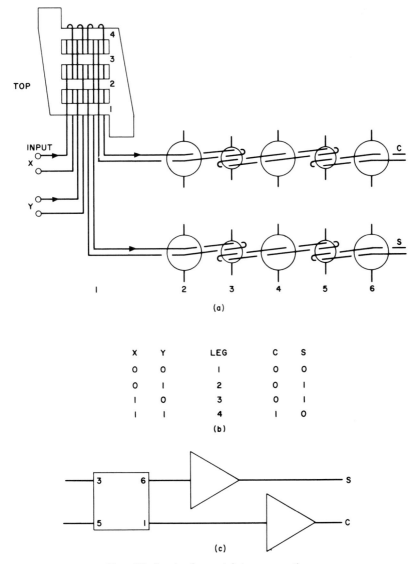

FIG. 25. Logic element interconnection

under column C the binary number 1 appears. A 1 appears in this position in the symbol for the logic element.

For reference purposes, define the "top" of a four-legged or two-legged element as the side the flux enters at the time of pump. Input and output windings are placed on the logic element starting at a point 90° counterclockwise from the top. With this convention the binary code in Fig. 25(b) represents the way in which the windings link the legs if "0" is interpreted as over. For example, the winding carrying the X input when traced in the reference positive direction goes over legs 1 and 2 and under legs 3 and 4 corresponding to the pattern shown in Fig. 25(a). The same convention applies to windings Y, C, and S.

6.2 Binary Counter—Lock-up Circuit

The symbol for a logic stage which will generate the sum and carry outputs for a binary counter stage is shown in Fig. 25(c). The logic element is pumped and tipped during the first occurrence of phase 1. During the second occurrence of phase 1, the sum and carry outputs are cleared from elements 5 [Fig. 25(a)]. The sum may then be re-applied as input as shown in Fig. 26. The feedback amplifier shown in

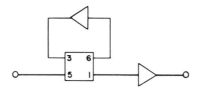

FIG. 26. A binary counter stage.

Fig. 26 is then more than an amplifier, it is also a memory. If this memory has been cleared, then its "0" will be applied to input 3 at the same time as a "1" is applied to input 5. The 6 output will generate a "1" and the carry output a "0". During the next occurrence of phase 1, the "1" stored in the feedback loop will combine with the "1" input to input 5 giving a sum output of "0" and a carry output of "1". It is then clear that this can act as the first stage of a binary counter. Succeeding stages are identical.

A so-called lockup circuit is shown in Fig. 27. Whenever Y is a "0", it is intended that a "1" input to X will send Z to a "1" which will then remain a "1" regardless of the value of X. The circuit is cleared if Y is sent to the "1" state. First consider the truth table for Y, Z, and F'. Whenever Y is a "1", the output is "0". However, whenever Y is "0" the output is identically equal to the input Z. This truth table then represents a gate which will pass Z faithfully if Y is "0"; however, if Y is "1" it will output "0"'s. Now as discussed previously, the F function is a 4. Note, however, a $\overline{4}$ is shown in the logic diagram. This inversion of the output winding on the structure is required as the second stage receives the output from the first stage at the time

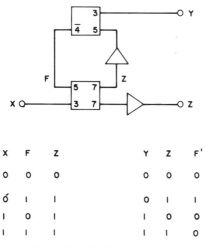

X	F	Z		Y	Z	F'
0	0	0		0	0	0
0	1	1		0	1	1
1	0	1		1	0	0
1	1	1		1	1	0

FIG. 27. A lock-up circuit.

the first stage is pumped, not the time it is cleared. Suppose Y is set at "0" and consider the truth table of X, F, and Z. If F is "0" and X is "1", then Z is "1". During the next occurrence of phase 1, F will be a "1" and Z will be a "1" independent of X. Thus a single "1" will cause the circuit to lock up in a "1" state. It will stay in that state until Y is made a "1" for at least one clock cycle.

6.3 Testing Logic Stages

Figure 28(b) shows two binary counter logic stages in line diagram form. Stage 2 is to be tested. This involves fixing one of the variables and measuring the input–output gain for the other. In this case, the first stage is used to deliver a carry input to stage 2 from the same circuit and of the same size as would occur in normal practice. The carry input C_{in} was first set to a "0". Using a hairpin probe and a program generator the signal in transformer A was overwritten. The subsequent sum output signal was measured and regarded as the input. The value of this signal after one trip around the feedback path (a frame—three clock phases) was also measured and regarded as the output. Note that the signal at A was not overwritten every frame. The difference flux signals were measured using a set of diode gates, gated at the appropriate clock times and fed to an X–Y plotter. The measurements were repeated for a series of inputs and outputs (varied by varying the overwriting signal). The results are shown in Fig. 28(a). The first and third quadrants show the case where $C_{in} = 0$. It is clear

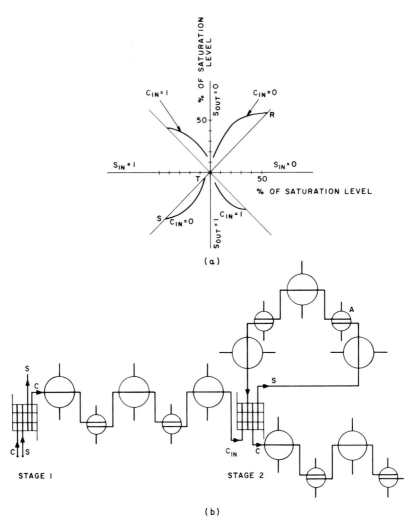

FIG. 28. Testing a logic stage by perturbation from its operating points.

there is gain around the loop involving the sum winding. The normal stable operating points are where the s-shaped curve crosses the unity gain line. The difference flux is expressed as a percent of a full tip. Here a full tip occurs if all the pumped flux switches down one leg of the logic element.

The discontinuity at the origin occurred when the overwrite signal was just large enough to change the sense of the transformer output. At point T in Fig. 28(a) the overwrite signal is large, the normal stable level in this quadrant is S and the stage would go to that level in the absence of an overwrite. Thus at point T the overwrite is in the opposite direction from the signal coming into the transformer. A slight additional value of overwrite causes buildup to start toward R not S, and now overwrite and feedback signal are in the same direction, causing a jump in the plotter from point T to point R. To measure the curve in quadrant I, the sense of the overwrite signal must now be reversed. The discontinuity in the $C_{in} = $ "1" curve occurred for the same reason.

This technique of measuring circuit performance by perturbing the system, without changing the wiring, and examining its recovery is satisfactory if the circuits can be expected to be operating and we wish to measure how close the circuits are to failure. It is not satisfactory if initial designs are being tested. In this case, it is necessary to open the feedback loop, put on a dummy load, and measure the gain curves. Systems have been measured both ways, and for all practical purposes the same gain curves result. Other logic stages may be tested in a similar manner.

7. Logic Operations Realized on a Two-Path Balanced Circuit

The ability of a four-legged magnetic structure to realize all Boolean functions of two variables has been discussed. There is an alternative way to mechanize some of the most commonly used logic functions of two or more variables on the simpler two-path balanced magnetic circuit by applying more than two windings on a single aperture [22]. Since the operation of such an aperture depends on the net magnetic drive, the term "threshold logic" is sometimes used.

7.1 Linearly Separable Logic Functions

If an aperture is fitted with several input windings, the tipping of flux in a circular sense around the aperture during a pump pulse results from the cumulative effect of several signal currents. Coming from similar apertures, the signals will be similar, differing only by the amount of variation in flux switched between the several sending apertures and the variation in coupling loop losses.

To avoid a zero drive or null condition on the aperture an odd number of input windings is necessary. All of the linearly separable functions of two variables (i.e., all but the exclusive OR functions) may be realized on a three-winding aperture. One input, serving as a bias, carries an unchanging "0" or "1" signal, and acts both to select the particular function realized and to prevent a null output.

Figure 29(a) shows the manner in which an aperture is wired to realize a logic function. Figure 29(b) shows the truth table for the

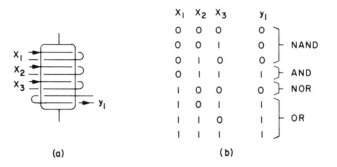

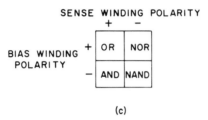

(a)   (b)

SENSE WINDING POLARITY

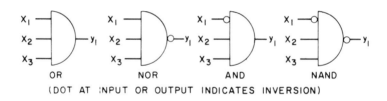

(c)

(DOT AT INPUT OR OUTPUT INDICATES INVERSION)

(d)

FIG. 29. Threshold logic element.

aperture. In brief, the AND and OR functions of X_2 and X_3 are obtained by applying a "0" and a "1", respectively, to the X_1 or bias winding, and the NAND and NOR functions obtained by reversing the polarity of the output winding.[4] Figure 29(c) makes the same statements in tabular form, and Fig. 29(d) shows the symbols for the four commonly used functions.

---

[4] The same winding convention is used here as discussed previously. It is assumed the output is taken at the time of clear.

The utility of the multiple input winding logic gate depends critically on its operating margins, or allowable variation of input signal level without disturbing the desired output response. For example in a 3-input threshold logic unit with input magneto motive forces (mmf's) M_1, M_2, and M_3, the following three inequalities must be satisfied if the unit is to operate properly:

$$M_1 + M_2 > M_3$$
$$M_2 + M_3 > M_1 \qquad (41)$$
$$M_3 + M_1 > M_2.$$

If the inequality signs are replaced by equalities, each of the resulting equations defines a plane, and the three planes taken together define a triangular cone. Inside the cone all of the inequalities are satisfied, and outside it at least one is violated. Thus, the region of successful operation can be predicted.

The actual region of successful operation was searched by driving each of 3 input windings from a common pulse source so that wave shape and timing were uniform. Current-varying resistors were inserted in each input line. Although there was cross coupling between resistor adjustments, this was compensated for by sensing the input current with current probes. The operating region can be visualized as a three-dimensional volume for a device with three inputs. The boundary between proper and improper response was searched in this three-dimensional figure by varying the input signal levels, and for each combination of levels, stepping through the eight possible combinations of signal polarity and monitoring the output voltage for amplitude and proper logical response. Such a test was performed using the circuit shown in Fig. 30, and the results of some 200 measurements yielded the figure shown in Fig. 31. The nominal drive to be expected from a balanced magnetic aperture is approximated by the geometric center of the cube. The region within which proper operation can be expected is defined by the triangular cone. Test points are shown on the figure. The open circles lying outside the cone do not give proper operation of the logic aperture, and the solid circles generally lying inside the cone do give proper operation. The slight discrepancies near the cone boundary are probably due to asymmetries in the windings and inherent aperture unbalances. The permissible variations in input signal shown in the figure represent satisfactory operating margins.

Another useful test of operating margins uses inputs derived from other balanced magnetic apertures. These act as voltage sources and have the advantage of testing the logic aperture in the environment

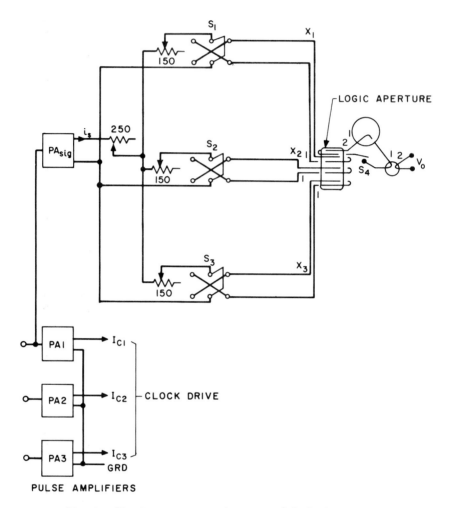

F<small>IG</small>. 30. Circuit arrangement for a test of the logic aperture.

in which it normally operates. The procedure is to hold two input
signals fixed, vary the third, from maximum negative through zero
to maximum positive excitation, and monitor the output during the
variation. The input and output signals are gated and integrated so
as to produce signals proportional to input and output flux, respectively. When the two inputs held fixed are of opposite polarity, the
input–output transfer curves are a characteristic s-shape, from which
can be read the small signal gain (slope at the origin), the offset (X
and Y intercepts), and a rough measure of the operating margin (the
area between each limb of the curve and a 45° line passing through the

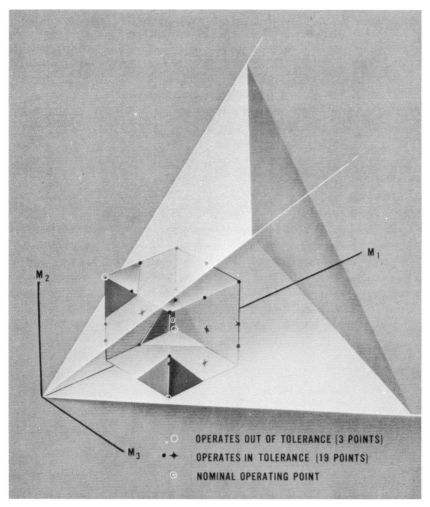

Fig. 31. Operating margins for the threshold logic gate.

origin). Figure 32 shows representative curves for a logic aperture. Figure 32(a) depicts an acceptable aperture, while the margins for Fig. 32(b) are not acceptable.

7.2 Exclusive OR and Lock-up Circuits

The exclusive OR $(X_2 \overline{X}_3 + \overline{X}_2 X_3)$ and its complement $(X_2 X_3 + \overline{X}_2 \overline{X}_3)$ are not linearly separable, in the sense that no plane can be found which is capable of separating these functions from the other

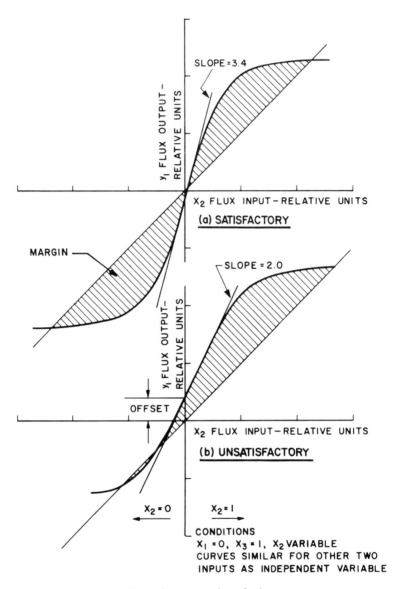

FIG. 32. Transfer curves for a logic aperture.

functions in the space representing all Boolean functions of two variables. It is possible to realize the exclusive OR using three balanced magnetic logic units, and one such circuit is shown in Fig. 33. It consists of a NOR and an AND gate which in turn drive a NOR gate. With the buffering and isolation provided by the interposed buffers, the gate works with adequate margins. In fact although Fig. 33 implies a full bit of delay between the two stages of logic apertures, it is possible to operate the circuit with the two stages separated by only a single buffer, producing the logical output in less than a full bit time. The exclusive OR was found to be a frequently occurring function in the work on balanced magnetics.

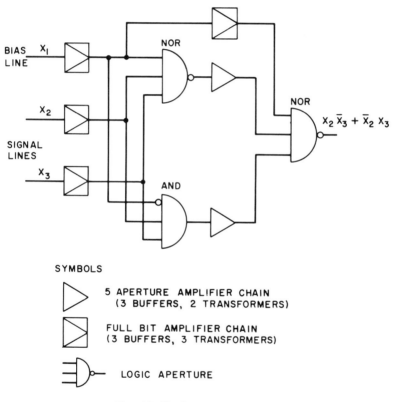

FIG. 33. Exclusive OR circuit.

Another frequently used device functioned in the manner of an R–S (Reset–Set) flip-flop, and can be realized by feeding back the output of a logic aperture through a stage of gain to its input. Figure 34 shows the circuit diagram and the state table for this circuit. It ordinarily exists in either state 1 or 2 (reset or set), and it operates under the cyclic excitation of the clock. Simultaneous application of a set and reset signal normally does not occur, but if it does, the circuit state remains unchanged. The circuit takes a minimum of two clock cycles

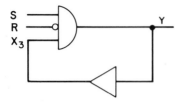

NOTE: DOT AT INPUT SIGNIFIES
INVERSION

CIRCUIT

STATE	S	R	X_3	Y_1	NEXT STATE	COMMENTS
1	0	0	0	0	1	S (STABLE)
2	0	0	1	1	2	S
3	0	1	0	0	3	S
4	0	1	1	0	3	UNSTABLE - RESET CONDITION
5	1	0	0	1	6	UNSTABLE - SET CONDITION
6	1	0	1	1	6	S
7	1	1	0	0	7	S (NOT USED)
8	1	1	1	1	8	S (NOT USED)

LOCK SEQUENCE: 1 − 5 − 6 − 2
UNLOCK SEQUENCE: 2 − 4 − 3 − 1

STATE TABLE

FIG. 34. Bistable circuit using a two path element and an amplifier.

to complete a set or reset cycle, but can take longer if the application of the actuating signal is prolonged.

The flux-input–flux-output characteristic is shown in Fig. 35. Point 1 on the curve corresponds to R, S, and Y all "0". If R is held "0" and S changed from a "0" to a "1" the curve 1,2,3,4 is followed. The jump at point 2 occurs when the feedback variable changes from a "0" to a "1". S is changed from a "1" to a "0" between points 4 and 5. The output stays a "1". With S held at "0" the reset curve 5,6,7,8,9 is followed as R is changed from "0" to "1" to "0".

7.3 Subtractor Circuit

A related problem which arose in the course of work on an automatic positioning mechanism was to form the difference of two binary numbers representing commanded and actual table positions in two directions. The numbers were presented in time serial form, least significant bit first. What was needed was a subtractor which could accept a

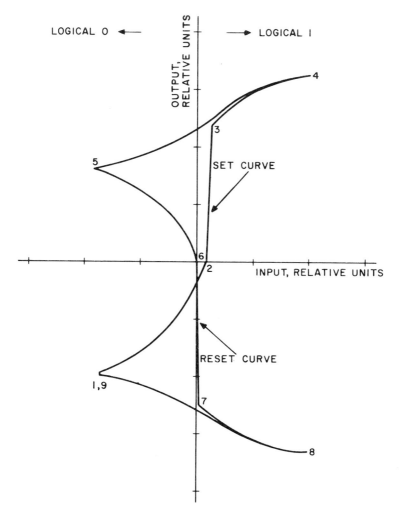

FIG. 35. Transfer characteristics of a lock-up circuit.

subtrahend S_i, minuend N_i, take into account any borrow propagated from a previous operation B_i, and produce a difference D_i, meanwhile storing any borrow newly generated, B_{i+1}. The truth table relating the input and output quantities is shown in Fig. 36. (In a strict sense, the borrows are neither input nor output quantities. A borrow can be generated by the first pair of digits entering the subtractor or at any time thereafter. The function of the borrow circuit is to keep up to date the presence of a borrow from one bit column to the next, and will

INPUTS			OUTPUTS		A $M(B_i,\bar{S}_i,N_i)$	B $\bar{B}_i$	C $M(B_i,S_i,\bar{N}_i)$	$M(A,B,C)$
BORROW B_i	MINUEND S_i	SUBTRAHEND N_i	DIFFERENCE D_i	NEXT BORROW B_{i+1}				
0	0	0	0	0	0	I	0	0
0	0	I	I	I	I	I	0	I
0	I	0	I	0	0	I	I	I
0	I	I	0	0	0	I	0	0
I	0	0	I	I	I	0	I	I
I	0	I	0	I	I	0	0	0
I	I	0	0	0	0	0	I	0
I	I	I	I	I	I	0	I	I

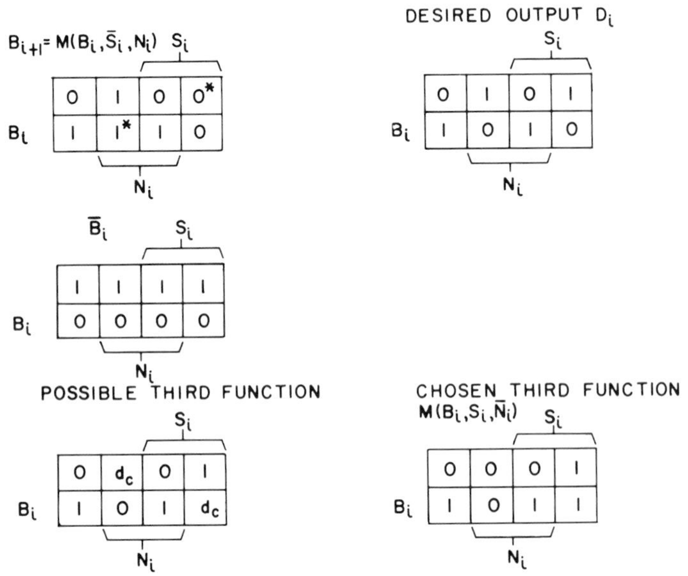

Fig. 36. Design of a subtractor circuit.

only be sensed as an output quantity at the end of the calculation for the purpose of underflow detection.)

It can be seen by inspection that the difference D_i is the exclusive OR of S_i and N_i, when $B_i = $ "0" and the complement of the exclusive OR when $B_i = $ "1". The borrow B_{i+1} is the majority function of $\bar{S}_i$, N_i, and B_i. The borrow can be generated directly using a single three-winding aperture. Direct generation of the difference by the exclusive OR gate described above might be awkward. The method to be described below was suggested by K. V. Mina, and it illustrates a useful design approach.

Observe that the borrow function $B_{i+1} = M(B_i, \overline{S}_i, N_i)$ differs from the desired difference in only two entries of the truth table, the third and sixth. These locations are also starred in the Karnaugh map for B_{i+1}, in Fig. 36. Notice also that at these locations the desired output is identical with inputs $\overline{B}_i$, S_i, and $\overline{N}_i$. Consider combining B_i and B_{i+1} in a majority logic circuit with another as yet unspecified function to generate D_i. The Karnaugh maps of $\overline{B}_i$, B_{i+1}, and D_i have been used to establish this third function as shown in Fig. 36. The resulting map has two "don't care" positions, which if chosen correctly, enable the third function to be made a threshold function, whose Karnaugh map is shown on the bottom of Fig. 36. Threshold functions in a three variable Karnaugh map can be recognized by a characteristic "T" shape, with the apex of the T identifying the arguments of the function. Thus the required third function is the majority function $M(B_i, S_i, \overline{N}_i)$.

The resulting subtractor circuit diagram, complete with required delays and fan-out amplifiers, is shown in Fig. 37. It can be seen that the

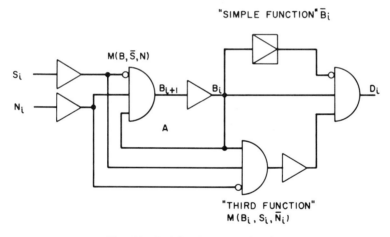

FIG. 37. Serial subtractor circuit.

loop "A" is the R–S circuit described previously. It is the means of storage for the propagated borrow from one digit to the next. The only precaution that must be taken is to send a precursor 1 signal down the S line before starting to take the difference of two new numbers. This initialization step clears any spurious signal from the feedback loop.

If instead of arbitrarily chosing $\overline{B}_i$ as the simple function, one choses either S_i or $\overline{N}_i$, the same design procedure can be followed, leading to two other subtractor configurations. The other two circuits differ in the fan-out requirements on the borrow output (3 instead of 4) but otherwise are similar. The three circuits are exhaustive of this design. Although the circuit diagram of Fig. 37 shows only two bits of delay through the circuit, the operating circuit has additional buffering and initialization stages which result in a front to back delay of 4 bits.

7.4 Larger Threshold Logic Units

It has proved possible to fit a logic aperture with more than three input signal windings. By increasing the number of turns in the input coupling loops, a logic aperture was operated successfully with three inputs weighted 3, 2, and 2. In certain important respects this can be looked at also as a 7-input unity-weighted threshold logic unit. The unit was built and tested successfully. Another unit, with five unity-weighted coupling loops, was also built and operated successfully, but this was the maximum number of inputs achieved before output performance became marginal. A rough limit on the number of inputs is

$$N \simeq 1/\varepsilon \tag{42}$$

where ε is the maximum per-unit variation in flux switched among the input loops. The trend toward greater compositional and mechanical uniformity in ferrite structures will enable larger fan-ins in the future.

By using a combination of two input AND gates and multiple input OR gates, it is possible to construct an arithmetic unit capable of forming sums, differences, and products of two input numbers at the same time. Such an arithmetic unit using the residue number system has been built successfully and reported [23]. In principle it is possible to obtain the results of the arithmetic operation two clock pulses after the numbers are input. In practice, for counting ranges of 1000 or less, an estimate of six clock pulses (two complete 3-phase clock cycles) is more realistic.

8. An Experimental Machine Control System

The control for an experimental programmed wiring machine has been constructed using the balanced elements shown in Fig. 22. A block diagram of the machine is shown in Fig. 38. The mechanical portion of the machine consists of a programmable Y–Z table, traveling needle carriage, and movable vacuum boxes for storage of slack wire. The control portion of the machine involves a teletypewriter (TTY) to read in Y and Z position commands, a magnetic interface for the TTY, a magnetic decoder, magnetic Y and Z comparison circuitry which compares desired and actual position to generate digital stepping signals, and resolvers to encode the table position.

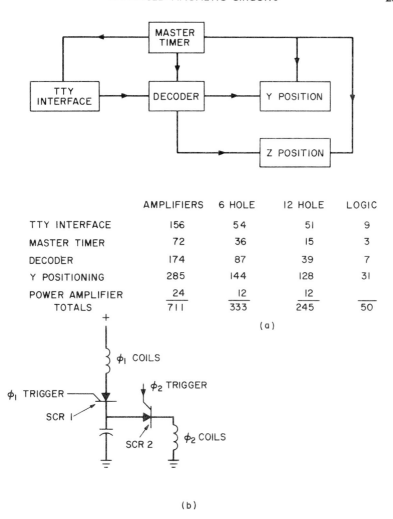

	AMPLIFIERS	6 HOLE	12 HOLE	LOGIC
TTY INTERFACE	156	54	51	9
MASTER TIMER	72	36	15	3
DECODER	174	87	39	7
Y POSITIONING	285	144	128	31
POWER AMPLIFIER	24	12	12	
TOTALS	711	333	245	50

(a)

(b)

FIG. 38. Clock supply, flow chart, and element usage in an experimental wiring machine.

The machine logic inside the TTY and up to the resolver interface was constructed using the balanced circuits described previously. A threshold logic subtractor was used in the positioning circuitry; four-legged logic elements were used elsewhere. The types of elements and their numbers are listed in Fig. 38(a). The power amplifiers were also magnetic and were used in fanning out from the master timer. The basic system clock repetition rate was 25.6 kHz. A 3-phase clock system was used throughout; the basic clock driver used two units of the type shown in Fig. 38(b). Since the balanced elements used do not require careful waveshaping of the drive currents, this simple circuit could be used. Phase 1 occurs whenever silicon-controlled rectifier (SCR) 1 fires, charging the capacitor. This capacitor is discharged and phase 2 generated by firing SCR 2. Although the circuit is simple, spurious triggering of the SCR's was a problem.

An illustrative portion of the logic is shown in Fig. 39. This is a portion of the TTY interface. The signal from the TTY is of the form shown, consisting of 11 time slots, each approximately 9.2 μs long. Of these, at most, time slots 1–8 contain information. Time slot zero performs a synchronizing operation. Normally the current from the TTY is at a nonzero level termed "marking." Reduction to zero (spacing) is the start signal which must synchronize the magnetic logic. The remaining time slots are filled by a nonreturn to zero signal. A typical signal is shown. The magnetic logic must strobe this signal, and does so at the points shown in Fig. 39. The machine control requires a 24-bit word which is obtained from the TTY by reading four ASCII characters and taking six bits from each word, hence the six strobing points shown. The magnetic circuitry must synchronize on the change from marking to spacing, begin strobing, strobe six bits, ignore the remaining two bits, shut off and wait for the next marking to spacing change, which occurs when the next character starts. The strobed information must be buffered until the control computer can accept it.

The circuit labeled A detects a change in the TTY input from marking to spacing. An examination of the truth table will show that this circuit will put out a single "1" whenever the input changes from a "1" to a "0". This latches the circuit labeled B, which in turn gates a 1600 pulse per second source through to the binary counter stages labeled D-1 through D-7. This source has been obtained by counting down the 25.6 kHz clock. The carry output from stage D-4 will occur with a 10 μs spacing. This provides a strobe to gate the "1" or "0" from the TTY into the holding buffer labeled E. An examination of the truth table will show that if the input to the "3" terminal of the holding buffer is a "1", then the input from the TTY will be gated into the stage. Whenever the input to the "3" terminals is a "0", the feedback input will circulate in the stage. Therefore, the 10 μs strobing pulse will gate a "1" or "0" from the TTY into this stage, and it will then circulate until accepted by the control computer.

Gate F delivers a 1 to the control computer whenever a valid bit is present in E. This gate will deliver a "1" for each of the first six strobe pulses. Whenever the binary stages D-1 through D-7 have counted past 6, stages D-6 and D-7 will have "1"s in their sum feedback loops. These "1"s are ANDED to inhibit gate F. Therefore, the

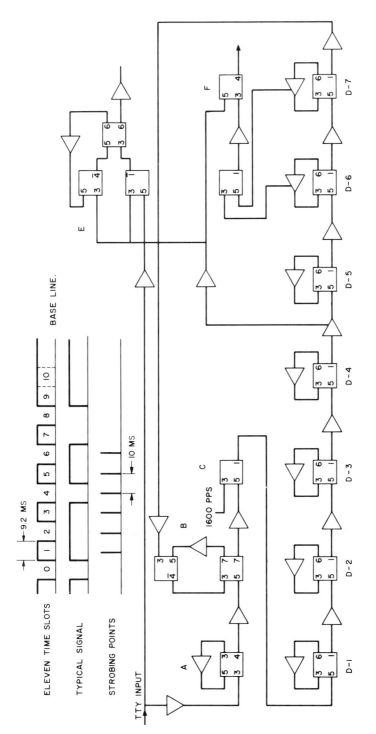

FIG. 39 Magnetic teletypewriter interface in an experimental wiring machine.

computer control only responds to the first 6 bits as required. Whenever the eighth strobe pulse occurs, a carry output from the last stage D-7 unlocks B which then ceases gating of the 1600 pulse per second signal. The cycle is restarted by the next transition from marking to spacing.

The mechanical motions required for automatic wiring are shown in Fig. 40. The structure to be wired is mounted on a positionable

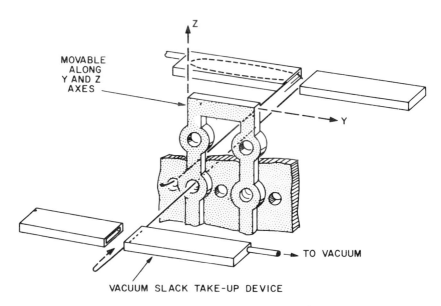

FIG. 40. Basic mechanical motions in experimental wiring machine.

Y–Z table. Two traversing carriages, one on either side of the positionable table, pass a needle carrying the wire back and forth. Between passes the table is positioned in accordance with the desired winding configuration. At the end of each pass, the needle can be rotated clockwise or counterclockwise. The direction of rotation is chosen with due regard for the direction in which the Y–Z table can be expected to move. The direction of rotation is chosen such that on the return pass the needle will not pass over the wire emanating from the board. This keeps the wire loop in a plane, avoiding kinks.

A photograph of the experimental machine is shown in Fig. 41(a). The vacuum boxes are movable on a plane inclined at a 45° angle. In Fig. 41(b) the needle carriage has accepted the needle from an identical carriage on the opposite side. The vacuum box on the right-hand side has come into position, and with the aid of the drop roller

Fig. 41. (a–e, see pp. 293–295). Photographs of a cycle of experimental wiring machine.

the wire is being drawn from a vacuum box on the opposite side. Once into the vacuum box on this side, the wire is held flat in the box by the vacuum. In Fig. 41(c) the vacuum box has dropped back and the needle rotation direction has been chosen by energizing the solenoid labeled RNS1. The left and right vacuum boxes operate in similar fashions. Figure 41(d) continues the sequence, but with the wire shown

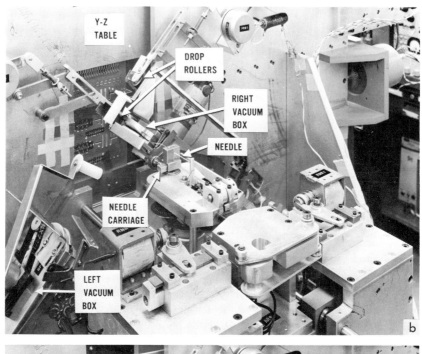

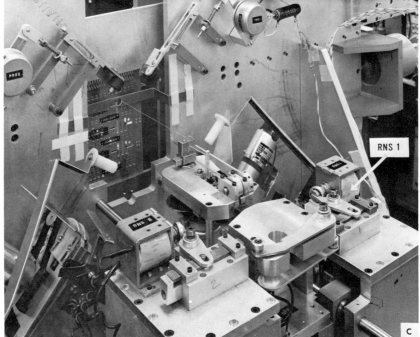

FIG. 41 (b) and (c). See caption p. 293.

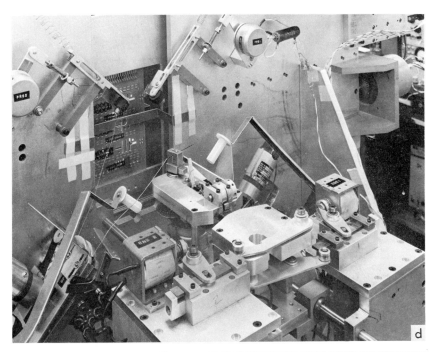

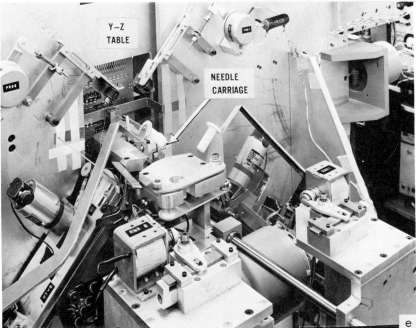

Y–Z
TABLE

NEEDLE
CARRIAGE

FIG. 41 (d) and (e). See caption p. 293.

in the left-hand vacuum box. The needle carriage has started to move back toward the Y–Z table, and the needle holder is rotating in preparation for another pass through the ferrite structure. In Fig. 41(e), the needle carriage is against the Y–Z table, the needle is being passed to the carriage on the opposite side, and soon the wire will be fed out of the left-hand vacuum box on the near side to another one on the far side. This completes a half cycle of operation.

The experimental machine succeeded in making passes at the rate of 1 per second, and wire lengths up to 40 inches could be handled. A very light coating of nonabrasive material was necessary on the ferrite structures to prevent removal of wire insulation.

9. Clocking Arrangements

The 3-phase clocking scheme previously described is preferred over the 4-phase schemes to be described for several reasons: Three phases are preferable to four from a driver point of view; all phases are symmetric in the 3-phase case. However, in attempting to regenerate flux patterns in sheets, or sense a magnetic store, four phases are necessary.

The 3-phase scheme is shown in block diagram form in Fig. 42. The elements could be cores (unipolar system) or balanced circuits (bipolar system). From the previous discussion the element characteristics can be summarized.

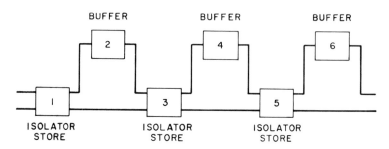

FIG. 42. Block diagram of a 3-phase system.

Isolator: Dependent on the applied clocks it can prevent coupling between adjacent loops or transfer signals with a minimum of attenuation; whenever it is isolating, it presents a very low impedance to coupling-loop current flow at its input and output terminals.

Buffer: Dependent on the applied clocks, it acts as a high or low impedance to coupling-loop current flow.

Store: Acts to store information.

The various element states can also be summarized.

Saturated : Element does not contain stored information; current flowing in a coupling winding linking the element ideally may take on any value without generating a back voltage.

Idle : Element contains stored information; however, current flowing in a coupling winding must rise to a threshold before generating any back voltage.

The actions performed by clock and bias windings on the elements can also be summarized.

Clear : Element is driven by current in the clock winding to the saturated state.

Pump : Element is readied to receive information. In the case of balanced circuits, this is a clock pulse. In the case of cores it is a bias. The magnetomotive force to tip or switch comes from the signal path.

It is clear from the previous discussion that the elements labeled *buffers* in Fig. 42 perform only as variable impedance elements. The elements labeled *isolators* act in the capacity of storage elements in addition to acting as isolators. They store information when pumped and deliver that information when cleared.

A 4-phase system is shown in Fig. 43. Operation involves first storing

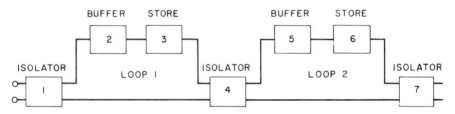

FIG. 43. Block diagram of a 4-phase system.

the information in the storage element of a loop, isolating that loop in both the forward and backward directions, opening the forward path, transferring information to the next loop, closing the forward path, and so forth. Operation of the stages shown in Fig. 43 is summarized below.

Phase 1—loop 1: Element 4 isolates loop 1 and loop 2; isolator 1 passes information to element 3; element 2 is in the cleared state.

Phase 1—loop 2: Element 6 is cleared; element 7 passes the stored information to the next loop; element 5 is in the idle state.

Phase 2—loop 1: Element 4 isolates loop 1 and loop 2; isolator 1 is sent to the clear state; to prevent destroying information stored in 3 element 2 is pumped and acts as a buffer.

Phase 2—loop 2: Buffer 5 is cleared in conjunction with isolator 7, their voltages canceling in the common coupling loop; elements 5 and 6 are now ready to receive information from loop 1.

Phase 3: Element 1 isolates loop 1 from preceding loops; element 7 isolates loop 2 from succeeding loops; element 3 is cleared, element 4 passes the stored information to element 6; element 2 idles; element 5 is in the saturated state.

Phase 4: Element 1 isolates loop 1 from preceding loops; element 7 isolates loop 2 from succeeding loops; element 4 is cleared; to prevent destroying information in element 6, element 5 is pumped and acts as a buffer; element 2 is cleared in conjunction with element 4, their voltages canceling in the common coupling loop.

At the termination of phase 4, phase 1 can be reapplied. This type of system allows information to be passed through an isolator and the isolator returned to the saturated state without destroying the stored information. The information is left in both the buffer and the storage element. They could be cleared together and their voltages would cancel in the common coupling loop. This type of circuit has been used to sense a balanced circuit store [24]. Using bipolar elements, the operating characteristics are very similar to the 3-phase circuit and the same analytical techniques apply. During phase 2 elements 4 and 6 act as a load, while element 3 acts as a flux source with element 2 the internal impedance. It follows that for maximum energy gain the control curve for the load made up of elements 4 and 6 must match the disturb curve of element 2. During phase 3 element 4 acts as the flux source, element 6 as the internal impedance, and element 5 as the load. The manner in which the buffer and storage elements can be increased in size to maximize the energy gain at each transfer can easily be determined.

A modified four-phase scheme is shown in Fig. 44. This scheme will accept input bits at twice the rate of the scheme in Fig. 43. If bipolar elements are used, the input winding is wound around apertures 1

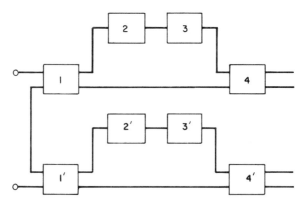

Fig. 44. A 4-phase system which operates at a double bit rate.

and 1′. Element 1 is pumped during phase 1 and cleared during phase 2. Element 1′ is pumped during phase 3 and cleared during phase 4. Thus the first bit travels down the upper rank and the second bit travels down the lower rank. A common winding linking the last stages delivers the bits in their original time sequence. For an n-stage shift register, this arrangement requires the same number of elements, and the same number of clocks, however, can operate at twice the bit rate of the four-phase system shown in Fig. 43.

In Fig. 20 a stage was shown in which storage and amplification capability were clearly separated, the storage capability delegated to the magnetic elements and the amplification capability to the diodes. A shift register using this arrangement is shown in Fig. 45. The clocking is summarized below.

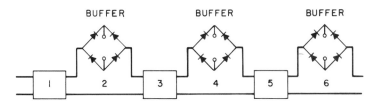

Fig. 45. A 2-phase magnetic–semiconductor shift register.

Phase 1:   Element 1 is pumped; element 3 is cleared; buffer 2 presents high impedance; buffer 4 conducts; element 5 is pumped; buffer 6 presents high impedance.

Phase 2:   Element 1 is cleared; buffer 2 conducts; element 3 is pumped; buffer 4 presents high impedance; element 5 is cleared.

In this case some reflection shows that a single shift register bit is made up of elements 1, 2, 3, and 4. Element 5 and element 1 perform the same operation. Thus this arrangement makes possible a reduction from 6 to 4 elements per bit and reduces the number of clock phases to 2. The buffer in this arrangement alternately presents high and low impedance; it differs from a magnetic gate, however, in that it does not require resetting. A magnetic circuit organized in the same manner is shown in Fig. 46; however, the diode buffer has been replaced by a buffer which must act alternately as a high and low impedance. With the areas shown it is impossible for the flux source to saturate the hole linked by the signal winding. The element will act as a high impedance to signal current whenever it is pumped, and a low impedance (up to a threshold) when it is not pumped. However, now we must reset the buffer; this increases the number of phases required

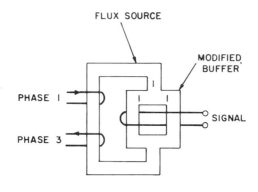

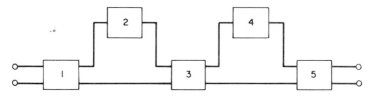

FIG. 46. A 4-phase register requiring four elements per bit.

from 2 to 4 but leaves the number of elements at 4 per bit. The clock sequence is summarized below.

Phase 1: Element 1 is pumped and element 3 is cleared; element 2 is pumped and isolates; element 4 idles; element 5 is pumped.

Phase 2: Element 1 is cleared; element 2 idles; element 3 is pumped; element 4 is pumped and isolates; element 5 is cleared.

Phase 2: Identical to phase 1 except that element 2 is pumped in the opposite sense.

Phase 4: Identical to phase 2 except that element 4 is pumped in the opposite sense.

The increase in the number of phases from 2 to 4 is required because of the need to reset the buffer element. There are other schemes for performing this reset using the elastic flux in the element. In this case a separate clock phase is not required; however, time must be allowed for this reset to occur.

There are other unipolar core arrangements which may be mapped into a balanced bipolar arrangement. In particular, a core arrangement described by D. C. Engelbart [25] using eight elements per bit has been tested. This arrangement allows one to obtain operating difference flux levels approaching 100%.

10. Regeneration of Signals within Ferrite Sheets

There are several distinct approaches to the propagation of information-bearing flux patterns without attenuation: flux pumping [13]; fan-out and flux addition; prepulsing to create low coercive force walls [12]. The first two will be discussed in detail here, the third properly belongs in a discussion of thin film domain wall technology, although ferrite properties do exist which permit this mode. The work of G. W. Dick on symmetric all-magnetic shift registers is also related [28].

Consider the 4-phase circuit shown in Fig. 47(a). Suppose transformers 1, 4, and 7 have a 1 : 1 turns ratio; then flux gain is not possible in the conventional sense, however, energy gain still exists. Flux gain

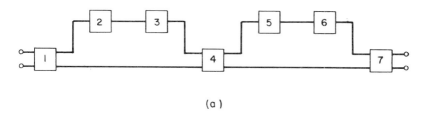

(a)

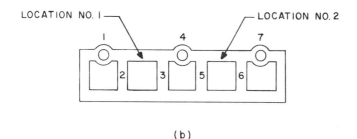

(b)

Fig. 47. Flux pattern regeneration by flux pumping in a unipolar system.

may still be achieved by a technique termed flux pumping [10, 13]. Consider one half of the usual 4-phase cycle. Suppose elements 1 and 7 are isolating and we are concerned with transfers of information from elements 2 and 3 into 5 and 6 through element 4. Suppose elements 2 and 3 both contain the stored information. They have previously been set to this state by information which has been advanced through

element 1. If element 3 is cleared and 4 and 6 pumped, information
will be delivered to element 6. If a 1 : 1 turns ratio is used on element 4,
the set in element 6 will be less than that in 3 due to coupling-loop
resistance losses. As such, the system will not propagate signals without
attenuation. Next, as in a conventional 4-phase system, element 4
is cleared and element 5 pumped. Element 4 will go to a saturated
state, element 5 to the information state. However, rather than clearing
element 2 in conjunction with the clearing of 4, element 3 is pumped.
The information stored in element 4 will be restored in element 3.
The cycle may now be repeated delivering additional flux to element 6.
In summary, 3 is used to deliver information to 4 and 6; whenever 4
is cleared, information is set back into 3 and the cycle can be repeated.

The elements in Fig. 47(a) may be either cores or balanced circuits.
The core version again lacks two natural stable states and artificial
means must be used to achieve stabilization; however, a discussion is
useful for illustration. The sheet version of the core circuit is shown
in Fig. 47(b). Suppose elements 1 and 7 isolate: a figure-eight winding
is used to hold flux closed around the hole, there is no net flux through
the leg (neutral). Suppose a "1" is stored in location 1: this is represented by clockwise set (leg 2 up and leg 3 down). Suppose a "0" is
stored in location 2: this is represented by a counterclockwise set (leg 6
up and leg 5 down). We wish to move the "1" in location 1 to location 2.
As in Fig. 47(a), we attempt to clear leg 3, biasing leg 6 to switch.
The flux in 3 will close through 6. Leg 4, however, now contains the
stored information. Leg 4 is sent back to neutral by energizing a figure-
eight winding; leg 5 is biased to switch in preference to leg 6; leg 3
to switch in preference to leg 2. At this stage, we are at a point where
a "1" is stored in location 1 as well as location 2 (both locations clockwise). The "1" in location 2 may not be as full a set as the original "1"
in location 1. However, the process may be repeated to further enhance
the "1" in location 2. Note, if a zero is initially stored, leg 3 is already
up and ideally no transfer of flux occurs to leg 6. Leg 4 stays neutral
so that a zero remains in locations 1 and 2 even after several flux
oscillations. This ideal situation does not exist, however, as elastic
flux will cause some buildup of a "0" into a "1". This same difficulty
exists in unipolar core circuits. As before, balanced elements may be
introduced to overcome this difficulty. It may be possible to stabilize
this unipolar scheme by adding additional area to leg 5 to absorb the
elastic flux.

A balanced circuit stage suitable for flux oscillation is shown in
line diagram form in Fig. 48(d). This circuit has been obtained using
a straightforward mapping of the circuit shown in Fig. 47(b). This

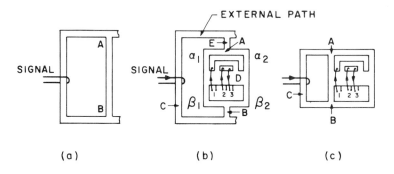

(a)   (b)   (c)

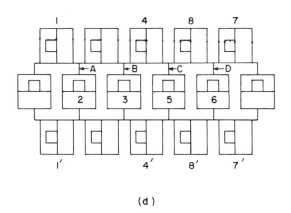

(d)

FIG. 48. Flux pattern regeneration by flux pumping in a bipolar system.

mapping technique is easily understood if it is recognized that information is to be stored in Fig. 47(b) by perturbations from a neutral
state. In wire-coupled balanced circuits, a "1" is represented as a
perturbation from an equal flux splitting condition. In the sheet
circuit, a "1" will be represented as a clockwise perturbation and a
"0" a counterclockwise perturbation. We must, however, develop a
technique for biasing legs so that they can accept either sense of flux
input. Suppose for example the path between points A and B in
Fig. 48(a) is to be biased so that the path will switch in preference to
some parallel path whenever signals are input. In a bipolar arrangement,
the input signal may be positive or negative, so conventional biasing

techniques are not suitable. Consider adding a balanced element as shown in Fig. 48(b) and suppose the path $\alpha_1\alpha_2\beta_1\beta_2$ has been saturated by energization of winding 1. Then if winding 3 is energized, part of the flux switched will be shunted through the leg placed in parallel with winding 3 so that considered as a flux source it cannot deliver enough flux to saturate the parallel paths in opposite sense. Winding 3 then acts as a pump in the usual sense. Applying the dynamic form of Ampere's law and taking into account the bridge nature of the circuit, it is clear that the net magnetomotive force introduced across points A–B will be zero, independent of the pump magnetomotive force applied. This will be true in Fig. 48(b) and Fig. 48(c) even though the balanced element itself is switching. We have a dynamic method of biasing which will respond to either sense of signal input. For example, in Fig. 48(b) if a signal of the sense shown is present in coincidence with pumping, the path α_1, D, β_2 will experience a magnetomotive force to increase its switching rate, whereas the signal magnetomotive force will decrease the rate of switching in α_2 and β_1. The flux entering at point A from the signal source will prefer leg α_1 to leg α_2, and leg β_2 to leg β_1. In the ideal case, all the pumped flux would switch in legs α_1 and β_2 and through the signal source; nothing would switch in legs α_2 and β_1. If the pump source is now reversed by energizing winding 2 (reverse pump) and the signal remains in the same sense, legs α_2 and β_1 will switch in preference to α_1 and β_2. This successively energizing windings 2 and 3 on the balanced circuit which exists between points A and B may be regarded as a method of biasing the path between these points beyond the threshold for switching, without introducing a net magnetomotive force into the connected external path.

If the external path starts in a neutral state, it may be sent in either direction from this state, dependent on the sense of the applied signal. However, whenever the balanced element is cleared, legs α_1, β_1, α_2, and β_2 must go to a saturated state, and from flux continuity consideration leg E must switch back to neutral. The flux which switches in E must also switch in the external path shown in Fig. 48(b) or some other parallel path dependent on the dynamic biasing used. The general observations above may be confirmed by drawing the usual arrows and insisting on flux continuity at each stage.

The transition from Fig. 47(b) to Fig. 48(d) is now straightforward. Dynamic biasing is added to every leg; a "1" is now represented by a clockwise perturbation in a location from the neutral condition. For example the state of legs A and B in Fig. 48(d) is indicative of the state of location 1, C and D of location 2. The behavior is then analogous to that discussed in connection with Fig. 47(b), however, in this case buildup of a "0" into a "1" is no longer a problem. As before assume elements 1, 1', 7, and 7' are isolating and location 1 is set partially clockwise.

Phase 1: Element 3 is cleared; elements 4, 8, 6, 8', 4' are pumped. Under these circumstances leg B must go to neutral and the flux which switches closes through the path 4, 8, 6, 8', 4'. The perturbation of leg A from neutral is now repeated in leg D.

Phase 2; Elements 4 and 4' are cleared, elements 3 and 5 are pumped. The legs leading into 4 and 4' must go neutral leaving equal perturbation from neutral in locations 1 and 2. The process may now be repeated using reverse pumping in legs 5 and 6. As the tip builds up a natural limiting action will occur as in wire-coupled balanced circuits.

A second method of flux pattern regeneration termed fan-out and flux addition is shown in Fig. 49. Suppose in Fig. 49(a) two loops are coupled to the transformer 1, each with a 1 : 1 turns ratio. Flux gain will not exist in the usual sense. Elements 3 and 3' are pumped and receive information from 1; next 2 and 2' are pumped and 1 cleared, as in the usual 4-phase system. Next consider combining the sets in elements 3 and 3' in element 4. First pump 4 and clear 3, delivering the set in 3 to 4. During this phase element A' must be present and pumped to prevent excessive coupling-loop flow in the lower loop. Next element 3' is cleared, 4 is pumped again accepting the set in element 3' and A is pumped to decouple the upper loop. In the absence of losses the set in element 4 will be the sum of the sets in elements 3 and 3' or twice the original set in element 1.

A unipolar sheet version of this circuit is shown in Fig. 49(b). Suppose elements 1, 1', 7, and 7' isolate. Suppose location 1 is set clockwise with a "1" and legs Q and R are neutral. Location 2 is set counter-clockwise.

Phase 1: Element 3 is cleared up and the path 4, 6, 6', R biased to the theshold. Ideally the flux switched from leg 6 will equal that in leg 3.

Phase 2: Element 3' is cleared up and the path Q, 6, 6', 4' biased to the threshold. Ideally the flux switched in leg 3 will further switch leg 6 down.

Phase 3: Legs 4, Q, R, and 4' are driven to neutral using a figure-eight winding on each of the four holes. Leg 5 is biased to switch in preference to leg 6.

Ideally the flux delivered to leg 6 will be the set which was down in 3 plus the set which was down in 3', providing the necessary flux gain. Ideally if a "0" has been stored in location 1, legs 3 and 3' will not switch and location 2 will also remain a "0". The usual problems associated with zero buildup can be expected.

The balanced circuit version is shown in Fig. 49(c). The mapping described previously has been used and the operation is analogous

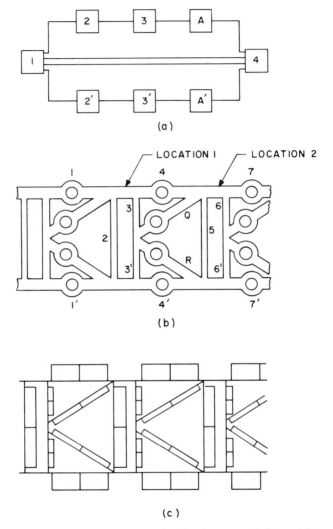

FIG. 49. Flux pattern regeneration by fan-out and flux addition.

to the operation of the circuit of Fig. 49(b). A "1" is represented as a clockwise perturbation from neutral and a "0" a counterclockwise perturbation.

11. A Compatible Storage Element

A method of magnetically sensing a magnetic store without encountering disturb problems has been described [24]. The store was word-organized and the sense amplifiers arranged as shown in Fig. 50.

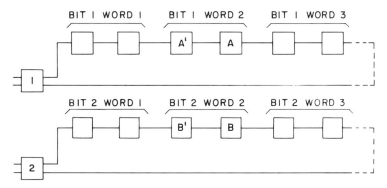

FIG. 50. Magnetic sensing of a magnetic store.

For example, if a word is to be stored in word locations 2 bit 1 is passed through isolator 1 to location A by pumping 1 and A simultaneously. Bit 2 is passed to location 2 by pumping 2 and B simultaneously, etc. Usually A and B are series-connected balanced circuits in the same sheet and all bits in the same word are pumped in coincidence. The isolator can be reset by clearing and pumping A′, B′, etc., at the same time. The organization is similar to that of one half of a 4-phase clocking scheme. Once the isolators have been cleared they may accept information for storage in other words. Words may be read from the store by clearing A, B, etc., and pumping 1, 2, etc. The isolators may then be returned to a cleared state by clearing 1, 2, etc., in coincidence with clearing of A′, B′, etc. New information may then be written into A, B, etc. Whenever isolator 1 has been pumped and information stored in A then in order to be able to clear isolator 1 without disturbing the information stored in element A element A′ is required.

A basic storage element capable of storing 24 bits is shown in Fig. 51(a) and (b). The bits are stored in the two outside legs, the inside legs between A and A′ are used for word selection. The selector holes permit one sheet to be selected from among thirty-two sheets. The sheets are punched from plasticized ferrite and selectively notched before firing. A typical pattern is shown in Fig. 51(b). Thirty-two sheets are stacked, each sheet having a distinctive set of notches. Five variables and their complements are applied to the stack to select one and only one sheet. Consider the way in which variable X_1 is applied to the sheet shown in Fig. 51(b). If $X_1{}'$ is present in the two positions shown it will hold the selective portion of the structure between A and A′ saturated in a clockwise sense. From symmetry considerations or simple magnetomotive force considerations it is also clear that any elastic flux generated by $X_1{}'$ will not generate a magnetomotive force between A and A′. This will be true for the other variables as well and is the

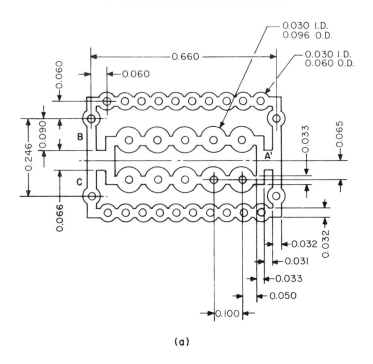

(a)

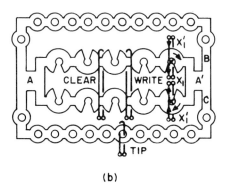

(b)

FIG. 51. Balanced circuit storage element.

reason for locating the selective holes symmetrically. It is an important consideration, as the sum of the holding magnetomotive forces may be large compared to the coercive force and considerable elastic flux generated.

Provided the hold current in X_1' is sufficiently large then application of current to the clear winding will not cause any switching in the select portion of the sheet. However, if X_1 is present it will not hold the structure, as the material in the notch has been removed. Therefore current in the clear winding can switch flux in the path linked by X_1'. Some reflection shows that if five variables are applied to the select holes in the same manner X_1 is applied, then whenever a clear pulse is applied one and only one sheet will switch. In this sheet the upper leg of the selector portion will switch causing legs B and C to saturate reading out any stored information. In the unselected sheets flux will be held closed around the selection portion leaving A in its initial neutral state. If a write pulse is now applied only the previously selected sheet will switch. The write pulse will reverse the flux in the upper leg of the select portion, driving legs B and C to neutral. Nothing will happen to the unselected sheets. Writing may be done at this time. A stacked array is shown in Fig. 52.

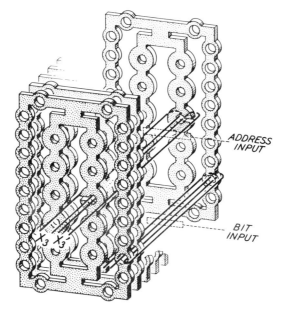

FIG. 52. Balanced circuit store.

12. Circuit-Gain and Material Characteristics

12.1 Disturb Measurements

This section discusses the manner in which material properties influence the amplification of a standard amplifier shown in Fig. 53. Although this amplifier was proposed as one suitable for digital control

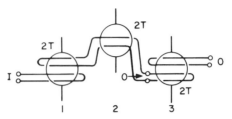

Fig. 53. Input–output points for measurement of tip disturb characteristics.

circuits, it is also capable of amplifying signals of varying amplitude, such as the sampled-data version of a speech wave. The discussion here applies to both the digital and analog cases. In this type of amplifier a signal is accepted as a sample during a particular clock phase. During a later clock phase a sample of higher energy is delivered. The output sample will be higher in voltage and/or current amplitude than the input sample.

During phase 1 element 3 isolates and elements 1 and 2 are pumped. Element 2 should act as a high impedance. Suppose at this time the input energy in the signal path is E_I. During phase 2 element 1 is cleared, element 2 idles, and element 3 is pumped. Element 2 should act as a low impedance. Suppose the energy delivered to terminals O is E_O. Then

$$E_G = E_O/E_I \tag{43}$$

where E_I is the energy input at terminals I, (Fig. 53) during phase 1, and E_O is the energy output at terminals O, during phase 2. Now E_I will be small if element 2 offers a very high impedance during phase 1, and E_O can be made large if element 2 offers low impedance during phase 2. The energy gain depends primarily on element 2 and its ability to act as a controllable impedance.

We seek a method of measuring the ability of element 2 to act as controllable impedance. Now in Fig. 53 during phase 2 the same coupling-loop current acts on elements 2 and 3. If 2 offers a low impedance and 3 offers a high impedance, the flux change in 3 will be greater than that in 2 and 3 will absorb most of the voltage from 1. Conversely, if elements 2 and 3 are identical, then by measuring the relative flux change in these elements during phase 2, the ability of a single element to act as a controllable impedance can be determined. An arrangement in which these measurements were made is shown in Fig. 54. Each element had three pump turns and three clear turns. The switching time was set at 1 μs. A signal was applied to the diode gates at the time of phase 2. This gated the signals from elements 2 and 3 to the X and Y input of the plotter, which produced a deflection

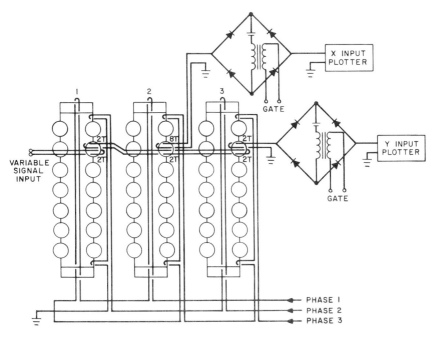

FIG. 54. Circuit for measurement of tip disturb characteristics.

proportional to the integral of the applied wave shapes, and this was proportional to the flux switched in the respective elements. The X and Y deflection sensitivities were identical; however, an attempt was made to expand the X-scale by using eight figure-eight turns on element 2 and two on element 3. Some reflection shows that we obtain a direct measure of K/K_B given in Eq. (40).

Some of the results are shown in Fig. 55(a) and (b) for two different samples. The sample whose characteristics are shown in Fig. 55(a) was doped with thoria and that shown in Fig. 55(b) with calcium [26]. In obtaining these results the signal input to element 1 during phase 1 was varied and the flux switched in elements 2 and 3 during phase 2 was measured. If a point on the plot had an ordinate of 100 and an abscissa of 0 this would correspond to a condition in which element 1 was fully tipped and all its flux was delivered to element 3 during phase 2, tipping it fully. The slope at the origin is a measure of the element's ability to act as a controllable impedance. From these measurements it appears as if the thoria-doped sample shown in Fig. 55(a) is better than the calcium-doped sample shown in Fig. 55(b). In Fig. 55(a) it is apparent that there is a region where very little switching occurs in element 2. Element 2 appears to have a definite

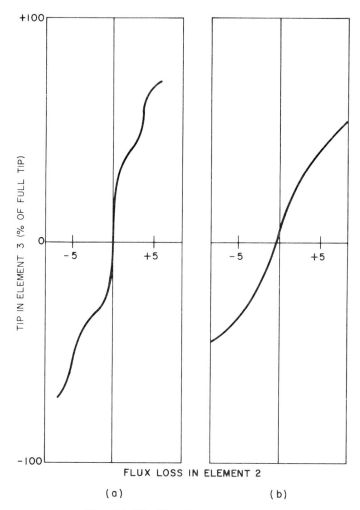

Fig. 55. Tip disturb measurements.

threshold. This is not the case in Fig. 55(b). It is believed that this difference is related to the so-called "soft threshold" of a partially set core. When a core is driven from remanence to neutral it may subsequently exhibit a soft threshold as previously discussed in connection with Fig. 4.

For small signal inputs, element 2 in Fig. 53 is almost in a neutral state when it is required to provide a low impedance, and consequently if it has a soft threshold, it will exhibit the type of performance shown in Fig. 55(b). Here switching starts around element 2 even when very small currents are transferring information from 1 to 3. By contrast in Fig. 55(a) a definite or hard threshold exists.

Although there is some correspondence between the soft threshold behavior of a single core and the behavior of the balanced element there are some distinct differences. In particular, a single core usually exhibits an even softer threshold if the minor loop is measured with the field applied so as to send the core back to the saturated state at which it started. By contrast, element 2 in Fig. 53 is symmetrical in its response to the disturb current because the parallel paths arrive at neutral having both started in the down state, and a disturb current will continue the switching of one leg and reverse the switching of the other.

12.2 Sample Preparation

The basic composition was $Fe_{1.7}Mg_{0.42}M_{0.50}Zn_{0.38}O_4$ as expressed in atoms per formula unit. To obtain different microstructures for a given heat treatment, three lots of this ferrite were made. To one 0.5 wt% ThO_2 was added to serve as a nonmagnetic second phase inclusion [27], to the second, 0.15 wt% CaO to promote discontinuous grain growth, and to the third, no addition for comparison. Standard ceramic processing techniques were used in their preparation. In brief, the raw materials were mixed in water, filtered, dried, granulated, and presintered at 900°C for 16 hours in air. The clinker was then milled for 16 hours under water with a $1\frac{1}{2}$ wt% addition of polyvinyl alcohol to serve as a binder. The ThO_2 and CaO were added to their respective lots in this last step. The milled slip was evaporated to dryness and granulated to a -20 mesh powder.

Multiaperture structures similar to that in Fig. 22(a) were formed by dry pressing at a pressure of 35,000 psi. These were fired at 1265°C for a period of 4 hours. An oxygen atmosphere was provided during heating, and while at temperature, with nitrogen during cooling. Specimens for microscopic examination were prepared and etched with a $C_3H_6O_3$ HF–HNO$_3$ solution. Densities were determined by the displacement method and for each composition approximated 97% of the X-ray density.

The microstructures for the lots with the ThO_2 and CaO and zero additions are shown in Fig. 56(a), (b), and (c) respectively (see pp. 314 and 315). With no addition the grain size has a relatively narrow distribution and averages 14 microns. Large grains up to 0.1 mm in diameter in a matrix of smaller grains with an average 7 microns appear with CaO present. For the lot containing ThO_2, grains fairly uniform in size and averaging 6 microns in diameter occur.

12.3 Energy Gain of the Sample With ThO₂ Addition

The previous analysis showed that maximization of the energy transfer may be handled in a manner similar to that of impedance matching in conventional circuitry. From this analysis a parallel type of load connection was suggested if maximum energy transfer was to occur from element 1 to element 3. This type of loading is shown in Fig. 57. The material used was Mn Mg Zn ferrite with ThO_2 doping,

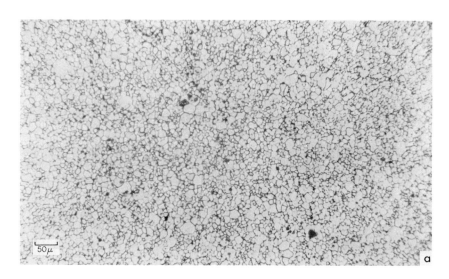

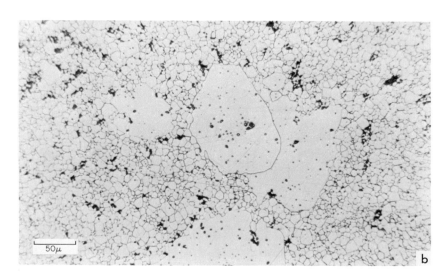

Fɪɢ. 56 (a) and (b). See caption on facing page.

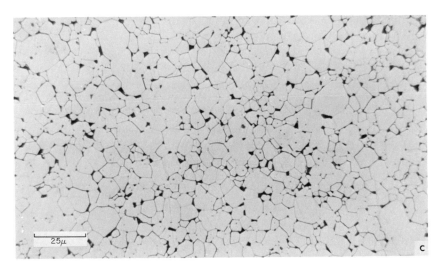

FIG. 56. Microstructure: (a) ThO_2-doped Mn Mg Zn ferrite; (b) CaO-doped Mn Mg Zn ferrite; (c) Mn Mg Zn ferrite without additions.

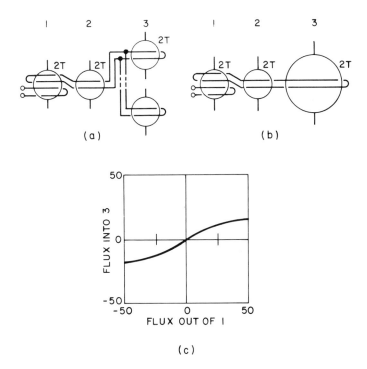

FIG. 57. Fan-out measurements.

whose characteristics are shown in Fig. 55(a). All the elements connected in parallel were in structure 3. The number of elements was increased to the point where, during phase 2, the flux loss in element 2, plus resistance loss, accounted for approximately half the flux from element 1, the other half being absorbed by the load. This point was reached when the number of parallel elements reached twelve. A plot of the flux transfer during phase 2 is shown in Fig. 57(c). The tip input to element 1 during phase 1 was varied to achieve this plot. It should be noted that the timing was different in this experiment from that described in connection with Fig. 54. The load switching time was held constant at 1 μs and three turns were used on the receive winding. However, five turns were used on the send winding of element 1 so its switching time was slightly less than 1 μs. From Fig. 57(c) it is clear that when the flux out of element 1 reaches approximately 25% of a full tip, about half of the flux from element 1 is lost in element 2 plus resistance loss; the other half reaching element 3. A line with a slope of 2 : 1 would be the loci of points where this occurs. For tips of less than 25% the flux lost in the transfer is less than 50%.

From the limited observations made to date it is concluded that a small amount of ThO_2 acts to inhibit the growth of large grains, providing a dense fine-grained structure, whose threshold in the partially set state is significantly better than is normally observed. This improved threshold increases the amplifying capability of a balanced amplifier as well as improving the tip-disturb characteristic of a balanced memory element, or two core per bit memory arrangement.

REFERENCES

1. Papian, W. N., A coincident current magnetic memory cell for the storage of the digital information." *Proc. IRE* **40**, 475–478 (1952).
2. Rajchman, J. A., and Lo, A. W., The transfluxor. *Proc. IRE* **44**, 321–332 (1956).
3. Wanlass, C. L., and Wanlass, S. D., Biax high speed magnetic computer element. *Proc. Western Joint Computer Conf., San Francisco, 1959*, pp. 40–54.
4. Gianola, U. F., and Crowley, T. H., The laddic: magnetic device for performing logic. *Bell Syst. Tech. J.* **38**, 45–72 (1959).
5. Gianola, U. F., Integrated magnetic circuits for synchronous sequential logic machines. *Bell Syst. Tech. J.* **39**, 295–332 (1960).
6. Crane, H. D., A high speed logic system using magnetic elements and connecting wire only. *Proc. IRE* **47**, 63–73 (1959).
7. Bennion, D. R., MAD–Resistance type magnetic shift registers. *Proc. Nonlinear Magnetics and Magnetic Amplifiers Conf., Philadelphia, Pennsylvania, 1960*, pp. 96–112.
8. Bennion, D. R., and Crane, H. D., All-magnetic circuit techniques. *Advan. Computers* **4**, 54–132 (1963).

9. Carbonel, M., DeChanteloup, V. C., and Sicot, J-P., Design of all-magnetic guided-flux systems. *IEEE Trans. Magn.* **MAG-4**, 689–697 (1968).
10. Newhall, E. E., and Perucca, J. R., Energy gain and directivity achieved using balanced magnetic circuits. *Int. Solid State Circuit Conf. Digest of Technical Papers, Philadelphia, Pennsylvania.* February 1963.
11. Newhall, E. E., The use of balanced magnetic circuits to construct digital controllers. *Proc. Int. Conf. Nonlinear Magnetics, Washington, 1963,* pp. 10-3,1–10-3-6.
12. Newhall, E. E., and Perucca, J. R., Exploitation of initial conditions to achieve flux gain and nondestructive readout in balanced magnetic circuits. *IEEE Trans. Electron. Comput.* **EC-13**, 278–284 (1964).
13. Newhall, E. E., U.S. Patent 3182297 issued May 4, 1965.
14. Galt, J. K., Motion of individual domain walls in nickel–iron ferrite. *Bell Syst. Tech. J.* **33**, 1023–1054 (1954).
15. Menyuk, N., and Goodenough, J. B., Magnetic materials for digital computer components. *J. Appl. Phys.* **26**, 8–18 (1955).
16. Becker, J. J., Domain boundary configurations during magnetization reversals. *J. Appl. Phys.* **30**, 387–390 (1959).
17. Hesterman, V. W., and Nitzan, D., Flux switching in multipath cores. *Stanford Res. Inst. Repts. 1–4.*
18. Baldwin, J. R., Circuits employing toroidal magnetic cores as analogs of multipath cores." *IRE Trans. Electron. Comput.* **EC-11**, (2) 218–223 (1962).
19. Newhall, E. E., All magnetic digital circuit fundamentals. *Int. Solid State Circuits Conf. Digest of Technical Papers,* February 1964.
20. Newhall, E. E., Balanced circuit shift register. *Electronics* **37**, 54–59 (1964).
21. Russell, L. A., Diodeless magnetic core logical circuits. *I.R.E. Nat. Convention Rec.,* Part 4, pp. 106–114 (1957).
22. Guilford, E. C., and Kieburtz, R. B., Using multiaperture ferrites for logic functions. *IEEE Trans. Magn.* **MAG-4**, 535–537, (1968).
23. Kieburtz, R. B., Residue arithmetic using balanced magnetic circuits. *IEEE Trans. Magn.* **MAG-4**, 698–701 (1968.)
24. Farmer, W. D., Sensing a magnetic memory using magnetic circuitry. *Proc. Int. Conf. Nonlinear Magnetics, Washington, 1964,* pp. 16-3-1–16-3-5.
25. Engelbart, D. C., Orthogonal magnetic systems and a new example of all-magnetic logic. *Proc. Int. Conf. Nonlinear Magnetics, Washington, 1963,* pp. 10-1-1–10-1-4.
26. Monforte, F. R., Newhall, E. E., and Perucca, J. R., Some observations concerned with microstructure, soft threshold and gain of magnetic digital circuits. *Int. Conf. Magnetics, April, 1965,* pp. 4.6-1–4.-7.
27. Baba, P. D., Gyorgy, E. M., and Schnettler, F. J., Two phase ferrite for high speed switching. *J. Appl. Phys.* **34**, 1125–1126 (1963).
28. Dick, G. W., Symmetrical all-magnetic shift registers. *Proc. 1965 Intermag Conf.,* pp. 4.8-1–4.8-9.

Command and Control: Technology and Social Impact

ANTHONY DEBONS

University of Pittsburgh
Pittsburgh, Pennsylvania

1. Introduction

1.1. Purpose and Approach

The purpose of the present article is to examine our understanding of command control and to attempt to relate the developments in military command control systems to similar systems now being envisaged for the private enterprises and to assess the underlying implications to the functioning of society at large.

The first approach is to attempt to provide the reader with a broad view of the field which is subsumed under the title of "command and control." The second effort attempts to present in brief detail those areas in science and technology which are now contributing directly to matters of command and control. Next, the present efforts in developing systems like command and control for application to the civic sector will be examined and finally an attempt will be made to assess whether or not the combined knowledge gained from such developments contribute to the basis for creation of a new science and profession of information.

1.1.1 Major Thesis

The major thesis advanced here is that the science and technology related to the command and control functions is primarily directed in achieving one objective, namely, aiding man to make the best use of the data about his environment for decision making. In the attempt to achieve this objective, efforts underlying command and control in four main areas have revealed the importance of the transformations that occur from the initial acquisition of the raw signal from the event world to the time it is received and processed by the human brain. Concepts in communication, computer, behavioral science, and system theory provide the core of our present understanding of these processes.

1.2. Background

1.2.1 Definition of Command and Control

Command and control both deal with the manner in which data can be elicited, processed, and used to effect acts. Command, control imply *environments* of equipments, procedures, and men—the purpose of which is to purposefully influence events and the directions and use of men and weapons. The central mechanism underlying both command, control is the feedback obtained on the state of the event world as a function of the data that is gathered after action regarding the event world is consumated. In control, the data is gathered on the event world to insure its regulation after the decision has been made as to its direction and objectives. In command, the decision function is imperative and the gathering of the data is a feedback to the exercise of decision.

By and large, the terms "command and control" when used in the conjunctive form are military terms and may be considered synonymous to military science in the broad sense, inasmuch as the terms imply the full spectrum of directing and correcting/adjusting functions underlying military operations at large. The planning, monitoring, analyzing, assessing, directing, and manipulating of resources are implied.

The term "command and control" may appear in the hyphenated form "command-control" or in the nonhyphenated form, "command, control." The context in which such terms appear in the literature suggest that they should be considered as synonymous to "command and control". Yet Kroger [81] has suggested, for example, that command, control imply different functions. Kroger views command as involving assessing functions enabling a commander to make decisions in which objectives may be changed while control involves the direction of weapons in which the objectives are fixed.

Other definitions of the collective term "command and control" are widespread in the literature [40]. Moreover, additional expressions as "communications, command and control" have been used [108]. The proliferation of definitions and views as to what constitutes command and control supports the general belief that use of such terms in the scientific and technical literature is ambiguous and in certain other areas vague.

The term *command and control systems* signifies environments where data are gathered to direct and regulate resources to meet specific operational objectives. When command and control systems are established for the major purpose of acknowledging resources (men and material), with the employment of such resources being a secondary consideration, such systems are often referred to as *management information systems*.

1.2.2 Historical Sketch of Command and Control

The exercise of command and control functions by humans responsible for the safeguarding of the national interest is as old as the military institution itself. Historically, command meant those personal skills and attributes a military leader possessed by which he could apply his resources to counteract the intentions of an adversary. Such personal attributes and skills were generally applied through his presence in close physical proximity to his adversary.

The contemporary meaning of military command and control can be distinguished from the historical counterparts in several significant ways. For one thing, the historical meaning placed a distinct emphasis on the personal responsibilities that were related to the exercise of command and control. The commanders' responsibilities were to exercise their prerogative of command and control, and this was vested in them by virtue of a legalistic relationship established between the officer and the state. Rank conveyed the officer's authority and bound the extent to which he could effectively exercise command and control, particularly over human resources. This was interpreted to mean that the officer brings within the domain of his authority all those personal attributes (through selection and training) upon which presumably his rank was vested.

The contemporary meaning of command and control, includes the former implications of what constitutes the exercise of command but places greater emphasis on the collective *attributes of environments* (physical and social) which provide the base for the exercise of command and control by individuals. The present concept retains the notion that the commander is responsible for his decisions, but the major source of his decision is no longer entirely dependent on his personal attributes, but rather on the functional relationship that exists between himself and the environment of men and machines that surround him.

The second aspect deals with military doctrine and the exercise of command and control. Historically, command and control centered around the exercise of functions within the established norms regarding military behavior. Contemporary command and control is more information bound and less doctrinally oriented.

The rules are there to be obeyed, but more information is available upon which to defend actions which are against established norms. The availability of data is a more significant force for military behavior in operations. Behavior which is based largely on a prescribed code of conduct is to be found less than formerly. Because of the influence of data availability, contemporary command and control entertains greater freedom of action during operations than heretofore envisaged. Such freedom has raised questions on the adequacy of prevailing organizational concepts (hierarchal) which heretofore were rigidly conceived and accepted.

The emergence of command and control as a matter of scientific interest and significance, was the natural outcome of several conditions. The United States after World War II faced the realities of maintaining military operations and personnel around the globe. The state of the art in electronics, finding expression in communication technology, made possible greater surveillance over larger land masses, with the consequence that sensor devices (radar, satellites, etc.) provided greater amounts of information regarding events that could critically influence the military policies and activities in such areas. Meanwhile, the work with digital data processing systems, particularly that done in the 1940's on ILLIAC at the University of Illinois, SAGE, NORAD, etc., applied to Air Defense problems of the 1950's, provided the possibility of creating computer systems for the processing of military data of kinds and amounts heretofore unrealized. The understanding in electronics that provided the basis for such trends also gave the impetus for the emergence of other technologies of equal significance.

Of particular importance was the attention paid to transmission of data as the result of advances in radar technology and the creation of new ways of presenting data which originated from the sensor and which were processed by the computer and eventually reached the military decision maker. Electronically generated displays interfaced the human, the data processing elements, and the event world. Now that the remote world was closer to the military commander, questions as to how such devices could be coupled to effectively assure greater command and control of resources both at home and at remote areas became of foremost interest. Systems philosophy, given definition by the military in the 1940's in its application to weapon development, was now extended to the matter of the design of large data systems. With a significant increase in data, military scientists were awakened by new interest in decision making, initially instigated by economists early in the 18th century. The new technology in the acquisition and treatment of data provided a new dimension to the commander's capacity to deal with the complex nature of the world around him.

The early 1960's saw events which clearly pointed to the increasing importance of command and control to the military. Several activities converged at once to give meaning to the area. The initiation of the so-called "L"[1] systems by the Air Force in the 1950's, the development at the Lincoln Laboratories of the Semi-Automatic Ground Environment (Sage), the Navy's program in undersea surveillance, the Army's efforts in introducing automated data processing for handling tactical nuclear weapons [128] represent one class of activities.

A second class of activities relates to the initiation of new laboratories and in some cases, the redirection of existing laboratories to the problems of command and control. At Bedford, Massachusetts, the center for the development of electronic technology for the Air Force, the then existing Operations Application Laboratory was redesignated as the Decision Science Laboratory and its attention was directed to the decision functions of commanders and the application of command and control systems to such functions.

In addition to the Decision Sciences Laboratory, the System Design Laboratory was activated at the same center. The major function of the laboratory was to extend the research to be conducted in support of command and control systems. The laboratory was a joint Air Force, Mitre Corporation enterprise, where the combined scientific and engineering resources of the two organizations concerned with command and control could be applied to the study of related problems. The Air Force provided personnel to the System Design Laboratory from its Directorate of Computers which was established early in 1962 and consisted of young military scientists in both the physical and behavioral sciences. The Directorate of Computers was instrumental in developing in conjunction with the Mitre Corporation the outline of a study program in the sciences pertinent to command and control.

At Rome Air Development Center (RADC) in Rome, New York, scientists and engineers of that center were extending advances made in solid state electronics to the problems of processing and the presentation of information. In addition, RADC continued its work on the development of sophisticated transmission devices, and included studies of computer language translation activities—all these being particularly relevant to the development of the new "L" systems.

---

[1] "L" systems refer to the class of electronic environments established to provide improved data acquisition, transmission, processing, and utilizing capabilities for the Air Force.

Such well-established laboratories as the Applied Physics Laboratory at John Hopkins University, and the Aerospace Medical Laboratory in Dayton, Ohio, directed their activities to command and control issues. As part of the research program of the Aerospace Medical Laboratory, a new experimental simulation facility at Ohio State University was established. The Naval Research Laboratory (NRL) initiated new research programs in command and control under the auspices of the Office of Naval Research. New command and control systems were now being conceptualized with respect to naval operations, and the work done by NRL provided the base for the creation of the Naval Tactical Data System (NTDS).

The foregoing are but a sampling of laboratory activities that represent the scientific and technological activities associated with command and control.

A third set of endeavors concerns the attempt to formulate the theoretical structure underlying the command and control area. These endeavors consist of the identification of technical problems and the identification and recruitment of scientists and engineers that were to constitute the professional body of the field.

In 1961, Jacobs and Degan of the Mitre Corporation drafted a report [74] which identified technical and scientific areas pertinent to command and control problems as existing at that time. Jacobs and Degan referred to the relevant areas as constituting *Systems Sciences* and linked the particulars of each of the respective sciences to progress made in electronic data processing. Thus, command and control became defined within the sphere of "Information Sciences," "Organization Sciences," "Computer Sciences," and Systems Theory. Two years later, in the first annual report presented on the subject by the Air Force Office of Scientific Research in 1963, Wooster alluded to the term "Information Science" and discussed in his introduction to the Research and Development Program representing that name [72] ". . . researches of the logicians, the cyberneticist, the linguist, the psychologist and even the philosopher . . ." An examination of the program in information science structure offered by Wooster complimented the earlier presentation offered by Jacobs and Degan. The areas included by Wooster were

Concepts of Machine Organization
Adaptive and Self-organizing Systems
Information Extraction and Classification
Transmission of Information
Language and Linguistic Research
Theoretical Foundations of Information Sciences

Meanwhile, the professional community associated with the foregoing technical problems gained identity. In 1962, the Mitre Corporation and the U.S. Air Force sponsored the first annual Congress of Information Sciences which was held in Hot Springs, Virginia. These meetings enabled scientists and engineers from many disciplines to gather, examine, and discuss the problems facing the military command and control functions. In 1963, the first Symposium in Computer and Information Sciences was held at Northwestern University. Other established organizations of scientists and engineers, such as the IEEE and the Military Operations Research Association began to include technical matters directly identified as command and control. In 1963, the Society of Information Display was established as the result of the interests of scientists and engineers in information presentation problems generated out of command and control systems.

In brief, the 50's and 60's saw the birth of command and control as a basic segment of military science if not synonymous with it. New command and control systems involving functions at the national level were being conceptualized. Scientists became more interested than ever in the human decision process. There continued to be experienced an increasing sophistication in the development of hardware and the growing awareness of the difficulty with related software. Throughout the military, some concern was emerging as to the influence of such systems in the military hierarchal structure.

1.2.3 Command and Control as a Concept

(a) Command and Control as an Environment   Command and Control imply an *environment* consisting of men, machines, and procedures which enable the manipulation and handling of data in support of the formulation and verification of a decision. Sackman [*119*] refers to the Air Force definition of this environment as a "composition of equipment, skills and techniques that enable a commander and his staff to exercise continuous control of assigned forces and weapons in all situations." Vaughn and Gillette [*146*] have pointed out that such systems are more often identified with content categories (weather, intelligence, traffic control).

The fundamental issues underlying command and control as an environment concern characteristics of components and the inherent properties of the interactions that exist between equipment, procedures, and people in achieving specific goals. How such things are put together to achieve specific ends is the domain of systems theory and systems engineering and as such are pertinent to the consideration of command and control as an environment.

Several elements serve to define the command and control environment. Of course, these elements do not necessarily have to be physically located in one area. The elements that have been proposed are (1) the event world that represents the physical states and the energy emitted from such states which identify their existence and presence; (2) the elicitation agent which may be the human (viz. eye, ear, smell, etc.), or physical sensor (mechanical or electronic); (4) data processing elements (computers, typewriter, punchcards, etc.); (5) data depiction element (CRT, TV, hardcopy printout, etc.); and (6) the decision agent (man). These elements all interface with each other and provide feedback. Man interfaces with the event world through some activator. The activator may be the display, data processing communication element, or other devices through which he modifies the state of the world. This is depicted in a model presented in Fig. 1 [34].

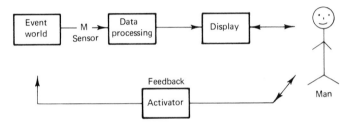

FIG. 1. Depiction of the essential components of a command and control (information) system.

In 1967, Yovits [157] proposed a description of a command and control system or information system (see Fig. 2). In the discussion accompanying this model, Yovits stresses the importance of the decision function to the entire information process.

McDonough and Garrett [95] provide a version of a management

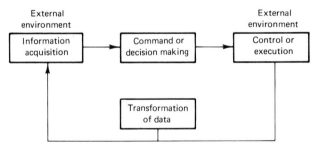

FIG. 2. Components of an information system as proposed by Ernst and by Yovits [50, 156a, 157].

information system which has a close analogy to the military command and control system (see Fig. 3).

An essential feature of command and control environments is their particular hierarchal nature. Command and control environments may consist of one or several command and control subsystems integrated into a total command and control environment as presently constituted in the National Military Command and Control System (NMCCS) and more recently as the World Wide Military Command and Control System (WWMCCS).

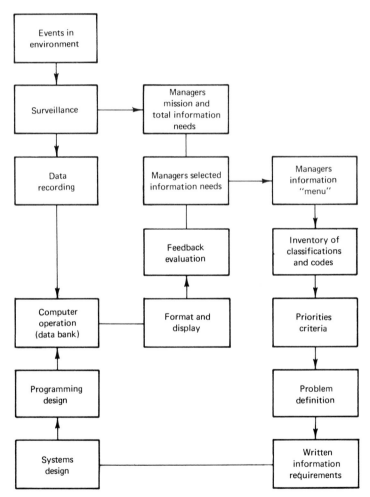

FIG. 3. Summary diagram depicting the design processes involved in the development of management information systems. (From McDonough and Garrett [95] "Management Systems," page 203; courtesy of Richard D. Irwin, Inc.)

(b) *Command and Control as Operations*   Command, control imply both human and machine functions or operations. Command and control as operations concern the primary matter of how data becomes transformed from a raw signal to information and how such transformations influence the human decision function.

Stated differently, command and control as operational terms always infer some act of selection (choice in response to some environmental condition) or state. The processes underlying such acts are postulated to involve certain transformations of the signals from the event world to the user. These transformations (such as experienced in translating raw signals in transmission to codes) may be incurred by the physical state of the environment, by the state of equipment, or by the user.

The manner in which such transformations occur, the principles that govern their influence on man and machine functions constitute the subject of command, control as an area for scientific investigation.

Command, control involve human and machine functions. The human functions refer to those sensory, cognitive, and motor attributes of the human organism that singularly or collectively enable the instigation of a directional act. The machine functions refer to those properties of mechanical elements or structures which enable the instigating, directing, assigning, aligning, and regulating of physical forces and states.

Some of the human and machine functions have been identified in the command and control system [*108*]:

Receive and analyze mission assignment.
Designate targets and/or objectives.
Calculate and maintain timely planning factors.
Prepare and maintain operations plans.
Decide on timing and implementation of plans.

(c) *Command and Control as a Theoretical Concept*   Command and control as a theory concerns the primary matter of how data becomes transformed from a raw signal to information and how such transformations influence the human decision function.

Using as a base the information problems centered around command and control, Ernst and Yovits [*50*; see also *108a, 156a*] have extended the descriptive model of the command and control environment (see Fig. 2) to provide an initial formulation of the transformational factors which are implied in the data acquisition–data utilization processes. Ernst and Yovits detail several formulations of the decision function in such a concept. Their hope is that the formulations can provide quantifiable means for evaluating the role of the decision function in information processing. The evaluation of these formulations must await experimental validation.

It is of interest to contrast the Ernst and Yovits formulation on information processing with that presented by McCormick [94] (see Fig. 4). McCormick differentiates information processing in manual, semiautomatic, and automatic systems. These formulations were derived

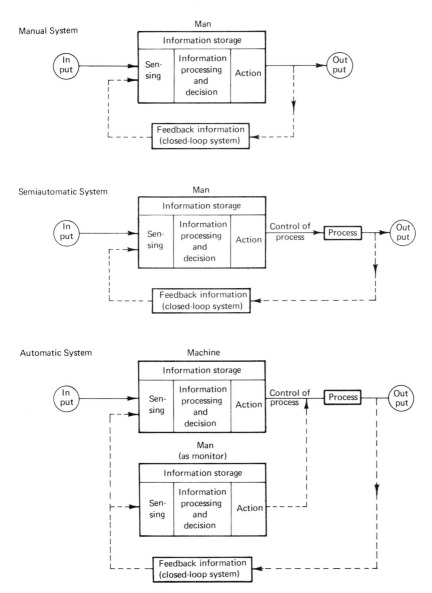

FIG. 4. Information processing flows for different types of system configurations (McCormick [94]).

to describe control mechanisms involved in aircraft operations. There
are apparent similarities between these two conceptual models, which
are generated to describe the decision function. What appears to be
necessary is to determine experimentally the significance of the differences that exist.

From a different point of view, George E. Briggs [13] at Ohio State
has attempted to study the human information process through a
detailed understanding of the cognitive (brain) functions which
accompany such processes. Expanding the model for human information processing postulated by E. E. Smith [132], Briggs outlines
conceptually (Fig. 5) the various elements which intervene between
the time a signal is received by an information processor to the final
execution of the response.

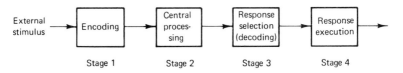

FIG. 5.   Depiction of the data transformation processes discussed by Briggs
[13] and E. E. Smith [132].

Brigg's experiment with human subjects include the measurement of
human reaction time to stimuli which differentially influence their
reception by the human sensory mechanisms. Initial experiments have
suggested that man is a sequential processor of information. But perhaps
more significantly, the work undertaken by Briggs is providing the
methodology with which related command and control functions can be
tested and studied.

These foregoing models, of course, do not represent the entire spectrum of considerations which underly command and control as a theoretical concept. In fact, much of the discussions that are included under
the respective technical areas in Section 2 reflect many aspects of
command and control that are theoretically pertinent. Concepts underlying language, data organization, and other areas discussed in Section
3 provide a base for a theoretical concept in command and control.

2. The Science and Technology of Command and Control

2.1 General

When electronic sensing devices complimented the human ear and
eye in their ability to detect and estimate different states of the physical
world and when electronic data processing machinery significantly
altered the amount of time and the kinds of manipulation possible with

data about the physical world, the possibility then emerged that such capabilities could effectively be marshalled to aid the human decision maker. Communications and computers are necessary and fundamental elements of command and control.

Behavioral Science in this context contributes to the science of command and control in two ways. First, it establishes the understanding required as to those properties inherent in man which provide him with the capacity to respond to the physical environment. Such capacity is not limited to the potential for application of mechanical energy available to him by his motor systems, but more importantly in his capacity to use the energy available to him for purposive ends.

Second, behavioral science provides the base from which the design of objects and environments can be made consonant with man's inherent and acquired capabilities. If communications and computers are indeed to serve man in command and control functions, then the technologies related to communications and computers must correspond to man's ability to handle, understand, and accept the technology.

Communications, computers, and *man* are the basic constituents of what we call the command and control environment. These elements constitute an effective resource for human endeavor when they are interlinked to the extent that the processes of each component become consistent and harmonize with the limitations and capabilities of each in the achievement of an objective.

The principles that guide the interlinking are often referred to as constituting *Systems Theory.* The practice of considering the functional relationship of different components in the design and engineering of systems has been referred to as the systems "attitude." It is this attitude that has materially influenced and continues to influence the development of command and control systems both in the military and civic sector.

We will attempt to look at each of the basic technical constituents of the command and control environment from the point of view of identifying those aspects which are particularly pertinent to the execution of military command and control functions and which can also be considered relevant in their application to the civic sector. In Section 2.3, we will attempt to highlight the impacts of such developments to civic community.

2.2 Major Technological Components of Command and Control

2.2.1. Communications (Transmission)

Communications may be discussed in terms of two separate but mutually related contexts. When the term "communication" refers to the conveyance of a signal from the event world, through a physical medium to a processor (which may be a human being or a computer), and when the major properties of the signal, the carrier, and the medium are the main objects of concern, then communications can be identified as being synonymous to signal transmission (physical aspect of communication). The transmission of signals (or data) is concerned with the following:

(1) The number of signals that can be rendered through a medium (channel) for any particular unit of time.

(2) The amount of protection possible in maintaining the identity and integrity of the signal.

(3) The fidelity with which a signal may be rendered through a medium without loss of signal character.

(4) The coding of information to facilitate its transmission without loss of information in the presence of signal distortion, noise and interference.

When communication is used to refer to an act in which signals are used to convey *meaning and intention*, the convention has been to refer to this second form of communications as *human communications* (semantic aspect of communication) which in this sense is synonymous with information transfer. In human communications the attribute of intentionality (semantics) is primary and the properties pertaining to the nature of conveying (transmitting) of signals from one place to another is of secondary relevance. Human communication will be discussed in Section 2.2.3 [*41, 91*].

Military command and control are highly dependent on effective transmission of data for a number of reasons. The actions that a military commander chooses to take during a military encounter depend largely on the "up to date" quality of the data he receives, his ability to obtain data from diverse sources, and his ability to check the source of his data within reasonable bounds of security and delay time. Of these, the ability of a communications system to provide maximum security dictates the nature of the communications technology incorporated in command and control systems.

"Rice (2) has captured the importance of communications in command and control: 'If you can't communicate you can't command and control [*67b*].'" Horveth [*70*] has provided a rich account of the history of communications as it occurred in the Navy. Horveth traces the technology of communications from the early use of fire (through smoke signals) for the transmission of messages, the use of artificial light by the Spaniards, the introduction of flags by the British Navy, and subsequently to sound signals which led to wireless communication and to the international code in digital communication. Horveth's account is important because it shows how the transmission of messages actually influenced the political and social framework of the military and the practice of command and control by the Navy. His account is relevant to the entire military structure.

The following are brief descriptions of some contemporary developments in technology that have influenced and continue to influence the transmission of data. Basically all the developments are the result of the rapid advances made in solid state electronics stimulated by military needs during the early 1960's.

(a) *Microminiaturization (Microelectronics)*   Advances in electronics which have been directed at achieving maximum output of signal power with maximum conservation of energy and minimum consumption of space have been referred to as microminiaturization.

Microminiaturization techniques represent a significant advance in electronics of relevance to command and control. Microminiaturization techniques in the form of integrated circuits and transistors provide the basis of high speed computers and have been instrumental in the design of space vehicles. Microminiaturization has facilitated satellite communications and have made possible telephone switching centers that many civic communities are experiencing. Microminiaturization appeals to and satisfies the need for standardization of equipment, which insures greater production efficiency and reduction of cost. The producer of microminiaturization techniques can be considered the foundation of our future transmission capabilities in Command and Control Systems. Considerable research is being undertaken on microminiaturization techniques that has applicability to the development of third and fourth generation Command and Control Systems.

(b) *Digital Transmission*   Military command and control functions require a highly rapid signal transmission system capable of submitting large quantities of data over great distances. Developments in solid state electronics have made possible new ways for the transmission of digital and analog signals.

Of particular relevance to command and control are digital transmission and switching and associated pulse-code modulation (PCM) systems. By digital transmission is meant the electronic conveyance of any form of information in digital, normally in binary, form over distance. Digital transmission provides the capability for transmitting both digital signals and analog (e.g., speech) signals. Analog signals have to be converted to digital form before they can be transmitted.

Because digital communication is based on binary signals the amount of noise that enters the system can be more controlled when compared to the analog signal. This is achieved by coding to detect transmission errors and to correct those. This offers a substantial advance in insuring greater reliability of communication required in command and control.

An important practical factor underlying digital transmission is the potential for standardization that it provides. Inasmuch as all functions are capable of being digitalized, this allows for a modular approach in the design of circuits which in turn provide for the interchangeability of the transmission units.

The relaying of data which is very important to command and control requires intermediate storage of data. Data in digitalized form is renderable to standard ways of storage which are not available for data in analog form.

Another factor related to digital transmission concerns the distribution and switching of signals. Digital transmission provides for switching that eliminates the necessity for extra conversion terminal units and the resulting degradation resulting from their use.

Last but certainly not least, is the question of secure communications. Security of transmitted data is of vital concern to military command and control. As best as it is known, there is no easy way of making analog data secure, while high degrees of security by cryptographic encoding of digital data are possible.

(c) *Satellites*   Military communications in command and control has favored radio communication because of the inherent cost involved in wire communications. Radio communication, on the other hand, does not provide the required reliability when long distances are involved. Because of the changing characteristics of propagation characteristics over terrain, radio transmission is often limited to line of sight. It is these limitations that have induced the creation of satellites for communication functions. Satellite communication in principle provides long distance communication by the cascading of two or more line-of-sight communication links.

Artificial satellites are now being established at varying altitudes. Such satellites will be directed at facilitating radio and TV transmissions as well as providing hundreds of the 3K telephone channels originally transmitted in limited numbers through the submarine cable for transpacific or transatlantic communication.

Belden and Schwartz [9] have discussed the use of satellite systems (COMSAT) to meet military command and control requirements. They cite the advantages of satellites in affording high quality reliability, high capacity and long range links. Belden and Schwartz indicate that "Science can be established at any location within 'view of satellite' by providing an earth terminal at location." They allude to the conferencing capability offered by satellite as well as providing a "clandestine transmitter some protection against radio direction finding."

Satellites can also be said to provide a low cost medium for transmission, but there are problems which are inherent in the delays that are instigated in the signal transmission process and which are important to command and control. The propagation delay time does not favor using this means where short reaction time decision feedback is required as it is in some control operations. For example, the delay in satellite transmission between New York and London is eight times that of transmission over submarine cable between the same points. This factor makes satellite communication unsuitable for telephone circuits over these distances (e.g., the signals from the respondent which interface with the speech of an inquiring agent).

But perhaps the greater consequence to command and control is the nature of the reliability in communications that satellites afford. The danger of early knockout by nuclear blast could negate the advantage of this element of communication, particularly if the communications systems were highly dependent on its operation. However, the importance of satellite communication for command and control systems in the civic sector should not be underestimated.

(d) *Microwave Systems*   In 1934, Clovier (see [48]) developed a microwave radio system for transmitting messages across the English Channel. Microwaves are radio waves of thousands of megahertz which permit transmitting of signals over line-of-sight paths at very high data rates.

Microwave communication is of importance to military command and control because of the advantages in security and transmission efficiency it provides. Ideally, command and control communications requires the capability of direct contact with the source of information without compromising the military information. Because microwaves come close to light waves, the possibility of bundling the transmisson energy is feasible. The capability permits the creation of a single, very narrow beam in which the signal can be transmitted. This narrow beam provides the directionality of the signal not possible with transmission energy at lower frequencies. Because of the high level of energy concentration there is greater transmission efficiency with less requirement of power.

The microwave techniques developed during World War II in conjunction with developments in radar accelerated the development of microwave communication systems.[2] One transcontinental microwave radio-relay transmission system is now available and more are contemplated. Television systems are now directly tied to microwave systems

---

[2] Cascades of microwave links in the form of relay systems permit the transmision of of large amounts of data over very long distances. Because of their transmission bandwidth microwave links, are particularly suitable for picture transmission as required for TV.

and possess considerable potential in their application to information systems in the civic sector.

(e) *Lasers and Masers*   The term "laser" refers to a device which operates on certain optical frequencies and which amplifies light through "stimulated emission of radiation." Masers are similar in operation to lasers but operate below the light frequencies in the microwave region of the radio spectrum. Developments in lasers may ultimately allow the capability of carrying as many as 80 million TV channels or 50 billion telephone conversations in practical hardware systems. There are some rather severe limitations to the use of lasers, however, inasmuch as a light pipe is needed to protect the signals and control the path of the light beam. The present research being conducted in this area is directed at the use of the laser in satellite communications. The use of lasers in satellite communication applications will probably be preceded by the rise of the device in fixed installations. The major problem concerns tracking the satellite with a narrow beam that is characteristic of the laser.

It should be acknowledged that practical laser systems are still quite a way off and that they do not constitute a present capability of significance to the application of military command and control technology to the civic sector.

Further developments in transmission technologies will continue to influence the military command and control environments. With continued world crises, the continued wide deployment of personnel, equipment, and facilities in the military, and the extended development of sensitive sensor devices, the need for reliable, high capacity, wider coverage capability transmission is apparent. With time-sharing of computer resources to be expected in both the military and the civic sector, the cost of telephone lines and other transmission media will be increasingly an important factor in the acceptance of much of the military technology by the civic sector. Table I lists the differential

TABLE I
OPERATING TRENDS IN TRANSMISSION TECHNOLOGIES

Transmission technology	Reliability	Time	Capacity	Coverage	Cost
Microminiaturization	Increase	—	—	—	Decrease
Microwave	Increase	—	Increase	—	Decrease
Satellites	—	—	Increase	Increase	—
Digital transmission	Increase	Decrease	—	—	—

advantages of the transmission technologies that have been discussed. Because of the developmental nature of lasers, they were not included in the tabulation.

2.2.2 Computers

(a) *General* Military command and control systems may be distinguished in time as those existing before the 1950s and those existing after. Pre-1950 command and control systems were largely dependent on the manual processing of data from the event world. Those after the 50s were influenced by the technologies related to the automated processing of data or Electronic Data Processing (EDP), as they are often called. Vast studies in sensor technologies provided the means for the collection of signals, both covert and overt from the event world. Sophisticated communication technologies enabled the transmission of a large number of such event signals over greater distance with considerable greater retention of signal identity and fidelity. Electronic displays enabled the presentation of processed data to the user quickly and efficiently. Such technologies made possible, therefore, the design of an environment whose sole purpose is to aid the decision maker cope with military situations of increasing complexity.

Research and development in the application of computer technology to military command and control has been active in several areas. All these efforts are relevant to the application of such systems to the civic sector. The major R & D activities of concern to command and control are in the following areas.

1. Increasing the capacity of the computer to process, receive, and store data more rapidly and reliably.

2. Reducing the cost of hardware production and the cost of operating the hardware.

3. Developing principles for the mutual sharing of the computer (time-sharing) by a number of subscribers or users.

4. Achieving adequate reliability of operation of computer-based systems.

5. Permitting better interface between computer and man as the user.

Kroger [81] and others in their assessment of military command and control systems have suggested the complex character of military command information processing and the consideration of the following factors in the use of computers in such systems.

(a) The establishment of an understanding of the principles which underlie the direct use of computers by man (man–machine symbiosis).

(b) The need for conceiving of computers as part of an information system that is continuously evolving, modifying itself.

(c) The careful consideration of the users' needs and the matching of the capacities of the computer to these needs.

(d) The importance of the computers to simulation and modeling of command and control problems.

(b) Hardware Development   In 1947, the report titled "Preliminary Discussion of the Logical Design of an Electronic Computing Instrument" by Burks *et al.* [*14a*] established the basic idea that computers consist of five parts, namely, memory, arithmetic–logic unit, input unit, output unit, and content unit. Several technologies made such units initially possible—the vacuum tube, magnetic core and film technology, transistors, and integrated circuits. Demands for higher speed mass memories led to new memory technologies. Magnetic thin films, cryogentric thin film, miniature ferrite core or ferrite film, ferrielectrics, and electroluminescent photo conductors contributed substantially to the production of computer memories with greater and greater capacities for data storage.

(1) Architecture.   The architecture of the computer has been affected by and in turn has had an effect on present command and control systems. Demands of speed, simultaneous requirements, reliability, and cost have all had their impact on hardware architecture. The areas affected most radically have been the memory/control interface, i/o interface, register stacking, and multiplication of the functional elements of the arithmetic–logic units (ALU).

Functional element speed has been improved by providing multiple functional elements (adders, comparers, multipliers, dividers, etc.), all available within an arithmetic–logic unit for simultaneous operation. Speed has been multiplied by increasing the number of elements available per cycle for the execution of instruction.

In i/o interface, the problem of getting enough data through relatively inefficient channels to feed an increasingly more efficient processor has been attacked in several ways. First, and one of the earliest solutions, was the independent programmable channel. One instruction from the control unit establishes a sequence of operations that the channel itself performs in transferring data between memory and the i/o device. Later developments have consisted of placing more routine data processing chores at the remote device end (with small special purpose computers) so that the data arriving at the main processor is preformatted, tagged as to processing to be done, etc. Another direction in which this problem has led is in the establishment of multiple device channels. Here they accept data from many devices at once, decode which device has sent which data, and transfer this information to main memory.

In hardware, the heightened speed and multiplicity of elements have responded to the needs of command and control, for much processing must be accomplished in as little time as possible. Further, additional elements provide greater reliability for an ALU can operate (with the appropriate switching and software design) despite the failure of any single functional element.

(2) Speed. When the military commander is faced with a situation in which the timeliness of the response is critical to the outcome of the operation, then the speed that data elicited from the receiving element can be processed may be critical to the outcome of the operation (see Fig. 6). Computer processing of data, of course, provides a substantial advantage over similar data provided manually. The last 5 years have seen a substantial increase in the quantity of data that can be processed [25, 26], and further increases in this capability are likely to be achieved in the future. Often the limiting factor corresponding to this capability has been the relative slowness of inputting of data to the processing units. Most systems are still restrained by the fact that much of the data are entered by means of largely mechanical devices, or manual inputs which are relatively slow compared to the capability of the data processing unit, to manipulate such data. Research in I/O devices still lags research in the basic units of the main processing elements.

The speed of computation is not expected to influence seriously the acceptability of these units by the civic sector. The slowness of the input devices is not presently a serious impediment; although increasing sophistication in the use of the computer by individuals engaged in civic enterprises, will place more demands on the computer to respond quickly to data demands.

There is one aspect of speed, however, that appears to be critical to the acceptance of the computer both for military and civic functions. Although the evidence is not based on experimental fact, there does seem to be a conviction that there is an upper time level for the computer to respond to human inquiry beyond which the tolerance of the individual to wait for a response becomes lessened. Much of this evidence comes from studies that have been conducted on the use of the computer to the user's demands seems to weaken the user's motive to pursue the request, despite the importance of the data to his needs. If such facts are verified through careful experimentation, the speed with which the computer responds to user's needs may have serious consequences to the acceptability of such devices whether in the military or civic sector.

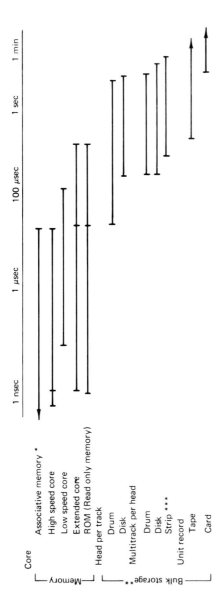

FIG. 6. Data retrieval speeds by devices. The times of the devices are reported in terms of the cycle time for finding and transfer of a basic processing unit, referred to as a byte, word, or character, depending on manufacturer.

*In associative memories the functional process is done over the entire memory so that the effective retrieval rate, when compared to other types of memory is actually a small fraction of the actual cycle time. That cycle time, however, may be as high as 600 μseconds. **Multiple devices in a system. ***The maps manufacturers are NCR—CRAM; IBM—Data Cell; RCA—MSU. See [31, 26, 3].

(3) Storage.   In earlier computers there was no need for the extension of memories inasmuch as the major task was arithmetic computation and no large amounts of data processing were involved. With the development of command and control networks, varied and unusual storage needs emerged since command and control requires extremely fast retrieval of some amount of predigested data and relatively slow (but still within the "immediate access" range) retrieval of vast amounts of "historic and precedent" type information. Storage devices are, for convenience, divided into memory, direct or immediate access, and unit record (see Fig. 7). In memory we have the various types of storage of instructions and data which is directly addressable by the main control unit. In direct access storage we have those types of storage in which data are continuously accessible to the processing elements of the computer. (In unit record devices, we have that storage of data which is accessible only through some form of human intervention.)

The trend in storage is away from the use of unit record devices except for the input of data. Instead a mix of direct access devices of various speeds is being incorporated for long-term storage and various speeds of memory are being employed for intermediate data and instruction storage.

One critical direction is the development of the concept of data migration based on use and device speed. It is almost a truism to point out that the higher the theoretical retrieval rate of a device, the more

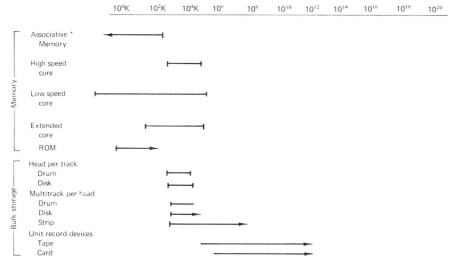

Fig. 7. Data storage capacity by device (in 1000 units). Multiple devices in a system. See [31, 26, 3].

costly the per-bit rate of storage. It is also evident that most of the data needed at any one point will be only a very small percentage of the data required to fill a system's needs. In one case, it was found that some 90% of all accesses were made on 35% of all data available. Most systems with extremely large amounts of data can make use of similar empirical facts to increase retrieval rate, while decreasing storage cost. Migration is simply a matter of keeping track of the number of accesses to particular records and during slack periods of changing storage devices on which they are resident, based upon these utilizations. The same concept of migration may be utilized on noncritical programs in memory, and for the same reasons. As a result of migration the effective retrieval time of all records in the system approaches that of the fastest bulk storage device in the system.

Another trend is the development of larger and larger capacity storage devices, mostly at the expense of speed. Two such devices are microform retrieval systems and laser record systems. Both devices have application only in archical (nondynamic) storage because of the *read only* nature of their storage.

Such devices provide another example of developments in storage—multiple access to a single device. This trend began with the introduction of head-per-track disk and drum devices and has continued to multiple spindle disks and the devices mentioned above which can handle, in one case, seven simultaneous requests (microform retrieval) and in the other 36 simultaneous requests (laser-optical storage). It is obvious that by proper utilization of this property the effective device efficiency can be increased many fold.

It is clear that these developments are to some measure developments in response to the needs of command and control systems, for it is in these systems that the combined needs of large volume and high speed exists

(4) Costs. Reduction of hardware as well as software costs stimulate user acceptance of computers, although they do not necessarily insure it. The application of computers to human endeavors whether military or not will depend essentially on the ability to purchase and maintain such hardware and to effectively use them. A current deterrent to the widespread use of computers to both the military and civic sector is their high cost, both in terms of purchasing and operating such systems.

The costs of computers have not undergone major changes in either rental or one-sum price. But there are trends which are important in reducing the burden of the costs of the computer to the user. For example the large production of integrated circuits has decreased the cost/performance ratio of computers. The price of smaller computers has remained substantially unchanged while their data processing capability has increased. In general, there is a conviction that with development costs largely out of the way, the cost of hardware components will decrease. This is true also for peripheral units, where the price of the units have not changed substantially since 1965, but performance has improved.

One aspect which will materially influence the cost of computers and their acceptance is the research conducted in time-sharing. Through computer resource sharing, via satellites and communication technology, reduced costs both in purchasing and operating data processing machinery may be realized.

(5) Reliability.   The matter of computer reliability concerns the down-time that data processing hardware experiences in operations. Reliability is quite critical to military operations and less critical to the application of such devices to the civic sector. In both cases, however, reduced reliability increases the cost of the computer operation. Perhaps of greater significance is the fact that reliability is an essential ingredient of user acceptance of the technology.

Facts on data processing component reliability are scarce. Manufacturers of data processing equipment are slow to reveal down-time records on their equipment. Much of the remorse experienced with down-time is alleviated by modular design that permits the easy replacement of data processing units. For critical operations as those to be expected in military crisis situations where data processing may be quite essential, dual systems may be available for turn-on when equipment failure is experienced. In general, data processing equipment design has proceeded with considerable sophistication from the earlier models in providing for quick readout of equipment failure, and for maintenance techniques which insure a lower degree of probability of failure.

One issue of data processing reliability concerns the equipment operator's confidence level in the hardware to produce results that can be "trusted" and relied on. Fortunately, present programming techniques insure cross-checking capabilities that can reassure the user that in effect the results are reliable, provided results are obtained.

At present, the problem of computer reliability is a matter of interest to the user in the civic sector, but not essentially in the same context as to the military user. At present, computers in the civic sector are largely employed for control purposes, where the major aim is to relieve the human agent from tedious and difficult monitoring tasks, i.e., transportation flows, etc. Reliability of equipment in these instances may be quite critical, requiring fairly sensitive alarm components connected to automated data processing systems. Such alarm components alert the user to failure arrest, the consequences of such failure to the environment being influenced by the system.

(c) Software Development Israel [73] has aptly stated that computer programs, or software, are of central importance, since they direct the data processing equipment, and hence the operation of the system. The development of computer programs represent perhaps the most costly as well as the most technically difficult aspect of data processing technology.

In command and control computers, system response and complexity demand that compilers and operating systems be integrated to make full use of all system elements while limiting human intervention to that of system testing, decision making at the highest levels only, and system posture establishment. By system testing we mean overall querying of elements to establish absence of malfunction. By decision making, we mean reaching top level command decisions and communicating those decisions to the system. And by system posture we mean arming those elements of system control which direct automatic or semi-automatic armament elements [*150*].

In essence, the operating system controls which programs are resident, programs priorities, utilization of i/o channels, and utility programs (such as Readers, Writers, Indexers, etc.). In command and control systems incoming data may trigger the operating system to call upon specific sequences of programs to deal with this data. The complexity of the decision that must be made at the control level of the computer in command control systems is clearly so great that the development of entirely automating the job control process is of highest importance. Such developments are demanded by the World Wide Military Command and Control System and by such peripheral systems as the advanced logistics system.

Compilers in the command and control field cannot afford convenience at the expense of efficiency of code generation. Where in the purely commercial or scientific application the full capabilities of a computer facility can be ignored for the sake of programming language simplicity (as in COBOL or FORTRAN), it is these very capabilities that must be taken advantage of in command and control programming. Further, there are two additional but conflicting requirements which must be satisfied by a command and control compiler. These are machine code high efficiency (upon which program running time and memory utilization are dependent) and high compile speed.

In response to the first requirement, the language called JOVIAL, e.g., provides the programmer with the ability to address the functional elements from a high (procedure) level, low (bit-operation) level, or any level in between.

In answer to the other concerns, systems have been developed which allow the programmer to decide the level of tradeoff desired. A programmer of such a system may specify the particular level of compiler to be used, knowing that the level of the compiler determines the speed and efficiency of machine code produced. Further developments have matched compiler generation to hardware architecture. The look-ahead compilers are designed to produce coding which makes most efficient use of stacked registers and multiple functional elements.

In general, the limiting factor in programming is the language used in directing the computer to action. The matter of computer language is too complex to present at length in this discussion. It is sufficient for the present purpose to indicate the following [84, 16, 37].

(i) That the structure of the programming language applied limits the range of processing capabilities which can be generated in the data processing unit via that language. There are different languages varying in complexity and capacity.

(ii) That with increasing complexity of the decision problems to which the data processing equipment is applied, the greater the need for new concepts of the computer programming.

(iii) With real time, on-line, time-sharing capabilities the greater the need for sophistication in the development of computer languages that can increase the flexibility of the data processing elements.

In addition to the development of the hardware, computer programming has occupied the greatest attention of computer scientists engaged in the development of military command and control systems. Licklider and Taylor [87] describe three programming concepts that have drawn the attention of research in this area. They identify the *Implicitly Programmed System* conceived by the Air Force which entails the development of computer hardware that would possess the computer program tailored to do a specific job. *Coherent programming* implies a progressive building up of software base by cooperative effort of users that could be modified through experience with the program. The third concept discussed by Licklider and Taylor was based on the assumption that computer programs already in existence *could be linked and arranged* by procedures which were established as the result of experience with problems

It is not possible to evaluate the present state of the art in computer programming. There is a paucity of data on debugging times for the various programs that are currently being employed. Computer languages have not been standardized and there is little likelihood that they will be in the foreseeable future. Interactive languages are in greatest demand because of the desire to provide interactive capability in time-sharing, real-time, on-line models.

Based on the present needs of the civic sector, it is unlikely that the limited advances made in programming will be a deterrent to the use of the computer. Yet, the greatest appeal of the computer in the civic sector is the application of time-sharing problems in education, transportation, etc. Project MAC [52][3] and the efforts at System Development Corporation [125] have pioneered in this area, and there is some evidence to suggest that programming problems involved with time-sharing in this area may be resolved, but this has yet to be seen. If a truly interactive capability is to be achieved in the man–display–computer interface, much work must be done to develop a language which is close to man's "natural" language and which permits him to interact freely with processing equipment in the application of such equipment to problem solving tasks.

2.2.3 Behavioral Sciences

The interest of behavioral scientists in command and control focuses in several areas.

(1) The Nature of the Human Decision Processes. Man is continuously faced with the need to select alternatives to action based on the data that may or may not be immediately available to him. Such action is influenced by many psychological processes including learning and perception as well as personality variables which may influence these processes. The determination of data requirements to facilitate the human task of selecting alternatives during critical situations as well as the identification of the principles which govern the processing of data by the decision maker are the concerns of the behavioral scientist involved in command and control problems.

(2) Human Communication. Man directs and controls his environment, both physical and psychological, through language and devices which utilize some form of symbols. Language may be explicit as exemplified in the various ways cultures have established to communicate among each other, or they may be implicit as found in the subtle changes in tonality of auditory and facial expression. Similarly, language is always influenced by the medium (media) within which it is transmitted (light, sound, tapes, displays, etc.).

There are several aspects of human communication which are important to command and control:

(i) The function of language structure in conveying accurately the state of events and the intentional states of the human transmitter and user of data.

(ii) The efficacy of data coding and data formating techniques in

---

[3] MAC is an acronym for "Machine Aided Cognition" or "Multiple Access Computer." Project MAC was begun in November, 1963 at M.I.T.

conveying meaning (cause and effect relationship) and state of events.

(*iii*) The manner in which man and the technology can be coupled for mutual and reciprocal assistance during the command and control operation.

(3) Acceptance of the Technology. Although technology very often provides the means for facilitating tasks, there is no assurance that the technology will be used by man to facilitate the accomplishment of the task. The incorporation of technology in the operational environment may be accompanied by personal attitudes of inadequacy and threat.

The upper bounds of performance of command and control technology (computers, displays, etc.) stress the capacity of man to respond to such capabilities. When such incongruencies exist between the man and the machine, the tendency is for man to retreat to more comfortable arrangements in his environments. The lack of acceptance of technology in this case may be a function of equipment design philosophy which denies the matching of machine capabilities with those of the human.

(a) *Decision Processes* (1) Decision making in military. Webster defines *decision* as the "act of making up one's mind; a judgment or conclusion reached or given."

There are a number of problems which are apparent in arriving at an understanding as to what constitutes the decision function in military command and control.

The first problem is a general problem that relates to the decision phenomena itself and is not specific to the military environment. Decision making can constitute and involve all the broad considerations of behavior. A decision is a response, varying possibly in kind and degree of complexity. Questions about decision making may relate to learning perception, thinking, motivation, etc. Decision making often becomes synonymous with behavior.

The second problem relates to the institutional structure in which the decision making operates. Decision making is a phenomenon that occurs at every level of human endeavor, from the simplest to the most complex. Depending on the level in which the decision function is executed, however, consequence of the decision may differ in importance. The character and significance of these consequences may be apparent, but they have not been rigorously defined and studied.

The third problem concerns the relationship that exists between military doctrine and individual responsibility in executing command functions. Both established doctrine and the interpretation of such doctrine by commanders influence the latitude in which decision making functions are exercised in military operations. Furthermore, the content of the doctrine passed down from higher levels has a complex but a complimentary relationship with the information passed upwards from the lower levels of decision makers.

The fourth problem is the result of the rapid advances in transmission and computer technology. The amount of information available to a commander for making operational decisions has increased and is continuing to increase significantly. The tendency of military commanders to demand more data than they may actually need could influence the decision making functions. Presently, much of the data and its form of presentation is selected by the individual commander based on individual preferences (see Fubini [56]).

An added problem may be stated related to the foregoing. The availability and quick processing of data is raising questions concerning the appropriateness of present military organizations. With much of the data on specific operations available to the top echelon, the question that is being asked is whether intermediate commanders can contribute to the command decision function. Intermediate levels of command are undergoing change in their organization and management theory.

The foregoing statements do not intend to exhaust all of the possible problems that are related to the military decision function. In addition, the problems themselves, although they are oriented to the military, can be attributable to problems influencing decision makers in other environments as well. But there are some characteristics of the military problem which appear to be peculiar to the military.

1. The emphasis on the criticality of the consequences or outcomes.

2. The dynamic nature of military decisions; there are few static decisions.

3. Major military decisions are always the result of processing, wherein the channels of processing are well defined.

4. Control of information throughout the command structure is an accepted axiom of operation. Decision making by lower echelons is usually devoid of higher level information. Higher levels are restricted by information they obtain from lower levels.

5. The standard operating procedures and customs are well established in the military. This restricts the degree to which latitude of behavior can be exercised.

6. The population of decision tasks is wider and quite diversified.

7. Because of the nature of the staff structure, it is possible that major decision makers are obtained from a restricted, narrower source, i.e., field commanders, pilots, fleet commanders, line officers, rather than technicians or support personnel. Commanders know about combat operations, but only hopefully about technology.

8. The criteria for determining the effectiveness of decision making functions are varied and intricate as opposed to such stable criteria (i.e., profit) enjoyed by other enterprises. Depending on the situation (i.e., peace, time training, all-out war, limited war, etc.) different factors (i.e., safety, cost) become paramount. For each situation, the frame of reference is radically different.

9. In military situations, time is of the essence because commanders are usually

faced with time constraints which are more severe than those imposed on decision makers within other environments.

The speed of modern military weapons provides an example of the time constraints which a military commander must operate. This problem has been recognized and partially solved by the upgrading of communications and information processing facilities.

In brief, it would appear that the following could be considered as representing some of the dimensions that could distinguish military decision making from other decision making contexts.

(a) Criticality of the consequences (risk).
(b) Differential character of the leadership in terms of the kind of training and experience applied to the formulation and execution of the decision functions. Military executives come from a different population distribution, thus implying different value systems, knowledge and personalities.
(c) The institutional prerogative which often governs framework upon which decisions are made.
(d) The unstable nature of the frame of reference which governs different situations.
(e) Criticality of time as a dimension for effective military decision making.

(2) Decision theory.   An action directed at achieving military objectives involves the selection of choices. Decision theory is the underlying construct which attempts to determine systematically what variables influence choices [46, 71].

Historically, decision theory has been concerned with man's need to deal with circumstances in his environment that offer alternatives differing in value and significance.

In the past several decades decision theory has undergone a number of transitions.

1. The concept of man as being "infinitely rational, infinitely sensitive and completely informed" emerged largely from economics (Edwards [43]). The attributes of the economic man were assumed to allow him to organize the information into probabilistic form. The use of probability notions led to differentiating features of man's use of such probabilities in dealing with alternatives. At first, these objective probabilities were thought to be ordered in hedonistic manner, but the more sophisticated concepts of utility and subjective probabilities soon arose.

2. The concept of economic man applied to static, riskless situations. The concept of utility attempted to integrate risk into the economic model (that man observed, acted, and was knowledgeable about things).

Risk was always under conditions of uncertainty. Utility was assigned a value that corresponded to the subjective value the individual placed on selecting the correct response (Siegel [131]). In much the same way, subjective probabilities were thought to be a determining factor in the selection of an alternative.

3. Clearly, experiments revealed that man does not respond in decision situations as if he were maximizing utility or subjective probability based on the objective probabilities underlying the occurrence of the alternatives (Edwards [42], Neimark [104], Toda and Shuford [142]). However, these concepts have proved useful in the design and interpretation of experimental situations and will continue to be useful terms.

4. The efforts of von Neumann and Morganstern [148] offered possibilities in dealing with decision situations that were primarily concerned with conflict and the rules to select strategies that would cope with such conflict. Von Neuman and Morganstern developed a theory that attempted to predict the behavior of man in terms of selecting a strategm which would allow minimizing the maximum loss thus obtaining the maximum gain. One of the difficulties inherent in this approach was that the value of the utilities changed with each decision made, and consequently, the probabilities were constantly reordered (both subjective and objective probabilities). This has been a continuing problem in any attempt to measure utility or subjective probability within the confines of *game theory*.

5. The need to incorporate man as an interacting, dynamic source in the decision process found expression in the restatement of Bayes theorem by Savage [121] and was articulated within a behavioral framework by Edwards *et al.* [45]. The inadequacy of static decision that man applied conditional probabilities was based on *a priori* and *a posteriori* distribution in optimizing the outcome of alternatives (Rappaport [114], Shuford [130], Wiesen [152], Southard *et al.* [135]).

6. The potential of Bayes theorem in describing man's behavior in dealing with decision situations has led to (a) attention to those factors which precede the decision process and which influence decision behavior (Shuford [130], Roby [116]); (b) the inclination to derive simple models of the decision process incorporated in carefully defined environments in which such processes can be studied (Shuford and Toda [130, 141]); (c) relating decision functions within a broader context of behavior theory (Swets *et al.* [139], Massengill [93]); (d) considering personality factors as variables in decision functions (Scodel *et al.* [124], Atkinson and Cartwright [2], Lanzetta [83], Kogan and Wallach [78]).

The foregoing developments have basically achieved the following:

(*i*) Attempts at better description of the decision situations; Shuford and Toda see an important demand for such description in order to deal effectively with such situations.

(*ii*) Scrutinized utility as a criterion for decision behavior and have provoked attempts to scale such utilities (Siegel [*131*]).

(*iii*) Demonstrated the need for the development of experimental designs which are appropriate to the difficult problems encountered in substantiating decision theory hypothesis (Edwards and Tversky [*46*]).

(*iv*) The incompleteness of the present decision theory formulations in incorporating more behavioral parameters (i.e., learning, personality, physiology, perception) (Atkinson and Cartwright [*2*], Berlyne [*11*], Lanzetta [*83*]).

What is the adequacy of present decision theory in coping with the kinds of decision situations which are peculiar to the military, and which may have applicability to similar problems in the civic sector?

(1) Attempts have been made to orient decision theory from static to more dynamic concepts. This is both desirable and useful in approaching military decision problems because very few military problems are static; they are continuous rather than discrete.

(2) Utility as a major criteria for the evaluation of decision behavior is rather restrictive when applied to military situation.

(3) The kinds of decision situations that have been used to study decision behavior have been largely restricted to simplified, rather artificial, environments where the stimuli for decision action were within narrow range of complexity. Such studies have not provided the basis for the initiation of simulation studies more realistic to the military environments and its related operational problems.

(4) From available studies, it is not clear as to whether training is an influence on decision behavior. If it is, the kind of training that would be optimal for the kind of military situation likely to be encountered is to be determined. At present, training is largely a function of assignment experiences and other related environmental influences.

(5) The nature of decisions suggests that they may be influenced by the organizational strata in which the individual decision maker functions. The very fact that the decision is based largely on the strata from which the problem emerges, insures interaction with decisions emanating from other strata. These interactions are considered as extremely important in military operations where coordination of actions often measures the success of a military mission. Communications theory has long recognized the problems inherent in these interactions, but there is no visible evidence from decision theory for coping with problems in this area.

(6) That personality variables influence decision making behavior has long been recognized. A review of the bulk of the literature does not reveal a clear or ordered picture of the relationship. One of the problems is the *criteria for describing differences in decision making behavior*. Bruner *et al.* [*14*] described the major criteria for individual differences in decision making, namely, the broad vs. narrow categories (cautious vs. noncautious). This appears to be a consistent phenomena supported by a number of experimenters. The second difficulty relates to the fact that decision making is correlated with the specific *task variables*. The third factor relates to the experimenters who either refuse to acknowledge the difference or confuse the personality *traits* with personality *states* (set) that the individual brings to the situation. By and large, decision theory as is presently constituted does not adequately account for personality variables.

(7) A military commander brings a constellation of personal and professional value systems to his decision assignments. Such value systems are difficult to identify and study.[4]

(3) State of development.   From decision theory we hope to gain tools and precepts which, when applied, will allow commanders to make better decisions. By better decisions we refer to more exact solutions, more productive solutions, and generalized approaches which will facilitate solution of yet unrecognized problems.

Bayesian statistics seem to offer the most comprehensive method for building descriptive and normative models of human decision behavior. If the Bayesian paradigm best describes human behavior (Rappaport [*114*]), and humans are assumed to be acting in an optimal manner considering their constraints (Massengill [*93*]), an inclusive theory of decision behavior can be founded. Research along the lines of this theory would necessarily be concerned with individual differences as a dependent variable. In this way, the shape of the prior distribution for the population and the relationship between individual factors and decision behavior may be discovered.

In brief, it would appear that if decision theory is to provide contributions to the kinds of decision problems that the military is likely to face, more emphasis has to be placed in the study of decision functions within operational contexts. In this sense, (a) more thorough description of actual military decision appears to be required; (b) studies of experiments are needed in which military executives are confronted with realistic military problems and are required to respond to them; (c)

---

[4] Value in this context has a much broader reference than utility and refers to the beliefs, personal judgments, sets, attitudes, etc., which very often unduly effects response to alternatives.

careful studies should be undertaken to determine how value systems influence decision behavior in realistic, on-line operational problems; (d) the character of decisions to specific military tasks differentiated with respect to the intensity and complexity of the decision demands must be determined; and (e) finally some research must be aimed at isolating and describing the military population in whose decision behavior we are interested.

An example of a research effort in this direction is provided by experiments conducted by Hanes and Gebhard [66] with Navy Commanders. These scientists attempted to determine how such personnel interact with the computer as an aid to tactical decision making and found that Commanders readily accept computer inputs; find the computer to be a good companion as well as a challenge to their own ingenuity. Moreover, it is interesting to note the problems these scientists allude to in their study of man–computer interaction. Hanes and Gebhard point out that the computer's response to the operator's needs may be an important factor. Some operators of computers think that they are too slow in responding to their need, while others regard the problem to be the converse—that computer solutions may be presented too swiftly for the Commander to be able to assess them properly. The credibility of the data base upon which computer solutions are based may be another problem which leads to the nonacceptance of the computer as a decision making aid. These factors plus the added consideration that the way the data is presented to the Commander after it is processed by the computer (through hard copy or display) may be critical. This suggests that further advances in computers are not as much needed as our understanding of how man can be efficiently interfaced with them.

The work done by Miller et al. [100] is another step in the attempt to derive meaning of the decision processes within operational contexts. Although basically exploratory at this state, the research being conducted is to determine whether value judgments can be effectively studied to understand human decision processes. Miller and his colleagues report an initial experiment in which experienced military personnel were engaged in judging mission requests in a Tactical Air Command proposed system and one that was similar to their own operations. The results of the investigation revealed that a "Judged Utility Decision Generator (JUDGE)" can be used to enable personnel to allocate missions to requests based on operational requirements. The authors indicate that JUDGE is based on two notions; namely, the estimation of military worth associated with requests can be made explicit and in real time by experienced personnel and that the system should maximize "the aggregate utility over the dispatching decisions that it makes."

Studies on human value systems have been conducted in other than military contexts. Howard [*68*] explored the matter of value in information theory. Howard's approach is to assign numerical values to the change in uncertainty that may occur. He postulates that the "joint elimination of uncertainty about a number of even independent factors in the problem can have a value that differs from the sum of the value of eliminating the uncertainty in each factor separately."

There is some basis to the belief that decision theory is far from being able to answer all the questions, even some of the most important ones. By and large, the impression is that decision theory is very often expressed in terms that are insufficient to account for the decision process as most people experience it. What does appear, however, is that decision theory can, in effect, become a bridge in joining the many aspects of cognitive function in some orderly and purposive fashion. The fact that memory, learning, thinking, and problem solving all can be subsumed as being involved in the decision process requires that some effort be made to relate them in a meaningful theory and to establish the tenets of such theory by experimentation.

(*b*) *Human Communications*   (1) Language. Language is a direct concern to military command and control for several reasons. Understanding the structure of a language provides the means for developing a machine language which facilitates the man–machine interaction required in such systems. Much of the research conducted at M.I.T. by Chomsky [*21*] and his colleagues have direct application to the efforts undertaken by military scientists to develop such languages for computer operations in military command and control systems. By and large, the theoretical studies made in this area, however, have not as yet led to any appreciable success in the development of a natural language for computer applications.

Frazer [*54*] indicates "Language is an access vehicle." In this sense, language dictates the possible ordering of data in computer storage and its retrieval. The way that the data is organized in the computer may limit its information capabilities. Consequently, the issue of linguistic analysis becomes critical to the matter of providing military commanders with the most efficient data accessibility to meet their needs. As Frazer has indicated, research is very much needed to determine the extent of linguistic analysis necessary, the relationship between the type of information requested, and the organization of the data.

But of foremost concern to command and control is the matter of meanings and intentions that are generated through the symbols and codes that constitute the message structure. Such symbols and codes are often part of the language with which the message is structured and transmitted [*117*].

The problems generated in the use of symbols and codes are not peculiar, to command and control. Nevertheless, their importance is stressed because of the major role of communications in military operations.

Wohlstetter's account of the events that preceded Pearl Harbor clearly illustrates the breakdown in communications. This can occur as a function of the differential interpretability of signals (both symbolic and physical). As Wohlstetter states: "To say that a signal was available is not the same as saying that it was *perceived* in the sense it was taken as evidence or necessitating a specific course of action in response" [*154*].

In general, the issue of the use of symbols and codes in military command and control operations is significant for a number of reasons.

1. The use of symbols and codes in language is subject to wide variety of meanings and interpretation of such meanings.

2. Symbols and codes possess varying characteristics of legibility that are sensitive to the influence of noise and other aberrations that constitute the communication environment.

3. Use of symbols and codes can be compromised during periods where security of messages may be vital to operations.

All the foregoing factors could independently or collectively influence the outcome of operations.

(2) Media: presentation of data.   When a state of the event world is captured by a sensor and transformed into signals, such signals are then transmitted in pure form (energy) or coded element to a processing element for storage and subsequent retrieval. The signals (or data) can then be presented to the user on demand by various media.

Media are hardware vehicles for implementing human communications. Command and control operations require different forms of media; the primary ones concern media such as the telephone and radio which permit *direct access* to resources in the environment whose contact is often essential for effective operations. Media in the form of electronic devices such as CRT, TV, and film permit interlinking of data acquisition sources to data processing elements for the presentation of data to a user remote from the event site. Paper forms as media represent still other means for the presentation of data. Factual media where the skin surfaces are stimulated to present data to the user have been applied to a much lesser extent.

The rendition of data on visible surfaces so as to enable a user to respond to situational states underlies the subject of *data presentation*. Data presentation has assumed different titles in military systems development. The technology that underlies the subject of visual presentation of data historically belongs to aeronautical systems development and has been referred to in the literature as *visual display*.

The term *information display* has emerged in connection with command and control functions and is differentiated from visual display by the fact that information displays are ground based and restricted to size, are connected to interlinking data processing hardware, and have major functions that include a wide range of management and operational applications. We shall use the latter term in the present discussion.

Several areas govern the design and use of information displays in command and control. (a) Determination of the data required for decision making, (b) compatability of hardware design with human source potential, (c) interfacing of the hardware with the human user as well as other hardware.

Information displays are an important, almost indispensable, component of command and control systems. They represent the governing link between the outside event world, the processing machinery, and the decision maker.

Information displays are particularly sensitive to the capacity of other components of the command and control system to capture and retain the integrity of the data as they are transformed from the event world to the input elements of the display device. Because a number of transformations may occur throughout the system process prior to its presentation on a display, data may suffer distortion. Nevertheless, the critical distortions may occur between the display–man interface where the human cognitive machinery may serve to abort data content as a function of highly complex behavioral processes. (The function of language in this respect has been previously discussed.)

It is through the information display that the human is in a position to utilize and extend his own sensory and cognitive capabilities. Displays enable man to reach the remote aspects of the event world which previously he enjoyed by having immediate and intimate physical contact with his environment through his visual and auditory senses [*36*]. Another factor which further suggests the importance of information displays is that such devices enable the direct interaction of the user with the data processing element. Such interaction provides the possibility for flexibility in the use of computer facilities through the possible symbotic relationship, which can be realized through a careful matching of computing and human potential. Licklider discusses symbiosis as the behavior representative of dynamic interaction with the communicative partner, in this case the computer [*86*].

(3) Data requirements. The decision maker in a command and control situation requires data that is appropriate to the situation with which he is confronted. This means that the data the decision maker records must be timely, accurate, and meaningful to him. Some estimate must be made of the situation he is likely to encounter so that the data that is elicited from the event through the sensors and processed by the com-

puter is organized in a fashion that will enable him to respond quickly and efficiently.

The question of what commanders project to be their data requirements centers around several problems:

1. The lack of distinction that is made between data requirements (raw signals of events) and information requirements (transformed or organized data) causing confusion in the attempt to derive an intelligent estimate of the user's needs. Information requirements imply that certain principles of data organization are available that permit system designers to optimize the way the data is presented to the user for decision purposes. Data organization and decision function are yet to be studied systematically.

2. Uncertainty of the commander of the data requirements corresponding to operational contingencies likely to be encountered. Due to the criticality of the operational outcome, commanders may require much more data than the command and control system can provide, both practically and economically.

3. Unavailability of investigating techniques that can provide for substantive evidence as to the nature of data requirement for specific operational situations [59].

4. The differences that exist between individuals in the amount of data they require to substantiate their choice of action [58, 59].

5. The tendency for technology to set the pattern for the data needs of the user with the consequence that the user has minimal comprehensions as to how the system will help him during operations [9].

The approach of scientists in resolving some of the foregoing problems has been to provide greater computer complexity through program structures that are susceptible to on-line updating and debugging. From another direction but for a similar purpose, several professional societies like the American Psychological Association, The American Physical Society, American Ceramic Society and others are attempting, through research, to determine the information needs of their constituents and the nature of the environment (system) that can be established to satisfy such needs.

(4) Hardware design. Design of displays for command and control has moved from mechanically generated display systems to sophisticated electronic systems. Many publications exist in the literature which describe these display developments in considerable detail [68, 129, 134]. Developments in laser, holography are recent additions to the technology that has been applied to the presentation of data for command and control systems. By and large, three areas have influenced the development of command and control displays:

(i) *Physiognomics.* Apparently certain displays characteristics and designs provide greater appeal to the user and are preferred based on their aesthetic qualities. A predominant instance of this has been the use of color to depict information as opposed to black and white. Data to substantiate the benefit of color to black and white in support of the higher cost of color in terms of performance have not been conclusive.

(*ii*) *Costs.* Command and control displays are costly because of the research and development that often accompany the requirement specifications that are generated. Kennedy [*77a*] and Teichroew [*139a*] have discussed the various parameters that influence cost.

(*iii*) *Size.* The size of the display and whether individual as well as large group displays are required for effective command and control operations has been a source of considerable study by command and control system designers.

There are three issues which are relevant to the use of large group displays and individual (console) displays, namely, need, efficiency, and cost. The command and control system centers around a large operations room where commanders can be presented large situational displays. Accompanying these large situational displays are individual display consoles which enable individuals, whether in command or in other managerial positions related to the command and control function, to view the situation in privacy. What privacy means in this case is that the individual has the option of reviewing in detail (by optical zooming, perhaps) any aspect of the data presented to him on the larger display. Further, the individual display provides the officer using such a display the ability to interact directly with the computer in providing him with additional data that he may require for his analysis of the situation. At present, large group displays are mainly intended to provide a kaleidoscopic view of the operational situation to top military leaders who are more concerned with overall trends and can depend on the finer details of the situation for study and analysis by elements of his staff. The major question centers around whether such large displays influence the decision process, regardless of the status of the user.

Loewe [*89*] has indicated that "it is impossible to derive meaningful generalizations regarding groups and console displays." He has suggested, however, a number of advantages that can be cited for each category of displays.

Some of the studies reported in the literature support some of the advantages listed by Loewe. Studies by Smith and Duggar [*133*] suggest that the group display may benefit from the fact that individuals interact in the process of the use of such displays. Hammer and Seymour [*65*] studied the differential efficiency of individual versus group displays in light of the fact that if the updated information were to be made conspicuous that time to search and errors would decrease.

Their study did not provide evidence in support of individual or group displays but did suggest that individual displays may provide a greater opportunity for the viewer to assimilate information on the display. Nicholson [103] found that the size of the display on which data is presented does not affect the user's ability to handle the data that is presented on the display.

(5) Specific human dimensions. *Human processing potential.* When displays and man are interfaced in a command and control environment, the question invariably arises as to the amount of data loading on the display that man can undertake without the probability of incurring breakdown in performance. In a critical command and control situation, the decision maker may want as much of the data as is available to be presented to him. Inasmuch as computers have the capability of receiving and processing data from the sensors as a fast rate, and a large amount of data from the event world becomes readily available for presentation on the display, it is quite possible that the display system can provide the user with so much data that it will be a deterrent to his decision-making function. Baker and Goldstein [5] have alluded to a number of experiments which have shown that amount of data that is presented on a display invariably influences human performance [22, 62, 122]. The more data presented to the observer the more the likelihood of a decrease in performance. Baker and Goldstein studied the ability of individuals to solve problems when the display provided the problem solver, under one experimental condition, all the data he needed for that task; the other experimental condition involved the presentation of the data at the particular point in the problem that he needed it for solution. Baker and Goldstein state that when the individual is presented with added data, search time always increases and as such is a detriment to his problem-solving abilities. Although not tied directly to the same displays parameters, the work by Paul Fitts [53a] Newell *et al.* [102] are particularly relevant and should be kept in mind in attempts to understand how man processes data that reach the senses, and the way man utilizes such data to effect control of his environment as well as the means through which he solves particular problems. The many studies conducted by the Carnegie-Mellon group in the Graduate School of Industrial Management are particularly pertinent to the field of command and control.

(6) Interfacing.   When the data is received by the computer, is stored and ready for processing at the call of the user, one way the user achieves this recall function is through the display device. Typical of this interaction and rather significant in its implication to command and control is the research conducted by Sutherland [138] at the M.I.T. Lincoln Laboratories. Sutherland designed an interactive computer-display

system which enabled him to solve mechanical engineering problems on-line with the computer through the display system. Ideally, the decision maker of a command and control system should possess the capability of interacting in similar fashion in the test of contingency plans and strategies. The essential ingredient of this capability, of course, is the programming structure in the computer which would allow for a broad flexibility in the ability of the user to manipulate data in terms of his needs. At present, this capability is a research objective and not an operational reality.

There is another facet of interfacing of equipment and man in command and control that does not include the information display as a visual device, but rather the telephone (a transmission device).

The military command and control environment is replete with instances in which individuals are required to communicate over telephone lines. Very often the telephone in this environment supplements the visual display, the teleprinter, television, and the teletypewriter in presenting critical, logistical, strategic, and tactical information to the commander.

The telephone is a particularly sensitive information device in such situations because of its accessibility and because of the advantages of personal contact that it affords. Despite its inherent security limitations, it may at times indeed represent the only media for information transfer and for the verification of information available to the commander.

Teleconferencing as defined in the IDA reports is referred to "as meetings in which more than two people communicate via such media as telephone, teletype, or television" [140].

Despite the importance of the problem, insufficient data as to the best uses that can be obtained from teleconferencing and the consequences of its misuse are available [145]. Data must be obtained to provide guidelines for the most efficient and economic use of the teleconferencing media.

Bavelas [8] refers to two classes of variables which must be considered in the study of teleconferencing problems, namely, "structural aspects of the teleconferencing machines, and second, the dynamic aspects of the problems to be dealt by that machinery." Bavelas emphasizes that these variables are interactive and the distinction is made to highlight differences in experimental control which are implicit in the study of these variables.

Some of the variables to which Bavelas alludes are contained in the findings of the preliminary study by IDA scientists contained in previously identified report [140].

1. Teleconferencing is often preferred to face-to-face meetings.
2. Teletype is more effective than telephone when exchange of information is the only requirement.

3. Group interactions are significant in teleconferencing situations and that roles played by individuals affect outcome of the teleconference.

4. There is a lack of data on bilingual, multiparty conferencing via telecommunications technique.

5. The need for research on the influence of channel characteristics such as noise, capacity, reliability on teleconferencing.

(c) *Acceptance of Technology* The rapid developments of computer and display technology and their incorporation in command and control functions have demanded the development of new skills in data processing by operational personnel in the military services. Training programs have generally not been able to keep pace with the changes that have occurred to equipment as the result of systems evolution. As a consequence, individuals faced with assignments with command and control systems have often been at bay in understanding the purpose of such systems in the military environment. Faced with the possibility of conducting the operations through standard, manual procedures as opposed to computerized procedures, the individual not trained in understanding the operations of such systems is inclined to accept the manual ways of doing things despite the economy of effort that is available to him through the computerized systems.

But perhaps more vital to the future of command and control is the acceptance of such systems by the higher level echelons of the military [35]. It is not possible to ascertain conclusively to what level such personnel accept such systems as necessary elements of the military environment, but several indications raise several questions concerning the role that such systems can exercise in the military environment. Significantly, these considerations apply to data processing systems in the civic sector as well.

1. Data processing capabilities of such systems are correlated to the human intellectual function and as such are considered as pre-emptive of the human decision function. They are perceived as a threat to the intellectual integrity of man.

2. Data processing capabilities dilute human communication functions by depriving the utility of inter- and intrapersonal relationships (and the communication possible in such relationships) in achieving objectives. Individuals can obtain the state of events from the system rather than obtaining it through personal contact.

3. Because data distribution can be achieved simultaneously across the breadth of the organizational hierarchy through data processing and communication, individuals at the higher levels have immediate access to lower level echelons—bypassing the middle echelon. Such bypass creates attitudes of frustration and inadequacy.

2.2.4 Systems Theory

(a) General   The concept of a system was formalized in the military by the Air Force in the 1950's [*104*]. The early application of the concept was toward the development of weaponry (missile, aircrafts, etc.) and then applied to command and control.

The development of the Semi-Automatic Ground Environment (SAGE) was one of the first real application of systems theory in the command and control area. Since then, the systems approach has prevailed in the development of most if not all military weapons and command and control environment.

As the result of the emergence and application of the systems approach to systems development, the terms "Systems Engineering" and "Systems Design," "Systems Analysis," "Systems Management" and "Systems Science" have gained importance. *Systems engineering* includes a number of technical activities (invention, design, and integration) directed at achieving some goal or objective. *Systems design* is an activity specifically oriented to establishing and specifying the optimum system component configuration for achieving specific goal or objectives. As Bushnell cites the design is "where, when, with what, and with whom you must accomplish, what, for whom and where" [*15*]. *Systems analysis* involves the description and assessment of the "internal relations of the system as well as the interactions with the environment" [*112*]. It includes *requirements analysis, capabilities analysis,* and *feasibility analysis* [*73*].

There are two ways that the concept of a system in military command and control can be regarded. First, a system can be considered in terms of hardware (equipment) and software (procedures that make the hardware function). Wilson and Wilson [*153*] define systems as "a set of components to perform some wanted operation on an object." Zadeh and Polak [*156*] state that a system "is a collection of objects united by some form of interaction or interdependence." The second way that system can be regarded is that the term represents an approach or an *attitude* that is assumed toward the development of technology or the perceptions of phenomena in general. The approach or attitude consists of the recognition that parts and wholes interact and that each need to be accounted for in the development of science and technology.[5] The "systems" attitude includes the tacit recognition that the man–

[5] Ludwig Von Bertalanffy in 1952 discussed the application of systems theory to the understanding of all living organisms citing that "a living organism is not a collection of separate elements but a definite system possessing organization and usefulness." (From [*120, 147*]).

machine interactions constitute the important dimensions of an operational environment as contrasted to the hardware, which formally guided weapon design and development.

Systems management is a broad term which implies the operations which insure the proper functioning of the system to attain stated objectives. The term may also imply the activities incident to the system design prior to the actual implementation of the system as an operational environment. The term *systems science* includes the application of the theories and principles from a number of applied and theoretical sciences to the development and implementation of systems. Often, organizational science is included as part of systems science. The term *information system science* [81] has arisen in respect to the application of systems theory to the design of command and control systems.

(b) Systems Theory in Military Command and Control   The major contribution of military command and control environments to systems theory has been in establishing methods for the conceptualization and evaluation of systems whose major functional objective is not solely the behavior of machines, but principally in the behavior of men. Command, control systems have generated the following perceptions pertinent to the design of such systems.

(1) The Importance of Evolutionary Approach to Systems Development. There have been two major concepts employed in the design of command and control systems. The "template" concept provides for the design of a system based on the specification of equipment configurations that meet defined requirements. Such a design is largely constructed on system models that are derived from a logical analysis of the environmental states, both present and projected. The premise is made that such requirements are not likely to change in the foreseeable future. Consequently, one can afford to live with a system that is not renderable to frequent change and retrofitting. The "evolutionary" concept, on the other hand, includes the design of a system which provides for continuous changes in the environmental and functional requirements.

The "evolutionary" concept is highly receptive to "modular" equipment design and system configuration inasmuch as such equipment and configuration permit the addition and modification of units in response to changes both in the environments and the needs of users operating in such environments.

To the best of knowledge there is no formal evidence other than the rationale cited above which would support either the template or evolutionary concept of system design. Yet experience with command and control systems has almost dictated the evolutionary design in their conceptualization. The fact that the question of the effectiveness of such systems as aids to decision making is largely undetermined, and the fact that the changes in technology are rapid, all suggest that an evolutionary design is the design of the greatest feasibility in the information systems field.

(2) Dangers Inherent in the Hardware Technology Dictating the System Design. During the early years when command and control systems were being conceived as part of the military weapon systems, the design of the systems were largely dictated by available hardware. Design was largely a function of an attained consensus of engineers and salesmen of hardware, with little or no attention paid to the user. One of the major contributions of command and control to the development of information systems has been their emphasis on the importance of understanding the needs of the users of such systems. This had provided considerable emphasis on the methods of obtaining an insight into the user requirements as a preliminary to and as an important part of the system design process.

There are several consequences to the practice of emphasizing hardware technology without considering the needs of the user. One of the consequences is that the final hardware configurations that are included in the system may not find ready acceptance by the user. Absence of human factors considerations related to the hardware may lead to configurations that are not compatible with the physical or psychological constitution of the user.

Yet, there may be more devastating consequences. It may be that in the design of the equipment the human factors considerations have been accounted for, yet the system may be totally incompatible with the user. If the user's needs are not taken into consideration, and the design and the appropriate equipment and related training philosophy established, the user may never fully realize how the system can assist him in those functions for which the system was designed in the first place.

(3) The Value of Simulation and Modeling as System Design Techniques. The expansion of interest in military command and control provided some impetus to the creation of new analytical tools to be applied in the study of complex environments. Simulation and modeling were initially envisaged as techniques to be applied in the conceptualization of systems. These techniques together with *exercising* emerged more as evaluation tools, although the distinction between conceptualization and evaluation in the application of such tools may be tenuous.

The classic simulation in military command and control were the

Leviathan studies conducted by the RAND Corporation. Such studies attempted to reproduce the Air Defense environment to determine the data processing problems likely to occur in such situations. In the 1960s Mitre Corporation attempted, as part of the activities of the System Design Laboratory, to create command and control situations wherein the decision-making functions of military and high government officials could be observed and studied [*38*].

Similar simulations have been attempted since then by all Federal Department of Defense agencies. Sackman [*119*] alludes to the work of Parsons [*107*] in bringing together all the work done on simulation conducted by the military. Sackman's discussion is also valuable for the functional distinctions that are implicit in simulation.

Related to simulations is the model of the environment generally expressed in *mathematical* terms. Such a *model* is an attempt to apply rigor to the analysis of the environment and subsequently to permit the test of the model through experimental procedures. Many mathematical models have been formulated to represent aspects of the command and control environment.

Another practice often associated with simulation is *gaming*. A game involves the activities of opposing parties with similar objectives involving similar or different strategies in their attainment. Military command and control provides the appropriate setting for the application of gaming techniques; although in practice this has not actually occurred.

Exercising developed by Proctor [*112*] attempts to determine the behavior of a system by systematically interjecting into the environment the guidance required to meet particular system objective. It is to be understood that in exercising the system is optional, and that the exercising is a form of evaluating the system. The outputs from such exercises, however, can be used in modifying the design of the system.

The significance of the application of simulation, modeling, gaming, and exercising to command and control environments, and thus to their application to the civic sector, is in the requirement for rigorous analysis that such environments demand. They point to the many difficulties of analysis within such environments.

2.3 Social Impact of Military Command and Control

This discussion has alluded to the importance of electronics, particularly solid-state electronics, to the development of communications, data processing machinery, behavioral science, and systems theory. The fact that technologies in general have influenced the total social structure and its related value systems has been discussed in some detail by Ferkiss [53], illustrating the point that the considerations underlying their influences may be more complex than is normally realized. McLuhan [97] is more direct in imparting the impact of electronics and particularly communications technology on man. Such change in man's concept of himself emerges from the fact that electronic devices (media) like TV are really extensions of man's sensory system and as a consequence require man's involvement with electronic media in ways that lead to unprecedented psychological and sociological consequences. The point that emerges from most of such discussions is that technology may have pervasive effects, and that the effects from any one technology or combination of technologies on one or several aspects of human endeavor to other endeavors may be difficult to assign.

At this point, it may be appropriate to raise the question as to the purpose of impact statements and the service they provide.

Impact identifications can provide an understanding of the prevailing state of the environment and the conditions which influence and establish its directionality. Through this understanding, ecological factors may be appreciated and utilized in assessing the function of the technology in its present state. Such an understanding should enable the generation of countermeasures (social/physical) for the control of any deleterious effects that may be the product of the technologies. Identification of impact could lead to the formulation of standards and other regulating procedures which attempt to achieve maximum benefits from the technology. In this connection, impact acknowledgments provide the means for the identification of new technological requirements and technologies.

If impact statements are to serve the useful functions mentioned previously, then an attempt should be made to realize their exact nature. In general, the attempt to pursue and identify the impacts of command and control in the civic sector faces a major hazard. Command and control is not one technology, as has been presented in Section 2 of this article, but rather a collection of a number of isolated as well as interdependent technologies.

In what sense can the impacts from the separate and interdependent nature of the technologies be realized? There are actually two different classes of impacts, easily distinguishable, and each requiring two different intellectual approaches toward their understanding.

First-order impacts of technologies represent those effects from the technology which pertain to the direct function that the technology was intended to perform. For example, the first-order impacts of computers concern their ability to increase the data manipulation function and to keep better records: display technology provides greater flexibility in the presentation of data; communication technology increases the availability of individuals located in distance, etc.

Second-order impacts of these technologies represent those influences which are the result of the combination of the first-order impact of several of the independent technologies. For example, a second-order impact of computer technology is that when directly interfaced with the human, computers provide the capability to improve the human decision action. In general, therefore, first-order impacts concern the influence of technological components on specific functions, while second-order impacts relate to the influences of integrated technologies in system contexts.

i. First-Order Impact. The clearest case of the first-order impact of military command and control on the civic sector has been the emergence of new services that support civic functions. Baran [6] of the RAND Corporation points this out in his discussion of the effects of communications and computers. ". . . these electrical switches are not believed to be more economical than their electromechanical switch counterparts. But their prime advantage lies in the new additional services that they offer because of the general computer nature of the control mechanism of the switching center."

ii. Second-Order Impact. This more clearly identifies the influence of command and control as an environment and as an operational philosophy. The following are several identifiable second-order impacts:

1. There has been an increasing realization of the value of data manipulation and organization in support of decision functions.

2. The greater availability, accessibility, and distribution of data has led to the reassessment of organizational theory and philosophy. Hargreaves [67] has pointed out the influence of computers in inducing changes in the organizational structure, particularly in reducing the number of echelons in the chain of command. Whisler [151] and Mensh [99] have discussed the issue of centralization of control as well as other issues that may occur as the result of implanting command and control technology in the organization.

3. The need for greater precision in predicting social trends has encouraged the application of systems theory to the study of social phenomena. Sackman [119] presented a detailed account of the impact of command and control on the study of social phenomena. The work by the Systems Development Corporation, the RAND Corporation, and Mitre Corporation all attest to the impact of command and control in this area.

4. The importance of data to the conduct of all human endeavors suggests the creation of the new interdisciplinary science of information. Perhaps this represents the most significant impact that can be specifically and directly attributed to command and control, both as an operational philosophy and an environmental concept.

Myers [*101*], Gavin [*58a*] and others have discussed the effects of computers on organizations and individuals in these organizations. Martin L. Ernst [*49a*] cites three major social impacts of computer technology. Inasmuch as computer technology is fundamental to the development of command and control, such impacts are relevant to the latter. These social impacts bridge the first- and second-order reports which have been discussed in the previous paragraphs. Ernst cites the impacts as being *depersonalization, talent bias*, and *vulnerability*. Depersonalization is brought about by the requirement for computers to standardize the data manipulation procedures and equipments involved. Standardization of data procedure is essentially a just order impact. Yet, the fact is that individuals regard that such procedures as placing their lives in molds is a second-order impact—the result of the standardization of the technology. Clearly a second-order impact is Ernst's assertion that computer technology in effect creates training requirements in individuals in the mathematical and analytical sciences as opposed to the humanities. In this connection, command and control can be considered as installing a need for individuals with broad interdisciplinary views and skills. Finally, computers tend to deprive the individual of the privacy he previously enjoyed with less sophisticated data processing systems, which makes the individual vulnerable to wide exposure of his personal habits and practices. Ernst states ". . . the fact that management itself will become more vulnerable in its decision making. As we use more complex decision making tools, and rely more heavily on large data banks, there will be more filtering of information by staff personnel before materials for decisions are presented to senior management . . . . As the decision-making apparatus becomes more complex, it will be harder for managers to exercise effective personal control". [*49a*] These statements are a clear reflection of the impact of command and control technology on the individual and the society at large.

2.4 Science of Information

In 1965, Ruth Davis [32] in examining the research falling within the area of command and control concluded that she could not assert that there was a science of information. Since then, the science of information has been considered by some to fall within the domain of library science, mathematics, linguistics, and psychology, as well as other areas [*12a*, *67a*, *131a*]. Yovits [*156a*] in 1970 stated that if information science is to be a science "it must have a set of concepts and analytical expressions that apply to the flow of information is a general way." Otten and Debons (106a) conceive of information science as a metascience wherein "the body of knowledge describing these phenomena (information and operations on information) and relations will evolve ..."

In general, the term "information science" suffers by ambiguity in application. For example, the term information *science* has been used interchangeably with the term information *sciences*. It is maintained there are indeed information scien*ces* (e.g., computer science, communication science, library science). It is also maintained that there is a base for the *development* of a science of information. This science of information would ultimately be the basic science of the information sciences.

The phenomenon of information is the most pervasive in human endeavor, and a matter germane to his development and survival; as such it justifies the attempt and promise of systematic investigation. With further developments in information technology, our understanding of information will gain further importance.

The experience and research engaged on behalf of command and control systems can provide the base for the development of theories regarding the transformations that underlie the acquisition, transmission, processing and depiction, and use of data. Command and control systems were generated as a reaction to the "data explosion." The technology that responded to this explosion clearly pointed to the power of the data resource, and the sparsity of available insight as to how such a resource could be effectively channeled to best serve man. What military command and control systems provide is the ability to manipulate the data resource. This capacity now has to be matched by an understanding of the underlying processes which make this data resource a valuable resource for man's purposes.

Ultimately, the many theories from psychology, linguistics, management, library science, automata, etc., which provided the impetus for the development of command and control technology, will provide the basic structure for the development of a science of information.

2.5 Non-Military Applications

2.5.1 Information Systems in Civic Sector

Table II summarizes some of the information systems now operational in the civic sector. In many of these systems, it may be claimed that either the hardware or the software design or both have their derivatives in the technological development that accompanied military command and control systems. An attempt has been made here to completely identify such systems, but because of the rapid emergence of such systems, a claim for completeness cannot be made.

2.5.2 Application to Civic Functions

Table III summarizes the several civic functions for which information systems have been contemplated or presently exist in the civic sector. Such systems have technological properties common to military command and control systems.

TABLE II: INFORMATION SYSTEMS IN THE CIVIC SECTOR

Field	Name of project	Location	Function	Equipment	Command and control application	Reference
Weather	Weather modification	University of Georgia under contract from U.S. Navy	1. Through 40 local automatic weather recording stations, it collects 16 weather parameters. 2. The statistics are to determine the most opportune time to seed clouds to produce rain for that particular environment. 3. Study of weather pattern. 4. The rainfall probability studies to guide planting crops to receive rain at optimum point in growing cycle. Used for southern Georgia vegetable growers.	IBM/360 terminals include teletypewriter, and graphic display. Time-sharing FORTRAN, COBOL, PL/1, and assembly language; conversational capacity	Control	[17]
Law enforcement	LEADS	Ohio, access by all law enforcement agencies	Central data base, information on stolen articles, vehicle registration, connection through it to other law enforcement agencies throughout U.S. by LETS connection to Natl. Crime Information Center, D.C.	200 odd teletypewriter terminals via telecommunications. Two 360/40 processing units in Columbus, Ohio	Control	[20]
Airline reservation		Eastern Airlines	Handles seat availability information for 24 other airlines. 10 regional centers connected over data lines to central processor Miami display terminals at reservation centers, provides scheduling information; makes and confirms reservations.	360/65 (3) disk packs, tape drives, transmission, control lines, IBM	Control	[75]
Banking	Audio-response	Bank of Delaware; Wells Fargo Bank, San Francisco; Manufacturers National Bank, Detroit	By dialing the customer's account number to a central file through a telephone, the computer checks the account and bring back the information by a computer-simulated voice	The combination use of computers and communications. On-line, real-time	Control	[106]
Banking	On-line account changes	Howard Savings Institutions, Nebraska; Union Dime Savings Bank, New York; the Society for Savings, Hartford; Citizens National Bank, St. Petersburg; Bank of Delaware	Through a special teller machine terminal, the customer's account on the computer as shown by the pass book, is updated automatically whenever deposit or withdrawal happens	The combination use of computers and communications. On-line real-time	Control	[106]
Banking	Automatic payment and deposit	Bank of America	Corporations submit payrolls to bank by tape or punched cards; employees' salaries can be automatically deposited to their accounts.	The combination use of computers and communications. On-line, real-time	Control	[106]
Banking	Automatic utility bill payment plan	A bank in Louisville, Ky.	It allows the bank to debit the customer's account and credit the account of any of the local utilities	The combination use of computers and communications. On-line, real-time	Control	[106]
Aerospace	NASA Regional Dissemination Centers	See reference, p. 25	Assists in transfer and use of aerospace technology in other areas; emphasis on NASA-supported journals; abstract journal publication; support 6 information centers	Varies with centers at University of Pittsburgh IBM 360/50 OS IBM 7090	Information dissemination	[101a]
Chemistry	NSF Office of Science Information Service	See reference, p. 38	Provides review and retrieval resources for literature	Varies; at Pittsburgh IBM 360/50 (OS/MVT/HASP)	Information dissemination	[72a]

Field	Name	Location/Developer	Description	Technology		Ref.
information	information through electronics)	of Pittsburgh and IBM under contract from USAF now serving the Department of Defense (DOD)	retrieve the information of (DOD) fiscal and accounting regulations, administrative decisions of Comptroller General affecting DOD, appropriation acts of Congress, or a body of selected international agreements affecting DOD areas of responsibility	Document processing system. (130,000 core storage) for the document processing system program, and 2311 disks for text, bibliographic data, key words, and index data	Control	[137]
Education	Computer-Assisted Instruction (CAI) Project Plato (Illinois)	Stanford University, Univ. of Illinois, Pennsylvania St. Univ., Univ. of Pittsburgh, Univ. of Michigan, Univ. of Texas, Florida State Univ., Univ. of Calif., Santa Barbara (IBM, SDC)	Computer assists the learning processes through terminals with a primary emphasis on the development of computer hardware, to the construction of short courses in subjects ranging from physics to typing	On-line, time-sharing, real-time	Control	[27]
Education		East Palo Alto, Calif.	Brentwood 1st grades—Stanford program to find out how well students learn to read and teach arithmetic. 2 TV screens per pupil. (1) words and numbers. (2) pictures of people. Received taped instruction while pictures are placed on screen. Children answer by speaking in microphone or touching screen with light pen	2 TV screens/pupil, keyboard, earphones, microphone, light pen Developed by Stanford, Dr. Patric C. Suppes working with IBM. Brentwood teachers agree computers better at teaching math than reading	Control	[29]
Education	CAI	University of California; developed by SDC	Provides computations for problems after student chooses correct formula. Introduces realism into college statistics course by enabling student to manipulate large complex data bases.	Source Language—PLANIT	Control	[29]
Education	CAI—"Samerian Game"	Westchester County, N.Y.	Student rules mythical empire through his actions at critical decision points. Results of decisions on allocation of manpower and resources are analyzed by computer; interaction of economic factors are displayed graphically to student.	CRT, typewriter, console link, Ed to computer	Control	[29]
Education	CAI Management	SDC Claremont Colleges, New Jersey	6 colleges—scheduling courses	Several computers	Control	[125]
Medicine	ABIIS (Automated blood inventory information system)	Milwaukee blood center as a prototype system to demonstrate feasibility of automated blood control	Blood inventory control and management for southeastern Wisconsin area. 1. Convert whole blood units into blood components. 2. Draw, process, and add a unit of blood to the bank. 3. Ship blood units to and from member hospitals. 4. "Cross-match", blood units to insure donor-recipient compatibility. 5. Transfuse blood into a recipient or otherwise dispose of it. 6. Maintain a file of blood donors. 7. Maintain a file of blood recipients.	Data Systems Sigma 2 Computer; IBM-360 time-sharing. FORTRAN and QUERY are used. QUERY is a specially designed language for ABIIS	Control	[136]
Medicine	Medidata sciences general medical history	Developed by Sciences, Inc., Waltham, Mass.	1. Patients are interviewed by the computer in through a plastic card reader terminal. At the end of the interview, a complete, organized and analyzed medical history will be printed out. 2. There are many conveniences for both the patients and the doctors.	PDP-81—Time-sharing system and special designed plastic card reader questionnaire terminal used. On-line, time-sharing	Control	[63]

TABLE II (*continued*)

Field	Name of Project	Location	Function	Equipment	Command and control application	Reference
Legal information	Computerized legal search system	Being used in the states of N.Y., N.J., Pa., Ohio, Iowa, Kansas, Hawaii, Mass., W. Va., Texas	Search of textual information such as judicial decisions, ordinances, department codes and regulations, results of agency adjudications, review decision of courts, material, bodies of official memoranda		Control	[57]
Sports	SCOUT (football scouting)	University of Georgia	1. Football scouts can look over the opponents one week in advance. 2. The system gives a complete report on the strength and weakness of the offensive and defensive maneuvers of the opposition, including the frequency and relationship to position on the field	IBM 360—terminals include teletypewriter, and graphic display. Time-sharing FORTRAN, COBOL, PL/1, and assembly language. Conversational capacity	Control	[17]
Engineering	CLAD (Cover layer automated design program)	Guidance and Control System D.V. of Litton System, Inc.. Woodland Hills, California	1. Through CRT display unit, individual engineers can use the CLAD as an automatic graphic method to define the cover of a multi-layer laminate. As soon as the cover layer is defined graphically information is transmitted to the magnetic tape. Then the tape becomes input to another program which automatically routes the interconnects of the laminate. 2. CLAD has replaced the manual procedures of coding, keypunching	Several big computers interconnected. Terminals: CRT display units	Control	[90]
Architectural design	M.I.T.		Immediate access by designer to results of precise operations CRT, light pen to adjust curve or equation and get other change from computer	Model 40		[148]
Traffic control		Toronto, San Jose, West London, England, Wichita Falls, Syracuse	1. Timing control traffic signal 2. Operate speed signs to maximize flow at signals on green phase. 3. Quantity control traffic backup. 4. Routing	Transistorized detectors, underground cable, Univac 1107 Thin-film Mim. closed circuit TV, monitors Variations of similar equipment	Control	[1]
Education medical		Main osteopathic hospitals—6 from Chicago and Philadelphia also NY University to Davis Clinic, Marion, Indiana, Penn., and Syracuse	Allow lecturer to address and discuss current developments in specialized areas or any subject of current interests with groups in different locations. Cuts travel time and expense. Questions handled from their assistants through monitors. The names of participants in the audience and their questions are projected on screen to lecturer	TELELECTURE—conference calls set up allowing 2-way voice transmission. Transmission between lectures and each audience. Audio visual aids, mailed (slides) in advance to groups.	Control	
Education share facilities		Two colleges, one at Louisville, Ky., one at Nazareth, Ky., also engineer at Grand Rapids, Mich. took course from Mich. State 90 miles away	Adds "blackboard" facilities to remote lecturer from lecturer's desk to larger screen in "remote classroom" (Aero-space Equip. Corp.)	Linked with TELEWRITING		

(a) *Legal Practice*   The practice of law requires the continual referral to previous case documents to determine legal policy and doctrine. The lawyer is confronted with a huge library problem if indeed he is to practice law effectively. The matter of computerizing legal abstracts is now being undertaken in the hope that future lawyers may have at their disposal, via a desk console, the capability of satisfying their case search requirements quickly and more efficiently. Much of the research on document retrieval and the problems of relevancy thereto are pertinent to the lawyer. Many of the questions raised in the process of the development of military command and control concerning the classification of data (indexing, etc.) and their placement in the computer for quick retrieval is pertinent to the legal profession. A significant contribution in this area is the microfilming of documents which allows a considerable reduction in size of the legal library and the automated retrieval and visual presentation of such documents on a display. But perhaps of more significance, data technology makes possible the updating of legal files on almost a real-time basis. Although this capability is yet to be achieved, a centralized data source of legal action on a day-to-day basis available on demand by the lawyer can serve to alter the entire character of legal practice. The further ability of the user to analyze legal documents through time-sharing, interactive computer procedures will represent a formidable capability that will enable the lawyer to achieve greater control in the exercise of law.

(b) *Policing*   The function of the police is to maintain order in the community. The police achieve this objective through surveillance and control of environment forces. The police establishment is similar to the military establishment inasmuch as both have the function of surveillance and control. As such, the police in a civic community is a miniature military establishment with prescribed function in specific areas of control. It has both command and control jurisdiction: authority to direct action affecting the security of the citizen and to insure that whatever laws are constituted are in effect carried out.

The achievement of police objectives is highly dependent on the data, both covert and overt, available on the state of the population and the facilities that make up the community. A police data system consists of the means of acquiring, transmitting, and processing data required to maintain law and order in the community. As now constituted police data systems are data management systems and serve as instruments for control of crime and the safeguard of people and facilities.

At present, police departments of local communities have only partially benefited from the advances which have their beginnings in command and control. The capabilities which are possible from the use

TABLE III: CIVIC FUNCTIONS, COMMAND AND CONTROL ACTIVITIES, AND STATUS OF RELATED INFORMATION TECHNOLOGY

Civic function	Description of civic function	Civic environment	Description of related C^2 function	Primary functions involved[a]	Activities related to primary related functions	Description of technical requirement	Availability of science and technology[b]	Related technology	Related science or field
Legal practice	Establish precedent for specific legal cases; determine outcomes, legal implications of court cases, etc. Abstracting of documents to derive case for action	Legal establishment; courts, law firms	Checking of possible decision actions against available operational directives	C	Documentation, identification, documentation crosscheck	Rapid content identification, knowledge of user needs, automated data synthesis quick updating	MA MA MA MA	Data recording media, I/O devices	Content analysis law, logic
Policing	Accounts for criminal action by counteraction; survey areas of crime potential; traffic control	Local, state, national law enforcing agencies	Tactical control, intelligence threat evaluation	C_M P	Detection, diagnosis, assessment	Same as Data Management *plus* sophisticated sensors, data transmission devices, large electronic displays	A MA MA	Same as Data Mgt. plus quick data cross checking, time sharing, detection devices	Law; communication; pattern recognition
Weather control	Detection of weather trends; alerting for significant disturbances and related emergency actions when necessary	Weather stations air pollution analysis	Weather prediction for operations planning chemical warfare	C_M D	Detection, identification, diagnosis, prediction, assessment	Sophisticated sensors, data transmission devices, large electronic displays	A MA MA	Displays, seismographics, communication (satellites)	Meteorology
Organizational management	Day to day alignment of human and personnel resources to achieve objectives	Institutional complexes (private and public) consisting of hierarchal structures and individuals working within such structures	Unit-Command Administration acknowledgment of unit status; personnel and material resources. Status of attainment of objectives; relationship with other operational units; reporting patterns, communications; relevancy of unit objectives	C_M P	Evaluation, screening, estimation	Simulation/modeling new organizational concepts, quick feedback, realize need for change	A A MA	I/O devices, displays, computers	Organization theory, management, business admin., psychology
Data management	Handling of published materials	Library, sales establishments, IRS, banks	Receipt and categorizing of intelligence data; estimate enemy's capabilities; inventory of personnel and supplies (logistics); historical accounts; reports operational record	C	Documentation identification, storage retrieval, referencing, categorizing, indexing	Quick updating, error identification, reduce cost of equipment relevancy in retrieval, knowledge of users' needs, rapid reporting and crosschecking data, priority handling,	MA MA MA MA MA MA NA	I/O devices; data recording media; displays (electronic) computers (large memory, etc.) microfilming, transmission facility, time sharing,	Philosophy (logic), classification systems, etc.); computer science

Application area	Function description	Institution examples	Military analogy	Symbol[a]	Function	Requirements	Availability[b]	Technology	Disciplines
						large data storage capacity, fast retrieval	A / A		
Transportation	Manage vehicular traffic flow: avoid bottlenecks, emergency action control, insure safety of vehicles, establish new routes	Air traffic control centers; air terminals	Movement of personnel and supplies to operational areas; inventory of vehicular resource	C$_{MD}$	Vehicular surveillance, scheduling	Area coverage, fast reporting of breakdown (unusual conditions)	A / MA	Displays (CRT, etc.) programming; sensors (radar)	Math (ops. analysis), electronics, systems theory
Education	Teaching functions for all educational levels, different course materials CAI, remote training stations	Schools, any circumstances where special information requirements facilitate primary functions; i.e., dentist office in describing why cavities develop	Use of data systems by commanders; feedback and interaction with data source to develop new ideas for using resources	COM	Man–machine communication	Man–machine interaction: Student progress monitor Lesson update Student query Course difficulty escalation	A MA A A	Computer time-sharing; programming; displays, satellites	Language, psychology (learning theory; cognitive theory), journalism
Medicine	Collection of data from many sources centrally enabling physician as well as medical researchers to check data on particular case studies against national trends	Hospitals; patient–physician interaction, medical research centers	Determining the pattern of enemy operations; analysis of operational states; intelligence data consequences of operational breakdown	Dp C$_M$	Diagnosis assessment; detection, identification	Feedback concepts on diagnosis, internal detecting mechanisms, data analysis, time-sharing	NA MA A MA	Telemetry; electronic displays; sensors communication	Physics (optics) medicine, electronics; psych. (decision theory), visual theory
Community affairs services development	Status and activities of civic population is surveyed to determine the satisfaction of human needs and related institutions; accounting of physical resources	Office of City Managers and Administrators; vital statistics and related agencies	The status of operational units to determine employment, deployment of resources; need for creation of new organizations	P C D O	Evaluation; screening, estimations	Large data storage, man–machine interaction, same as Organization Management	A A	ADP I/O computer device, data recording media, data security	Sociology, political science, statistics systems theory

[a]Symbols represent related abbreviation of functions: C, Control; M, Monitor; P, Planning; D, Decision making or command; O, Operating. Vertical alignment, e.g. $\frac{C}{P}$ $\frac{D}{}$ signifies that planning (P), control (C), and decision (D) are all primary functions of equal involvement and importance. Diagonal alignment, e.g. M^{C}_{O} signifies that this is primarily a control (C) function where monitoring (M) and operating (O) functions may be involved as *subsidiary* functions.

[b]A, available, now existing; MA, moderately available, technology is only partly available to do the job; NA, not available.

of sophisticated data sensing and processing devices in detecting possible areas of disturbances, violence, and crime have only been considered recently. Although the police functions of the national government have incorporated such devices for crime analysis and detection, the integration of such facilities with local agencies is still to be achieved.

The centralized "control centers" now in existence in police departments consist of sophisticated displays and communication media, but data acquisition media still depend largely on human inputs. The problem of the reliability of such inputs makes the data acquisition function inadequate. In general, therefore, the major impact of military command and control in police functions has been largely in the realization of retrieval of data on crime history.

There are instances, however, that provide considerable hope to the application of command and control technology to police functions. One instance in fact is the New York State Identification and Intelligence Systems (NYSIIS) which enable the surveillance of stolen automobiles entering city tunnels [4]. By and large, however, police data systems remain largely control systems. The use of automated data processing to enable such command functions as predicting and acting on the next outbreak of violence, and determining what measures are most effective to be applied to specific forms of crime based on the data available is still to be achieved.

(c) *Weather Control*   The surveillance of seismographic and climatic conditions is now a matter of sophisticated treatment. The analysis of weather data by computers has now achieved a sizeable degree of scientific sophistication. With the dependence on satellites as weather sensors—their great degree of space coverage and ability to elicit variation in radiation—greater sophistication in weather prediction is to be expected. Again, weather control systems are largely data management systems centered around a particular function.

In addition to the capabilities which have been made possible through satellites and developments in computers, the research undertaken for military command and control in displays is significant to weather prediction. Large displays generated by computer output of data enable the assessment of weather trends in real time. Weather control displays are now permanent fixtures in air traffic control centers; these displays enable traffic controller interaction with the computer in assessing critical weather patterns. Still, such weather data systems are of limited help in establishing the decision functions that the weather man must assume in protecting human life and property from severe weather. In projecting disturbances of a very dynamic sort, the meteorologist requires a data processing system that will enable him to interact in real time in the context of those weather parameters that help him to predict weather behavior. A weather information system should provide the capability for predicting with a high degree of accuracy the course and form of a weather disturbance and the possibility of alerting particular areas of a community of weather patterns and their consequences.

The detection and control of air pollution can be considered to involve the same technical problems as those encountered in weather control. Air pollution has gained the interest of a large percentage of the population because of its apparent effect on health. The measurement of air polluters has achieved considerable sophistication but the control of such pollution seems to have suffered because of the lack of sophistication in the management of community life in general. There are particularly encouraging signs, however, that the technology derived from military command and control can now be applied to the problems of air pollution. The city of Pittsburgh, for example, has now established an air pollution control information system which permits the detection of concentrates of pollution and to identify the physical area related to the concentration. The detection is achieved by special sensors located in buildings and on highways. The detector then leads to alerting the source contributing to the pollution to take corrective action. The analysis of the levels of concentration is achieved through computer analysis [109].

(d) *Organizational Management*   The application of automated data processing to the execution, planning, and control functions of an organization has been considered as constituting a Management Information System (MIS). Prince [111] in discussing information systems for management cites that "a traditional Information System is a *closed* system encompassing all of the major information flows within a business organization." Golding [61] details six (6) functions that such a system is intended to perform—namely, reviewing, estimating resources, programming and planning, accounting, flagging (tasks on which time or resources is expended), and retrieving. A Department of the Navy report defines a management information system as "the aggregate body of people, policies, procedures, methods and equipment, both manual and automated, which serves the primary purpose of collecting, storing, processing, analyzing and disseminating useful information in an organization [30].

The broad effects engaged by the military in applying systems design to the assemblage of automated processing equipment and data presentation components have considerably influenced the civic sector to apply similar concepts for the use of such devices in organizational management. The experience now being gained from military command and control in their attempt to achieve information system status will materially have an impact on the development of such systems in the civic sector.

(e) *Data Management*   A data management system is an environment consisting of an assemblage of equipment and procedures directed to insuring the availability of data when needed by a user (man or machine).

A data management system includes procedures for the inputting of data to a central store, the storage of data, and the outputting of data on demand, either in printed hard copy form or on an electronic display. The data may be in the form of transmitted signals from a sensor source or in the form of printed material. Data, in this sense, may undergo several transmissions by either man or machine, but the implication is that the character (substance-content) of the data remains theoretically intact. Errors or transformations that are likely to occur in the process of transmission are considered part of data management systems corrective procedures. One of the objectives of data management systems is to maintain the integrity (reliability, reproductivity) of the data intact, and to insure that whatever interface that occurs with the user that the data submitted to him is relevant to his purpose. Most so-called "information systems" are basically data management systems because the user when included in such systems is considered as a passive (receiver) agent rather than interactive (modifying) element. The function is to make the data available rather than to enable the most effective integration of the available data with the human purpose. The latter is the function of the "true" information system as defined here.

The purpose of data management systems is to reduce the time and cost of the processing of data. Specifically, data management systems are established to reduce the paperwork involved in accounting for the state of the organization, and for relating events that may be pertinent to the life of the organization. With the large increase in the vital statistics generated by the census, with the complexity of industrial production and the personnel employment practices as well as politics, the need for accounting of data has gained considerable interest by many sectors of the civic community. Of particular interest, is the change in the habits of the citizen in handling the debits and credits incurred in his day-to-day encounters. Cashless societies are now being seriously contemplated. This form of society can only be conceived if sophisticated data management systems covering a wide range of human activities (such as would be found in retail and banking functions) can be designed and implemented.

One of the social institutions benefiting highly from data management systems has been the library; this institution seems to be one of the major institutions of our time that can benefit most from the advances made in data management technology. Most certainly, the libraries are facing the greatest challenges, the result of "information" (data) explosions. The library is now seen as being in the best position to reap the benefits of data technology, but in so doing, it will probably constitute the clearest instance of how such technology can truly modify the entire character of the institution. The processing of huge amounts of printed material, the transformation of such material into microform and other data reduction technologies, the alteration of the habits of the user of published data all will serve to alter the character of the library as we know it today [85].

It is believed that the most significant contributions to the civic sector made by military command and control in the area of data management are the following: (a) reduction or elimination of the manual processing of data; (b) availability of increased capabilities in data processing equipment (speed, capacity, and reliability of digital computers); (c) real-time data processing and time sharing of data; (d) the possibility of centralizing data processing facilities, and the accessibility of data to some people; (e) the use of automated data processing for planning and control function.

(f) *Transportation*   With more and more vehicles in air and space and on the ground, and at sea, the greater the need for the control of these vehicles. The matter of controlling vehicles in space has always occupied the attention of both the military and civic sectors. With the birth of aviation, the requirement for aircraft control has been of prominent interest. The aircraft constituting a military weapon requires control to insure its destination and the achievement of its mission. When aircraft assumed civilian roles, the security of passengers emphasized the need for control. With the increase in the range of such vehicles in space, and the increased density in the number of available vehicles, the matter of control gained even greater attention.

The military command and control required that vehicles at any particular point in time and space be accounted for so as to insure their efficient employment when needed for operations. The accounting concerned the accurate knowledge of the character (potential effectiveness) of the vehicle and its capabilities (range, weapon load), etc. Several crises which emerged during the 1950's in which our nation was involved required a quick reach capability for deploying such vehicles. This led to the possibility of deploying, scheduling, and assigning vehicles entirely by the computer. With increased complexity in air traffic control patterns, the computer began to be used more frequently in the assignment and scheduling of aircraft. Eventually with the increase in nonmilitary passengers, computers were used to allocate space on aircraft and for airlines to project schedules and aircraft needs.

The application of computers to centers for the control of ground vehicles has been realized much slower. Operations analysis of transportation problems has been aided considerably by the introduction of computers to traffic control and is continuing to do so. Many large cities have entertained rather sophisticated data management systems for effecting control of traffic. Such systems resemble miniature command and control systems inasmuch as they contain all the objectives of the latter systems—controlling the vehicles (weapons) and providing the data for effecting decision actions that can substantially alter traffic patterns on a real time basis.

The matter of adding sophisticated sensors in the form of lasers and satellites to automatically control traffic patterns without human intervention is the area of transportation information systems, but this is yet to be realized.

(g) *Education* The linking of a data processing element (computer) to a data-presentation device with the human acting as the response element and the computer as the input element in a performance modification operation constitutes an instructional subcomponent (instructional module) of an educational system. An educational system consists of a composite of such instructional units integrated by a central data processing element(s). Evaluative subsystems that attempt to show the progress of the student may be tied directly or indirectly to the instructional module. In addition to central processing and display elements, educational systems are envisaged as being tied to sophisticated communication devices (satellites).

Instructional technology has a long and extensive history. Saettler [120] treats the initial concepts of programmed instruction as emerging from Ancient Greece, with the work of Montessori in Rome and Pressey, the psychologist at Ohio State, representing some of the early work done in this area. The concept of computer-aided instruction emerged fundamentally from the earlier "teaching machines." The teaching machine was an outgrowth of the reinforcement theory of learning advanced by B. F. Skinner. In 1954, Skinner presented a paper "The Science of Learning and the Art of Teaching" in which he provided the basis of programmed instruction as we have it today. The early concepts of programmed instruction consisted of breadboard console models which permitted the mechanical presentation of instructional material visually and sequentially to the trainee. More contemporary models consist of the presentation of instructional material through an electronic display. The material on the display is generated via the computer program. In present day models, the trainee can interact directly with the computer through electronic display.

The instructional module of an educational system can be compared to the computer–display–man interactive elements of the military command and control system. Similar man–machine functions may be envisaged in both. In the CAI, the trainee initiates the action for the presentation of the material that he intends will increase his store of knowledge and modify his behavior. His response to the data presented to him will be checked against criteria relating to the correctness or incorrectness of his response. Essentially, the behavior of the trainee in this instance consists of a number of human cognitive functions that are largely regulated by the nature of the stimuli presented to him on the display device used for the instruction. In the military and command and control case, the commander uses the display to gather the data he needs to conduct satisfactory operations. The data is programmed to respond to certain queries, and the response to the queries may be generated through certain rules which contain certain corrective formulas.

As far as the computer–display–man subcomponents of a military command and control are concerned, military command and control may be considered to constitute, in part, instructional systems, inasmuch as they include the same processes. Seidel [126] in discussing an instructional situation stated "a set of control processes passing 'info' (quotes are mine) back and forth between one another, the capacity to change and adapt over time to improve the system, that which we call the instructional environment." There is analog of this in the military command and control system.

The foremost contribution of military command and control technology to educational systems has been in the area of displays.

In the development of *electronic displays* which enable the presentation of instructional material, the significant advances have been in the following:

1. The development of large group displays which permit the presentation of instructional material to large audiences in well-lighted rooms without loss of data resolution and perspective.

2. The development of individual consoles which permit the viewer to interact directly with the computer (Sutherland [138]).

3. The development of color in electronic displays to enhance coding and highlighting (emphasis) of data.

4. The development of three-dimensional displays which provide the means for improving the presentation of material that requires the use of perspective.

(h) Medicine   The greatest promise for the application of military command and control technology is in the practice of medicine. Of considerable importance to medicine is the function of diagnosis. Diagnosis is intimately linked to the act of deciding.

There are several factors which make medicine a potent recipient of military command and control technology. First, the growth of population has made the old time patient–doctor relationship rather obsolete. The practice of medicine now requires attention be paid to organizational techniques for its successful execution. There are more people to care for today with fewer than required trained personnel to perform medical functions. Second, and also of importance, is the fact that medical research has received unprecedented attention and support from the government and private individuals alike. More research is now being conducted on health problems than ever before. This trend will continue and as a result, the amount of available data to the physician can reach staggering proportions. The average physician is unable to keep pace with the development in his own specialization much less the entire field of medicine. With more people and more research, theory and fact in medicine have achieved considerable richness both in quality and significance.

The space program's requirement for insuring the physical and mental health of the astronauts has placed demands on control and monitoring mechanisms which have led to rather sophisticated telemetry. This capability is now being applied to general medical problems.

The application of X-ray and other photographic techniques have led to further data on medical states. The coupling of such capacities with sophisticated displays provides a formidable capability to the diagnostic function of the physician.

The practicing physician as well as the researcher in this field, therefore, is now deluged with data, which could be of vital importance to him if he could manage to get to them, and perhaps more importantly, at the time he needs them. The development of medical data systems and medical information systems are moves in this direction. Presently, large centralized data systems for the storage of medical data in specific areas (i.e., cancer, TB) are in the state of development and refinement. Such systems include provision for diagnostic analysis services to physicians when needed; although such capabilities are presently only in the conceptual state.

(i) Community Affairs Services   Community affairs services is similar to organizational management [Section 2.5.2(d), page 369]. A data management system comprises data elicited from numerous civic agencies to provide planning and control operations and decision-making capabilities to the executive management echelons of the community.

The major impact of military command and control in this area has been the application of systems theory to community problems. The important emphasis in this development is centered on the capability in data technology to provide projection of trends and to establish models concerning the interactive features of the community which then can be simulated and an estimation of community behavior established. Several such systems have been conceptualized. There is very little evidence to suggest that such systems will work however. Although there has been general acceptance of such systems, very little has been done to implement them. It is particularly interesting and exciting to note that the creation of information systems are now being considered in conjunction with urban renewal and model city programs [*39, 77, 79, 105*].

Acknowledgments

The author wishes to express his appreciation for the efforts of many individuals who assisted in the preparation of this article in various ways. Particular gratitude is expressed to Professor K. Otten, National Cash Register Corp.; M. Yovits, Ohio State University; William La Plant, United States Air Force; Logistics Command; Ray Sabeh, Defense Communications Agency; H. Rienstra, System Development Corporation (SDC); Gary Haug, NCR; Margaret Scheurer, Frank Na, James Falter, Robert Remm, Tom Featheringham, and Jack Martell, Adams & Associates; Robert Yaple, University of Dayton; and Ralph Tuttle and Col. Ashley of the U.S. Naval Research Laboratory. I am indebted to the efforts of Mrs. Annette Feely whose patience sustained the many drafts of this paper. The substance of the paper was completed while the author was Professor of Information Science at the University of Dayton, Dayton, Ohio.

References

1. *The American City.* July, 1966, May, 1966, September, 1968, April, 1967, June, 1966.
2. Atkinson, J. W., and Cartwright, D. P., Some neglected variables in contemporary conceptions of decision and performance, in *Proc. Symp. Predecisional Processes in Decision Making, 1964*, Rept. No. AMRL TDR–64–77, pp. 179–192. Behavioral Sciences Lab., AMRL, AMD, AFSC, Wright-Patterson AFB, Dayton, Ohio.
3. Auerback *Standard EDP Reports*, Volume 1.
4. Bairdain, E. *Information display in a vehicular traffic control system of the post-1970 era. Information Display* **2**, No. 3, 34–37 (1965).
5. Baker, J. D., and Goldstein, I., Batch vs sequential displays: effects on human problem solving. *Human Factors* **8**, 225–235 (1966).
6. Baran, P., *Communications, Computers and People* **27**, Part 2, 45 (1965). Thompson Book, Baltimore, Maryland.
7. Bates, F. L., The impact of automation on the organization and society, *Georgia Reliance Symp. Automat. Soc.* Atlanta,Georgia, 1968.
8. Bavelas, A., Teleconferencing: guidelines for research. IDA Res. Paper, P-107 IDA/Hq 64–2312, Arlington, Virginia, November, 1963.

9. Belden, T. G., and Schwartz, J. W. Application of communication satellites to military command structure. IDA Rept., Arlington, Virginia, January 1969.

10. Bennett, E., Degan, J., and Spiegel, J., *Military Information Systems.* Praeger, New York, 1964.

11. Berlyne, D. E., Attention, curiosity and decision, in *Proc. Symp. Predecisional Processes in Decision Making, 1964,* Rept. No. AMRL TDR–64–77, pp. 101–116. Behavioral Sciences Lab., AMRL, AMD, AFSC, Wright-Patterson AFB, Dayton, Ohio.

12. Bernstein, G. B., A fifteen-year forecast of information-processing technology, Naval Supply Systems Command, Research and Development Division, Washington, D. C., January, 1969.

12a. Borko, H. Information science, What is it? *Amer. Doc.* **19**, 3–5 (1968).

13. Briggs, G. E., Reaction time and uncertainty in human information processing, Tech. Rept. 69–5. Ohio State University, Columbus, Ohio, 1969.

14. Bruner, J. S., Goodnow, J. J., and Austin, G. A., *A Study of Thinking.* Wiley, New York, 1956.

14a. Burks, A. W., Goldstine, H. H., von Newman, J., Preliminary discussion of the logical design of an electronic computing instrument, cited in *Advan. Computers* **1**, 308 (1960).

15. Bushnell, D. D. (ed.), The automation of school information systems. Monograph 1. p. 126. Dept. Audiovisual Instruction, National Education Association, Washington, D.C., 1964.

16. Carbato, F., Merwin-Daggett, M., and Daley, R., *An Experimental Time-Sharing System, Programming Systems and Languages* pp.67–83. McGraw-Hill, New York, 1967.

17. Carmon, J. L., Education through remote terminals—The University of Georgia computer network. *Comput. Automat.,* **17** (1968).

18. Carroll, D. C., and Zannetos, Z. S., Towards the realization of intelligent management information systems, *3rd Cong. Inform. Syst. Sci. Technol, 1967,* pp. 151–167.

19. Carzo, R., Jr., and Yanouzas, J. N., *Formal Organization: A Systems Approach.* Richard Irwin and Dorsey Press, Illinois, 1967.

20. Chiaramonte, Col. R., A report on Ohio's law enforcement automated data system. Ohio State Highway Patrol, 1969.

21. Chomsky, N., *Aspects of the Theory of Syntax.* M.I.T. Press, Cambridge, Massachusetts, 1964.

22. Coffey, J. L., A comparison of vertical and horizontal arrangements of alpha-numeric material—Experiment I. *Human Factors* **3**, 93–98 (1961).

23. Computer-aided instructional management. *Systems Development Corporation Magazine* **10**, No. 4.

24. Atkinson, R. C. and H. A. Wilson, Computer-assessed instruction, *Science* **162**, No. 3849, 73–77 (October 4, 1968).

25. Computer directory and buyer's guide. *Comput. Automat.* **13**, No. 7 (June, 1964).

26. Computer directory and buyer's guide. *Comput. Automat.* **18**, No. 6 (June, 1969).

27. The Computer goes to first grade. *The Parents,* pp. 46–47 (June, 1968).

28. Computers and communications: Ingredients for revolution. *Communications Designers' Digest,* pp. 20–21 (May, 1969).

29. Computers find school is tough. *Business Week,* pp. 106–108 (July 1, 1967).

30. Concept of the Department of the Navy, management-information control system, MICS Concept for the Advisory Group Rept., August 24, 1967.

31. McLaughlin, R. A. The IBM 360/195. *Datamation*, **15**, No. 10, 119 (1969).
32. Davis, R. Classification and evaluation of information system design Techniques. *2nd Cong. Inform. Syst. Sci.*, pp. 77–84. Spartan Books, Washington, D.C., 1965.
33. Dearden, J., and McFarlan, F. W., *Management Information Systems Text and Cases*, p. 105. Richard Irwin, Homewood, Illinois, 1966.
34. Debons, A., Introduction to display systems, in *Display Systems Engineering* (H. R. Luxemberg and R. L. Kuehn, eds.), Chapter 1. McGraw-Hill, New York, 1968.
35. Debons, A., The effects of ADP processing on Naval command, NRL Report Office of Naval Research, Washington, D.C., December, 1968.
36. Debons, A., Command and control. Paper presented at the 2nd ARDC Science Symp., Baltimore, Maryland, 1960.
37. DeFerranti, B. Z., The next three years. *Proc. 1968 IFIP Cong.* pp. 38–45. North-Holland, Amsterdam, August, 1968.
38. Dodson, J. D., Simulation system design for a *TEAS* simulation research facility. Rep. AFCRL 1112, PRCR–194. Planning Research Corp., Los Angeles, California, November 15, 1961.
39. Doelling, N., Computer resource sharing, *Comput. Automat.* **17**, No. 10 (October 1968).
40. Doucette, Dale, Towards a definition of the field of information science. American University, Washington D.C., 1966, unpublished.
41. Dorff, E. K., Computers and communications: Complementing technologies. *Comput. Automat.* **18**, No. 5, 22–23 (May, 1969).
42. Edwards, W., Information seeking to reduce the risk of decisions, in *Proc. Symp. Predecisional Processes in Decision Making, 1964*, Rept. No. AMRL TDR–64–77, pp. 1–5. Behavioral Sciences Lab., AMRL, AMD, AFSC, Wright-Patterson AFB, Dayton, Ohio.
43. Edwards, W., The theory of decision making. *Psychol. Bull.* **51**, 380–417 (1954).
44. Edwards, W., Behavioral decision theory. *Ann. Rev. Psychol.* **12**, 473–498 (1961).
45. Edwards, W., Lindman, H., and Savage, L. J., Bayesian statistical inference for psychological research. *Psychol. Rev.* **70**, 193–242 (1963).
46. Edwards, W., and Tversky, A., eds. *Decision Making*. Penguin Books, London, England, 1967.
47. Edwards, W., Miller, L. W., and Kaplan, R. J., Judge: A value-judgment-based TAC command system. Rept. RM–5147–PR, Rand Corp., Santa Monica, California, November 1966.
48. Encyclopedia Britannica, Integrated Circuits. *Encycl. Britannica* **12**, 340 (1966).
49. Encyclopedia Britannica, Information Theory. *Encycl. Britannica* **21**, 900 (1966).
49a. Ernst, R. L., What else will computers do to us? *The Wall Street Journal* **XLVI**, No. 80 (October 21, 1970).
50. Ernst, R. L., and Yovits, M. C., Information science as an aid to decision making, Tech. Rept. 69–13. National Science Found., Washington, D.C., September 15, 1969.
51. Evans, J. A., A methodology for command information system analysis. *3rd Cong. Inform. Syst. Sci. Technol., 1967*, p. 251.
52. Fano, R. M., The MAC system: The computer utility approach. *IEEE Spectrum* **2**, 42–46, January, 1965.
53. Ferkiss, V., *Technological Man: The Myth and Reality*, Mentor Books, 1969.

53a. Fitts, P. M., The information capacity of the human motor system in controlling the amplitude of movement. *J. Exper. Psychol.* **47**, 381–391 (1954).

54. Frazer B. J., The role of natural language in man-machine communication. *3rd. Cong. Inform. Sys. Sci. Technol., 1967* p. 21.

55. French, E. G., and Thomas, F. H., The relation of achievement motivation problem solving effectiveness. *J. Abnorm. Social Psychol.* **56**, 45–48 (1949).

56. Fubini, C., Command and control. *Armed Forces* **11**, No. 10, 52–54 (1965).

57. Furth, S. E., Automated retrieval of legal information: State of the art. *Comput. Automat.* **17**, No. 12, pp. 25–28 (December, 1968).

58. Gardner, J. F., Gebhard, J. W., Hanes, R. M., and Hayes, J. R. Inquiry into methods used to obtain military information requirements, Tech. Doc. Rept. No. ESD TDR. 62–302, Armed Forces NRC Committee on Vision, May, 1962.

58a. Gavin, J. M., The social impact of information systems. *Comput. Automat.* **18**, No. 8, 16–18 (1968).

59. Gebhard, J., and Hanes, R., Simulation studies of fleet command situations. Appl. Phys. Lab. Mem., 1964, Silver Springs, Maryland.

60. Glauthier, J. T., Computer time sharing, its origins and development. *Comput. Automat.* **16**, No. 10, 23–29 (October, 1967).

61. Golding, E. I., Management information system, Rept. Office of Economics and Systems Analysis, Office of the Secretary of Transportation, Washington, D.C., December, 1968.

62. Green, B. F., McGraw, W. J., and Jenkins, H. M., The time required to search for numbers on large visual displays, Rept. No. 36, ASTIA Doc. No. 21109. M.I.T. Lincoln Laboratory, Lexington, Massachusetts, 1953.

63. Haessler, H. A., Recent developments in automating the medical history. *Comput. Automat.* **18**, No. 6, 24–32 (June, 1969).

64. Halloway, B. K., Command control (AFRP–62, 1). *Aerospace Safety* **22**, No. 9, 2–3 (1966).

65. Hammer, C. H., and Seymour, R., Information assimulation from coded and uncoded individual and group diaplays. *Human Factors* **7**, 245–255 (1965).

66. Hanes, R. M., and Gebhard, J. W., The computer's role in command decision. *U.S. Naval Institute Proc. No. 763* **92**, No. 9, 61–68 (September, 1966).

67. Hargreaves, B. J. A., The place of computers in command and control of the Armed Forces; *J. Royal United Services Inst.* **CXIV**, September, 1969.

67a. Heilprin, L. B. Toward a definition of information science. *Amer. Doc. Inst. Meeting, 1963.* Short papers part 2: 239–41.

67b. Heiman, G., Navy emphasis swings toward strategic communication. *Armed Forces Management* **15**, No. 10, 62–68 (July, 1969).

68. Howard, J. ed., *Electronic Systems Displays.* Spartan Books, Washington, D.C., 1963.

69. Howard, R. A. Information value theory. *IEEE Trans. Commun. Technol.* **COM–14**, No. 5 (October, 1966).

70. Horveth, L. S., History of communications—Electronics in the United States Navy. United States Govt. Printing Office, Washington, D.C., 1963.

71. Hunt, D., and Zink, D., eds. *Proc. Symp. Predecisional Processes Decision Making.* AMRL–TDR–64–77 Behavioral Sciences Laboratory, AMRL, AMD, AFSC, Wright-Patterson AFB, Ohio, 1962.

72. Information Sciences—1963. Annual Report 64–0101, Air Force Office of Scientific Research, Washington, D.C.

72a. Information Services, 1970, Chem. Abstr. Serv. The Ohio State University, Columbus, Ohio.

73. Israel, D. R., Systems engineering experience with automated command and control systems. *3rd. Cong. Inform. Sys. Sci. Technol., 1967* pp. 193–214.
74. Jacobs, J. F., and Degan, J., System science research, TM 3126. Mitre Corporation, Bedford, Massachusetts, July, 1961.
75. Jenkins, W. E., Airline reservation systems. *Datamation* **15**, No. 3, 30 (1969).
76. Jordan, P. B., *Condensed Computer Encyclopedia*. McGraw-Hill, New York, 1969.
77. Kelley, R. A., and Andrews, F. T., Challenge in transmission, *Sci. & Technol.* **76**, 55–62 (April, 1968).
77a. Kennedy, E. J., Some pragmatic considerations influencing the selection of Air Force techniques, in *Proc. 3rd Nat. Symp. Inform. Display*. The Society of Information Display, Los Angeles, 1964.
78. Kogan, N., and Wallach, M. A., *Risk Taking: A Study in Cognition and Personality*. Holt, New York, 1964.
79. Kraaemer, K. L., The evolution of information systems for urban administration, Public Administration Review, July–August, 1969.
80. Kroger, M. C. *et al.*, Computers in command and control. Institute for Defense Analysis Report TR 61–12, Office of the Assistant Director of Defense Res. and Engrg, ARPA, Task 17, Con. SD-50. 1961.
81. Kroger, M. C., Introduction to tactical information systems, 2nd Cong. of the Information System Sciences, 1964, Preprints, pp. 145–150.
82. Luxemberg, H. R., and Kuehn, R. L., *Displays Systems Engineering*. McGraw-Hill, New York, 1968.
83. Lanzetta, J. T., and Sieber, J., Predecision information processes: Some determinants of information acquisition prior to decision making, in *Proc. Symp. Predecisional Processes in Decision Making, 1964*, Rept. No. AMRL TDR–64–77, pp. 125–172. Behavioral Sciences Lab., AMRL, AMD, AFSC, Wright-Patterson AFB, Dayton, Ohio.
84. Licklider, J. C. R., Languages for specialization and application of prepared procedures. *2nd Cong. Inform. Sys. Sci. Technol., 1962*, pp. 177–188.
85. Licklider, J. C. R., *Libraries of the Future*, p. 123. M.I.T. Press, Cambridge, Massachusetts, 1965.
86. Licklider, J. C. R., Man–computer symbiosis, *IRE Trans. Human Factors Electron.*, **HFE–1**, No. 1, 4–11 (1960).
87. Licklider, J. C. R., and Taylor, R. W., The computers as a communications device. *Sci. & Technol.* **76**, 21–31 (April, 1968).
88. Livingston, R. T. *The Engineering of Organization and Management*. McGraw-Hill, New York, 1949.
89. Loewe, R. T., System design, coding, formats and programming, in *Display Systems Engineering* (H. R. Luxemberg and R. L. Kuehn, eds.), pp. 24–69. McGraw-Hill, New York, 1968.
90. Logan, R. J., Computer graphics in electronic circuit design. *Comput. Automat.* **17**, No. 11, pp. 28–30 (November, 1968).
91. Lynch, C. J., A communications revolution. *Sci. & Technol.* **76**, 14–20 (April, 1968).
92. Martin, J., *Programming Real-Time Computer Systems*. Prentice-Hall, Englewood Cliffs, New Jersey, 1965.
93. Massengill, H. E., Purposive systems: Theory and application ESD–TDR–64 531, Decision Sciences Laboratory, L. G. Hanscom Field, Bedford, Massachusetts, 1964.
94. McCormick, E. J., *Human Factors Engineering*. McGraw-Hill, New York, 1964.

95. McDonough, A. M., and Garrett, L. J., *Management Systems*, p. 4. Richard Irwin, Homewood, Illinois, 1965.

96. McKay, K. G., Network. *Sci. Technol.* **76**, 45–50 (April, 1968).

97. McLuhan, M., *Understanding Media: The Extensions of Man.* McGraw-Hill, New York, 1965.

98. Mealy, G. H., Operating systems (excerpts), in *Programming Systems and Languages* (S. Rosen ed.). McGraw-Hill, New York, 1967.

99. Mensh, M., Multiprogramming, what it is: when to use it: what to look for . . . , *Comput. Automat.* **17**, No. 2, 22–25 (February, 1968).

100. Miller, L. W., Kaplan, R. J., and Edwards, W., Judge: A value–judgment–based tactical command system. REMO RM5147–PR, Rand Corp., Santa Monica, California, March, 1967.

101. Myers, C. A., ed., *The Impact of Computers in Management.* M.I.T. Press, Cambridge, Massachusetts, 1967.

101a. The NASA Scientific and Technical Information System . . . and How to Use It. National Aeronautics and Space Administration, Office of Technology Utilization, Code US, Washington, D.C. 20546.

102. Newell, A., Shaw, C. J., and Simon, H. A., Problem solving in humans and computers. *Carnegie Tech. J.* **21**, No. 4, 34–38 (1957).

103. Nicholson, R. M. Maximum information-handling rates for sequentially presented visual stimuli. *Human Factors* **4**, (1962).

104. Neimark, E. D., Information gathering in diagnostic problem solving. A preliminary report. *Psychol. Rec.* **11**, 243–248 (1961).

105. Nievergelt, J., Computers and computing—Past, present, future. *IEEE Spectrum* **5**, 72–79 (1968).

106. O'Brien, J. A., The bank of tomorrow: today, *Comput. Automat.* **8**, 30–32 (1968).

106a. Otten, K., and Debons, A., Towards a metascience of information. *J. Amer. Soc. Inform. Sci.* **21**, No. 1, 89–94 (1970).

107. Parsons, H. M. Review and analysis of man–machine system experiments and laboratories. Aerospace Med. Res. Labs., Wright-Patterson AFB, Dayton, Ohio, 1967.

108. Parsons, H. M., and Perry, W. E., Concepts for command and control systems. TMWD–227/000/00–SDC., December, 1965.

108a. Pepinsky, H. B., *People and Information.* Macmillan (Pergamon), New York, 1970.

109. Pittsburgh System. Personal communication.

110. Preston, M. G., and Baratta, P., An experimental study of the auction value of an uncertain outcome. *Amer. J. Psych.* **61**, 183–193 (1948).

111. Prince, T. R., *Information Systems for Management Planning and Control.* Richard Irwin, Homewood, Illinois, 1966.

112. Proctor, J. H., Normative exercising: An analytical and evaluative aid in system design. *Proc. 1st Cong. Information System Sci.*, ESD-Mitre Corp., November, 1962.

113. Rakoczi, L. L., A fourth generation concept. *IEEE Computer Group News*, March, 1969.

114. Rappaport, A., Sequential decision making in a computer controlled task. *J. Math. Psych.* **1**, No. 2, 351–374 (1964).

115. Reisbeck, G., *Information Theory.* M.I.T. Press, Cambridge, Massachusetts, 1965.

116. Roby, T. B., Belief states, evidence, and action, in *Proc. Symp. Predecisional Processes in Decision Making, 1964*, Rept. No. AMRL TDR–64–77, pp. 27–46. Behavioral Sciences Lab., AMRL, AMD, AFSC, Wright-Patterson AFB, Dayton, Ohio.

117. Rubenstein, H., and Pollack, I., Work predictability and intelligibility, *J. Verb. Learn. Verb. Behav.* **21**, 147–158 (1962).

118. Sabeh, R., Determination of requirements, in *Electronic Information Display Systems* (J. Howard, ed.), p. 52. Spartan Books, Washington, D.C., 1963.

119. Sackman, H. *Computers, System Sciences, and Evolving Society: The Challenge of Man–Machine Digital Systems.* Wiley, New York, 1967.

120. Saettler, P., *A History of Instructional Technology.* McGraw-Hill, New York, 1968.

121. Savage, L. J., *The Foundation of Statistics.* Wiley, New York, 1954.

122. Schroeder, H. M., Driver, M. J., and Streupert, S., *Human Information Processing.* Holt, New York, 1967.

123. *Science and Technology,* October, 1968. Command and Control Staff Report, pp. 40–52.

124. Scodel, A., Ratoosh, F., and Minus, J. S., Some personality correlates of decision under conditions of risk. *Behavioral Sci.* **4**, 19–27 (1959).

125. System Development Corporation Project—*Time Sharing.* Totschek, R. A. An Empirical Investigation into the Behavior of the SDC Time-Sharing System. Rept. SD 2191/001/00 (undated).

126. Seidel, R. J., Computers in education: The Copernican revolution in education systems. *Comput. Automat.* **18**, No. 3, 24–26 (1969).

127. Seitz, F., The Science Year in Review: A Perspective, pp. 282–285. Britannica Yearbook of Science and the Future, 1969.

128. Shoemaker, H. L., A technical progress report on the army's CC15–70 Project, in *Proc. 2nd Cong. Information System Sci..* Spartan Books, Washington, D.C., 1965.

129. Sheer, S., *Displays Systems.* Wiley—International Science Series, New York, 1970.

130. Shuford, E. H., Predecisional process related to psychophysical judgment, in *Proc. Symp. Predecisional Processes in Decision Making, 1964,* Rept. No. AMRL TDR–64–77, pp. 53–74. Behavioral Sciences Lab., AMRL, AMD, AFSC, Wright-Patterson AFB, Dayton, Ohio.

131. Siegel, S., *Choice, Strategy and Utility.* McGraw-Hill, New York, 1964.

131a. V. Slamecka, *Proc. Conf. Training Inform. Specialists,* p. 155, October, 1961, April, 1962, Georgia Institute of Technology.

132. Smith, E. E. Choice reaction time: And analysis of the major theoretical positions. *Psych. Bull.* **69**, 77–110 (1968)

133. Smith, S. L., and Duggar, B. C., Do large shared displays facilitate group effort? *Human Factors* **7**, 237–244 (1965).

134. Sinaiko, H. W., and Buckley, E. P., Human factors in the design of systems, NRL Rept. 4996, Naval Research Lab, Washington, D.C., August 1957.

135. Southard, J. F., Schum, D. A., and Briggs, G. E., An application of Bayes theorem as a hypothesis–selection aid in complex information-processing systems, AMRL–TDR–65–51, BSL, AMRL, Wright-Patterson AFB, Ohio August, 1964.

136. Stelloh, R. T., An automated blood bank system for the Milwaukee blood center. *Comput. Automat.* **18**, No. 6, 16–19 (1969).

137. Suppes, P. *The Use of Computers in Education, Information.* A Scientific American Book, Freeman, 1966.

138. Sutherland, I. E., Computer inputs and outputs, in *Information* (D. Flanagan, ed.). Freeman, San Francisco, 1966.

139. Swets, J. A., Tanner, W. P., Jr., and Birdsall, R. C., Decision Processes in perception. *Psychol. Rev.* **68**, 301–340 (1961).

139a. Teichroew, D., Data display in business information systems, in *Management Information Data Displays*, Bull. 10, p. 30. Center for Technology and Administration, The American University, Washington, D.C., 1964.

140. Teleconferencing: Summary of a preliminary study, IDA Study S–138 IDA/Hq 63–2123, November, 1963.

141. Toda, M., Pre and post decisional processes of the fungus eater, in *Proc. Symp. Predecisional Processes in Decision Making, 1964*, Rept. No. AMRL TDR–64–77, pp. 81–92. Behavioral Sciences Lab., AMRL, AMD, AFSC, Wright-Patterson AFB, Dayton, Ohio.

142. Toda, M., and Shuford, E. H., Utility, induced utilities and small worlds, ESD–TDR–63–662, Vol. IV, pp. 40. Decision Science Laboratory, Air Force Systems Command, Maryland.

143. TR 66–558–22–Office of Naval Research.

144. Truitt, T., *Data Systems News* (1969).

145. Unold, R., Communications command and control (C^3) *Telecommunications*, March, 1968.

146. Vaughan, W. S., Jr., and Gillette, P. R., Command control: analysis of basic concepts and developments of requirement methodology. Office of Naval Research Report, Washington, D.C., December, 1965.

147. Von Bertalanffy, L., *Problems of Life: An Evaluation of Modern Biological Thought.* Wiley, New York, 1952.

148. von Neumann, J., and Morgenstern, O., *Theory of Games and Economic Behavior.* Princeton Univ. Press, Princeton, New Jersey, 1944.

149. Walker, P. D., and Catalano, J. Where do we go from here with MIS? *Computer Decisions* 1, No. 9 (September, 1969).

150. Walker, P. D., Systems engineering experience with automated command and control systems. *3rd Cong. Inform. Syst. Sci. Technol., 1967*, p. 102.

151. Whisler, T. L., The impact of information technology on organization control, in *The Impact of Computers in Management* (A. C. Myers, ed.), pp. 16–49. M.I.T. Press, Cambridge, Massachusetts, 1967.

152. Wiesen, R. A., and Shuford, E. H., Bayes strategies as adaptive behavior, in *Biological Prototypes and Synthetic Systems*, pp. 303–310. Plenum Press, New York, 1963.

153. Wilson, I., and Wilson, M., *Information, Computers and System Design*, pp. 182–187. Wiley, New York, 1967.

154. Wohlstetter, R., *Pearl Harbor, Warning and Decision*, p. 73. Stanford Univ. Press, Stanford, California, 1962.

155. Woodford, H. A., ed., *The United States Air Force Dictionary*, Air University Press, Maxwell AFB, Alabama. 1956.

156. Zadeh, L., and Polak, E., *System Theory*, pp. 3–5. McGraw-Hill, New York, 1968.

156a. Yovits, M. Information science: Toward the development of a true scientific discipline. *Amer. Doc.* **20**, No. 4, 369–376 (1969).

157. Yovits, M. C., and Ernst, R. L., *Generalized Information Systems—Electronic Handling of Information: Testing and Evaluation*, p. 281. Thompson, Washington, D.C., 1967

Author Index

Numbers in parentheses are reference numbers and indicate that an author's work is referred to although his name is not cited in the text. Numbers in italics show the page on which the complete reference is listed.

A

Adansom, M., 68, *122*
Abramson, A. S., 181, *226*
Akhmanova, O. S., *52*
Alt, F., 15, 32(55), *54, 56*
Alter, R., 200, *222*
Andrews, F. T., 383(77), *387*
Antony, J., 168(2), 184(2), 190(2, 143, 153), *222, 228, 229*
Atkinson, J. W., 350, 351, *383*
Atkinson, R. C., *384*
Austin, G. A., 352(14), *384*

B

Baba, P. D., 313(27), *317*
Bach, E., 16(20), *55*
Baille, A., 38(74), *57*
Bairdain, E., 376(4), *383*
Baker, J. D., 359, *383*
Balandis, L. S., 204, *222*
Balashek, S., 204, 210(28), *223*
Baldwin, J. R., 239(18), *317*
Ball, G. N., 87, *122*
Baran, P., 367, *383*
Bar-Hillel, Y., 2, 3, 4(1), 6(1), *54*, 173(4), *222*
Barney, H. L., 186, *223*
Bates, F. L., *383*
Bavelas, A., 360, *383*
Baxendale, P. B., 84(33), *124*
Becker, J. J., 235(16), 237(16), *317*
Bekesy, G. von, *173*
Belar, H., 153, *163*, 186(110, 111), 205, *227*
Belden, T. G., 334, 357(9), *384*
Belzer, J., 69(75), *125*

Bennett, E., *384*
Bennett, J. L., 84(33), *124*
Bennion, D. R., 232(7, 8), *316*
Benzécri, J. P., 89, *122*
Berlyne, D. E., 351, *384*
Bernick, M., 67, *122*
Bernstein, G. B., *384*
Bezdel, W., 205, *222*
Birdsall, R. C., 350(139), *389*
Bloom, B. H., 211, *222*
Bobrow, D. G., 60, *122*, 207, *222*
Booth, A. D., 7, *52, 53, 54*
Borko, H., 67, *122*, 173, *222*, 368(12a), *384*
Borst, J. M., 214(20), *223*
Brandwood, L., *52*
Bratley, P., 172(148), *229*
Bridle, J. S., 205(5), *222*
Briggs, G. E., 330, 350(135), *384, 389*
Broadbent, D. E., 173, *222*
Brower, R. A., 15(11), *54*
Brown, A., 41(86), *58*
Bruner, J. S., 352, *384*
Bryden, B., 214(13), *222*
Buckley, E. P., 357(134), *389*
Burger, J. F., 173(138), *228*
Burks, A. W., 338, *384*
Buron, R. H., 195(11, 12), *222*
Bush, V., 60, *122*
Bushnell, D. D., 362, *384*

C

Carbato, F., 345(16), *384*
Carbonel, M., 232, *317*
Carmon, J. L., 370(17), 372(17), *384*
Carroll, D. C., *384*
Cartwright, D. P., 350, 351, *383*

Subject Index

A

Acoustically controlled machines, 217–218
Acoustic waveform, 172, 179
Air Traffic Control
  displays in, 217
  speech in, 170
ALPAC (Automatic Language Processing Committee) report, 44–48
Ampere's law, 240
Amplifiers, balanced circuit, 266–272
Aspiration, in speech production, 176
ASR, *see* Automatic Speech Recognition
Association hypothesis, 102
Association map, 66
Astronauts, man–machine interface and, 170
Audiovisual displays, automated, 217
Auditory system, human, 179
AUDREY, 210
Automatic print reader, 4
Automatic Language Processing System, 45
Automatic Speech Recognition (ASR), 182, 197, 211, 213–217
  applications of, 219–221
Automatic syntactic recognition, 16
Automatic translation, *see* Machine translation

B

Balanced magnetic circuits, 231–316
  binary counter and lock-up circuit in, 274–375
  circuit characteristics of, 255–266
  circuit-gain and material characteristics in, 309–316
  clocking arrangements in, 296–300
  compatible storage element in, 306–309
  core equivalent and, 243–247
  disturb measurements in, 311–316
  element characteristics in, 250–255
  experimental machine control system and, 288–296
  ferrite sample preparation in, 313–314
  flux sources and states in, 246–250
  gain limits in, 259–266
  information transfer between apertures in, 255–266
  logic operations in two-path circuit, 277–288
  multiple-path parallel circuits and logic elements in, 272–277
  and regeneration of signals within ferrite sheets, 301–306
  sample preparation in, 313
  storage elements in, 306–309
  teletypewriter and, 289–296
  three-phase circuits in, 266–272
  unipolar and bipolar, 270–272
BASEBALL, 60
Behavioral sciences, command and control systems in, 346–361
Belgium, machine translation in, 39
Biax logical element, 232
Binary counter lock-up circuit, 274
Bipolar circuits, 270–272
Bistable circuit, 284
Blind persons, speech-generating devices for, 220

C

CAI system, 213–216
Canada, machine translation in, 38, 213–217
Channel vocoder, 183, 194
Chinese–English translation, 34
Classification
  association hypothesis in, 102–103
  constraints in, 86–90
  defined, 78
  indexing and, 65–70

Contents of Previous Volumes